Children's Language
and the Language Arts

Children's Language and the Language Arts

A Literature-Based Approach

Third Edition

CAROL J. FISHER
University of Georgia

C. ANN TERRY
Baylor University

ALLYN AND BACON
Boston   London   Sydney   Toronto

Series Editor: Sean W. Wakely
Series Editorial Assistant: Carol Chernaik
Production Administrator: Annette Joseph
Production Coordinator: Sue Freese
Editorial-Production Service: Kailyard Associates
Cover Administrator: Linda Dickinson
Manufacturing Buyer: Bill Alberti

See page 510 at the end of this book for permission acknowledgements.

Library of Congress Cataloging-in-Publication Data
Fisher, Carol J.
  Children's language and the language arts : a literature-based
approach / Carol J. Fisher, C. Ann Terry.
    p. cm.
  Includes bibliographical references.
  ISBN 0-205-11431-8
  1. Language arts (Elementary) 2. Children—Language
  3. Literature—Study and teaching (Elementary) I. Terry, C. Ann.
  II. Title.
  LB1576.F44 1990   89-18127
  372.6—dc20   CIP

Printed in the United States of America
10 9 8 7 6 5 4   95 94 93 92 91 90

Photos by Nickki Ann Spretnak (pages 3, 24, 197, 237, 315, 339, 373),
Raymond Groscrand (pages 27, 46, 48, 57, 63, 67, 133, 146, 163, 176, 290,
295, 321, 354, 356, 357, 362, 416, 451, 475, 481), and Ann Terry (pages
15, 75, 91, 124, 255, 279, 309, 363, 425).

Brief Contents

Contents

Chapter 10   Listening and Language   309

Preface

This third edition of *Children's Language and the Language Arts: A Literature-Based Approach* is linked to a cognitive perspective of learning in which students actively organize information and construct meaning. It reflects a psycholinguistic view of language acquisition and development that requires a rich language environment and offers opportunities to find patterns in language, revising them according to the response received. The language arts program developed in this textbook is based on literature, which provides a diverse language environment as well as much of the content within which language skills are developed.

Those familiar with the previous editions of *Children's Language and the Language Arts* will recognize that adding the subtitle *A Literature-Based Approach* is a change only in emphasis. In the earlier editions, children's literature was referenced in each of the chapters. This edition gives literature even greater attention, reflecting a commitment to a literature-based language arts program. Chapter 2, "Literature in the Language Arts," establishes a foundation and understanding of literary values, elements, and genres that support a literature-based program and provide guidelines for selecting excellent books for such a program. The remaining chapters suggest how to use literature to influence speaking, listening, writing, and reading.

While Part I of the book is devoted to the foundations of the language arts, Part II presents the components of language, including vocabulary, grammar, and language variations. Since more and more teachers are faced with teaching children whose native language is not English, information about teaching the bilingual learner is provided throughout the text. Chapter 7, "Describing Linguistic Variations," has been expanded to include more information on this subject.

Part III presents the substance and strategies for teaching the language arts. The first three chapters in this section discuss oral discourse, dramatic expression, and listening. The next three chapters are companion chapters that deal with teaching composition. Chapter 11 establishes the framework for teaching writing as a process. Chapter 12 focuses on modes of written discourse and on how to implement a writing program. It includes an extensive presentation on poetry writing. Chapter 13 gives a thorough overview of supportive writing skills and suggestions for teaching these skills within the context of writing. Chapter 14, the final chapter of the book, broadens the scope of the language arts. This discussion extends the language arts into the content areas and across the curriculum.

Acknowledgments

The authors wish to thank and acknowledge the many special people who have helped to make *Children's Language and the Language Arts: A Literature-Based Approach* a published reality. We extend our appreciation to Karen Buchanan for her word-processing and proofing efforts. A number of people were most helpful in providing photographs to illustrate the text. We particularly want to thank Mary Ward, Hazel Johnson, Terry Piniola, Jody Stevenson, and the children at Westwood Elementary School in Friendswood ISD, Friendswood, Texas. We also are grateful to photographers Raymond Groscrand and Nickki Ann Spretnak.

We also wish to thank the following reviewers for their helpful comments and suggestions: Victoria Chou Hare, University of Illinois-Chicago; Linda Gambrell, University of Maryland; Pose Lamb, Purdue University; Mary Lou Maples, Huntingdon College; Jessie Roderick, University of Maryland; and Timothy Rush, The University of Wyoming. Last, but certainly not least, we are grateful to Charlotte S. Huck and Martha L. King, who inspired us to write a text for the language arts and from whom we still draw inspiration.

Part I

Foundations for the Language Arts

Language, Literature, and Learning

The basis for a good language arts program is derived from the theories of how children learn and how they learn language. Learning and language are set within a framework of literature that provides the context for development.

Although some kinds of learning can be explained by behaviorist theories, cognitive theories may better explain the complexities of language acquisition and the development of the thought processes that language learning requires. Language acquisition is a complex process in which children are active participants. Learning, especially language learning, needs a rich experiential setting for development, and literature coupled with firsthand experiences provides such a context.

Chapter 1 defines the language arts and the characteristics of a good language arts program in elementary and middle schools. It demonstrates through different examples what a literature-based language arts program might look like and gives three ways such a program might be organized. In these classrooms the language arts are integrated with each other and with other curricular areas, instruction is individualized so that students have choices and do not spend time on concepts or skills they have already mastered, and students are actively involved in their own learning.

Chapter 2 highlights aspects of literature for children from kindergarten through eighth grade that teachers involved in a literature-based program need to know. The various genres of literature are described with examples. This chapter provides the information about literature that teachers should have as a foundation for planning language arts activities based on books, stories, and poems. Parts II and III of the text explain how literature is actually used in the language arts program.

Chapter 3 provides the learning theory on which the examples of classroom environments in Chapter 1 are based. Students have the capacity to organize new information and experiences and to incorporate them with other experiences and concepts. The processes through which learning takes place form the foundations for the skills that students use in obtaining, interrelating, and evaluating information.

Chapter 4 discusses in detail how children acquire and develop language. The emphasis is on the children's ability to process the language in their own linguistic environment and to develop, test, and revise their rules about how language operates. Linguistic research is cited to show a developmental sequence in children's language acquisition, and the major implications of this research for teaching are presented.

Chapter 1

The Language Arts Defined

The Language Arts Defined

An Overview of a Language Arts Program

Individualization

Involvement

Integration

An Interaction Model of the Language Arts

The Whole Language Approach

Literature-Based Language Arts

Developing a Literature Base

Literature-Based Language Arts Webs

Integrating Several Texts

The Teacher and the Language Arts Program

Needed Directions in the Language Arts for the Future

Valuing Oral Language

Emphasizing Language Use

Becoming Readers and Writers

Preventing Testing from Determining Teaching

Using Literature as a Context for Learning

Bibliography: Children's Literature

Language arts is the term currently used to describe the various areas of the curriculum related to language. This includes listening, speaking, writing, and reading, and their component parts such as spelling, drama, handwriting, or debate. The language arts curriculum focuses on language, literature, and composition. Children's experiences form the basis for any quality language arts program. These experiences include those the children have in their everyday lives, those planned by the teacher in the classroom, and those encountered by students in the literature they read. To understand what is involved in teaching the language arts, look at what goes on in primary, upper elementary, and middle school classrooms where children are actively involved in speaking and listening, writing and reading.

An Overview of a Language Arts Program

Students in good language arts classes today are not sitting silently at their desks in rows answering questions in their English books and doing duplicated worksheets. Instead, they are often working on different projects. For example, some are writing in their journals or conferring with a writing partner as they edit their writing. Others are listening to a tape they prepared of mock interviews with authors whose books they have been reading. One pair is planning their display of the early settlement in St. Augustine to go with their research on Spanish settlements. The children are engaged in listening, reading, writing, and meaningful conversation. They are active participants in their own learning—choosing their own books, listening to others as they share their reading, asking for help when they need it from other students or from the teacher. Their classrooms reflect three important aspects of any good language arts program that is based on current theory about how children learn and how they acquire and develop their language. A good language arts program is characterized by (1) *individualization* of the experiences children encounter, (2) active *involvement* in their learning activities, and (3) *integration* of communicative or creative language arts skills with one another as well as with other areas of the curriculum.

Individualization

When you observe children in the classroom, you notice almost immediately that some excel in one area and others are better in another. Some children have a background of experience or a temperament that makes learning easier for them. Some children develop more slowly than others and are not yet ready for increasingly more complex tasks. If an entire class is given a single assignment, some children will quickly complete it, others will work along methodically, and still others will not be able to do it at all. Teachers who are concerned about helping each child to develop fully need to vary children's assignments, thus individualizing children's learning.

Involvement

Children in the elementary school learn best when they are actively involved in each learning situation. What they are doing must seem important to them in a very personal way. Active involvement means working with specific, concrete materials and experiences instead of abstract ideas or materials from a textbook or some other secondary source. Children need things to touch and examine, build and construct, collect, observe, and categorize before they move into reading about more distant ideas or places. As fantasy must be grounded in reality, abstractions must touch experience.

Integration

Instead of setting up a whole series of small blocks of time for each of the curricular areas—8 to 8:10 A.M. for handwriting, 8:10 to 9 A.M. for reading groups, 9 to 9:15 A.M. for spelling, 9:15 to 10 A.M. for library on Monday, creative writing on Tuesday and Friday, and so on—the various areas of the language arts need to be integrated with each other and with other content areas such as science, mathematics, and social studies. Reporting on a science experiment or acting various occupational roles develops language arts skills and at the same time promotes basic understanding in other content areas. This type of integrated study provides for large blocks of time and allows the teacher to capitalize on teachable moments instead of letting the clock dictate when a learning experience is to end.

These are the characteristics of the language arts program you will find described in this book. The basis for such a program is found in current linguistic theory, which describes how children acquire and develop language, and in cognitive psychology, which describes a developmental learning process. The program values both communicative and creative language and recommends a classroom environment in which (1) learning is individualized, (2) children are actively involved in what they are doing, and (3) content and skills are integrated. It emphasizes both written and oral aspects of the language arts, allowing time for discussions, listening experiences, dramatizations of stories and situations, and an oral sharing of ideas and experiences as well as the development of skill in reading, spelling, handwriting, conventional punctuation, and capitalization. Perhaps most important, each child feels good about what he or she can do and about attempting new things.

An Interaction Model of the Language Arts

The language arts have traditionally been divided into four parts: listening, speaking, reading, and writing. This sequence was, until recently, believed to reflect natural language development. But new research, which has studied children in their home environments, indicates that speaking and listening develop together as adults interact with children. And, many children write, although it may be considered scribbling, before they read or at the same time. In this early writing there may only be letter-like shapes or forms, or perhaps a single letter such as *D* will stand for *Daddy*, representing the intention to write *Daddy*. As for early reading, even very young children recognize—read—and can pick out their favorite cereal. They know when you have passed McDonald's or Wendy's. They probably can't read c–o–r–n f–l–a–k–e–s if you printed it on a sheet of paper, but they can get the right box from the cupboard. Speaking and listening and later writing and reading therefore support each other.

The relationships among the language arts are represented in Figure 1.1. There is an obvious similarity between speaking and listening, which are both oral and usually occur at the same time as people take turns listening and speaking. A parallel relationship exists in the written language arts between writing and reading, which both involve written language. We write down things that others can read, and we learn to read things that others have written.

Less obvious but perhaps more important are the relationships between speaking and writing and between listening and reading. Although writing is certainly more than "talk written down," many of the same decisions must be made in both speaking and writing. You must decide in what order you want to present your ideas or retell the events. You have to decide what details to include and which to omit, and you must choose the words that will communicate your ideas and give the right tone. These decisions are part of the composing process, and they apply to both speaking and writing.

There are also differences. In speaking you can use your voice to emphasize, exaggerate, or indicate sarcasm. That is why in personal letters we might use underlining, capital letters, and smiling faces to suggest how we would say something. In writing we are more deliber-

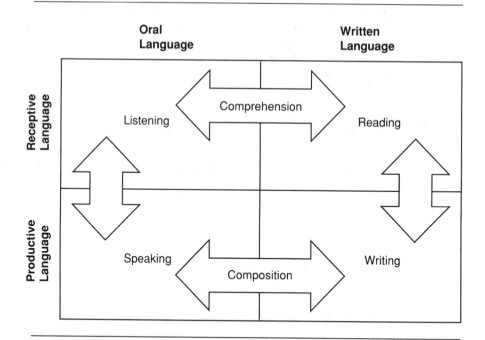

FIGURE 1.1 *An interaction model of the language arts*

ate, better organized, more precise. We must also be concerned with spelling, punctuation, and other writing skills. We are composing, however, while we talk as well as while we write.

There is also a special relationship between listening and reading. Both involve comprehension and critical thinking skills. In both, we must follow a line of reasoning or sequence of events, understand the ideas, respond sensitively to the words used, and critically evaluate the author's or speaker's purpose, logic, authority, and so forth. We continually match what the author/speaker is saying with our knowledge of the world as we figure out a meaning. Reading a sentence is very different from hearing it, and deciphering print has difficulties that we do not encounter when listening to someone. But the comprehension process is nearly the same in listening and reading, and a critical examination of the content involves the same criteria of adequacy and relevancy.

In these ways, the language arts are inextricably bound together. Each one supports the other and draws from the other. For this reason it is important to help children work with language in real situations without artificially dividing language into discrete lessons on final consonant clusters or practice on writing topic sentences.

The Whole Language Approach

In opposition to those who would divide the language arts into tiny pieces and teach them one bit at a time, the whole language approach emphasizes both the integration of the language arts and the use of language for real purposes in meaningful contexts. Goodman describes whole language as a concept based on a learning theory with the following characteristics.

- Language learning is easy when it's whole, real, and relevant; when it makes sense and is functional; when it is encountered in the context of its use; when the learner chooses to use it.
- Language is both personal and social. It's driven from inside by the need to communicate and shaped from the outside toward the norms of the society. . . .
- Language is learned as pupils learn through language and about language, all simultaneously in the context of authentic speech and literacy events. There is no sequence of skills in language development. Teaching kids about language will not facilitate their use of language. . . .
- Language development is empowering: the learner "owns" the process, makes the decisions about when to use it, what for and with what results. Literacy is empowering too, if the learner is in control of what's done with it.
- Language learning is learning how to mean: how to make sense of the world in the context of how our parents, families, and cultures make sense of it. Cognitive and linguistic development are totally interdependent; thought depends on language and language depends on thought.
- In a word, language development is a holistic personal-social achievement.[1]

Such a view of language forms the basis for classrooms in which the language arts are integrated, learning is individualized, and students of all ages are involved in their own learning. The skills that were traditionally taught in isolation are taught when they are needed or relevant.

Literature-Based Language Arts

Literature may be used in different ways—as an enrichment of the basic program or as the core of the language arts program. The following sections examine how three teachers at different grade levels used literature in their language arts programs.

Developing a Literature Base

In one third-grade class, Ms. Watson was expected to use a traditional language arts textbook. It was set up in units with most lessons involving instruction in traditional grammar, a few lessons on study skills or mechanics, a few on composition, and one on listening or speaking. No literature at all was included. Ms. Watson decided to take the lessons from this textbook and set them within a more meaning-centered context that included literature. The lessons from Unit 2 of the textbook included the following topics:

Nouns
Plural Nouns
Common and Proper Nouns
Nouns in a Sentence
Singular Possessive Nouns
Plural Possessive Nouns
Abbreviations
Using *A, An,* and *The*
Using Commas
Capitals and Commas in Letters
Messages
Letters of Invitation
Listening to Messages

Ms. Watson looked at the skills to be taught in this unit and realized that the work on nouns could be done through lists. She selected several published poems that were in a list format, several list poems that children had written, and a book from the library entitled *I Packed My Trunk* by B. Walker. This list story resembles the repetition game in which members of a group take turns naming items to put in the trunk, in alphabetical order. Each person repeats the previously named items and adds one. The teacher also saved some of her shopping lists and an address list from a party she had given at the end of the summer.

One of the poems was "The Right Place" by Myra Cohn Livingston, a list that she was sure would make third-graders giggle. She copied it on chart paper.

The Right Place

Shoes and socks and underwear,
Books and batteries,
Games and cards and nails,
Fritos,
Hershey bars,

Mad *magazines,*
Scotch tape,
Baseball cards,
And whatever you need in a hurry
   is much better to keep
   where you can find it,
under the bed.[2]

The children began by listening to this poem and giggling as Ms. Watson read it, and then they read it along with her. Although it didn't rhyme, they liked the poem, and they liked the phrases that started with the same letter, like "shoes and socks" and "*Mad* magazine." They talked about items in the poem and other objects that could be found under their beds. The teacher listed what they said on the chalkboard. She suggested that they probably had as many strange things in their desks as under their beds, and they added to the list some of the funny items found in their desks. There were jacks, balls, bubble gum, toy racing cars, a long-forgotten pumpkin cookie, a whistle, and some doll clothes. Then she read a list poem written by children.

What Is Exciting?

Christmas
Parties
Making all A's
Polka dots
Birthdays
Getting an allowance
Knowing a movie star
Long fingernails
New records
Exciting is different things
to different people.

Then the teacher selected a book by L. Ward, *I Am Eyes—Ni Macho,* in which a child from Kenya describes the things she sees. "I see sunflowers and skies. I see grasses and giraffes. I see stars and starlings."[3] The students noticed right away how the word pairs started with the same letter. Ms. Watson explained the concept of alliteration—when words begin with the same sound—which poets and writers often use. She suggested that they write their own "I Am Eyes" or a list poem. The next day she read *I Packed My Trunk,* and the students participated.

I packed my trunk and in it I put an apple.
I packed my trunk and in it I put an apple and a book of jokes.
I packed my trunk and in it I put an apple, a book of jokes, and a
   chocolate cookie.

They included dirty dogs, high hats, lipstick, pens, a taxi, and items borrowed from the book—a yak and a zoo. Ms. Watson noticed the children used *a* and *an* perfectly. She put up two short lists of words to check that they really did know to use *an* with words beginning with a vowel. One list had words with initial consonants and the other had words with initial vowels: *apple, egg, iris, oak tree, umbrella*. They quickly read the lists, saying *a* or *an*, and they were right. Because the children recognized that *an* went with the words that began with a vowel, the teacher knew there was no need to teach a lesson on that topic.

While the children were playing "I packed my trunk," she listed their items and added the words to the list from "under my bed" and "in my desk." It was a long list of words, all nouns. At that point she asked the children to look at all the words they had named in the last few days. She explained that these were called nouns and asked them how they could identify a noun. From their explanations, they wrote their own definition and compared it to the one in the textbook. Their definition was in a little different order, but it included all the same elements. They then tried identifying nouns in the sentences in the book and did very well.

Ms. Watson realized that the word list contained only common nouns. The next day she got out a map of their state, a map of the United States, and the address list from her end-of-the-summer party. The children went up to the maps and pointed out the places where family members or people they knew lived. They pointed out where the President lived, where their favorite movie stars lived, and other locations. As they did this, Ms. Watson listed the names of cities, states, and persons. Sometimes the children needed help finding places on the map and remembering how to pronounce them. They generated a long list and picked favorites in each of several categories, as in the following sample.

person	Aunt Susan
place to visit	Disneyworld
national park	Grand Canyon National Park
mountains	Appalachian Mountains
city	Chicago
state	Georgia
tall building	Empire State Building
football stadium	Sanford Stadium
street	Baxter Street

The children quickly figured out which words should be capitalized—the name of a special person, place, or thing. Ms. Watson told them that the "special" ones are called *proper nouns*, while the "ordinary" words are called *common nouns.* She knew they would work with proper nouns when they wrote invitations and worked on social studies and map skills later that year.

The students then worked with the lessons in the textbook, easily identifying nouns and learning to make singular nouns plural using both regular and irregular nouns. They did the review section together on common and proper nouns, holding up a 3″ × 5″ card for each noun that they thought was a proper noun. Most of the students were correct each time and had the opportunity to practice without embarrassment if they were wrong on a particular item.

Later the children shared their list poems in small writing conference groups and made a display. Three children who were especially interested in *I Am Eyes—Ni Macho* made their own version, using alliteration and illustrating each page. The librarian was glad to catalog it and include it in the school library collection.

Ms. Watson felt comfortable extending the language arts textbook this way because the children seemed to learn more by starting out with words of their choice—words that were meaningful to them. They enjoyed the stories and poems, and writing gave them an immediate opportunity to use the newly learned skills. Although Ms. Watson did not set out to teach literary concepts, she assisted children in using the ones they noticed and identified them by the correct name. Instead of separating English from literature and from composition, this approach allowed the children to work on all of them together. They felt proud of their poems and books as well as their ability to do the textbook exercises.

Literature-Based Language Arts Webs

In another school system, the first-graders did not use a language arts textbook but were expected to develop what are regarded as essential language skills. The teacher, Ms. Carmen, worked out literature-based webs for her planning in language arts. Webs are a planning concept in which clusters of activities and/or books related to a topic or to a particular book are listed. She included in the webs science or social studies lesson activities. She developed one web around Frank Asch's *Bear Shadow.* In this adventure, Bear goes fishing, but when he stands up to throw his line into the water, his shadow scares the big fish away. He tries to get rid of his pesky shadow—by running away from it, nailing it to the ground, and burying it. When it is noon, Shadow is nowhere to be seen, so Bear takes a nap. Afterwards, Shadow is still there so Bear makes a deal with him.

Ms. Carmen included four other books by Frank Asch in which Bear is involved: *Happy Birthday, Moon, Mooncake, Skyfire,* and

Moongame. She also included *Nothing Sticks Like a Shadow,* by Ann Tompert. In this story Rabbit tries to lose his shadow to win a bet with Woodchuck. The teacher added some old favorites with bears, such as *Bearymore* by Don Freeman, *Blueberries for Sal* by Robert McCloskey, and *Winnie-the-Pooh* by A. A. Milne. Poems included "Shadows" by Lillian Moore, "Look" by Charlotte Zolotow, and other poems about bears, which were displayed in the room. Figure 1.2 shows the web Ms. Carmen developed.

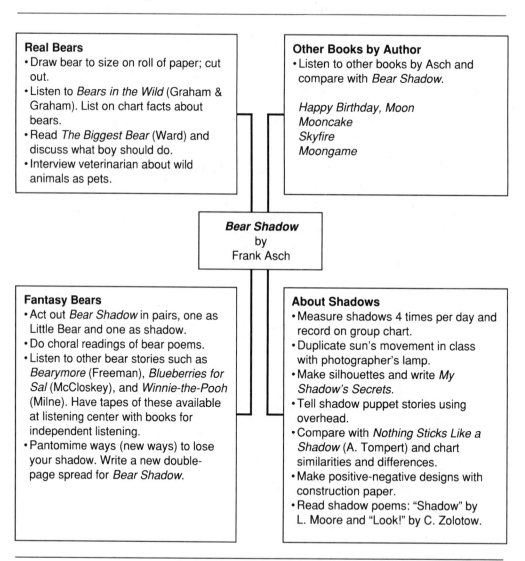

Real Bears
- Draw bear to size on roll of paper; cut out.
- Listen to *Bears in the Wild* (Graham & Graham). List on chart facts about bears.
- Read *The Biggest Bear* (Ward) and discuss what boy should do.
- Interview veterinarian about wild animals as pets.

Other Books by Author
- Listen to other books by Asch and compare with *Bear Shadow.*

  Happy Birthday, Moon
  Mooncake
  Skyfire
  Moongame

Bear Shadow
by
Frank Asch

Fantasy Bears
- Act out *Bear Shadow* in pairs, one as Little Bear and one as shadow.
- Do choral readings of bear poems.
- Listen to other bear stories such as *Bearymore* (Freeman), *Blueberries for Sal* (McCloskey), and *Winnie-the-Pooh* (Milne). Have tapes of these available at listening center with books for independent listening.
- Pantomime ways (new ways) to lose your shadow. Write a new double-page spread for *Bear Shadow.*

About Shadows
- Measure shadows 4 times per day and record on group chart.
- Duplicate sun's movement in class with photographer's lamp.
- Make silhouettes and write *My Shadow's Secrets.*
- Tell shadow puppet stories using overhead.
- Compare with *Nothing Sticks Like a Shadow* (A. Tompert) and chart similarities and differences.
- Make positive-negative designs with construction paper.
- Read shadow poems: "Shadow" by L. Moore and "Look!" by C. Zolotow.

FIGURE 1.2   *Web of* Bear Shadow

One of the first things the students did was to measure their shadows at different times of the day and then record their findings. Ms. Carmen wanted to be sure they understood the shadow's movement in *Bear Shadow.* They went outside the next morning, chalked an X on the sidewalk where one of the children stood, and then marked and measured the child's shadow. They went out again at 10:00 A.M., noon and at 2:00 P.M. before leaving for the day. Each time they had Juanita stand on the X while they measured and marked her shadow. They also observed the sun's position in the sky each time. The next day the children wrote up what they had discovered about shadows—when they are long or short and why they change direction. Ms. Carmen also brought a bright photographer's lamp on a stand, darkened the room, and used the lamp to demonstrate the sun's movement across the sky and the changing shadows.

They then used the lamp to make silhouettes of each other that became the covers for books they wrote on "The Secrets My Shadow Knows about Me." The children learned from each other how to make shadow animals on a screen by shaping and moving their hands. The teacher made simple paper cut-outs for shadow puppets and told a

Inspired by the book Bear Shadow *children take turns measuring their shadows.*

story using the overhead projector. The children all wanted to make shadow puppets and tell a story, which they did.

They also made positive/negative designs by cutting out a shape from the center of a sheet of colored paper and pasting it in the center of a sheet of another color. Another sheet of the second color served as the backing for the "negative"—the sheet from which the original design was cut. This created two matching designs, each the opposite of the other. These images were used as a border for the large bulletin board on which they displayed their writing.

The students did choral readings of the bear poems, experimenting with different styles of reading. After listening to *Nothing Sticks Like a Shadow*, they pantomimed the ways of losing a shadow that Bear and Rabbit tried, as well as new ways they invented. As each child mimed a way to lose a shadow, the others tried to guess the method. Another day they acted out Bear's story with one child playing Bear and another in an old black robe playing Shadow. As the children retold the story, Ms. Carmen had to help them only once by showing the scene where Bear tries to nail his shadow to the ground. Immediately Li Su called out, "No, he nailed it to the ground before digging the hole." It was so much fun to be the shadow and to copy everything Bear did that all the children wanted turns. So, Ms. Carmen had them find partners and, while she played "If You Go Out in the Woods Today" on the piano, the pairs moved as bears and their matching shadows.

The children wrote two individual pieces of writing in the course of the *Bear Shadow* experience in addition to the group writing of their experiment with shadows. One piece was a two-page spread for the book describing a new way for Bear to lose his shadow. These were illustrated and displayed. Some children could write on their own with the teacher only checking in with the students and giving them some spelling help. Others dictated their text after completing their illustrations, and the teacher printed the text on scrap paper for them to copy on the page. The other piece of writing was the text for the covers on their books *The Secrets My Shadow Knows about Me*.

Part way through this web of experiences, Ms. Carmen considered the possibility that the children might not know what real bears are like. The small zoo in their town lacked a bear. The children might think that real bears are as cuddly as teddy bears. She made a quick trip to the library for some informational material on bears. She brought back the encyclopedia section on bears and had the children draw a life-size bear shape on brown paper. She also found *Bears in the Wild* by Ada and Frank Graham, which had some interesting information, although it was intended for older children. She read parts to her students, and they all enjoyed the illustrations. She also read *The Biggest Bear* by Lynd Ward, which graphically shows what happens when a cuddly baby bear grows up. A veterinarian was invited to come and talk with the children about the similarities and differences between wild animals and pets. The children prepared a list of questions to ask the veterinarian, which Ms. Carmen wrote on chart paper, and they read aloud together. The children enjoyed their work with *Bear Shadow*, and Ms. Carmen was pleased to check off on the list of essential skills the things they had done.

> Respond to storytelling by drawing or painting.
> Identify main ideas of a speaker's messsage.
> Engage in creative dramatic activities and nonverbal communication.
> Sequence events appropriately when relating them.
> Present poems chorally.
> Give a short sequence of directions for others to follow.
> Use information and ideas from personal experience as source for writing.
> Write stories.
> Recognize that rewriting and editing are done with a particular purpose and audience in mind.
> Use basic conventions of capitalization and punctuation.
> Write legible manuscript letters.[4]

In addition to teaching a wide variety of skills, one advantage of integrating the language arts work was saving time by using the literature and experiences with shadows as bases for writing and discussion. It was unnecessary to brainstorm topics for children to write about or to provide motivating ideas. Their writing flowed from the books and poems they were reading and from the related activities. Because of the dramatic activities and discussions, no one had to wait for the rest of the class to finish. The children genuinely enjoyed hearing each other's ideas about getting rid of shadows. Ms. Carmen could compliment them on their printing as their displays went up and praise their "Secrets" books. The wide variety of activities in the literature-based web kept up an exciting pace. Every morning Ms. Carmen found the children waiting expectantly for the new and different things they would do that day.

Integrating Several Texts

Integrating literature into the middle school curriculum presented different problems for Mr. Heffler, who teaches seventh grade. His school provided an English anthology as well as a regular English textbook.

The anthology was divided into units that focused on either an author or a topic such as discovery, animals, or myth and legend. It included lessons on literary understandings, such as theme or point of view, and on vocabulary, reading skills, and composition. The English book was also divided into units that covered elements of grammar, writing or study skills, and composition in describing events, writing letters, or writing biographies.

Most of the teachers in Mr. Heffler's school alternated a unit from the anthology with one from the English text. He found that he never had enough time to do it all, and the kids groaned every time he told them to get out their English books. Because each book had different writing assignments, the students' writing didn't flow from their experiences. There was never enough time to share the writing, edit it, and polish final drafts. Each day was chopped into small bits of time, leaving little time for discussing things that really mattered or doing drama and choral reading.

Mr. Heffler realized that grammar and usage were taught every year, and that some students knew much of it already. He set up that strand on a mastery basis, using the "Review" sections within each unit as a kind of pretest. Since the reviews were designed to correspond with the preceding lessons in the text, if the students passed the pretest, they could skip the corresponding pages. If they did not do well on parts of the pretest, then they completed the corresponding pages of explanation and practice.

Mr. Heffler kept on file a master checklist for each peer writing group. The writing groups served as the main organizational feature of his class. They functioned as discussion groups when small groups were desirable and as conferencing and sharing groups for writing. When Mr. Heffler studied the master checklist for the grammar and usage lessons, he sometimes assembled a group for instruction if there were several students with the same deficiency. Otherwise his class was essentially a writing workshop with an ongoing strand of literature and twice weekly literature discussions.

The week was structured so that on Mondays and Wednesdays most class time was used to discuss the literature they were reading and to do other literature-related response activities. On those days about 15 minutes was used for writing—conferring with Mr. Heffler, drafting, revising, looking up information, or reading. Fridays were group sharing time. Students shared with each other their week's work, received help from one another, cooperated on proofreading drafts, and took responsibility for "publishing" writing from their group. Tuesdays and Thursdays were work time—writing, teacher conferences, small group instruction, grammar mastery, and reading. Mr. Heffler always had extra books relating to the unit they were reading from the public library, the school library, or from the teacher's private paperback collection. The students were immersed in reading and writing and in conversations about what they were doing. Most instruction in writing conventions was given individually during teacher-student conferences as specific needs arose. Students worked at their own pace on grammar mastery, although Mr. Heffler occasionally insisted that procrastinators deal with grammar before the next conference. He knew everything they were doing, even though he spent only about 20 minutes per peer group each afternoon checking over that day's records.

The Teacher and the Language Arts Program

The three teachers described in this chapter taught language arts with an emphasis on literature. They integrated the various aspects of their programs, doing away with separate lessons on each aspect of the language arts. They found that the children in their classes—whether first grade, third grade, or seventh grade—seemed to learn more and to enjoy their work more with this focus on literature. Certainly these teachers enjoyed teaching more.

Teachers who implement an integrated language arts program need to structure learning situations just as traditional teachers do; they simply do it in a different way. Structure comes from the questions asked, from the materials made available in the classroom, and from the teacher's knowledge of the subject matter and of each person's interests and abilities. It is not a matter of just doing anything at all and having students learn; it is allowing them to meet challenging and purposeful situations from which they learn best.

The teacher keeps careful records of each person's progress. Through careful observations and individual conferences, the learning needs of each student are monitored. Evaluation and subsequent guidance by the teacher are part of the daily routine, and students are frequently engaged in evaluating their own work and establishing their own learning goals.

Students are constantly involved in activities that reflect an understanding of their learning needs and abilities. Work on skills is balanced with more imaginative activities. Oral experiences are part of the classroom, as are writing and reading experiences. Students have experiences with productive language as well as with receptive language. In essence, the environment is one in which students participate actively in their own learning, and school is an enjoyable place to be.

A good teacher may intuitively provide such a learning environment. The qualities that make a good or successful teacher are cited in a teacher competency report by Marvin Roth for the American Association of School Administrators. The findings were compiled from more than 400 related studies over the last 25 years. In the report, Roth identified specific characteristics of good teachers. His guidelines appear below, adapted in the form of a checklist. Read each statement carefully and decide how you would rank as a teacher.

Characteristics of Good Teachers

Yes   *No*

___   ___   You believe not only that children can learn and want to learn but also that you can help them.

___   ___   You believe that teaching children is more important than teaching subjects.

___   ___   You have empathy, and not only do you understand how the student feels, but you let the student know you understand.

___   ___   You listen to get information and listen to help the student.

___   ___   You listen to both sides and get information from those who will be affected before making a decision.

___   ___   You see people as individuals and not as blacks, Indians, or the kids who live in trailers.

___   ___   You have the drive to share your knowledge with students.

___   ___   You read and collect things—on vacation, for example—to bring to class.

___   ___   You use specific teaching techniques that you can describe.

___   ___   You derive satisfaction from your investment in your work—not from what you do as a teacher, but from what you see children learn.

___   ___   You have characteristics that activate learning and have a drive to build rapport.

___   ___   You balance organization with flexibility.

___   ___   You have high expectations for children, coupled with an acceptance of children as they are.

___   ___   You are innovative—for example, you have twenty years of experience, not one year of experience twenty times.[5]

Needed Directions in the Language Arts for the Future

Trends or educational movements seem to fade in and out of vogue. To cite one of many examples, numerous schools were built in the 1960s and 1970s around an open-space concept—one large area without walls to separate classes. This physical plan was designed to facilitate team planning and teaching and grouping for skills across grade levels. Now, educators are espousing the virtues of the self-contained classroom—the fashionable classroom of the 1940s and 1950s. And many are exploring ways to convert schools without walls to schools with walls where one teacher is responsible for children's learning needs.

Rather than dwell on issues, trends, or educational movements—which are usually short-lived—it seems appropriate to discuss needed directions in the language arts for the future on the basis of what we know currently about how children learn and what teaching methods promote learning.

Valuing Oral Language

There is a tendency to devalue oral communication in school, perhaps because, once spoken, it is gone. We usually do not grade talk the way we grade writing, and so we deemphasize it. We also tend to assume that all children can listen if only they would, which is probably true only at the base comprehension level. However, we cannot expect students of any age to be able to make the complicated interrelationships and judgments that are required for higher levels of listening without instruction and opportunity.

Writing is an important aspect of schooling, but as students leave school they spend considerably more time talking and listening than writing and reading. Information about news, current events, and politics comes more from listening to the radio or watching television than from reading magazines or newspapers. Certainly politicians and advertisers believe in oral communication since that is where the bulk of their expenditures go. Studies of how people spend their time indicate that much of it—far more than half—is spent listening and talking. We need to prepare students to get the most from listening and to present their ideas orally in the best possible way.

Emphasizing Language Use

In traditional English classes most of the time and energy is spent talking about language and labeling it in various ways, rather than developing skills for using it to accomplish real purposes. Teachers need to develop students who can explain their ideas, describe events, and retell things they have experienced or imagined, which is more important than preparing students to identify a noun clause or determine if a sentence is active or passive. The latter should be reserved for students interested in English as a discipline, not for those who need to focus on effective use of their language. Language should be used for a wide variety of purposes in the classroom, not just for answering the teacher's questions or those in the textbook. Students should be using language to describe, to clarify, to compare or contrast, to summarize, to make analogies, and to evaluate ideas.

Students develop their ability to use language by learning more words and more about the words they know. They become sensitive to the connotations of the words they use and to their audience. They refine their usage and become more adept at adjusting their usage to fit the situation and the mode of communication. Precision and art in communication are more important than identifying adjectives.

Becoming Readers and Writers

Although many children know how to read and write, they are not really readers or writers. That is, they do not choose to read for their own enjoyment. They do not think of themselves as writers. Teachers have taught the skills but missed the real purpose. Our task now is to go beyond teaching how; we must help our students become readers and writers.

Students do not become readers by reading only basal textbooks—even the best basals with good selections of literature. They do not become readers by answering questions about the events in a story or by doing exercises in a workbook. Those tasks may help children learn to read, but they do not make children readers. They become readers when they find books, stories, or poems that make them think, "Oh, I've felt just like that!" or "I wonder what I would do in that circumstance?" or even "What a perfect way to say that!" You know you have a reader on your hands when a student hides a book inside a textbook, or when you hear students telling each other about a good book to read.

For years teachers have taught students how to write and have had them write essays once a week to prove it, but they have not created many writers. Writers need an audience that responds to their work. Writers need to discover all the different ways they can use writing for their own needs. The once-a-week essay accomplishes none of these things. However, just as we can help students become readers by making connections with good literature, we can help them become writers by developing their knowledge of what good writing is by providing books and stories by fine writers.

Preventing Testing from Determining Teaching

In an attempt to be more accountable to the public and to ensure that children get a good education, we have created an almost overwhelming number of tests. There are pretests and posttests, mastery tests, criterion tests, standardized tests, system-wide tests, state tests, commercial tests, and so on. While a greater number of tests does not necessarily contribute to better learning or teaching, it too often determines what is taught. Part of the problem with tests is that they tend to measure the knowledge that is most easily tested in a machine-scorable format, whether or not that knowledge is important. The effect of tests on classroom teachers is to force them to spend class time on points that will be tested. This time is wasteful if the tests fail to reflect what is important for children to learn.

Composition is a good example. Commercial test developers try to measure students' ability to write by means of multiple answer, computer-scored tests. Composition teachers and researchers insist that writing ability can be measured only by having students write, which is expensive to evaluate. If teachers accede to pressure from commercial test developers, tests on writing skills will measure punctuation, spelling, usage, and vocabulary but will not measure a person's struggle to organize and sequence ideas, or to choose the right words for expressing their ideas according to what the reader can be expected to know. In short, the test will not measure students' ability to write.

Using Literature as a Context for Learning

While personal experience is important in learning and in language learning, it has limits. You cannot rely on first-hand experiences as the sole source of ideas and discoveries. Of the available secondary sources of experience, literature is one of the richest in language structure and vocabulary. It is also rich in presenting the past, the present, and the future. It presents reality and fantasy, introducing real people and imaginary ones. It takes us from our own town and state to foreign countries that we only dream of visiting.

When literature is well written, we are touched because we find that someone else has felt what we feel, thought what we sometimes think, and dreamed dreams not unlike our own. We can be swept away by the beauty of words or by the aptness of a phrase, or we can be angry when the words show an ugly reality. Literature has power to evoke

Literature provides a context for meaningful listening, talking, writing, and reading experiences.

strong emotional responses and strong images. It can truly provide a sense of living the experience. Literature establishes a context within which listening, talking, writing, and reading take place naturally—the perfect framework for the language arts.

Summary

Language arts is often described in terms of its modes—listening, speaking, writing, and reading—rather than in terms of its content—language, literature, and composition. This chapter describes the characteristics of a good language arts program in which children have opportunities to use their skills in real situations for their own purposes. The program is framed in literature, which serves to integrate language and composition work. Such a program involves students in learning, offers them opportunities to integrate what they are learning, and provides for individualization based on skills and interest.

The chapter describes three different classrooms in which such a literature-based program is implemented in different ways. In the first-grade classroom, the teacher does not have a language arts textbook. Instead, she uses a storybook as the point of departure for a wide variety of activities involving the language arts modes as well as science and mathematics. In the third-grade classroom, the teacher has a textbook but uses it as a framework for planning and to check student progress. The same topics are covered in literature-related lessons developed to use more student-generated thinking. In the seventh-grade classroom, the teacher has both an anthology of literature and an English textbook. He sets up a writing workshop with a specialized focus on responding to literature and teaches the grammar and usage language component through an individualized mastery program.

The final section of the chapter describes the directions that the language arts should follow in the future, with more attention paid to oral language, a emphasis on language use, a concern for developing readers and writers, an appropriate use of testing, and a foundation of literature as the context for learning the language arts.

Questions for Discussion

1. Why are individualization, involvement, and integration characteristics of a good language arts program?
2. What are some ways that literature can be used in language arts teaching?
3. Discuss the difference between "knowing how to read" and "being a reader." What will help students become readers?
4. How can tests be used appropriately in elementary and middle schools?

Notes

1. Kenneth Goodman, *What's Whole in Whole Language?* (Portsmouth, NH: Heinemann, 1986), 26. © 1986 by Kenneth Goodman. Published by Scholastic-TAB Publications. Used with permission.

2. Myra Cohn Livingston, "The Right Place," in *The Way Things Are and Other Poems* (New York: Atheneum, 1974), 10. Copyright © 1974 by Myra Cohn Livingston. Reprinted by permission of Marian Reiner for the author.

3. Leila Ward, *I Am Eyes—Ni Macho* (New York: Greenwillow, 1978), unpaged.

4. *Essential Elements for Elementary Education* (Austin, TX: Region IV Education Service Center, 1984), unpaged.

5. Marvin J. Roth, *Teacher Competency Report of the American Association of School Administrators* (Reno, NV: Selection Research, Inc., 1980), unpaged. Used with permission of the author, Selection Research, Inc., Reno, Nevada.

Bibliography: Children's Literature

Asch, Frank. *Happy Birthday, Moon*. New York: Prentice Hall, 1982.

Asch, Frank. *Mooncake*. New York: Prentice Hall, 1983.

Asch, Frank. *Skyfire*. New York: Prentice Hall, 1984.

Asch, Frank. *Bear Shadow*. New York: Prentice Hall, 1985.

Asch, Frank. *Moongame*. New York: Prentice Hall, 1985.

Freeman, Don. *Bearymore*. New York: Viking Press, 1976.

Graham, Ada and Frank Graham. *Bears in the Wild*. Illustrated by D. D. Tyler. New York: Delacorte Press, 1981.

Livingston, Myra Cohn. "The Right Place," in *The Way Things Are and Other Poems*. New York: Atheneum, 1974.

McCloskey, Robert. *Blueberries for Sal*. New York: Viking Press, 1949.

Milne, A. A. *Winnie-the-Pooh*. New York: Dutton, 1926.

Moore, Lilian. "Shadows," in *See My Lovely Poison Ivy*. New York: Atheneum, 1975.

Tompert, Ann. *Nothing Sticks Like a Shadow*. Illustrated by Lynn Munsinger. Boston: Houghton Mifflin, 1984.

Walker, Barbara K. *I Packed My Trunk*. Illustrated by Carl Koch. New York: Follett, 1969.

Ward, Leila. *I Am Eyes—Ni Macho*. New York: Greenwillow, 1978.

Ward, Lynd. *The Biggest Bear*. Boston: Houghton Mifflin, 1952.

Zolotow, Charlotte. "Look," in L. B. Hopkins, ed., *Me! A Book of Poems*. New York: Seabury Press, 1970.

Chapter 2

Literature in the Language Arts

Literature in the Language Arts

Values of Literature

Provides Enjoyment

Nourishes Imagination

Broadens Experiences and Background Knowledge

Influences Language and Reading Development

Enriches Writing

Selecting and Evaluating Literature

Plot

Characterization

Setting

Theme

Style

Point of View

Broadening Knowledge of Literature

Fiction: Realistic and Historical

Fantasy: Fantastic Stories, High Fantasy, and Science Fiction

Traditional Stories: Folktales, Fables, Myths, and Legends

Poetry

Nonfiction: Autobiography, Biography, and Informational Books

Picture Books

Bibliography: Children's Literature

Do you recognize the following Mother Goose rhyme?

> *Old Mother Hubbard,*
> *She went to the cupboard*
> *To fetch her poor dog a bone,*
> *But when she got there,*
> *The cupboard was bare,*
> *And so the poor dog had none.*

More than likely, you not only recognize this familiar rhyme, but can recite it from memory because you heard it as a child. Suppose you are asked to recite "Mary Had a Little Lamb" or "Humpty Dumpty." Can you do it? Considering children's stories rather than Mother Goose rhymes, can you answer the following questions? In what book will you find Charlotte, Wilbur, and Templeton? Which of these three book characters is the spider? With whom did Peter Rabbit find himself in trouble when he entered the garden?

If childhood years are enriched with an abundance of good literature, then adult lives are enriched as well. Huck, Hepler, and Hickman suggest, "Literature is the imaginative shaping of life and thought into the forms and structures of language. The province of literature is the human condition: life with all its feelings, thoughts, and insights."[1] We discover through books such as E. B. White's *Charlotte's Web* an in-depth understanding of what it means to be a devoted friend, and we grieve along with Wilbur when Charlotte, the spider, dies. We recognize Peter's plight when he finds himself in trouble in Mr. Macgregor's garden, yet we also recognize that Peter is in trouble because he does not heed his mother's warning. She told him explicitly not to go near Mr. Macgregor's garden. If you remember the end of Beatrix Potter's classic tale of *Peter Rabbit*, Peter is given a dose of camomile tea and sent to bed, while his three well-behaved sisters, Flopsy, Mopsy, and Cottontail, enjoy bread, milk, and blackberries at suppertime. Certainly, there is a subtle lesson to be learned here. Children's literature has value in the home and in school. Its value is priceless when we consider the inherent benefits—both personal and educational—that literature offers.

Values of Literature

Provides Enjoyment

Children can discover early the joy and laughter that accompanies the reading of one of Arnold Lobel's books about his humorous characters, as in *Frog and Toad Together* and *Frog and Toad Are Friends*. Students can read and reread Shel Silverstein's poems in *Where the Side-*

walk Ends and *The Light in the Attic* until they have learned many of them. A first-grade teacher read Silverstein's popular "Boa Constrictor" to her children and then gave them copies of the verse. Over a period of several days, the young children read the verse in concert with their teacher, dramatized it through movement experiences, read it to partners, and shared it at home with their parents. By the end of a week, all of the first graders could read "Boa Constrictor" as well as recite it. The children expressed delight in their ability to read and say the verse. Their enjoyment with this one verse led to reading and sharing other Shel Silverstein rhymes in the class, as well as verses by other children's poets such as Jack Prelutsky, David McCord, and Karla Kuskin.

In a fourth-grade classroom, a teacher read aloud Judy Blume's book, *Tales of a Fourth-Grade Nothing*. The students enjoyed the story so much that they asked the teacher to leave the book in the classroom library area, where they read it again. By the end of the school year, more than half the class had reread the book, and three students indicated they had reread it a third time. As an extension of the book, a small group of fourth graders wrote a new chapter, entitled "A New Tale of a Fourth-Grade Nothing," bound it, and presented their published work to the class. As you can imagine, this new chapter became a favorite addition to the classroom library.

If a love of literature and reading is created early through book and poetry experiences that promote enjoyment, children not only learn to read, they learn the pleasures associated with reading. And these same children grow into adults who pursue and sustain a habit of reading throughout their lifetimes.

Nourishes Imagination

"Children are natural fantasists," says Lively. "They have an elasticity of imagination that most of us lose in our adult life. What literature can do is nourish that imagination and give it something on which to feed and flourish and fly off into its own discoveries and adventures."[2] During an Academy Awards acceptance speech, Stephen Spielberg talked about the relationship between reading literature and the development of one's imagination. He lamented that the great screenplays of the future are in jeopardy of being written. Why? To paraphrase Spielberg, "Great writers are avid readers, and through their devotion to reading, they develop their keen imaginations. Today, unfortunately, fewer people are dedicated readers, and hence in the future, we shall have fewer great writers."[3]

Reading, unlike television viewing in most instances, requires an active mind. A reader is in control, creating mental pictures, rereading to ponder a point, stopping to share, rereading, and discussing some bit of thought-provoking content with someone else. Reading challenges the mind and imagination, and often encourages the reader to ask, "What if . . . ?"

Broadens Experiences and Background Knowledge

When children have vicarious experiences through literature, they broaden their knowledge of the world and consequently add to their background knowledge. For instance, if students have not experienced a day in the snow, they do so while reading Ezra Jack Keats's *The Snowy Day.* They will know how it feels to make tracks in the snow, how to make snow angles, and how to firmly pack a snowball they wish to keep. Most children know very little about China, especially from firsthand experience, but through Leonard Everett Fisher's book, *The Great Wall of China,* they can participate in a part of Chinese history and can understand the hardships and complexities that surrounded the creation of the Great Wall. After reading the book, students can close their eyes, use their imaginations, and mentally picture the Great Wall of China. For some children, Fisher's book may be only one of many stories they read about China. Jean Fritz's book *Homesick* presents middle-grade students with an authentic account of life in China in the 1920s. This story is autobiographical, and students who read it may become fascinated with the section that contains Fritz's family photographs from their days in China. Older readers will extend their knowledge of China when they read another Jean Fritz book, *China Homecoming,* a nonfiction work that also interests adult readers.

Reading comprehension and background knowledge are related. It makes sense that the more a child knows about a subject, the better the child will comprehend written material about that subject. The reverse is also true. If a child knows very little about a topic, the child's comprehension of material on that topic is usually less. Wide reading of literature provides children with world knowledge that helps them as readers. Wide reading also provides children with information that broadens and strengthens their cultural literacy.

Influences Language and Reading Development

How can something as simple as reading books aloud be so helpful to children who are learning to read? How can the language of stories and poems assist young learners to advance linguistically? Looking closely at literary language, students discover rhythmical words as in the following poem:

The Modern Hiawatha

He killed the noble Mudjokovis,
With the skin he made him mittens,
Made them with the fur side inside,
Made them with the skin side outside,
He, to get the warm side inside,
Put the inside skin side outside.
He, to get the cold side outside,
Put the warm side fur side inside.
That's why he put the fur side inside,
Why he put the skin side outside,
Why he turned them inside outside.[4]
    —George A. Strong

You discover emotional language as in Katherine Paterson's story *Jacob Have I Loved.*

> She flashed her eyes at me. I would've growed," she said like a
> stubborn child. "He run off and left before I had a chance." Then
> she put her head down on her gnarled hands and began to cry.
> "I turned out purty," she said between sobs. "By the time I was
> thirteen I was the purtiest little thing on the island, but he was
> already gone. I waited for two more years before I married Wil-
> liam, but he never come back 'til now." She wiped her eyes on
> her shawl and leaned her head back watching a spot on the
> ceiling.[5]

You also discover descriptive language as in Nancy Willard's *Firebrat.*

> A train rushed past and its roar sucked up Sean's words. The
> newsstand, the turnstile, the benches, the people waiting—
> everything seemed about to be swept away.
>   Then the train was gone. The air stood so still Molly could
> hear water dripping. She was about to ask Sean if he heard it too
> when a second train rushed through the darkness toward them,
> beaming its light on the walls, as if searching for something—a
> face, a sign, a window—before it screeched to a stop.[6]

From literature, children learn the complexities of language, the
diversity in its usage, the emotions of its tones, and the softness of its
beauty. When children hear and read literature, they also adopt literary
words and phrases and make them their own. Think how often children incorporate into their own stories the familiar words, "They lived
happily ever after" or "Long, long ago." Young children internalize the

structures and conventions of language through continued exposure to quality literature.

Research supports the above claims. Courtney Cazden conducted an experimental study to determine if the finding of certain grammatical constructions in young children's oral language was related to parents' frequent expansion of children's telegraphic speech.[7] In reviewing her findings, Cazden reported that children whose statements were expanded by adult responses scored higher than two other groups on six measures of language development. The significance of this finding for the use of literature in language arts is the study's reliance on reading stories aloud to this group to stimulate conversation and discussion. In citing implications of the research results, the investigator suggests that children be given extensive opportunities to discuss ideas out loud and that books are ideal for creating talk about the pictures or story content.

A similar study was conducted at New York University.[8] More than 500 black children, kindergarten through grade three, were involved in the year-long research effort. Approximately half the children (ten classrooms) assigned to the experimental group "participated in a literature-based language arts program intended to expand experience, conceptual ability, control over the structure of language and the range of language used."[9] Selected books were read aloud each day, followed by activities emphasizing the use of children's oral language. The control group—the remaining half of the participating children—enjoyed a literature program, but the enrichment activities were not based on oral language. The results of the research indicated that literature expanded language skills for both groups of children; however, students in the experimental group evidenced the greatest gains, with the most significant increase at the kindergarten level.

In view of these findings, the director of the study, Bernice Cullinan, makes the recommendation that the literature-based oral language program begin early. She further states that emphasis on oral language enhances children's mastery of standard dialect while maintaining facility in their own dialect.

From the results of these two well-designed and often quoted studies, we conclude that reading books aloud—and then allowing time for plenty of conversation and discussion—enhances children's oral language development. It appears too that students find greater opportunity to become proficient in a more socially acceptable dialect when they participate in this type of language environment.

As the second part of a linguistic study, Carol Chomsky directed an investigation involving children between ages five and ten.[10] She gathered extensive information about each child's exposure to reading. For example, data were compiled regarding the amount the child read and was read to, and the degree of complexity of the reading material. Additional data was provided by Charlotte Huck's *Taking Inventory of Children's Literary Background*, a measure indicating a child's knowledge of content from sixty well-known books.[11] The primary purpose of the study was to determine the relationship between reading exposure and a child's rate of linguistic development. Since Chomsky considered written language as potentially more complex than oral speech, she made the assumption that children who read and hear a variety of rich and complex materials receive greater linguistic benefits than children who are nonliterary. The findings on all reading measures were highly significant, leading to the conclusion that reading exposure and linguistic stages of development are strongly related. Huck's inventory proved an excellent measure since it consistently showed a positive relationship between scores and children's linguistic stages of development.

A summary of the results and their educational implications speak profoundly to the classroom teacher. Children's exposure to the more complex language available from reading seems to be related to increased knowledge of the language. This finding implies that children should experience wider reading of more complex texts containing rich language rather than restrictive, controlled reading materials.

Considering the relationship between literature and reading, Dorothy Cohen conducted an extensive study to determine the influence of literature on vocabulary and reading achievement.[12] Cohen identified second-grade classrooms containing children who were slow to learn to read. Each of the experimental classes received 50 books to be read aloud during the year, with some selections to be read more than once. The books chosen for the study dealt with universal experiences, permitted emotional identification with characters, and contained language that flowed smoothly and best conveyed ideas and images to children. No limitation was placed on vocabulary when selecting the texts. Throughout the academic year, experimental group teachers read stories aloud daily for twenty minutes. These reading aloud sessions were followed by a variety of activities, while the control group received no special attention. The results of the study showed that the experimental group developed significantly more than the control group in word knowledge, quality of vocabulary, and reading comprehension.

It is apparent from research that children should be exposed to books that contain complex language and vocabulary. They should not be limited to hearing and reading books that have controlled vocabularies, such as basal readers. In traditional basal reading lessons, children are introduced to new vocabulary words that they may encounter in a story. Teachers, however, cannot introduce every new word that children may discover in their reading materials. How, then, do children expand their reading vocabularies beyond those words that are taught directly? They broaden their word knowledge through reading—listening to stories read aloud and reading books independently. Madeleine L'Engle, Newbery Award-winning author of *A Wrinkle in Time*, confirmed through her own childhood experiences that wide and frequent reading contributes to one's acquisition of vocabulary. "There weren't any limited-vocabulary books in those days. I learned vocabulary by coming across new words in my reading for fun. . . . I didn't stop to look up the new words; I was far too interested in what I was reading. By the time I'd come across a word in two or three books, the shades of its meaning would automatically become clear, and the word would be added to my vocabulary."[13]

Reading literature aloud should be a common occurrence in all classrooms, kindergarten through high school. In elementary school classes, children should hear stories and poems read aloud every day. The educational rewards and benefits are far too great to omit such a simple, powerful activity from the daily classroom schedule. In reporting the results of his longitudinal study of the literacy achievement of children, Gordon Wells highlights the significance of reading stories aloud to young children.[14] He relates the story of Jonathan, who had heard more than 6,000 stories prior to attending school, and Rosie, who had not heard one. Jonathan ranked highest among all the children studied at age seven, while Rosie ranked at the bottom in achievement. At the end of their schooling, Jonathan still ranked the highest, and Rosie's achievement level remained unchanged.

Children should also have time to engage in daily recreational reading. Both teachers and students benefit from scheduled time for uninterrupted, sustained silent reading. In the words of Frank Smith, "Children learn to read by reading."[15] Children need to read more than a few pages each day in a basal reader if they are to become fluent, motivated readers.

Enriches Writing

Research studies substantiate the observation that reading and writing are related. In summarizing research findings, Sandra Stotsky says, "The correlational studies show almost consistently that better writers tend to be better readers (of their own writing as well as of other reading material), that better writers tend to read more than poorer writers, and that better readers tend to produce more syntactically mature writing than poorer readers."[16] Other research also suggests that pleasure reading and independent reading may improve writing as well as, or better than, grammar study.[17]

Conducting a four-year longitudinal study using children's literature to teach composition, Mills discovered that fourth graders who read or listened to and then discussed children's literature prior to writing scored significantly higher in their free writing than control group students who were not exposed to the literature stimulus.[18] The results appear to indicate that children can become effective writers from hearing, reading, and discussing quality literature.

In another study, Eckhoff compared children who read from a simplified basal text to students who read from a text that more closely matched literary prose.[19] She discovered that children's writing tended to resemble the type or style of writing in their reading texts. It seems clear that literature provides models for children's writing. Knowledge of this fact challenges the teacher to find the best, richest literature possible to share with students.

Selecting and Evaluating Literary Elements

The importance of children's literature in the classroom is clearly established, and the importance of selecting quality literature to share and use with students is clearly evident. How can a teacher select the best literature from the approximately 3,000 children's books published each year? What criteria should be applied when evaluating books for children? Without a doubt, each of us has a favorite book that was special to us when we were children. Why is that book memorable? Was it a good children's book? Answers to these questions emerge when we learn to recognize and evaluate such literary elements as plot, character, setting, and theme, as well as an author's style and use of point of view. In discussing the various literary elements, touchstone books—books that have stood the test of time or have received some critical acclaim—are used as examples in this section.

Plot

Children want action in their stories. The plan of action in a story is called the *plot.* It is the sequence of events or the order in which things happen. An author purposefully chooses a plot, thinking that a particular sequence or plan of action best tells the particular story. If the author makes the appropriate choice, the plot produces conflict, tension, and action that creates in the reader a sustained interest in the story.

Most children's stories, especially those that are written for young children, follow a narrative or chronological order. Events are told in the order of their happening. Flashbacks may occur within this sequenced pattern, as in Chris Van Allsburg's *The Wreck of the Zepher;* however, the young child sometimes finds a story difficult to understand if it contains flashbacks. Originality is an important consideration when we are evaluating plot. When an author combines original, fresh ideas with a well developed plot, a foundation is established for creating a good story that children will enjoy.

Characterization

True characterization, like a well-constructed and developed plot, is essential to a well-written story. Characters in children's stories may be human beings or personified animals or objects. The term *character development* refers to the way a character grows and changes over a period of time in a story. It also refers to the way an author shows the complexity and wholeness of a character. Major characters within stories should be well-developed and three-dimensional in nature.

How do we get to know characters within literature? One way is for the author to share with the reader what the character is thinking. We discover firsthand the character's innermost thoughts, desires, and dreams. Another way for the writer to reveal the character is through specific actions. As we observe actions, we discover that the character may be selfish, arrogant, timid, or shy. Actions are often accompanied by speech, so we learn about a character through what that character says or what other characters say. An author also uses description, showing the readers the physical appearance of the character. Finally, the reader may discover more about a character through the author's narration.

Book characters stand out in our memories. Some we get to know well: Arnold Lobel's Frog and Toad, A. A. Milne's Winnie-the-Pooh, Beverly Cleary's Ramona, and the list grows. These authors, and others like them, develop characters in such a way that we get to know them for life. We can describe their physical features, discuss their personalities, and talk about their unique behaviors. The characters come to life. Once a book character achieves this life-like quality in the reader's mind, the author has achieved a hallmark in writing. In books for older students, characters should show growth and change. It is more difficult to show character development in books for younger children because of their abbreviated texts. Stereotypes should be avoided in books intended for any age student.

Setting

The term *setting* refers to time and place, and both character and plot development occur within the context of the setting. A story may be set in the past, present, or future. The time and place may be viewed as essential or as relatively unimportant depending on the writer's purpose. For example, if the author wishes to convey a universal situation, the time period, season of the year, and location become irrelevant; whereas, if a story is set in the past during the Civil War, time and place become extremely important. In telling a believable story, the author must reconstruct a setting that is both accurate and authentic.

In evaluating the element of setting, we must consider first the significance of time and place to the story. Is a mere backdrop setting appropriate because the story has universal implications, or does the setting play an integral part in telling the story? Once we answer these questions, we must ask if the writer creates a setting that fits with the plot and presentation of the characters. The setting should work in the story. It should be credible and authentic.

Theme

If you ask, What is the author's primary purpose in writing this story? you are asking, What is the central *theme?* The theme may be growing up, accepting others, overcoming fears, surviving, or meeting the obligations of friendship. Children as well as adults often experience difficulty in identifying the central theme in some books because well-written stories can be read for several layers of meaning. These layers of meaning may be identified as minor themes that run throughout the story. In a discussion of E. B. White's *Charlotte's Web,* Huck, Hepler, and Hickman offer this example: "On one level of the story of *Charlotte's Web* by E. B. White is simply an absurd but amusing tale of how a spider saves the life of a pig; on another level, it reveals the meaning of loneliness and the obligations of friendship. A third layer of significance can be seen in the acceptance of death as a natural part of the cycle of life."[20]

If we consider E. B. White's own comments about the story, we realize that there are other meaningful messages: It is "an appreciative story. . . . It celebrates life, the seasons, the goodness of the barn, the beauty of the world, the glory of everything."[21] This well-written book clearly contains minor themes—many layers of meaning and subtle messages to ponder. However, if you are to identify a central theme in *Charlotte's Web,* the concept of friendship exists as an overarching or controlling idea in the story.

Since a theme carries a message to the reader, it is important for an author to lead the reader to discover new insights and truths associated with the theme. The author should avoid didacticism, or preaching a message to the reader. The theme also should be worth sharing with children.

Style

In the words of Rebecca Lukens, "Style is basically words, *how* an author says something as opposed to *what* he or she says. From an infinite number of words available, the writer chooses and arranges words to create a particular story. . . . Tone, word choice, grammatical structure, devices of comparison, sound, and rhythm are style. All of these elements vary with the author's purpose, as the idea, the incidents, and the characters vary. Style gives the whole work its distinction and makes the story memorable."[22]

Read the following descriptions. The first one appears in Cynthia Voigt's *Homecoming*. The second excerpt is taken from Bette Greene's *Summer of My German Soldier*. How might you decribe the two writing styles? What similarities do you detect between the two styles of writing?

> *The long beach was a flat crescent that marked the edge of a shallow cove. Children straddled the water's edge and a few bolder ones were actually swimming. Towels crowded the sand, like bright pieces of confetti. On the towels lay people in bathing suits, surrounded by picnic baskets, paper bags, canvas totes, blaring radios and coolers full of ice and drinks.*[23]

> *A playful breeze brought a scent of roses into the breakfast room where it mingled with the purely kitchen aroma of coffee perking, griddle cakes rising, and bacon frying. The table was set for two with real cotton napkins, the newest of everyday tablecloths, and our fancy dinnertime* made-in-Japan *china.*[24]

Both authors paint pictures for the mind's eye as they select words carefully to describe scenes in their books. They choose words that not only appeal to a reader's sense of sight but also to a reader's sense of smell, taste, touch, and sound. The two authors create texts that flow and read smoothly.

What questions should we ask when we are evaluating style? According to Huck, Hepler, and Hickman, "The best test of an author's style is oral reading. Does it read smoothly and effortlessly? Is the conversation stilted, or does it sound like people talking? Does the author introduce variety in the sentence patterns and his or her use of words?"[25]

Point of View

When an author decides the role or function of the narrator in a story, then the author has chosen a point of view. For example, if a story is told in the first person (*I*), then the writer has chosen the *first-person point of view* for telling the story. Karana tells the reader the story in Scott O'Dell's *Island of the Blue Dolphins*, for example, and the first-person narrator is in charge of revealing the story in Paula Fox's *The Slave Dancer*. Another choice for writers is the *omniscient point of view*. The omniscient narrator tells the story in the third person (*he, she, they*). Since the narrator is all-knowing, readers discover characters' thoughts, feelings, words, and actions through the voice of the narrator. E. B. White chose the omniscient point of view for telling *Charlotte's Web*. Another possibility is the *limited omniscient point of view*, as found in Katherine Paterson's *The Great Gilly Hopkins*. The story is still presented in the third person, but the reader learns the story through the eyes of only one character, usually the protagonist (main character).

In evaluating point of view, it is important to keep in mind that the young child may experience difficulty in understanding the first-person point of view. Because of young children's egocentricity, they may not identify or understand the *I* in a story; however, there are exceptions, including the Dr. Seuss stories. The narrator in stories such as *And to Think I Saw It on Mulberry Street* is not as significant as the nonsense, the sounds of the words, and the colorful cartoon-like illustrations. According to Huck, Hepler, and Hickman, we also "need to ask why the author chose this particular point of view and how the choice influenced the style of writing, moved the action, and revealed the character."[26] As a summary, the following lists questions that seem most pertinent in evaluating literary elements in children's literature.

Questions for Evaluating Literary Elements

Plot	Does it tell a good story?
	Is there action that moves the story along?
	Is the plot original, believable?
Characterization	Do you get to know the major characters?
	Are the characters convincing, believable?
	Are the characters three-dimensional?
	Does the author avoid stereotyping?
Setting	Does the setting work in the story?
	Does the setting fit with the plot and presentation of the characters?
	Is the setting accurate, authentic?
Theme	Does the author avoid didacticism?
	Is the theme worth sharing with children?
Style	Does it read smoothly?
	Does the conversation sound like people talking?
	Does the author use a variety of sentence patterns and words?
Point of View	Does this choice of point of view work in this story?
	Does the point of view fit with the writing style, move the action, and effectively reveal the character(s)?

Broadening Knowledge of Literature

Books can take us back in time, help us relate to the present, or project us into the future. They offer insights as we read about characters who deal with difficult but realistic situations, or they help us become better informed about subjects that reflect our personal interests. Literature offers choices of different kinds of books, which are often referred to as *genres*. The term genre refers to a type of literature, and within different genres we find *subgenres*. The following outlines the kinds of literature presented in picture books as well as in books for older children.

Genres	*Subgenres*
Fiction	realistic
	historical
Fantasy	fantastic stories
	high fantasy
	science fiction
Traditional stories	folktales
	fables
	myths
	legends
Poetry	verse
	narrative
	lyric
	ballad
	free verse
Nonfiction	autobiography
	biography
	informational

Fiction: Realistic and Historical

Contemporary Realistic Fiction

In the category of fiction, realistic stories prevail in popularity among upper-elementary age students. Beverly Cleary's *Dear Mr. Henshaw* and Judy Blume's books *Tales of a Fourth-Grade Nothing* and *Are You There God? It's Me, Margaret* continue to entice new readers. Why? Students relate to the characters and situations in these stories. Contemporary realistic fiction stories such as these favorites address problems and issues that students are dealing with in their own lives. Even though the stories are fictionalized, they are based on real life situations that could actually happen.

Two types of realism emerge in realistic books for today's readers.

One type involves a story that focuses on some kind of social issue. For example, the protagonist may be a victim of race or sex discrimination. The second type of realism centers on a personal problem; for instance, in *Blubber*, the protagonist is overweight and consequently a victim of other children's harassment. How should the following realistic books be evaluated? Rebecca Lukens suggests the following:

> In these kinds of realism the protagonist's problem is the source of plot and conflict, and that conflict may be with self, society, or another person. In a well-written book, character and conflict are both well developed and interrelated. In a poorly written novel, the character may either be stereotypical or seem to be made up only of problems. The physical problems, handicaps, the problems with drugs or sex, or divorce situations, the minority or gender issues become so overwhelming that they may blot out the credibility of the character as a whole human being made up of a mixture of feelings and thoughts, emotion and intellect. Furthermore, in poor fiction of these kinds, the protagonist's problems may be solved in too pat a manner.[27]

If contemporary realistic fiction enables children to understand themselves and others better, then teachers must guide students toward well-written stories that contain well-developed characters and believable conflicts. For example, when students follow the Tillerman children through Cynthia Voigt's two books, *Homecoming* and *Dicey's Song*, they get to know believable characters in plausible situations and conflicts. If students follow Voigt's development of Dicey Tillerman through the third book, *A Solitary Blue*, they know the protagonist at different ages and from all sides. Students relate to Dicey as a friend, seeing how she feels and behaves in various realistic situations. They judge how they might have handled a difficult situation in contrast to how Dicey handles it.

Historical Fiction

Stories that fall into this category take place in the past. The setting, a critical element in this type of literature, reflects the time and place in the past. For instance, the manner in which characters dress and talk reflects both the time period and place where the story occurs.

Any writer of historical fiction is faced with the challenge of combining the historical facts with an imaginative story. Newbery Award–winning author Patricia MacLachlan drew upon an actual event in her family history to write the story *Sarah, Plain and Tall*. The years since Momma died haven't been the easiest for Papa, Caleb, and Anna. Feeling the loneliness along with the pressures of rearing two children, Papa places an ad in a newspaper for a wife and receives an answer from a woman named Sarah. In the following excerpt, notice how the language of the characters fits the 1900 time period of the story and reveals the landscape of the midwestern prairie. The setting reflects the time and place as Sarah travels by train from Maine to the Midwest.

> *Sarah came in the spring. She came through green grass fields that bloomed with Indian paint brush, red and orange, and blue-eyed grass.*
>
> *Papa got up early for the day's long trip to the train and back. He brushed his hair so slick and shiny that Caleb laughed. He wore a clean blue shirt, and a belt instead of suspenders.*
>
> *He fed and watered the horses, talking to them as he hitched them up to the wagon. Old Bess, calm and kind; Jack, wild-eyed, reaching over to nip Bess on the neck.*
>
> *"Clear day, Bess," said Papa, rubbing her nose.*
>
> *"Settle down, Jack." He leaned his head on Jack.*
>
> *And then Papa drove off along the dirt road to fetch Sarah. Papa's new wife. Maybe our new mother.*[28]

Fantasy: Fantastic Stories, High Fantasy, and Science Fiction

Fantastic Stories

The challenge of the fantasy writer is to suspend the reader's disbelief, and to achieve this feat an author must excel at making imaginary worlds and their inhabitants so credible that readers want to believe they exist. In fantastic stories such as *Mrs. Frisby and the Rats of NIMH* and *The Wind in the Willows*, the animal characters are personified. They talk and act like real persons and assume human roles and behaviors. The characters seem so real that we sometimes forget Mrs. Frisby is a rat. In fantastic stories such as Natalie Babbitt's *Tuck Everlasting* real people combined with realistic details assist readers in suspending disbelief of the fantastic elements. Babbitt provided a contrast between the realistic, mortal character, Winnie Foster, and the Tucks, who will never die because they drank water from the secret spring in Treegap.

> *Winnie blinked, and all at once her mind was drowned with understanding of what he was saying. For she—yes, even she— would go out of the world willy-nilly someday. Just go out like the flame of a candle, and no use protesting. It was a certainty. She would try very hard not to think of it, but sometimes, as*

now, it would be forced upon her. She raged against it, helpless and insulted, and blurted at last, "I don't want to die."

"No," said Tuck calmly. "Not now. Your time's not now. But dying's part of the wheel, right there next to being born. You can't pick out the pieces you like and leave the rest. Being part of the whole thing, that's the blessing. But it's passing us by, us Tucks. Living's heavy work, but off to one side, the way we are, it's useless, too. It don't make sense. If I knowed how to climb back on the wheel, I'd do it in a minute. You can't have living without dying. So you can't call it living, what we got. We just are, we just be, like rocks beside the road."[29]

High Fantasy

What makes high fantasy different from fantastic stories? The sub-genre of high fantasy is characterized by its focus on the conflict between good and evil. Consequently, themes in high fantasy reflect a concern for humanity, and reveal universal values and truths that are associated with good and the fight against evil.

What characteristics make high fantasy stories believable to readers? First, the internal consistency of a new world compels and sustains belief, as in C. S. Lewis's seven fantasies about the country of Narnia. When students read books in this series, such as *The Lion, the Witch, and the Wardrobe,* they know and believe in Narnia as much as in their own city and neighborhood. Second, a protagonist's belief in his or her own experience suspends readers' disbelief. In Susan Cooper's *The Dark Is Rising,* Will Stanton is convinced that he is an Old One, a fighter for good in every age.

Setting can be extremely important in making high fantasy credible. If an author is creating new worlds—unrealistic worlds to readers of the story—then the setting must be developed and described fully to make the reader suspend belief. Jane Yolan creates such a setting in *Dragon's Blood:*

> *Austar IV is the fourth planet of a seven-planet rim-system in the Erato Galaxy. Once a penal colony, marked KK_{29} on the convict map system, it is a semiarid, metal-poor world with two moons.*
>
> *Austair IV is covered by vast deserts, some of which are cut through by small, irregularly surfacing hot springs, and several small sections of fen lands. There are only five major rivers: the Narrakka, the Rokk, the Brokk-bend, the Kkar, and the Left Forkk.*
>
> *Few plants grow on the deserts: some fruit cacti and sparse, long-trunked palm trees. The most populous plants are two wild flowering bushes called burnwort and blisterweed.*[30]

Science Fiction

What characteristics distinguish the subgenre science fiction from other types of fantasy? Certainly, scientific or technological advances are emphasized in most science fiction stories. Also, they are set in the future and often feature alien characters. However, at the heart of any good science fiction novel are human beings dealing with problems and searching for solutions. For example, consider the works of science fiction writers H. M. Hoover and Ray Bradbury. Both Hoover and Bradbury show as much concern for human beings in their stories as they do for scientific speculation.

A large and varied collection of works exist today for the avid, devoted science fiction reader. When we consider evaluating novels that fall in this category of literature, the same criteria for good fantasy apply. Science fiction authors, however, probably rely more on conflict than on characters to make their stories credible to the readers.

Traditional Stories: Folktales, Fables, Myths, and Legends

Folktales

Folktales exist today because they were told orally to one generation and then the next until they were finally recorded in written form. We often find many versions of the same folktale or fairy tale, for example, *Cinderella*, because the story is repeatedly retold in different cultures. Since different versions of these stories exist, students can compare such books as James Marshall's modern retelling of *Red Riding Hood*, Lizbeth Zwerger's traditional tale of *Little Red Cap*, and Trina Schart Hyman's uniquely illustrated version of *Little Red Riding Hood*.

Retellings offer students enjoyable opportunities to compare tales, as shown in the following chart developed by third- and fourth-grade students and presented by Diane Driessen.[31] The students looked for visual examples of good and evil in Fiona French's *Snow White in New York* and the Grimms' traditional *Snow White and the Seven Dwarfs*.

French's Snow White	*Grimm's Snow White*
Snow White is a blonde	Snow White is a brunette
New York Mirror	Magic mirror
city	forest
1920s	long ago
Newspaper reporter	Prince
Seven jazz-men	Seven Dwarfs
Bodyguard	Huntsman
Poisoned cherry	Poisoned apple
Singing in a club	Cleaning the cottage

| Stepmother arrested | Queen died in dungeon |
| Gun to kill | Knife: bring back heart |

Predictable is a word often associated with folktales. Why? The same characters appear over and over again in folktales—the prince and princess, the wicked stepmother, the wicked witch, the fairy godmother. The number three is used in many folktales, such as *The Three Bears, The Three Little Pigs,* and *The Three Billy-Goats Gruff.* Themes may vary, but they often stress human needs and wishes; and the notion that good is rewarded and evil is punished is conveyed over and over again in folktales. Finally, the way folktales usually begin and end is commonly known by all ages: "Once upon a time," "They lived happily ever after." Folktales, because of their predictable story structure, are excellent beginning-to-read materials.

Fables
Unlike folktales, fables are not intended for the very young child because they often contain abstract ideas. A fable is a short story, usually with talking animal characters, that presents a moral or a lesson. In

Children delight in reading and sharing Arnold Lobel's modern Fables.

attempting to illustrate a collection of Aesop's fables, Arnold Lobel found them so grim for young children to read that he created his own award-winning collection, *Fables.*

Myths

Myths, too, are handed down by word of mouth. Like fables, they are intended for older students. Unlike folktales or fables, however, myths are stories that attempt to explain natural phenomena, such as the existence of the four seasons. Myths often concern superhuman beings, including gods and goddesses, who deal with events in the story that have no natural explanation. Many books exist today that are beautifully illustrated retellings of ancient myths, such as Gerald McDermott's *Daughter of Earth.* In this story, although Prosperpina has eaten three of the forbidden seeds, Jupiter orders her release on the condition that she return to Pluto for only a third of the year.

> So to this day, once a year, Prosperpina descends into Pluto's gloomy realm to sit silently by his side.
> On earth this is the season of cold and darkness, and all growing things await her return.
> Then, when she rises from the ground in glory, the birds sing in welcome, and the wheat and the grass and all the flowering plants begin to grow. Once more life begins, and the world is filled with the joy of spring.[32]

Legends

Another type of traditional story is the legend, a fictitious tale about a real person, event, or place. Legends, like myths, may offer explanations about things that occur in nature. In *The Legend of the Bluebonnet* and *The Legend of the Indian Paintbrush,* Tomie dePaola retells and illustrates two beautiful old tales that explain the origin of the wildflowers bluebonnet and Indian paintbrush.

Poetry

Verse

Young children are most often exposed to verse or rhyme, such as Mother Goose, and it is because of children's familiarity with verse that they think all poetry must rhyme. For most, it probably is not important to distinguish between verse and poetry, but there is a difference. "Twinkle, twinkle, little star/ How I wonder what you are/ Up above the world so high/ Like a diamond in the sky" is obviously verse, whereas William Blake penned a poem when he wrote: "To see a world in a grain of sand/ And a heaven in a wild flower/ Hold infinity in the palm of your

Tomie dePaola's The Legend of the Bluebonnet *is a popular book choice among students.*

hand/ And eternity in an hour."[33] Exposing children to a wide variety of poems and verses should be your most important consideration since it is through hearing and reading poetry that students begin to develop an appreciation for the genre.

Narrative Poetry

Subgenres exist within the genre of poetry. Both young and older children enjoy narrative poems because they tell a story. Narrative poems may be written in one of several forms, such as lyric or free verse, and they may tell humorous or serious stories. John Ciardi's narrative poem remains a favorite among children:

Mummy Slept Late and Daddy Fixed Breakfast

Daddy fixed breakfast.
He made us each a waffle.
It looked like gravel pudding.
It tasted something awful.

"Ha, ha," he said, "I'll try again."
This time I'll get it right."
But what I got was in between
Bituminous and anthracite.

"A little too well done? Oh well,
I'll have to start all over."
That time what landed on my plate
Looked like a manhole cover.

I tried to cut it with a fork:
The fork gave off a spark.
I tried a knife and twisted it
Into a question mark.

I tried it with a hack-saw.
I tried it with a torch.
It didn't even make a dent.
It didn't even scorch.

The next time Dad gets breakfast
When Mummy's sleeping late,
I think I'll skip the waffles
I'd sooner eat the plate![34]
　　—John Ciardi

Lyric Poetry

The lyric poem has a song-like quality and often contains a refrain. Many of the poems written for children are lyrical. They are usually descriptive and express a personal feeling or thought. Lyric poems present a reader or listener with appealing sound qualities, evoking a feeling they should be sung, such as the following poem by David McCord.

Song of the Train

Clickety-clack,
Wheels on the track,
This is the way
They begin the attack:
Click-ety-clack,
Click-ety-clack,
Click-ety, clack-ety
Click-ety
Clack.

Clickety-clack
Over the crack,
Faster and faster
The song of the track:
Click-ety-clack,
Click-ety-clack,
Click-ety, clack-ety
Click-ety
Clack.

Riding in front,
Riding in back,
Everyone hears
The song of the track:
Click-ety-clack,
Click-ety-clack,
Click-ety, clack-ety
Click-ety
Clack.[35]
   —David McCord

Ballad

The ballad, like the traditional story, has its origin in folk literature. It is a narrative poem with song-like qualities. Other characteristics of the ballad include a heavy emphasis on rhyme, rhythm, repetition, and frequent use of dialogue in telling the story. The ballad of "John Henry" exhibits all of these characteristics, and, like most folk ballads, it was originally sung. Here are the first two stanzas of this familiar ballad.

When John Henry was a tiny little baby
Sitting on his mama's knee,
He picked up a hammer and a little piece of steel,
Saying, "Hammer's going to be the death of me, Lord, Lord,
   Hammer's going to be the death of me."

John Henry was a man just six feet high,
Nearly two feet and a half across his breast.
He'd hammer with a nine-pound hammer all day
And never get tired and want to rest, Lord, Lord,
   and never get tired and want to rest.[36]

Free Verse

Free verse, simply stated, is free of rhyme and a regular beat. Free verse allows poets to create their own rules about writing and shaping a poem. They have the freedom to develop their own rhythm and cadence when they use this verse form and can even decide how a poem will look on the page. Carl Sandburg's poem "Fog" is a classic example of free verse.

Fog

The fog comes
on little cat feet.

It sits looking
over harbor and city
on silent haunches
and then moves on.[37]
   —Carl Sandburg

Nonfiction: Autobiography, Biography, and Informational Books

Autobiography and Biography

An autobiography is an individual's own life story, whereas a biography is a documented account of a person's life that is written by someone else. It is possible for both types of books to show bias, depending on an author's point of view and perspective. In evaluating biography, consider that an authentic biography should be well researched. Only statements that were actually made by the person should be included in the text or as conversations. In fictionalized biographies, however, the story is based upon facts and careful research, but the author may invent dialogue, include unspoken thoughts of the subject, or even dramatize an event. One of the most intriguing biographies published in recent years for students is the Newbery Award–winning book *Lincoln: A Photobiography.* Russell Freedman combined an appealing, well-written story with photographs and prints that he selected from Washington, D.C., Springfield, Illinois, and other cities.

Informational Books

Quality informational books devoted to a wide range of subjects are available today for both younger and older readers. For example, David Macaulay's books demonstrate the author's knowledge of architecture and skill at drawing well-researched pen-and-ink illustrations. His books show readers the process of building a *Castle, Pyramid, City,* and *Underground.* Aliki has written and illustrated the fascinating book, *Mummies Made in Egypt,* which includes hieroglyphic writing and pictures arranged like the friezes that decorated the Egyptian tombs.

Considering the many different types of informational books published today, what criteria should a teacher use to judge their quality and worth for children? In judging any book of this type, it is important to see evidence of thorough and careful research on the topic. The facts should be accurate and the content up to date. Generalizations should be supported by facts, and there should be a clear distinction between fact and theory in any informational book.

Informational books once resembled textbooks, but that comparison cannot be made today. The format of informational books has changed to include more colorful illustrations and art work. Since illustrations play an important role in informational books, they must be evaluated along with the text. Pictures and line drawings should help explain and clarify information in the book, and should be appealing and attractive to a reader, helping to capture and sustain the reader's interest. Captions and labels should be used where needed to explain illustrations and emphasize material in the text.

Picture Books

Picture books cannot be placed into one genre because they cross genre lines. For example, Ezra Jack Keats presented a realistic story in the Caldecott Award–winning book *The Snowy Day*, while Leo Lionni created a delightful fantasy in his classic picture book *Inch by Inch*. Diane Stanley presented a well-researched and -illustrated biography of *Peter the Great*, while John Jakes and Paul Bacon wrote and illustrated *Susanna of the Alamo*, a documented historical fiction.

Although the text of picture books must be brief, the quality of the writing still should meet high standards of literary excellence. Because of the abbreviated text in a picture book, an author's careful choice of words and style of writing becomes even more important than in longer texts.

In evaluating picture books, it is important to consider the quality of the illustrations and how they work to extend the text, as noted by Lukens: "We expect color and style and story to be compatible. We ask that the placement of text and pictures move our eyes from left to right. The pleasing visual effect of the double-spread pages results from balance and rhythmic movement. Perhaps what we value most highly is the artist's unique personal style, style that does not duplicate the art of greeting cards nor the comic distortions of every Saturday morning cartoon show."[38]

In their text, *Children's Literature in the Elementary School*, Huck, Hepler, and Hickman suggested the following specific questions to use as guides for evaluating picture books. Not every question in their guide is appropriate for judging every book; however, if teachers consider the most applicable questions in the five listed categories, they can decide how well a given picture book achieves literary quality.

Guides for Evaluating Picture Books

Content

- How appropriate is the content of the book for its intended age level?
- Is this a book that will appeal to children, or is it really written for adults?
- When and where does it take place? How has the artist portrayed this?
- Are the characters well delineated and developed?
- Are sex, race, and other stereotypes avoided?
- What is the quality of the language of the text?
- How is the theme developed through text and illustrations?

Illustrations

- In what ways do the illustrations help to create the meaning of the text?
- How are pictures made an integral part of the text?
- Do the illustrations extend the text in any way? Do they provide clues to the action of the story?
- Are the pictures accurate and consistent with the text?
- Where the setting calls for it, are the illustrations authentic in detail?

Medium and Style of Illustrations

- What medium has the illustrator chosen to use? Is it appropriate for the mood of the story?
- How has the illustrator used line, shape, and color to extend the story?
- How would you describe the style of the illustrations? Is the style appropriate for the story?
- How has the illustrator varied style and technique? What techniques seem to create rhythm and movement?
- How has the illustrator created balance in the composition?

Format

- Does the size of the book seem appropriate to the content?
- Does the jacket design express the theme of the book?
- Do the cover design and endpapers convey the spirit of the story?
- In what way does the title page anticipate the story to come?
- Is the type design well chosen for the theme and purpose of the book?
- What is the quality of the paper?
- How durable is the binding?

On Saturday
he ate through
one piece of
chocolate cake, one ice-cream cone, one pickle, one slice of Swiss cheese, one slice of salami,

FIGURE 2.1 *Eric Carle's clever story delights children as they read about* **The Very Hungry Caterpillar.**   Illustrations by Eric Carle reprinted by permission of Philomel Books from *The Very Hungry Caterpillar,* copyright © 1969 by Eric Carle.

Comparison with Others

- How is this work similar to or different from other works by this same author and/or illustrator?
- How is this story similar to or different from other books with the same subject of theme?
- What comments have reviewers made about this book? Do you agree or disagree with them?
- What has the artist said about his or her work?
- Will this book make a contribution to the growing body of children's literature? How lasting do you think it will be?[39]

When we think of outstanding picture books that meet this criteria, many stories come immediately to mind. Among these stories, the clever text and format of Eric Carle's *The Very Hungry Caterpillar* entices children to follow the caterpillar as he eats his way through one piece of cake, one ice-cream cone, one pickle, one slice of cheese, and so one lollipop, one piece of cherry pie, one sausage, one cupcake, and one slice of watermelon.

That night he had a stomachache!

on, until he has a stomachache. The spread presented in Figure 2.1 shows the sequence. The creators of *The Napping House*, Audrey and Don Wood, present readers with a story to be read over and over again. In this cumulative tale, children delight in the language of the text as they are introduced to a snoring granny, a dozing dog, a snoozing cat, a slumbering mouse, and a wakeful flea. The illustrations go beyond the text, filling in details and adding humor as Figure 2.2 shows, and creating a rainy day mood that changes when the sun appears at the end of the story. Finally, Chris Van Allsburg's *The Polar Express* is likely to stand the test of time. The language of the text, rich in metaphor and description, reveals a memorable story. Readers are drawn into the story as close observers because of the artist's dramatic and engaging use of perspective, shown in Figure 2.3. These books are examples of quality picture books for children. If you consider them touchstone books, then other picture books should reflect the same quality text and illustrations.

Summary

At the beginning of this chapter, literature was established as an integral part of all the language arts. Literature contributes to children's understanding of language, broadens their vocabularies, serves as

FIGURE 2.2 *Don Wood's illustrations in* The Napping House *extend the text adding both humor and detail.* Illustration from *The Napping House,* text copyright © 1984 by Audrey Wood, illustrators copyright © 1984 by Don Wood, reproduced by permission of Harcourt Brace Jovanovich, Inc.

FIGURE 2.3 *Chris Van Allsberg's perspective gives reader's an aerial view of Santa's sleigh and the scene below in* The Polar Express. From *The Polar Express* by Chris Van Allsburg. Copyright © 1985 by Chris Van Allsburg. Reprinted by permission of Houghton Mifflin Company.

Children listen attentively to Chris Van Allsburg's Caldecott Award-winning book, The Polar Express.

models for students' writing, and forms the basis for any reading program. Since quality literature helps ensure an effective literature-based language arts program, a primary purpose of this chapter is to provide information about selecting and evaluating books for children. Specific questions about plot, characterization, setting, theme, style, and point of view help in determining the literary quality of a book. Since we choose different books for different purposes, it is important to gain a broad knowledge of literature, which includes an understanding of various genres and subgenres. Discussion focuses on the genres of fiction, fantasy, traditional stories, poetry, and nonfiction. Subgenres are subsumed under each of these genres. Nonfiction includes, for example, autobiography, biography, and informational books. Fictional stories include both contemporary realistic fiction and historical fiction. Picture books cannot be considered as a genre; they cross all genre lines. You acquire background knowledge in this chapter that is applied in later chapters when you read about how to use the many wonderful books that you select for your literature-based language arts program.

Questions for Discussion

1. Explain how literature broadens children's experiences and background knowledge.
2. According to research findings, how does literature influence children's language and reading development?
3. Identify and discuss the literary elements that you should consider when you are evaluating books for children.
4. Compare and contrast the following subgenres of literature:
   a. realistic fiction/historical fiction
   b. high fantasy/science fiction
   c. fables/myths
   d. autobiography/biography
5. Consider a picture book that you think is outstanding. What attributes contribute to the quality of this picture book?

Notes

1. Charlotte S. Huck, Susan Hepler, and Janet Hickman, *Children's Literature in the Elementary School* (New York: Holt, Rinehart & Winston, 1987), 4.

2. Penelope Lively, "Bones in Sand," in *Innocence and Experience: Essays & Conversations on Children's Literature* (New York: Lothrop, Lee & Shepard, 1987), 16.

3. Stephen Spielberg, Acceptance Speech (Hollywood, CA: Academy Award Ceremonies, 1987).

4. George A. Strong, "The Modern Hiawatha," in *Favorite Poems Old and New,* Helen Ferris, comp. (Garden City, New York: Doubleday, 1957), 337.

5. Katherine Paterson, *Jacob Have I Loved* (New York: Crowell, 1980), 187.

6. Nancy Willard, *Firebrat* (New York: Knopf, 1988), 29–30.

7. Courtney B. Cazden, *Child Language and Education* (New York: Holt, Rinehart & Winston), 121–125.

8. Bernice E. Cullinan, Angela Jaggar, and Dorothy Strickland, "Language Expansion for Black Children in the Primary Grades: A Research Report," *Young Children* 29 (January 1974):98–112.

9. *Ibid.,* 103.

10. Carol Chomsky, "Stages in Language Development and Reading Exposure," *Harvard Educational Review* 42 (February 1972):1–33.

11. Charlotte S. Huck, *Taking Inventory of Children's Literary Background* (Glenview, IL: Scott, Foresman, 1966).

12. Dorothy H. Cohen, "The Effect of Literature on Vocabulary and Reading Achievement," *Elementary English* 45 (February 1968):209–213, 217.

13. Madeleine L'Engle, *A Circle of Quiet* (San Francisco, CA: Harper & Row, 1972), 147–148.

14. Gordon Wells, *The Meaning Makers: Children Learning Language and Using Language to Learn* (London: Heinemann, 1983).

15. Frank Smith, *Essays into Literacy* (London: Heinemann, 1983), 35.

16. Sandra Stotsky, "Research on Reading/Writing Relationships: A Synthesis and Suggested Direction," in *Composing and Comprehending*, Julie M. Jensen, comp. (Urbana, IL: National Conference on Research in English/ERIC, 1984), 16.

17. W. B. Elley, I. H. Barham, H. Lamb, and M. Wyllie, "The Role of Grammar in Secondary English Curriculum," *Research in the Teaching of English* 10 (Spring 1976):5–21.

18. Editha B. Mills, "Children's Literature and Teaching Written Composition," *Elementary English* 51 (October 1974):971–973.

19. Barbara Eckhoff, "How Reading Affects Children's Writing," *Language Arts* 60 (May 1983):607–616.

20. Huck, Hepler, and Hickman, *Children's Literature in the Elementary School*, 19.

21. Dorothy L. Guth (ed.), *Letters of E. B. White* (New York: Harper & Row, 1976), 613.

22. Rebecca J. Lukens, *A Critical Handbook of Children's Literature* (Glenview, IL: Scott, Foresman, 1986), 147.

23. Cynthia Voigt, *Homecoming* (New York: Fawcett Books, 1981), 67.

24. Bette Greene, *Summer of My German Soldier* (New York: Bantam, 1973), 120.

25. Huck, Hepler, and Hickman, *Children's Literature in the Elementary School*, 24.

26. *Ibid.*, 25.

27. Lukens, *A Critical Handbook of Children's Literature*, 14.

28. Patricia MacLachlan, *Sarah, Plain and Tall* (New York: Harper & Row, 1985), 16–17.

29. Natalie Babbitt, *Tuck Everlasting* (New York: Bantam, 1975), 57.

30. Jane Yolan, *Dragon's Blood* (New York: Dell, 1982), 1.

31. Diane Driessen, "Snow White in New York," in *The Web*, Charlotte S. Huck and Janet Hickman, eds., 12 (Fall 1987):8.

32. Gerald McDermott, *Daughter of Earth* (New York: Delacorte Press, 1984), unpaged.

33. William Blake, "To See a World," in *Knock at a Star*, X. J. Kennedy and Dorothy M. Kennedy, comps. (Boston: Little, Brown, 1982), 40.

34. John Ciardi, "Mummy Slept Late and Daddy Fixed Breakfast," in *You Read to Me and I'll Read to You* (Philadelphia, PA: Crowell, 1962), 18. Reprinted by permission of Judith H. Ciardi.

35. David McCord, "Song of the Train," in *Far and Few* (Boston: Little, Brown, 1952), 87. From *One at a Time* by David McCord. Copyright 1952 by David McCord. By permission of Little, Brown and Company.

36. "John Henry," in *Knock at a Star*, X. J. Kennedy and Dorothy M. Kennedy, comps. (Boston: Little, Brown, 1982), 16.

37. Carl Sandburg, "Fog," in *Rainbows are Made*, Lee Bennett Hopkins, comp. (San Diego, CA: Harcourt Brace Jovanovich 1982), 71. "Fog" from *Chicago Poems* by Carl Sandburg, copyright 1916 by Holt, Rinehart and Winston, Inc., and renewed 1944 by Carl Sandburg. Reprinted by permission of Harcourt Brace Jovanovich, Inc.

38. Lukens, *A Critical Handbook of Children's Literature*, 26.

39. Huck, Hepler, and Hickman, *Children's Literature in the Elementary School*, 220.

Bibliography: Children's Literature

Aliki. *Mummies Made in Egypt.* New York: Crowell, 1979.

Babbitt, Natalie. *Tuck Everlasting.* New York: Farrar & Strauss, 1975.

Blume, Judy. *Blubber.* New York: Bradbury, 1974.

———. *Tales of a Fourth-Grade Nothing.* New York: Dutton, 1972.

———. *Are You there God? It's Me Margaret.* New York: Bradbury, 1970.

Carle, Eric. *The Very Hungry Caterpillar.* New York: Philomel Books, 1968.

Cleary, Beverly. *Dr. Mr. Henshaw.* New York: Morrow, 1983.

Cooper, Susan. *The Dark Is Rising.* New York: Atheneum, 1973.

DePaola, Tomie. *The Legend of the Indian Paintbrush.* New York: Putnam, 1987.

———. *The Legend of the Bluebonnet.* New York: Putnam, 1983.

Dr. Seuss. *And to Think I Saw It on Mulberry Street.* New York: Vanguard, 1937.

Fisher, Leonard Everett. *The Great Wall of China.* New York: Macmillan, 1986.

Fox, Paula. *The Slave Dancer.* New York: Bradbury, 1973.

Freedman, Russell. *Lincoln: A Photobiography.* New York: Clarion, 1987.

French, Fiona. *Snow White in New York.* New York: Oxford University Press, 1986.

Fritz, Jean. *China Homecoming.* New York: Putnam, 1985.

———. *Homesick: My Own Story.* New York: Putnam, 1982.

Grahame, Kenneth. *The Wind in the Willows.* New York: Scribner, 1908, 1940.

Greene, Bette. *Summer of My German Soldier.* New York: Dial Press, 1973.

Grimm, Jacob and Grimm, Wilhelm. *Snow White and the Seven Dwarfs.* New York: Farrar & Strauss, 1972.

———. *Little Red Cap.* Translated by Elizabeth Crawford. London, England: Picture Book Studio, Neugebauer Press,

Hyman, Trina Schart. *Little Red Riding Hood.* New York: Holiday House, 1983.

Jakes, John and Bacon, Paul. *Susanna of the Alamo.* New York: Harcourt, 1986.

Keats, Ezra Jack. *The Snowy Day.* New York: Viking, 1962.

L'Engle, Madeleine. *A Wrinkle in Time.* New York: Farrar, Straus, 1962.

Lewis, C. S. *The Lion, the Witch, and the Wardrobe.* New York: Macmillan, 1961.

Lionni, Leo. *Inch by Inch.* New York: Astor-Honor, 1960.

Lobel, Arnold. *Fables.* New York: Harper, 1980.

——. *Frog and Toad Together.* New York: Harper, 1972.

——. *Frog and Toad Are Friends.* New York: Harper, 1970.

MacLachlin, Patricia. *Sarah, Plain and Tall.* New York: Harper & Row, 1985.

Macauley, David. *Castle.* New York: Houghton Mifflin, 1977.

——. *Underground.* New York: Houghton Mifflin, 1976.

——. *City.* New York: Houghton Mifflin, 1974.

——. *Pyramid.* New York: Houghton Mifflin, 1973.

Marshall, James. *Red Riding Hood.* New York: Dial, 1987.

Milne, A. A. *Winnie-the-Pooh.* New York: Dutton, 1926.

O'Brien, Robert C. *Mrs. Frisby and the Rats of NIMH.* New York: Atheneum, 1971.

O'Dell, Scott. *Island of the Blue Dolphins.* New York: Houghton, 1960.

Paterson, Katherine. *The Great Gilly Hopkins.* New York: Crowell, 1978.

Potter, Beatrix. *Peter Rabbit.* New York: Warne, (1902), 1985.

Sendak, Maurice. *Where the Wild Things Are.* New York: Harper & Row, 1963.

Silverstein, Shel. *The Light in the Attic.* New York: Harper, 1981.

——. *Where the Sidewalk Ends.* New York: Harper, 1974.

Stanley, Diane. *Peter the Great.* New York: Macmillan, 1986.

Van Allsburg, Chris. *The Wreck of the Zepher.* New York: Houghton Mifflin, 1983.

——. *The Polar Express.* New York: Houghton Mifflin, 1985.

Voigt, Cynthia. *A Solitary Blue.* New York: Fawcett Juniper, 1983.

——. *Dicey's Song.* New York: Atheneum, 1982.

——. *Homecoming.* New York: Atheneum, 1981.

White, E. B. *Charlotte's Web.* New York: Harper, 1952.

Wood, Audrey. *The Napping House.* New York: Harcourt Brace Jovanovich, 1984.

Chapter 3

Learning and Thinking

Learning and Thinking

The Learning Process

Classroom Implications

The Teacher's Role

Characteristics of Children

Primary Grade Children

Children in Upper Elementary and Middle School

Ways to Learn

The Role of Language and Thought

Finding Information

Dealing with Experience

Focusing Our Attention

Clarifying Ideas

Retrieving Information

Developing Strategies Used in Thinking

Obtaining Information

Interrelating Information

Evaluating Information

Throughout the history of education, various theories have been advanced to explain how children learn and have been applied to the classroom. An understanding of how children learn is critical in planning educational events. How one looks at teaching and learning depends largely on one's view of how learning takes place.

In the early 1900s the behavioral tradition was predominant, but since the 1960s cognitive views of learning have come into ascendancy. According to Shuell, cognitive views represent the mainstream of thinking in both psychology and education.[1] Cognitive theories view learning as "an active, constructive, and goal-oriented process that is dependent upon the mental activities of the learner."[2] Students bring to the learning task an intention or desire to learn, and they try to make meaning from their experiences. They relate past experiences to new situations or problems. Most cognitivists agree that children acquire knowledge structures, which are like networks of information or operational rules. Learning is cumulative, and so the role played by prior knowledge is extremely important.

The Learning Process

The processes through which learning takes place are described somewhat differently by different theorists. Piaget focused on two basic processes, *organization* and *adaptation* with its two component parts—*assimilation* and *accommodation*. He believed that humans have the ability to organize information by developing categories, or schemata. This ability to organize information is one of the basic processes of learning. The second, adaptation, is the process by which we modify our existing organization (schemata). It involves two complementary processes: assimilation in which we take new experiences into our existing categories, and accommodation where we modify our existing schemata to fit the new information.

Rumelhart and Norman in their schema-based theory of learning suggest three kinds of learning: *restructuring*, or *schema creation*, which is the process by which a new schema is created; *accretion*, in which new information is encoded in terms of existing schema; and *tuning*, or *schema evolution*, which is the slow modification and refinement of a schema as a result of using it in different situations.[3] See Table 3.1 for a comparison of terms.

In many ways the two views are similar. Restructuring, or schema creation, is similar to Piaget's organization in which information is organized into schemata. Accretion and assimilation both involve taking new information into existing organizations (schema), and tuning, or schema evolution, is like accommodation in which existing schema are modified as a result of new information.

TABLE 3.1 *Comparison of Terms Used in Describing the Processes of Learning*

Process	Piaget's Term	Schema Theory Term
Develop or organize new mental structures or schema	Organization	Schema Creation or Re-structuring
Incorporate new information into existing structure	Adaptation: Assimilation	Accretion
Revise or refine structures to incorporate new information	Adaptation: Accommodation	Tuning or Schema Evolution

Leo Lionni's picture storybook for children, *Fish is Fish*, illustrates these processes in a meaningful and humorous way. (See Figure 3.1.) In this story a frog and a fish become friends. The frog grows legs and leaves the pond one day to explore the world. He returns much later to visit his friend the fish and tells him about the "extraordinary things" he has seen. He tells about birds. " 'Like what?' asked the fish. 'Birds,' said the frog mysteriously. 'Birds!' And he told the fish about the birds, who had wings, and two legs, and many, many colors."[4] Since the fish's world is organized into categories based on a fish's experiences, he pictures the birds as fishlike creatures with two legs and wings. He assimilates this new information into his existing categories of experience, but in doing so he changes his category to accommodate "birds" as he sees them.

To illustrate further, let's take the story beyond the book. Suppose the fish was caught one day and placed in a glass tank where he could see the world as the frog did. The fish would then create new schemata for the new things in his experience. He would also assimilate other experiences into his existing organization, thereby modifying existing schemata to accommodate these new things. Every new experience causes us to add to our existing schemata or to change the current ones, and this process continues at all ages.

Classroom Implications

What are the implications for the teacher of these learning processes from the cognitive view of learning? First, children should be allowed to organize learning in their own way. When everything is preorganized for them, learning is made more difficult, not easier. For example, writing and word-recognition skills are usually taught in a sequence

FIGURE 3.1 *Illustration from Leo Leonni's* **Fish Is Fish**   From *Fish Is Fish* by Leon Lionni. Copyright © 1970 by Leo Lionni. Reprinted by permission of Pantheon Books, a Division of Random House, Inc.

reflecting the regularity of their phoneme-grapheme correspondences. It seems logical to do consonants first (most regular), then short vowels, and finally long vowels (least regular). However, if children are using their preexisting knowledge of the alphabet as an entry into writing and reading, this sequence is more difficult not easier. The children know the long vowels and consonants from the alphabet but not the short vowels.

Next, children need a variety of new experiences, problems, and ideas to organize. The richness of experiences and ideas contributes to the complexity of mental structures or *intelligence*. As students encounter new information, they relate it to other new ideas and to their prior experiences. These new organizations and revisions of old ones are the mark of intellectual growth. If nothing is novel, there is no growth.

The third critical implication for the classroom is the need for students to handle concrete materials and to have many direct, first-hand experiences. This is especially true for younger children, but also for older children, who do not always learn by being told about something or by reading about it. The more direct, concrete, and meaningful our experiences, the better we learn at any age.

Although the processes of learning remain constant, older learners are different because they are better at differentiating stimuli. They have more complex networks of schema that are more detailed and refined, which allow them to make more accurate and complex responses. They can use indirect experiences more effectively and can apply reasoning skills. They also can sort through information and ignore what is not pertinent to the current problem.

The Teacher's Role

The teacher's role in a classroom based on the cognitive theory of learning is different from the teacher's role in a traditional classroom. If the students are active in their own learning, organizing new information and ideas, then the teacher does not divide what must be learned into separate skills and teach them in isolation. The teacher is not the source of all information. The correction of students' work is not the major task. Instead, the teacher's task is to involve students in activities that should result in learning, to suggest resources for acquiring information, and to structure the learning so that students get a variety of responses to their ideas.

This does not imply, however, that children can do whatever they want; it means that learning takes place through a child's inherent interests and natural curiosity. The teacher considers students' social, physical, cognitive, and linguistic development when structuring the learning environment. The curriculum, rather than being built around content, is built around the child. More specifically, children are active participants in their own learning. Reading, writing, and listening grow out of meaningful experiences. Conversation with peers is regarded as a significant part of a child's mental, social, and linguistic development. Concrete objects and events are always present in the learning environment. The children act on their environment, rather than being acted upon. This is the learning climate of the classroom based on cognitive theory.

The teacher is responsible for establishing the learning environment. The physical organization, concrete materials, and experiences are planned by the teacher. The teacher is the knowledgeable source in the active classroom, not the textbook materials. The teacher under-stands how children learn best and is aware of each child's needs, abili-ties, interests, background of experience, and level of development.

The teacher who forms the classroom curriculum around the child's needs, interests, and abilities becomes a facilitator or director of learning. The teacher is not in the role of the dispenser of knowledge. Through a teacher's intervention at the appropriate time, a child's learning may be extended or the quality of an experience raised. Ques-tions, comments, words of encouragement, or suggestions can all act as learning stimulants. A question at the right moment may extend a child's thinking or cause that child to study a problem in greater depth.

Trust is important in this type of learning setting. That is, a teacher must learn to trust children with their own learning. Trial and error are integral parts of the learning process. Children need to be given time to work out solutions to problems. Throughout this pro-cess, intervention by the teacher can be significant; however, interven-tion can become interference if it is not presented appropriately when the child needs the help.

It is important for the teacher to listen to children; their ques-tions, comments, and conversations offer insights into their thinking. Much can be learned about a child's level of development if one listens carefully and knowledgeably. Children's errors also reveal their think-ing; in fact, it probably is more beneficial for the teacher to look closely at children's mistakes than at what they say or do correctly.[5]

New materials, new information, and new problems to solve are a key to learning. Memorizing information is less important than figuring out how to find and evaluate information. The processes of learning and the ways of getting information become more important than learning particular content. What the student does in class is more important than what the teacher does. The teacher's major responsibility is to make sure the students are involved in meaning-making activities.

Characteristics of Children

As children mature, there are changes both in their behavior and in what they need to be successful learners. Here are some characteristics of children at different ages.

Primary Grade Children

1. They are active. Children move about within the classroom set-ting. Sitting all day is not natural for these children.

2. They are interested in themselves and will not be interested in their neighbor until later. These children need to be made to feel that they have something to say and contribute and to be allowed to carry out their own ideas.

3. They have their own world of fantasy. Children's imaginative play should be encouraged; they need to listen to both fantasy and realistic books and talk about them.

4. They are beginners. They learn through mistakes, and trial and error is a learning process. The teacher needs to be patient and understanding, giving children time to learn at their own rates.

5. They want stimulation. They have the desire to explore and experiment. Naturally curious, they may ask question after question. The teacher must provide a rich learning environment—things to observe, touch, handle, taste, explore, and so on.

6. They are talkative. They learn by talking and working actively; therefore, conversation is a natural part of the learning environment.

7. They are individuals. All children are different and have neither the same interests nor the same backgrounds of experience. They may be at different levels of development and therefore need choices; they should not be expected to be all together on the same page on the same day.

8. They need to be successful. Encouragement and praise should be continuous within the learning environment.

Children in Upper Elementary and Middle School

1. They require an abundance of concrete materials and experiences. Children during this period still think best with something in their hands. Therefore, the classroom is filled with a wide assortment of materials to manipulate and handle, small animals and plants are available for observation, field trips and environmental excursions are provided, writing grows out of real experiences, and so on.

2. They need a rich language environment. Their oral language is developing as well as written language. The teacher encourages conversation and discussion, makes a wide variety of books available to children, reads stories aloud, and provides a listening center with records and tapes.

3. They are active. These older students can sit for longer periods of time; however, they still need opportunities to move about and become actively involved in their learning.

4. They have individual interests. Learning can and should grow out of children's interests. The teacher recognizes this and encourages

individual pursuits through reading, constructing models, discussing, record keeping, and so on.

5. They want the approval of adults. Thus, encouragement and praise can stimulate and foster children's learning.

6. They are different from one another. They have different interests and learn at different rates. They will be at different levels of development. Teachers provide for these differences by offering learning choices and experiences that meet personal needs. The children have opportunities to decide about what they learn.

7. They are socially aware of others. Children this age want to communicate and exchange ideas with others. The classroom environment encourages and facilitates children's communication.

8. Students become increasingly able to work on purely verbal tasks and to reason about things. They are able to disregard nonsignificant appearances.

9. As children get older, they rely more on their peers and less on adults for information, support, and opinions.

10. They have increasingly divergent interests and need even more to select topics and areas for exploration.

Teachers who are aware of the ways their students think about things and who know their abilities and characteristics are much better prepared to plan appropriate learning activities.

Ways to Learn

The ways people learn can be described in terms of the following four methods:

1. Learning by observing others
2. Learning through doing and participating
3. Learning by having someone tell you about it
4. Learning through practicing the skills involved

Before students come to school, most of their learning is accomplished in the first two ways: watching others and having someone tell them to try things out. In school, however, they learn from having someone tell them or by practicing the component skills. This does not fit with what we know about children's learning. In the initial stages of learning, observing and trying out appear to be most effective. Verbal explanations or skill practice may be helpful after learners gain some initial understanding of a process such as reading, writing, or computing. It is especially important with younger children to provide some firsthand experiences with materials before having them read about or telling them about how to learn. The more meaningful the context is and the more realistic the need to master the skill, then the more effective the learning.

The Role of Language and Thought

Language plays a vital role in thinking, but language and thought are not the same. Although most of us cannot imagine thinking about something without thinking in words, it does exist. Before children can say any words at all, they certainly think. Just try to get a child who does not like carrots to take a spoonful and you know that thought exists apart from language. Artists and musicians often do not speak easily about their work; perhaps this is because they communicate best in form and line and color or in rhythm and tone.

Although words are not essential for thought, they facilitate thinking. Language plays many roles in thinking. Lindfors described several of them, including the following five roles language plays in thinking: to find information, to deal with experience, to focus attention, to clarify ideas, and to retrieve information.[6]

Finding Information

We use language to ask others about things we have observed or wondered about. Young children are prize question askers; in fact, they are exhausting to be around because they want to know about so many things. What are you doing? What is that for? Why did you say or do that? When are we going? They especially notice inconsistencies, But you said. . . . Why did you let him do that when you told me. . . . It is unfortunate that children abandon asking questions as a main source of information because asking questions is a useful strategy. Teachers need to see their students as question askers, not just as responders.

Dealing with Experience

As we try to make sense of the world around us, we talk about what has happened in the past, what is happening now, and what may happen in the future. Much of our conversation with family and friends is recalling events and describing what has happened to us. Even young children love to talk about when they were little, like when they first learned to skate or ride a bike. As we talk about what we have done or seen, what is going on in our lives, and what we might do or plan to do in the future, we use language to help us deal with problems and experiences.

Focusing Our Attention

Sometimes we talk about what we are doing while we do it, apparently to help focus our attention on the task at hand. Children do this often; adults do it when they are trying to remember many details at one time. Someone knitting in a pattern might say aloud, "Knit five, slip one, knit two, pass slip stitch over," and so forth. When children build something, they often accompany everything they do with verbal instructions. "Put that piece this way for the cabin, now this big flat one across it for the wings. Nail it down. Right, just like that. Now another nail. Now got to find a piece for the tail. That's too big. Ahh! That one is just right. Now get the glue and put it up." Language helps us keep our mind on what we are doing and makes it easier to ignore distractions.

Clarifying Ideas

Explaining something to someone else often forces us to clarify our own thoughts. Telling someone else about a problem often helps us solve it—not because the other person says what to do but because the solution becomes evident from the other's questions or just from the telling. Authors find that writing down an idea forces clarity. They think that an idea is perfectly clear, but when they begin to explain it to someone else, they discover that it is not very clear at all. They may start to write about something they think is well thought out, only to find that they need to do more research on the topic. Children also clarify their thinking by talking or writing. A clue that clarification is going on is sentences that begin, "Well, then. . . ," or "Does this mean that I. . . ," or "Then that must be why. . . ."

Retrieving Information

Language apparently helps in storing and later retrieving information. Having a name for something is useful in thinking about it and remembering it. Lindfors cites a study by Brown and Lenneberg on color name recall among monolingual Zuni Indians and monolingual English speakers.[7] The informants were shown 4 colors and then asked to select the same 4 from a chart of 120 colors. The Zuni, who do not have separate names for yellow and orange, had difficulty matching shades of these colors, but did as well as the English-speaking informants on other colors. The study showed that named colors were easier to match.

It is clear, then, that the development of language aids the development of thinking. A critical challenge for the teacher is to develop children's language and their effective use of language for thinking.

Developing Strategies Used in Thinking

Students of all ages need to develop expertise in using different ways of thinking to solve problems. The skills or strategies they use directly affect the quality of their judgments and decisions. Their ability to gain information and to relate ideas to each other are critical to everything they do. The strategies used in thinking relate to the three basic aspects of cognitive learning: obtaining information, interrelating information, and evaluating information.

Obtaining Information

Perhaps the most basic task in thinking is to obtain accurate and complete information. We obtain information in different ways in different situations and at different times in our lives. All the strategies focus on significant details of the object or concept, and each strategy provides a particular kind of information. Strategies for obtaining information include observing, drawing, sorting, and classifying.

Observing

Opportunities to observe closely are helpful in developing and extending children's thinking. What does it mean to observe closely? We have all admired a beautiful piece of furniture or lovely garment. Without close observation, however, it is difficult to evaluate the quality of the furniture or the garment. What about the workmanship? the design? the quality of the wood or fabric? These are questions that we answer by using and applying critical observations.

We need to help children become better observers. Having students observe details and describe them in writing is one way of doing this. For example, some children were interested in caring for a budding plant that their teacher had brought to school. To extend the learning experience, the teacher suggested that they record their observations of the plant each morning when they checked on it. Over a period of several weeks the students wrote their precise observations of the plant. They described the different stages of blooming and recording observations about its size, its shape, its color, the number of leaves, the quantities of buds and when each opened, and the amount of water that the plant required. One student wrote her observations in the form of a diary, and another student shared a poem that he had

Children become better observers when they are encouraged to describe details.

written about the plant. Their final project was to compare their writings and compose a group experience story about their observations.

These students were becoming close observers. A variety of experiences that will develop children's observational skills are available in most elementary school classrooms—observing the birds that come to the window each morning, the weather as it changes from day to day, the goldfish, hamster, or guinea pig, the trees as their leaves change to the autumn colors, or indoor plants that the students have planted.

Older students also need to work on close observations. In a study of energy, for example, they might monitor different materials used to collect solar heat, determining how long heat is retained and figuring the comparative costs of the various materials. They can record their observations on a chart and use the information as the basis of a report on solar energy.

As children grow older they tend to depend less on observation as a way of gaining information. However, many classroom activities can provide opportunities for students to observe as a means of obtaining information. In the lower grades students might observe birds that come to the window—comparing features of the males and females of various species, seeing what kinds of seeds or other food they like, observing how they interact with other species, and so forth. As part of a study of weather, older students might observe and record cloud formations, wind patterns, and temperatures. Students might examine the bone structures of different animal species through x-rays and dissection. The focus of observation can be different at different ages, but the use of observation skills to collect information is the same.

Drawing

This strategy may seem at first to be out of place in a chapter on developing thinking skills, but actually drawing is a productive way of getting information. People tend to see things in terms of preestablished categories. Learning to draw forces us to learn to examine objects and people in new ways. Just as learning to read and write makes a qualitative difference in thinking, so does learning to see by means of drawing.[8]

We use our knowledge of the world as a kind of screen through which we view people and events. Students asked to draw an American flag that was hanging from a flagpole drew the flag as if it were lying on a flat surface. They showed all the stripes in perfect rows and a square blue corner with fifty stars. Their idea of the flag interfered with drawing the flag as it actually looked.

Many artists, however, try to look at the world without preconceptions as if it were completely new. The skills necessary for drawing are the same skills that enable us to look at the world in a different way. As Edwards notes, "The most efficient way to attain that understanding is to learn to see by learning to draw, just as the most efficient way to learn to do library research on a subject is first to know how to read."[9] The need to draw something accurately forces us to look at it intensively and perhaps to see new aspects.

Sorting

Sorting requires paying attention to certain aspects of an object and ignoring others. Imagine you put together a group of buttons, some red, some yellow, and others white; most are round, but a few are square; some have two holes, some have four, and some have a shank. Young children who are asked to sort the buttons will probably put the white ones in one group, the red ones in another group, and the yellow ones in a third group, ignoring their shapes and how they are to be sewn on. If asked to sort by some criterion other than color, some children can do this easily and others with difficulty. As children mature, they become increasingly adept at sorting by one criterion and ignoring other obvious possibilities. Because we are all individuals, what is obvious to one person may not be noticed by another. It is important for thought development to be able to see alternative criteria for sorting, which permit a larger store of information and easier retrieval.

One second-grade teacher working on health and nutrition brought a large variety of fruits and vegetables to class. Some were familiar, such as apples, carrots, green beans, and corn. Some were more unusual, such as eggplant, apricots, and rutabaga, and others were exotic, such as kiwi fruit, mangoes, and tomatillos. She divided the class in groups of four or five and asked the children to sort the items into groups, making sure that they could explain their reasons. One group sorted them by color, putting corn, carrots, lemons, mangoes, and apricots together in one pile, the green fruits and vegetables in a second pile. A third pile included the eggplant and rutabaga. Another group sorted by shape and size with apples, tomatilloes, kiwi fruit, and lemons in one pile, corn, green beans, and carrots in another pile and eggplant, rutabaga, and mango ("sorta big and funny shapes") in a third pile. Since the children did not recognize the fruit-vegetable distinction, the teacher made that sorting herself. As each group completed the sorting task, the other students tried to guess the criteria. They concluded the activity with a tasting—making vegetable soup and a fruit salad. Each child got to taste each new thing. The students expanded their concepts of fruit and vegetables and learned several new words.

Older students too can learn from sorting activities. They might sort various rocks by type of composition and hardness or insect specimens by body parts, the number of legs, or the presence or absence of wings. Often, older students can accomplish the same results by classifying.

Classifying

Sorting and classifying are related activities. Both require a person to group items according to identifiable characteristics, and both involve the same type of thinking. However, classifying is usually a more complex and abstract task than sorting. Whereas sorting involves the manipulation of objects, classifying usually does not; therefore, classification activities are difficult for young children. They require not only abstract thought but also background knowledge and experience. For example, classify or group the following words: *Mustang, Rabbit, Datsun, Corvette, Honda, Mazda.* One way of classifying the words might be to group them in a class called *automobiles;* or they may be placed in a class called *small cars.* When we classify, we may also have subclasses. For example, some of the cars are made in America and others are made in foreign countries. When we classify objects, places, people, animals, and so on, it is possible to categorize them in a variety of ways.

Classification experiences can occur naturally in the classroom. As students prepare bulletin boards or set up science displays, they can classify and label objects. For example, collections of leaves, shells, rocks, or pebbles might be classified or grouped according to a number of their attributes (color: dark, light; weight: light, heavy; size: small, medium, large; texture: rough, bumpy, smooth; and so on). A small group of students might work together and plan several classification schemes based on related attributes. After a discussion they could decide which arrangement they preferred for their display. This type of activity helps students identify regularities and relations of things in their environment. A popular classification activity, which is certainly not new, is called *animal, vegetable, mineral*. Using these three classes, try grouping the following items: horse, paper, tire, gasoline, lettuce, broccoli, milk, bread, people, mink, pencil, and emerald.

As students progress in their ability to classify, they might be challenged to develop a matrix that graphically illustrates a cross-classification of items. They might begin with a matrix consisting of four squares as shown in Figure 3.2. A more complicated matrix might include more squares and show a number of related attributes. Look at Figure 3.3 and try completing the matrix.

There are an infinite number of possibilities for developing classification skills. *Thinking Goes to School*[10] is an excellent source for classification games that can be used with various age groups. As stu-

Animals

	Dog	Cat
Large	Saint Bernard	Tiger
Small	Chihuahua	Siamese kitten

Size

FIGURE 3.2 *Simple cross-classification*

Transportation

	Private	Public
Land		
Water		
Air		

FIGURE 3.3 *Classification matrix*

dents have more experience with classifying, they will readily comprehend how things around them may be grouped into classes and subclasses.

Interrelating Information

Another major intellectual task is to interrelate information. We must find ways of fitting new ideas, concepts, and observations with our existing information. Three ways of interrelating are comparing and contrasting, semantic mapping, and making analogies. In comparing and contrasting we focus on similarities and differences; in mapping we visually represent mental constructs. In making analogies we analyze new information in relation to what we already know. The mental process of interrelating information is perhaps the essence of learning.

Comparing and Contrasting
Because of the way we store information in our mind, we are constantly making associations between experiences. Every day we make decisions based on comparisons. Almost every decision involves judging the good and bad aspects of alternatives.

Experiences that involve comparing one thing with another can be included very easily in the school day. Students can increase their skills at recognizing likenesses and differences as well as making certain kinds of judgments. A teacher's questions can create situations where children are asked to make comparisons: How are these two shapes different? How is this story like the one we read yesterday? How are these two shells alike? What can you say about their size? Who is taller, Jimmy or Kay? Questions such as these can be asked during any part of the day.

Students may also enjoy comparing and contrasting books. A number of children's stories have similar themes, plots, characters, or illustrations. Book comparisons can inspire conversations between the teacher and young children; for older children, they provide opportunities for indepth discussions. Some suggestions for literature comparisons follow in Table 3.2.

Semantic Mapping

Semantic mapping is a visual structuring of information or ideas associated with a particular topic. These visual representations are referred to as mapping, clustering, or diagramming, depending on the graphic style used. In this discussion, semantic mapping will be used to include all styles. According to Buckley, "To map is to engage in a thinking process involving two types of symbolic expression: presentational or nonlanguage expression such as art, and discursive or language expression."[11] A semantic map presents in pictoral form the major and minor ideas as well as their interrelationships.

There is increasing evidence that having a visual referent aids memory. According to Johnson, "Semantic mapping has been shown to be an effective way to learn new words, a procedure for activating students' schemata, and a technique that improves both composition and comprehension."[12] In mapping and clustering, the supporting details are related to larger categories, which are remembered more easily. Bruner explains, "Perhaps the most basic thing that can be said about human memory, after a century of research, is that unless detail is placed in a structured pattern, it is easily forgotten."[13]

These visual representations of content serve three purposes: to establish categories and subcategories of the concept, to show the supporting details related to main ideas, and to show the relationships among ideas. There are different types or styles of maps. The types used most often in school are like those in Figures 3.4 and 3.5, which show how younger and older students visually represented ideas. Figure 3.4 is the mapping a fourth grader made to plan an essay about a trip to the Upper Peninsula of Michigan. Figure 3.5 is the clustering that an older student created in his research on Jamaica for a report in his social studies class. Clustering helped him plan his research as well as organize ideas.

Another kind of semantic mapping is the Venn diagram, which is especially suited for comparisons. Figure 3.6 shows a Venn diagram

TABLE 3.2 *Selections for Comparisons*

Point of Comparison	Titles
	Picture Books
Drawing takes over	*If You Take a Pencil* by F. Testa (Dial Pied Piper, 1982) *Simon's Book* by H. Drescher (Lothrop, Lee Shepard, 1983)
Shrinking problems	*The Little Father* by G. Burgess, illustrated by R. Egielski (Farrar, Straus & Giroux, 1985) *The Shrinking of Treehorn* by F. P. Heide (Holiday House, 1971)
Wishing to be different	*The Mixed-Up Chameleon* by E. Carle (Crowell, 1984) *The Magnificent Moo* by V. Forrester (Atheneum, 1983)
Animals in the rain	*Will It Rain?* by H. Keller (Greenwillow, 1984) *All Wet! All Wet!* by J. Skofield, illustrated by D. Stanley (Harper & Row, 1984)
Quilts are magical	*Lemon Moon* by K. Chorao (Holiday House, 1983) *The Quilt* by A. Jonas (Greenwillow, 1984)
Different versions of the same	*Jack and the Bean Tree* by G. E. Haley (Crown, 1986) *Jack and the Beanstalk* retold by L. B. Cauley (Putnam, 1983)
	Dawn adapted by M. Bang (Morrow, 1983) *The Crane Wife* retold by S. Yagawa, translated by K. Paterson, illustrated by S. Akaba (Morrow, 1981)
	Moss by W. H. Hooks, illustrated by D. Carrick (Houghton Mifflin, 1987) and *Cinderella* by J. Grimm and W. Grimm, illustrated by N. Hogrogian (Greenwillow, 1981)
	Middle-Grade Books
Time fantasy	*Beyond Silence* by E. Cameron (Dell/Laurel Leaf, 1980) *Building Blocks* by C. Voigt (Atheneum, 1984)
Civil War era with Indian involvement	*Winter of the Wolf* by G. C. Wisler (Lodestar, 1980) *A Month of Seven Days* by S. Climo (Crowell, 1987)

Continued

TABLE 3.2 *Continued*

Point of Comparison	Titles
Learning to live in the United States	*Sea Glass* by L. Yep (Harper & Row, 1979) *In The Year of the Boar and Jackie Robinson* by B. B. Lord (Harper & Row, 1984)
Strong female characters	*Sweetly Sings the Donkey* by V. Cleaver (Lippincott, 1985) *Where the Lilies Bloom* by V. Cleaver (Lippincott, 1969)
Dragon stories	*The Book of Dragons* by E. Nesbit (Dell, 1986) *The Drac: French Tales of Dragons and Demons* by F. Holman (Scribner, 1975)

Poems and Books for Younger Children

Fireflies	*Fireflies!* by J. Brinkloe (Aladdin, 1986) [picture book] "Firefly" by E. M. Roberts in *Listen, Children, Listen,* compiled by M. C. Livingston (Harcort Brace Jovanovich, 1972) [poem] "A Secret" by D. Aldis in *Favorite Poems of Dorothy Aldis* (Putnam, 1970) [poem] "If You Catch a Firefly" by L. Moore in *I Feel the Same* (Scholastic, 1967) [poem]
Mud	"Mud" by P. C. Boyden in *Time for Poetry,* edited by M. H. Arbuthnot (Scott, Foresman, 1971) [poem] "Poem to Mud" by Z. K. Snyder in *Today Is Saturday* (Atheneum, 1969) [poem]
Porcupines	*Ben and the Porcupine* by C. Carrick, illustrated by D. Carrick (Clarion Books, 1981) [picture book] "The Porcupine" by N. M. Bodecker in *Potato Chips & A Slice of Moon,* edited by L. B. Hopkins (Scholastic, 1976) [poem]

Poems and Books for Older Children

Biography	*Harrriet and the Promised Land* by J. Lawrence (Simon & Schuster, 1968) [book] "Harriet Tubman" by E. Greenfield in *Honey, I Love* (Crowell, 1972) [narrative poem]
Parents asking questions	"Where" by K. Kuskin in *Near the Window Tree* (Harper & Row, 1975) [poem] "Questions" by M. Ridlon in *That Was Summer* (Follett, 1969) [poem]

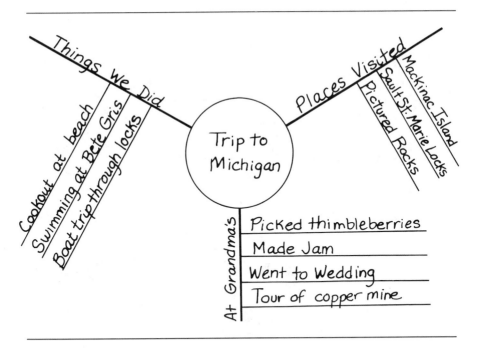

FIGURE 3.4 *Map of trip to upper peninsula of Michigan: plan for writing*

that a sixth grader, Sumon, used to show how the Earth and Venus are alike and different. The area where the circles overlap shows common features of the two being compared; the parts that do not overlap are unique. She included enough specific information to make her diagram a good learning device. After she displayed this as part of her project, the whole sixth-grade class wanted to make Venn diagrams; they "Venned" everything.

Mapping of any kind is useful in thinking about an idea, in seeing how each part is related to the other parts. Because they provide a kind of ideational scaffolding, maps may be used as advanced organizers for writing or for reading. In writing, as a part of rehearsal or prewriting, they help to organize ideas, to point out missing information, and to suggest a logical plan or order for writing. Organizing information for writing is difficult for students. Mapping as a prewriting activity may help students plan and organize before writing. In reading, mapping is useful in representing prior knowledge of key concepts in a passage. Mapping assists comprehension as students relate what they know to the new ideas and information in the selection. After reading, as students revise or add to their maps, they can confirm prereading ideas and add new information.[14]

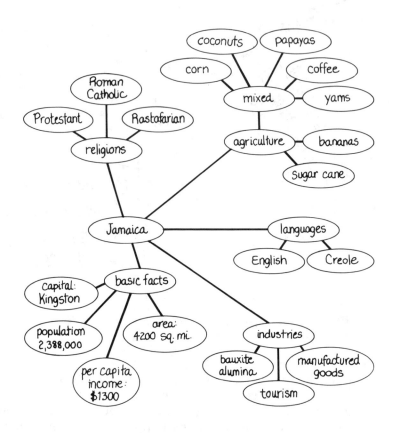

FIGURE 3.5 *Cluster of information for reports on Jamaica*

Making Analogies

Analogies in a literature study are more familiar than as a part of thinking, but they have a place in both. Analogies depend on some similarity of features on which a comparison is based. When we refer to the heart as a pump that circulates blood throughout the body, we are using an analogy. Analogies help us use our present knowledge to understand new information. We may not have seen a heart at work, but we have seen a pump; the comparison helps us construct meaning for the new idea. Belth suggests that an analogy such as a metaphor "becomes a kind of lens by which the familiar is seen in new light, new

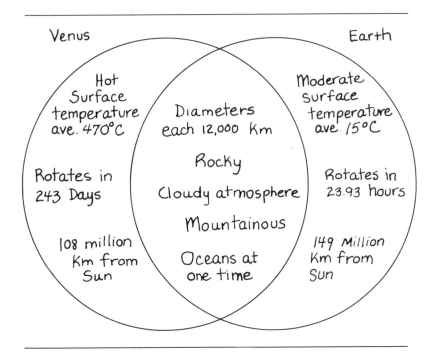

FIGURE 3.6   *Venn diagram of a comparison of Earth and Venus*

organization, new interrelationships of meanings. Terms and concepts that are normally understood as belonging to one context become the means for speaking of the other."[15]

Analogies may be metaphors (direct comparisons), similes (comparisons using *like* or *as*), or expressions of antonomasia (identifying a person by a term that is not his or her real name, such as the "Don Juan" of the seventh grade). The effectiveness of the analogy depends on the closeness of the comparison and the awareness it creates. Belth points out that every new metaphor or analogy we create or use shows us the structure and function of the world in a new way. In our attempt to understand the world more fully, analogies give us better explanations and more interesting and faithful descriptions to explain ideas in a richer way.[16] Analogies are a way to construct meaning for new concepts from old experience.

How are analogies useful in school? In science, a molecule of gas is analogous to a billiard ball, and nuclear fission to a drop of water breaking into smaller drops. Since we cannot observe firsthand either gas molecules or nuclear fission, familiar concepts facilitate our understanding of difficult concepts. Analogies are useful in the social sciences too. The Kennedy presidency was referred to as "Camelot." The analogy was effective because of the parallels that many people believed existed—the atmosphere of the times, the overall response of the nation to the president, and the attractiveness of the president and his wife. A congressional debate might be referred to as a "war of words" or a "war of ideas." This analogy suggests the conflict between the parties, the strategies used to win, and the minor battles before the big one.

Helping children learn to use analogies may enable them to see relationships in new ways. What is this like? What can I compare it to? Questions such as these prompt students to look for analogies. It is also helpful to point out analogies as you find them and talk about how they work. In what ways are two items alike? Is there a sense of discovery in the analogy? Does the analogy make you see or understand the concept better? Is there a better comparison you can think of?

This section has discussed three ways of interrelating information—comparing and contrasting, semantic mapping, and making analogies. Each helps students to relate new information more effectively to what they already know. Using specific strategies for fitting concepts and information together enables students to become better, clearer, more efficient thinkers.

Evaluating Information

Evaluating information is often called critical thinking. Critical thinking is reflected in critical reading and critical listening. Teachers need to help students think critically about what they read and hear because evaluating information is essential to intellectual development. Betts, one of the first to use the term, defined critical reading as the process of making judgments by "evaluating relevancy and adequacy of what is read."[17] This description seems to apply to critical thinking as well.

Adequacy
One of the first things to determine in judging information is its adequacy:

- Is the source reliable?
- Is the author credible—believable?
- Is the information current?

Answering these questions will determine the adequacy of the information we have.

Relevancy
Once we determine the adequacy of the information, we must determine if it is relevant in making a judgment. These questions determine the relevancy of the information upon which we base our evaluation:

- Is it fact or opinion?
- Is it pertinent to the problem at hand?
- Do the conclusions follow logically?

Consider critical thinking from the perspective of the reader or listener. What are the things a person does when he or she is evaluates information well? Harnadek's suggestions for critical readers also apply to critical thinkers:

- They do not believe everything they read or hear.
- They question everything which doesn't make sense.
- They question some things even when they do make sense.
- They reread when they think they may have missed something.
- They consider the type of material before deciding how much weight to give it.
- They admit that the effect of what the author says may be caused more by the style of writing (or speaking) than by the facts presented.
- They analyze arguments.
- They discount arguments based on faulty reasoning.
- They have good reasons for believing some things and disbelieving others—for agreeing with some authors (or speakers) and disagreeing with others.[18]

Students need to become aware of consciously evaluating the information they read or hear and basing their decisions on those judgments. They need to develop more independence and less reliance on authority—even if that sometimes means that students question their teacher.

Summary

How children learn and how they develop strategies for thinking and judging information are critical aspects of intellectual development. Thought development is one of the basic foundations for all content areas, and its close connection with language makes it a major responsibility of the language arts teacher.

Every teacher needs to consider the characteristics of students in his or her classroom to plan for experiences that will enrich the students' learning. In addition, there are a number of strategies used in thinking that should be taught and applied in every area of the curriculum. These strategies help students obtain, interrelate, and evaluate information.

Questions for Discussion

1. Describe the three processes through which people learn: organization, assimilation, and accommodation (Piaget) or schema creation, accretion, and tuning (the schema theory).
2. What are some of the characteristics of children in the age group you plan to teach. Give a specific example of behaviors that show this characteristic.
3. How does language help you think?
4. Describe specific activities that help develop students' ability to obtain information about a topic.
5. Describe specific activities that involve students in interrelating information.

Notes

1. Thomas J. Shuell, "Cognitive Conceptions of Learning," *Review of Educational Research* 56, no. 4 (Winter 1986): 414.
2. *Ibid.*, 415.
3. D. E. Rumelhart and D. A. Norman, "Accretion, Tuning, and Restructuring: Three Modes of Learning," in *Semantic Factors in Cognition*, J. W. Cotton and R. L. Klatzky, eds. (Hillsdale, NJ: Lawrence Erlbaum Associates, 1978), 37–53.
4. Leo Lionni, *Fish Is Fish* (New York: Pantheon, 1970), unpaged.
5. Eleanor Duckworth, "Piaget Takes a Teacher's Look," *Learning* (October 1973): 24.
6. Judith A. Lindfors, *Children's Language and Learning* (New York: Prentice Hall, 1980), 231–247.
7. R. W. Brown and E. H. Lenneberg, "A Study in Language and Cognition," *Journal of Abnormal and Social Psychology* 49 (1954): 454–462 as cited in Judith A. Lindfors, *Children's Language and Learning* (New York: Prentice Hall, 1980), 241.
8. Betty Edwards. *Drawing on the Artist Within* (New York: Simon & Schuster, 1986), 13.
9. *Ibid.*, 127.
10. Hans G. Furth and Harry Wachs, *Thinking Goes to School* (New York: Oxford University Press, 1974).
11. M. H. Buckley, "Mapping the Writing Journey," in *Teaching Writing: Essays from the Bay Area Writing Project*, G. Camp, ed. (New York: Boynton/Cook, 1982), 188.
12. Dale D. Johnson, "Foreword," in *Semantic Mapping: Classroom Ap-*

plications, J. E. Heimlich and S. D. Pittelman, eds. (Newark: DE: International Reading Association, 1986),v.

13. Jerome Bruner, *The Process of Education* (New York: Random House, 1960), 116.

14. D. L. Prater and C. A. Terry, "Effects of Mapping Strategy on Reading Comprehension and Writing Performance," *Reading Psychology,* 9 (1988): 101–120.

15. M. Belth, *The Process of Thinking* (New York: David McKay, 1977), 77.

16. *Ibid.,* 23.

17. Emmett A. Betts, *Foundations of Reading Instruction* (New York: American Book, 1946) as quoted in T. L. Harris and R. E. Hodges, *A Dictionary of Reading* (Newark, DE: International Reading Association, 1981), 74.

18. A. Harnadek, *Critical Reading Improvement* (New York: McGraw-Hill, 1978), 4.

Chapter 4

Acquiring Language

Acquiring Language

The Bases of Language Acquisition
Biological Factors
Environmental Factors
Psychological Structures

Processing Language from the Environment
How Adults Modify Language for Very Young Children
How Children Incorporate Adult Language

The Sequence of Language Acquisition
Early Language and Motor Development
Acquisition of Syntactic Structures
Acquisition of Semantics
Development of Complexity

Patterns and Variations in Language Acquisition
Patterns in Acquisition
Variability in Acquisition

Bilingualism: Learning Two Languages
Extent of Bilingualism
Goal of Bilingualism
Programs of Bilingualism
Children's Strategies for Learning Another Language
Code Switching
Two Methods of Teaching a Second Language
Characteristics of a Good Bilingual Program

Language Acquisition of Handicapped Children
Deafness
Mental Retardation
Speech Handicaps

Implications for Teaching
Need for a Rich Language Source
Opportunities to Engage in Language
A Natural Learning Environment

Children's first words bring joy and amazement to their parents. What a thrill and delight—they can talk! At first they may just say "Mama" or "Dada," but very soon they can express an entire idea. Telegraphic sentences like "Want cookie" or "All-gone doggie" become longer as they begin to speak more like the adults with whom they are in contact. Learning to talk seems so natural and children learn so quickly that most adults simply take it for granted. How do such young children do it? Are they born knowing how to speak? Do children imitate what they hear? Is it taught? Children move from saying single words to a two- or three-word sentence to full adult speech in a year or two. What explains this?

An understanding of how children acquire language is critical to any language arts program. It is especially crucial to a program like the one suggested in this text that aims to build upon each child's ability to use language both communicatively and creatively. The teacher needs to know what factors have been important in the child's development of language because they have important implications for classroom practices.

The psycholinguistic view of language acquisition presented here comes from cognitive psychology and linguistics. This view of acquisition suggests that children draw language from their linguistic environment, which is then internally processed to develop the common sets of rules used by adult speakers. Thus, language acquisition is similar to the scientific method in which observations are made, hypotheses are formulated, and the hypotheses are then tested against the data collected. As they learn to talk, children progressively amend their language until it becomes more and more like that spoken by adults with whom they are in contact. Smith said that "a child learning to talk is systematically trying out alternative rules to see which ones apply— that he is 'testing hypotheses,' literally conducting linguistic experiments, to discover specifically what kind of language is talked around him."[1] Basic to this view of how language is acquired is a consideration of the child's capacity for language, how language is processed, what sequence of development may be expected, and what variations may be involved.

The Bases of Language Acquisition

The source of language acquisition includes both the human capacity for language and the particular linguistic environment of the child. Language acquisition results from a complex combination of biological and environmental factors.

Biological Factors

Linguists do not agree on exactly how biological factors affect language learning, but they do agree that human beings inherit some capacity or facility for a spoken language. One view of the biological factors important to language development is that of Lenneberg, who explored those biological endowments that make language as we know it uniquely possible for human beings. His reseach suggests that language is a species-specific trait of humans.[2] Lenneberg also suggested that language might be expected from evolutionary processes and that the basis for language capacity might be transmitted genetically.

McNeill agreed that there is a biological basis for language, although his views differ from Lenneberg's. He suggested that human beings inherit the notion of a sentence as a way of organizing language. Virtually everything that occurs in language acquisition depends on prior knowledge of the basic aspects of sentence structure. Thus the concept of a sentence may be part of the human being's innate mental capacity.

> The facts of language acquisition could not be as they are unless the concept of a sentence is available to children at the start of their learning. The concept of a sentence is the main guiding principle in a child's attempts to organize and interpret the linguistic evidence that fluent speakers make available to him. What outside observers see as distorted or "telegraphic" speech is actually a consistent effort by a child to discover how a more or less fixed concept of a sentence is expressed in the language to which he has, by accident, been exposed.[3]

Others would argue that what the child inherits biologically is the ability to organize the surrounding language and figure out what substitutions can be made, how to indicate plurality or past time, how indeed language works to communicate ideas. There are not sufficient data at present to judge which view of biological factors is correct. There are, however, adequate data to support the idea that biological factors are involved in language acquisition.

Environmental Factors

In addition to the biological capacity of humans for language, an important factor in language acquisition is the environmental or experiential factor. Central to language acquisition is verbal contact with adult speakers of the language. Two early studies (those of McCarthy and Davis) established the importance of such contacts. A more recent investigation by Cazden indicates that within the adult-child interaction a particular kind of verbal stimulation may be important.

McCarthy and Davis, in two separate studies in the 1930s, examined differences in language development among twins, children with brothers or sisters (not twins), and only children.[4] Both researchers found that only children are superior in linguistic skill to the other two groups, and that children with siblings other than twins are superior to twins. The studies thus indicate that children who associate more with adults and with adult language are more linguistically mature than children who spend more time with other children.

The importance of the adult input in children's linguistic development was evident in an experimental study by Cazden.[5] One group received forty minutes a day of extensive and deliberate expansions of their telegraphic sentences. In this treatment the adult repeated in full sentence form what the child had said in telegraphic form. For example, "All-gone milk" might be expanded by the adult as "Yes, your milk is all gone." A second group was exposed to an equal amount of time spent in focusing attention on the children's ideas; but instead of repeating what they said, the adult continued the conversation with a related sentence. In this group, "All-gone milk" might be extended to "Do you want some more?" or perhaps "Then let's clean up and go outside." The third group received no special treatment. Contrary to expectations, the second group—who had received responses to their sentences, with the adult extending ideas and introducing different grammatical elements, word meanings, and relationships among ideas—performed better on all measures of language development than the first group, who had received only the simple expansions of their sentences into full-sentence form. Cazden commented that "semantic extension proved to be slightly more helpful than grammatical expansion" for several reasons that may have a bearing on language development programs for children.[6] In the extension treatment there was a richness of verbal stimulation and the focus was on the children's ideas instead of on grammatical structures. McNeill also suggested that attempts to expand children's telegraphic sentences into full sentence form may be inaccurate at least part of the time and thus may mislead or interfere with development. Cazden's research seems to indicate that the kind of adult contact that is particularly important involves using mature rather than simplified language to extend children's sentences and ideas.

Psychological Structures

Language is an intellectual response, and in Piaget's view (introduced in Chapter 3), particular intellectual responses are not inherited. Instead, children inherit a tendency to organize their intellectual processes and to adapt to their environment.[7] The theoretical framework suggested by Piaget indicates that biological factors affect intelligence in three ways: there are inherited physical structures that set broad limits on intellectual functioning; there are inherited behavioral reactions that influence the first few days of human life; and there are two basic inherited tendencies—organization and adaptation.

Organization

Organization is "the tendency common to all forms of life to integrate structures, which may be physical or psychological, into higher-order systems or structure."[8] The process of organization may be clearly seen in language acquisition as children apply their own organization to linguistic rules. In the early stages of language, important content words are employed in the child's speech and only the nonessential words (as far as meaning) are left out. For example, young children say, "No take bath!" or "Where kitty?" instead of "No, I don't want to take a bath" or "Where is the kitty now?" In later stages of acquisition, rule development or organization appears when rules are applied too generally to words that do not follow the overall pattern. This is quite obvious as the child says *catched, runned,* or *holded,* or says *mines* instead of *mine,* adding the /z/ sound used on *his, hers, yours,* or *theirs.*

Adaptation

Adaptation to the environment takes place through the two complementary processes of assimilation and accommodation. "Broadly speaking, *assimilation* describes the capacity of the organism to handle new situations and new problems with its present stock of mechanisms, *accommodation* describes the process of changing through which the organism becomes able to manage situations that are at first too difficult for it."[9] After accommodation the individual is able to assimilate increasingly novel situations: these are then accommodated, and an increasingly complex and more mature system evolves. Adaptation through these two processes as described by Piaget may account for the way new linguistic structures in the adult language children hear are incorporated into the existing language and how their linguistic rules are revised to fit the new evidence children get from trying out their language. Thus, the psycholinguists who describe the inherited capacity for learning languages and the researchers who have found important influences in the child's linguistic environment agree when we consider language to be an intellectual function.

Processing Language from the Environment

How children use the adult language in their environment is a key issue in language acquisition. It has strong implications for what teachers should do to help children develop their language, what methods are most effective, and even what content is appropriate.

Most children sound very much like their parents: they pronounce words the same way their parents do, and they use many of the same lexical items or vocabulary as well as many of the same grammatical or syntactic structures. From this, one could easily assume that children learn their language from their parents or other adults with whom they are in close contact. They do, but not merely by imitating the adult language they hear; instead, children incorporate the language surrounding them into their own rules system. If you examine the speech of two-year-olds, you find consistent patterns unlike those used by adults. Parents do not say "I holded" or "Ask me if I no make mistake." Imitation or copying of adult speech does not account for differences such as these. Processing and rule development does account for the similarities and the differences between children's speech and that of their parents.

How Adults Modify Language for Very Young Children

When children first begin to talk, adults typically change their language in a variety of ways. Thus, children are presented with language that is especially adapted for them—language that is adjusted to what they appear to understand. Clark and Clark[10] suggested that how adults talk to young children is influenced by three things: (1) making sure that children realize an utterance is addressed to them, (2) choosing the right words and sentences so that the child can understand, and (3) saying what they have to say in many different ways.

Getting Attention
Adults often use attention getters or attention holders to keep children involved and participating, such as using the child's name or exclaiming "Look!" before a statement. Adults also use a higher pitch when talking to very young children and sometimes whisper directly into their ears. Typically adults use a greater range of pitch with children, and so there is an exaggerated up-and-down quality to the talk. Touching the child, using gestures, and pointing also help to get and hold the child's attention.

Selecting What to Say
Adults make what they say to the child relevant by talking about what is going on in the child's world, often making a running commentary on the child's activities. They adjust the words they use to those they perceive are easier for children to pronounce, or words that are more useful, and those that are most easily understood. Instead of naming

the breed, adults say "There's a dog" (or *doggie*). They use fewer pronouns, saying "Daddy's going to wash Linda's hair now" instead of "I'm going to wash your hair now." Adults also encourage children to take turns by responding to their yawns or gestures as if they were part of the conversation and later by using question-and-answer formats or prompting-type questions like "You saw *WHAT?*" Adults seldom correct the form of what children say; instead, they correct the content "That a birdie house" would get a smile and "Umm-hmmm," while "That's a birdnest" might be answered by "No, that's a squirrel's nest." This emphasis on meaning or content rather than on form is a significant aspect of parent's talk that is too often missing in a school situation.

Altering Language

Adults change their language by slowing down their speech, using shorter, simple sentences, and repeating parts of what they say. By speaking slowly and pausing at the end of their utterances, adults separate one phrase from another and one sentence from another—perhaps making it easier for children to understand. One reason for a great deal of the repetition in children's language is the use of *sentence frames*[11] like the following.

> *Where's* _____.
> *Let's play with* _____.
> *Look at* _____.
> *Here's* _____.
> *That's a* _____.
> *Here comes* _____.

These are completed with a name of a person or thing, and the frame serves to mark off the beginning of the new word as it is put in the familiar place in the frame. Repetitions are frequently used by adults. "Pick up the *red one*. Find the *red one*. Not the green one. I want the *red one*. Can you find the *red one?*" These repetitions may give children information about the structures in language and also help children understand longer sentences because they can concentrate on only the repeated part.

It is not completely clear whether all these adaptations are either necessary or even helpful. Experiments to determine this without risking a child's development have not been conducted. Some evidence from children of deaf parents who use only sign language or from children exposed to a second language only on television suggests that it is at least helpful and perhaps even necessary for adults to talk to children using language specifically intended for them. Oversimplification is not helpful, but some adjustment of adult language when speaking to very young children seems to be valuable.

How Children Incorporate Adult Language

The psycholinguistic thesis is that children draw language from their linguistic environment and then process this language to discover regularities and induce generalizations or rules about its phonology and semantic and syntactic structures. The errors that children make are evidence of the rules they have developed. As they gain more experience with language and with mature language, their rules more closely approximate that of the adults.

Do Children Imitate Adult Language?

An interesting insight into this processing of language comes from a study that asked children to imitate sentences.[12] Their inability to do so is most revealing about the language rules they have, and at the same time demonstrates the ineffectiveness of direct copying or imitation in learning a language. The elicited imitation involved specific sentences to see what constructions the children would repeat accurately and which they would change or be unable to repeat at all. One such sentence given to a 2½-year-old was, "This one is the giant, but this one is little." It was repeated as, "Dis one little, annat one big." The researchers comment that evidently the child had comprehended the underlying meaning of the sentence, and then used that meaning in a new form when imitating. They pointed out how this process of filtering a sentence through one's own productive system would be described in Piaget's terminology: "a sentence, when recognized, is assimilated to an internal schema, and when reproduced, is constructed in terms of that schema."[13] This sort of recasting of sentences to fit one's productive patterns is especially obvious in repetitions such as "Mozart, who cried, came to my party," which was repeated as "Mozart cried and he came to my party," or "The owl who eats candy runs fast," repeated as "Owl eat a candy and he run fast." Evidently *who* clauses were not part of this child's productive system, and so they were changed as the child tried to repeat them.

Two other studies examined imitations in children's speech as a part of investigating the process of language acquisition. In these studies—unlike Slobin's and Welsh's work, in which children were specifically asked to imitate sentences—a whole body of the children's language was examined. Ervin studied grammatical differences between imitated and free utterances of one- and two-year-olds and concluded that there is no evidence that the child's progress toward adult grammar is greatly affected by imitation of adult sentences.[14] This same general conclusion may be drawn from a longitudinal study of two children, called Adam and Eve. A part of this study examined the children's imitations of their mother's speech. The researchers found that the children's utterances were not really imitative, and that grammatical mistakes the children made revealed their search for regularities in the language.[15]

What children actually do in using the adult language that surrounds them is to try to discover regularities in it, to organize it into patterns or rules. A child who hears *today* and *tonight* and then says *tomorning* is not imitating adult language, but is instead processing the language heard to discover how it works and then developing a rule to use. When the rule the child has developed is not actually used (as in this example), it becomes obvious what type of thinking, organizing, and processing is occurring.

Should Children's Language Be Corrected?

Just as children learn to behave in ways deemed acceptable to their parents by a process of being corrected when they do not act properly and being reinforced or praised when they do, it would seem that parents can and should use this process to shape their children's language. Think of all the times, though, that a parent says, "Say, thank you," or "Say please." Language develops very rapidly, and "so far no evidence exists to show that either correction or reinforcement of the learning of grammar occurs with sufficient frequency to be a potent force."[15] Cazden cited a conversation between an adult and a four-year-old to show how impervious to correction a child's rule system can be.

Child: My teacher holded the baby rabbits and we patted them.
Adult: Did you say your teacher held the baby rabbits?
Child: Yes.
Adult: What did you say she did?
Child: She holded the baby rabbits and we patted them.
Adult: Did you say she held them tightly?
Child: No, she holded them loosely.[17]

Another such conversation was quoted by McNeill about a parent who was deliberately trying to teach a child a form that was not within the child's own system.

Child: Nobody don't like me.
Parent: No, say, "Nobody likes me."
Child: Nobody don't like me.
Parent: No, nobody likes me.
Child: Nobody don't like me.
          (Seven more repetitions of this)
Parent: No! Now listen carefully. Say "Nobody likes me."
Child: Oh! Nobody don't likes me.[18]

An explanation for this resistance to correction is part of the principle of assimilation. In order for something to be assimilated, there must be a degree of only moderate novelty. Anything that is too new, too novel, is not assimilated, because it does not correspond to anything in the child's schemata or existing internal organization.

If they are exposed to mature adult language, children receive sufficient information from their environment to use in the process of adaptation without needing specific correction or reinforcement. When they are mature enough linguistically to make these changes, they will restructure their existing linguistic rules and incorporate the new items.

What Strategies Do Children Use?

In using the language environment to discover how language works, the child appears to rely on certain operating principles or strategies. Foss and Hakes pointed out that children learn to apply an increasingly complex and sophisticated set of strategies to the utterances they hear. Some strategies govern the surface forms of talk children pay attention to, and some govern the interpretations that children associate with the utterances. The strategies used in language acquisition may be similar to the general strategies children use with nonlanguage aspects of learning. Slobin described seven such strategies that seem to show how children operate. Language acquisition includes the following self-instructions.

1. Pay attention to the ends of words.
2. The phonological forms of words can be systematically modified.
3. Pay attention to the order of words and morphemes.
4. Avoid interruption or rearrangement of linguistic units.
5. Underlying semantic relations should be marked overtly and clearly.
6. Avoid exceptions.
7. The use of grammatical markers should make semantic sense.[20]

Children appear to attend to language they hear within the framework of the situation they are in. The strategies that are first used appear to relate to general, regular aspects of language. Later, children deal with the more narrow, exceptional parts of language.

What Strategies Should Teachers Use?

Perhaps the most important goal of teachers is the development of fluency in children. We want children to be able to explain things clearly, to describe events, people, and places, and to give directions accurately. We want children to develop expertise in using language effectively in both speech and writing. The model in Figure 4.1 shows a

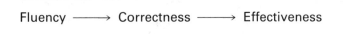

FIGURE 4.1 *Fluency sequence model*

sequence of development that suggests what teachers should do. This model suggests that fluency must come before either correctness or effectiveness. Our first emphasis with younger children is building ease in using language naturally and well. Fluency generally includes two aspects: amount and ease of production. You are not fluent in French if you can say only *bon jour* and count from one to ten. To be fluent, you should be able to say almost anything you wish in the language. You also should speak easily, without hesitations and corrections. This should be the teacher's aim for younger children—to enable them to talk and to write extensively and easily about the things with which they are familiar. In the early stages, worrying about correctness is counterproductive. Just as parents do not correct three-year-olds every time they say "holded" or "It's mines," teachers should not be too insistent on correct spelling, capitalization, and punctuation in early writing. That comes after the ideas are written down.

If too much emphasis is placed too early on correct usage or correct mechanics in writing, students may never develop to their full potential. After students write easily, producing good amounts of text, then we can place more emphasis on correctness. Effectiveness comes after the basic fluency and correctness have become almost a habit. At that point, students and teachers can deal with writing style, rhetorical devices such as repetition for effectiveness, the use of a controlling image, and connotative language.

There is a classic story of a child writing about the circus. She wrote that a lady was on the bar and then jumped through the air. When her teacher questioned her, the child said that she had wanted to use *trapeze,* but didn't know how to spell it. We want students to worry about choosing the right word, not about how to spell it. In editing writing, we can correct spellings and fix up punctuation or capitalization. However, we cannot retrieve the idea that is not there. This does not mean that spelling, capitalization, and punctuation should not be taught or used in the early grades; only that they should not be the central focus, especially in early drafts of writing. If we help children in the elementary grades become fluent writers and speakers, they will be prepared for more emphasis on correctness in the middle school grades. By the time the students enter high school, they are ready to learn how to make their writing more effective and their speaking more precise.

The Sequence of Language Acquisition

The developmental sequence leading from fluency to effectiveness is consistent with what is known about the sequence of language acquisition. As explained in the previous section, acquiring language involves systematic and progressive rule development and then verification or revision of these rules using evidence given by other speakers of the language. This systematic and progressive development is evident in the predictable order of acquisition of linguistic items. Although there may be wide variations in the rate of acquisition or in the age at which particular items are acquired, the order of acquisition of these items is strikingly similar.

Early Language and Motor Development

The chart of motor and language development shown in Table 4.1 is adapted from Lenneberg.[21] The approximate ages corresponding to each section have been omitted in order to focus on the developmental trends involved. The chart covers the period from six months of age to about four years of age.

Acquisition of Syntactic Structures

Numerous studies have been conducted to establish the sequence of acquisition of syntactic structures. In the study of syntactic acquisition by two young children called Adam and Eve, Bellugi and Brown found an identical order of appearance of certain inflections in both children's language although there was a considerable difference—between 8½ and 15 months—in the ages of the children when the inflectional forms first appeared.[22] The inflections were items such as -s for plurals and -ed for past tense of verbs. Moreover, the order of appearance of these inflections did not match the frequency of the forms found in the language of the children's mothers.

Stages of acquisition of syntactic structures were also identified by Menyuk in a study of nursery school and kindergarten children.[23] The language of the children was recorded in family role playing, in answering questions, and in talking about pictures. She found that certain transformations were used by significantly more first-grade children than by kindergarten children, showing maturation between nursery school and first grade.

A third study showing evidence of stages in the acquisition of syntactic structures was Chomsky's study of children between the ages of five and ten.[24] In an effort to determine the order of acquisition and the approximate age of acquisition, Chomsky examined four particular

TABLE 4.1   *Motor and Language Development: Selected Milestones*

Motor Development	*Language Development*
Supports head when in prone position; then plays with a rattle when placed in hand; then sits with props	Makes gurgling sounds usually called cooing; then responds to human sounds; then the vowel-like sounds begin to be interspersed with more consonant sounds
When sitting bends forward and uses hands for support; then stands up holding on and grasps with thumb apposition; then creeps efficiently and pulls to a standing position	Cooing changes to babbling; then vocalizations are mixed with sound play; differentiates between words heard; appears to try imitating sounds, but isn't successful
Walks when held by one hand; walks on feet and hands with knees in air	Identical sound sequences are replicated and words (*mama, dada*) emerge; shows understanding of some words and simple consonants
Grasp, prehension, and release fully developed; gait stiff and propulsive; sits on child's chair with only fair aim	Has a repertoire of 3 to 50 words; still babbling but with several syllables and intricate intonation patterns; may say *thank you* or *come here*, but can't join items into spontaneous two-item phrases
Runs, but falls in sudden turns; can quickly alternate between sitting and standing; walks stairs up or down with only one foot forward	Vocabulary of more than 50 items; "telegraphic speech" as tries to join vocabulary into two-word phrases; increase in communicative behavior and more interest in language
Jumps into air with both feet; takes a few steps on tiptoe; good hand and finger coordination.	Fast increase in vocabulary; frustrated if not understood; utterances have two to five words; characteristic "child grammar"
Runs smoothly with acceleration and deceleration; makes sharp and fast curves; walks stairs by alternating feet; can operate tricycle	Vocabulary of some 100 words; 80 percent of utterances intelligible even to strangers; grammatical complexity roughly that of adult usage
Jumps rope, catches ball, and walks a line	Language well established; deviations more in style than in grammar

constructions that are not usually present in the grammar of five-year-olds but are normally acquired by age ten. She found that one construction involving understanding of pronoun reference was quite rapidly and uniformly acquired by age five and a half. Two of the other constructions appeared to be under control from age nine on, and the fourth construction was not completely controlled by all the ten-year-olds.

These studies and others on the acquisition of various syntactic structures have found that individual structures are acquired in a particular order, although the age of acquisition may vary from one individual to another. There is, then, a sequence of acquisition that is quite regular. It seems independent of experiential factors except in the rate of acquisition.

Acquisition of Semantics

The acquisition of semantics, or word meaning, is less clear than that of syntax. Early studies dealt mostly with vocabulary frequencies and derivations of words. Linguistic investigations until recently concentrated on phonology and syntax. Although the details of the acquisition of semantics are not clear, there are many similarities between syntactic and semantic acquisition. There seem to be stages in semantic acquisition as children progressively amend their early language until word meanings approximate those of adults.

One view of semantic acquisition is that word meanings are learned by adding *features*, or meaning components, to the lexical meaning of words. Clark made the following suggestion. "When a child first begins to use identifiable words, he does not know their full (adult) meaning; he only has partial entries for them in his lexicon. The acquisition of semantic knowledge, then, will consist of adding more features of meaning to the lexical entry of the word until the child's combination of features in the entry for the word corresponds to the adult's."[11] For example, very young children may call anything on four wheels a car—including trucks and moving vans. As they have more experience with different vehicles, they refine *car* in various ways until what they call a *car* is just what an adult calls a car. In the process of refining the meaning of words, children both particularize (*car* to *Chevy, Ford*) and generalize (*car* to *pickup* or *van*).

With older children an indication of this process of refining meanings until they approximate the adult meaning may be seen in their use of words that have many overlapping features. In word pairs such as *boy/brother* or *girl/sister*, one word refers to a subset within the other word but has additional features. All brothers, for example, are boys, but not all boys are brothers. *Brother* is a subset of *boy* with the additional feature of family relationship. Many middle graders still have difficulty with this distinction, and when asked how many brothers or sisters they have, will include themselves.

Another view of the role of semantics in the language of young children was expressed by Bloom.[26] She examined the telegraphic speech of a number of children and found that grammatical explanations of sentences such as "Mommy sock" neglected to include the connection with cognitive-perceptual development and the inherent semantic relations that underlie the juxtaposition of words in these early sentences. "Mommy sock" meant different things at different times. Once it meant the child was picking up her mother's sock, and another time it described the mother putting on the child's sock. In Bloom's view of semantics, language has a surface structure and an underlying semantic (not grammatical) structure.

Menyuk also explored the context within which a particular word or lexical item is used and suggests that until the child is over age ten lexical items do not have meanings separate from the sentence contexts used by the child.[27] Menyuk points out that even when a word is understood and used in one sentence structure, the same word may not be understood in a different sentence structure. This would indicate, as Bloom suggested, that there are underlying semantic relationships reflected in the particular grammatical context.

In the acquisition of semantics, there is evidence of organization and adaptation in the development of mental structures. The sentence context serves as an organization for semantic properties, and adaptation is the process through which the child acquires increasingly more mature lexical references through interactions with the linguistic community.

Although we do not have definitive data on the process of semantic acquisition, we do know some of the factors that enable children to increase their vocabulary—the number of words and word meanings they can use and the precision of word meanings. One factor that aids development is meaningful contact with a wide variety of words, both in speech and in written material. Another is feedback from adults about word meanings as words come up in the context of a situation. A discussion of vocabulary development is included in Chapter 5.

Development of Complexity

Complexity in language involves compressing two or more simple structures into a single sentence through compounding, subordinating, and embedding. For example, the following sentences may be combined several ways.

I had a baseball.
It was new.
I took it to school.
I lost it.

They may be made into compound sentences: "I had a baseball, and it was new. I took it to school, and I lost it." They may be made into complex sentences by subordination: "My ball that was new was a baseball. When I took it to school, I lost it." Or they may be combined with embedding into a single sentence: "I lost the new baseball I took to school." In the latter case "It was new" is embedded as a single adjective.

As children mature, there is a developmental increase in the number and kinds of structures they use. This does not mean that young children use only simple sentences, for children at kindergarten age do use compounding, subordination, and embedding. However, there is an increase in the number of transformations used as age and ability with language increase. This is true of both oral and written language. A major study evaluating the development of children's oral language was conducted by Loban over a period of years. In 1952 more than three hundred children were selected and oral language samples were obtained annually throughout their school years. This study found that students showed an increase in complexity of language throughout the years with a noticeable rise about the time of fifth grade. The primary difference in grammatical complexity between the less mature and more mature children was in the dexterity of substitutions within patterns and not in the number of different patterns used.[28]

A key study on differences in syntactic maturity in written language examined students in grades four, six, eight, ten, and twelve and two groups of adults. They were all given passages containing very short simple sentences and were asked to rewrite it in a better way without omitting any information. Their rewriting was then checked on five semantic measures. Hunt found that as children mature, they tend to embed more of their elementary sentences or kernel strings, and that this embedding is done in different ways at different age levels.[29] As with oral language, older students tended to write significantly longer clauses and T units. A *T unit* is a minimal terminal unit—an independent clause with its modifiers. It is a more accurate measure of complexity than sentence length since it prevents run-on sentences from increasing length artificially.

These studies and others on complexity in children's language indicate a pattern of increasing complexity in both spoken and written language throughout the elementary grades. Although a variety of means to combine structures is used at all grade levels, children at first use mostly coordination and later subordination and embedding. One may expect many run-on sentences throughout the early elementary grades, which should decrease as children's language matures.

Patterns and Variations in Language Acquisition

While there is great variation in certain aspects of language and in the age at which certain structures or meanings are acquired, there are overriding patterns in the acquisition process that apply to all aspects of language.

Patterns of Acquisition

The process of language acquisition, like any cognitive process, exhibits patterns that may help us understand certain things that children say or do. Taylor points out that children everywhere master linguistic rules, forms, and functions in the following pattern.[30]

> Essential before less essential
> Simple and short before long and complex
> Few before many
> Gross and distinct before subtle and finer
> Salient before less salient
> Concrete before abstract
> Isolated items individually before items in relation
> Regular before irregular (unless irregular items are common and simple)
> Forms with more general application before forms with restricted application
> Basic functions before particular details of forms to express the functions

The acquisition of language takes place within this sort of framework. Variations in language are primarily differences in the structures acquired by a child at a particular time, or in the acquisition of a particular structure by children of the same age.

Variability in Acquisition

Individual Variability

A study discussed earlier in the chapter presented a very clear picture of the differences between children in the acquisition of particular structures. The researchers were investigating the appearance of various syntactic or morphological inflections in "Adam and Eve's" language.[31] Of the five inflections reported, the one acquired when the children were closest in age was the *-ing* on present progressives. Eve used this inflection at 19½ months and Adam used it at 28 months—8½ months' difference. The third person ending *-s* on present tense verbs was reported for Eve at 26 months, but not for Adam until 41 months, a 15-month difference. Despite such tremendous variations in the ages at which these children used the inflections, the order or sequence of use was the same.

Individual variability may be found for other syntactic or semantic structures, as well as for various elements of motor development. There is a great deal of variability in individual children's rates of development. In language acquisition, the factor that appears to be most important is the linguistic environment of the child. The individual linguistic experiences of children serve as the source from which children process their language. The words they hear, their pronunciations, and the structures used by people around them serve as a basis for developing linguistic rules. The particular linguistic environment of the child may determine the kinds of interaction opportunities available—opportunities for the child to test and revise particular linguistic rules.

Social Variability

People also vary their language within particular social contexts. Within any dialect of English there are varieties, or *registers*, of that dialect that are appropriate for use in particular situations. People vary their language depending upon their current situation and what they believe to be correct in their dialect for that situation.

Children use such registers of language. Just ask a seven-year-old to role play an adult and you will notice different inflections, different vocabulary, and different gestures. The use of different language in writing is also observed in children. By the time they are in middle school and have been exposed to a great amount of written material, children write differently from the way they talk, showing an understanding of a register of written language. (See Chapter 7 for further discussion of language variation.) Generally, variability in language arises from the particular situation in which language is used and from differing linguistic environments. It is this variability within language that the teacher observes so clearly in the classroom and that necessitates varying assignments or experiences for different children.

Bilingualism: Learning Two Languages

Bilingual people—those who speak two or more languages that involve differences in sound, vocabulary, and syntax—acquire their languages in one of several ways. Some children learn the two languages almost simultaneously at the time when they are first learning to talk. Other children learn one language at home and another when they go to school sometime after the age of five. Still others acquire a second language as a school subject during the elementary or secondary school years. The effectiveness of second-language learning and the process of learning differ among these three kinds of bilingualism.

In the United States attitudes toward people who speak more than one language differ greatly. For children who grew up speaking English, being able to learn another language is a high achievement. A person who can speak three languages may be regarded as brilliant. Consider, on the other hand, the child whose parents emigrated from Mexico or French-speaking Canada and who does not speak English at all. After six months in school, starting at age five, the child can say a few phrases, knows when to line up to go to recess or lunch, puts the date and his or her name on papers correctly, and understands some of what the teacher says. However, the child could not succeed in a regular classroom with the standard curriculum. Teachers are impatient. The family has been in this country for three years. Why can't they speak English? Such an attitude reflects the paradox that Americans who speak another language are respected, while those born in other countries are expected to learn English rapidly.

Although Americans may talk about bilingualism as a goal, Grosjean says, "Bilingualism in the United States is basically short-lived and transitional, in that it links monolingualism in one language—usually an immigrant language—to monolingualism in the majority language, English."[32]

Extent of Bilingualism

How many people are bilingual? An analysis of the 1980 census shows that of the total United States population of 225,361,000 more than 23 million speak a non-English language at home, and about 18.6 million speak English and another language. Almost half, 45 percent, of those who speak another language speak Spanish. Mexican Americans live primarily in the Southwest, often in its larger cities. Puerto Ricans have migrated to the mainland and live in New York City, other large cities of the Northeast, and on the West Coast. Most of the Cubans who came to the United States in the 1960s have settled in the Miami area, while Central and South Americans tend to be scattered throughout the United States, often in established Hispanic communities. The European language groups consisting of German, French, Italian, Polish, and Scandinavian are the next most populous group identified, although many of them speak English. Two other groups of non-English-language speakers are the Asian population, which now numbers 3.7 million and the 800,000 Native Americans. About two-thirds of the

Asians speak their native language at home, and they are concentrated in California, Hawaii, and New York. The Native Americans often retain their own language because over half of them live on reservations and because the native language is used in traditional religious practices.[33]

Goal of Bilingualism

Americans have not come to an agreement on what the goals should be for children whose native language is not English. Some seek a melting pot effect and others seek a mosaic. Should those whose native language is not English learn English as soon as possible and become American (melting pot)? Alternatively, should a diversity of languages, customs, lifestyles, and aspirations be encouraged (mosaic)? Bilingual education touches on more than educational issues concerning language; it involves race, poverty, state and federal funding, and job security for teachers. Historically, rapid Americanization has been stressed, often at the expense of children's happiness and security. The following excerpts attest to the painful Americanization experiences of bilingual children.

A Franco-American in New England

We have had our share of being called names, having stones thrown at us (as children), being laughed at in school, being overworked and underpaid by Yankee bosses. But today, in the 1980s I personally feel that the Franco-Americans have come a long way since being called "the Chinese of the East" in the 1880s.[34]

A Hispanic American

As a child my life seemed strange and confusing. At home, which meant brothers, parents, an aunt and uncle . . . and grandparents, the language was mainly Spanish and the culture distinctly Mexican. At school, the language was only English, and the culture was a cold and distant way of being treated—like the remolding process of an Army boot camp.[35]

A German-English Bilingual

As for my own experience, I felt a bitterness somewhat because I was "different," not only in language but also in culture and dress, from my primary school peers. I used to cry when the children called me "Little Hitler" and this prompted my own rebellion against the German forces within our family. . . . My "rebellion" resulted in my mother addressing me in German and me constantly replying in English.[36]

Forcing children to abandon their native language—the language of their home—to learn English also forces them to reject their own culture and family relations. Instead a program should help children add a second language while maintaining their own. This second language learning experience should maintain respect for the culture that surrounds the family language. Opponents of bilingualism insist that people who come to the United States should become American, speak English, and forget their foreign ways. There is also opposition from some parents of non-English speaking children, who feel that their children must learn English as soon as possible to avoid becoming second-class citizens. Others contend that we are wasting a precious national resource if we try to eliminate native languages and cultures, and that children can become bilingual without giving up their native language.

Programs of Bilingualism

In 1968 The Bilingual Education Act, or Title VII, was signed into law. It stated in part:

> In recognition of the special educational needs of the large numbers of children of limited English speaking ability in the United States, Congress hereby declares it to be the policy of the United States to provide financial assistance to local educational agencies to develop and carry out new and imaginative elementary and secondary school programs designed to meet these special educational needs.

In 1974 the *Lau* v. *Nichols* decision mandated that non-English speaking children have a meaningful opportunity to participate in the public educational program. Because of this decision, amendments to Title VII now provide that bilingual education must be offered in any school district with twenty or more students from the same language background who have limited English proficiency. The law was amended again in 1978 to include more parental involvement, evaluation and research plans, and participation by some native English speakers.

There are four general program categories for bilingual programs: immersion, transitional bilingual, partial bilingual, and full bilingual-bicultural. *Immersion* programs are typically used when students whose home language is that of the dominant culture learn a second language. It has been used extensively in Canada for English-speaking children who are learning French. The children are first heavily exposed—immersed—in the new language until they develop some degree of proficiency. Then their first language is used as another medium of instruction. *Transitional bilingual* programs use the native language in addition to instruction in the second language until children can use their second language for learning. Fluency or literacy in both languages is not the goal. While this has been a common pattern in the past, according to Alexander and Nava, school districts using a transitional program today must provide predictive data showing that students are ready to make the transition into English and will succeed educationally in such a program.[37] The third type of program is the *partial bilingual* program, in which fluency and literacy in both languages are fully developed. The cultural heritage of the native language is presented in social studies, literature, and the arts. In the *full bilingual-bicultural* program, the native language and cultural factors are used for fluency and literacy in the native language at the same time as students develop these skills in the second language and culture. The aim is to help students function fully in either language or culture.

The last three types of programs are used in the United States with children whose native language is not English. The programs differ in their emphasis on maintaining native language skills and in the position and value given to cultural aspects of the native language group.

Children's Strategies for Learning Another Language

What makes someone successful in learning another language? Some children in the same classroom and in the same program learn more quickly than others. Interesting information about successful second language learning comes from Fillmore's study of five monolingual Spanish-speaking children, ages five to seven, in a bilingual program.[38] After examining these children's progress in learning English, she described two sets of operating principles that seemed to represent the strategies used by the most successful children. These principles included a set of cognitive strategies and a set of social strategies. Fillmore described the following cognitive strategies.

1. Assume that what people are saying is directly relevant to the situation at hand, or to what they or you are experiencing. Metastrategy: guess.
2. Get some expressions you understand, and start talking.
3. Look for recurring parts in the formulas you know.
4. Make the most of what you've got. Use a word that is something like what you mean or add phrases you do know when you talk.
5. Work on big things; save the details for later.

Children's social strategies included the following.

1. Join a group and act as if you understand what's going on even if you don't.
2. Give the impression—with a few well-chosen words—that you can speak the language.
3. Count on your friends for help.

These strategies certainly do not reflect the way foreign languages have been taught traditionally in high school or college. Perhaps that is why few American students become fluent in a foreign language. Or perhaps foreign language teachers have been too concerned about correctness and not concerned about communication in the second language.

To some extent, the cognitive strategies for learning a second language are the same ones children use in learning their first language. Young children first learning their language tend to assume that what people are saying is relevant to the situation, to search for recurring parts, words, and patterns, and to work on the big things first. Second language learning is not entirely like the acquisition of one's first language, however. Second language learners are older and have more experiences with language to apply to new problems. At the same time the first language can interfere with the second in cases where the two differ. Many foreign language classes today approach second language learning more like first language learning, emphasizing the communication of ideas and the development of oral skills through experiences and conversation.

Code Switching

One of the interesting aspects of bilingualism is called code switching—the use of two or more languages in the same conversation. Sometimes words are mixed within the sentence; other times the speaker starts in one language and then switches to another. In one example, the wife says, "Va chercher Marc and bribe him avec un chocolat chaud with cream on top." In another, a Spanish bilingual says, "La consulta era eight dollars."[40]

Many bilinguals realize that they switch languages, especially when they are with others who speak the same two languages or who also switch codes. Sometimes switching occurs because the term in one language is more precise or more familiar; other times speakers seem unaware of changing languages in midsentence. Code switching is viewed—even by those who do it—as a grammarless mixture, impure and lazy. This is probably too harsh a judgment since such mixtures of languages often result in effective communication.

Two Methods of Teaching a Second Language

The two primary methods used in bilingual education programs are different in their psychological underpinnings as well as in their aims and methodologies. The *audio-lingual method* is based on a behavioral view of language learning that emphasizes modeling, correction, and repetition. In this method, the teacher sets up pattern sentences for practice or dialogues that students memorize and repeat. The purpose of these activities is to make the structures of the second language habitual and to make students master the forms of the language. In such a method you might hear the following exchange:

Teacher: This is a pen. Is it a brush?
Student: No, it is not a brush.
Teacher: Is it a pencil?
Student: No, it is not a pencil.
Teacher: Is it a book?
Student: No, it is not a book.
Teacher: Is it a tablet?
Student: No, it is not a tablet.
Teacher: What is it?
Student: It is a pen.

This method emphasizes correctness at the earliest stages and ignores meaningful and purposive interaction with others. At one time it was the primary method of teaching a second language, but is now being replaced with methods more like those used for original language acquisition.

The *communicative competence method* is based on a cognitive model of learning that gives the learner a central, active role in constructing meaning and interacting with the environment and other people. Its emphasis is on communication, and correctness is deferred until a later stage. Students learn the language by using it to talk with others about their activities, experiences, and thoughts. In this method you might hear exchanges like the following.

Teacher: Tomorrow is Anna's birthday. She will be seven.
Student: I am seven.
Student: I am eight. I have more years.
Teacher: Yes, Jose, you are eight now. How old are you, Paulette?
Student: I . . . I six. Yes?

Teacher: That is right, Paulette. You are six.
Teacher: Do you want to have a party for Anna?
All: Yes.
Teacher: What will we have for our party?
Student: Ice cream.
Student: Cake.
Student: We also have pizza?
Teacher: Well, I'm not sure about pizza!

Here the focus is on a real situation, and the children participate without being corrected for every mistake. After the children are older and more fluent, their teachers will correct them if they have not corrected themselves by listening to others and finding the patterns in this new language.

There seems little doubt that the latter method is preferable in second language learning experiences. As children become more fluent in the second language, explanations and drill practice may promote continued growth in language skill. However, until children become fluent in both oral and written language, the focus should be on meaning and not on form.

Characteristics of a Good Bilingual Program

The following list summarizes the features of a good bilingual program for children whose native language is not English. It is based on the same views of language acquisition and learning theory as the general language arts program. It does not ignore the differences between first and second language learning nor the aspects of culture that surround language learning. If we believe that children should become fluent in English while maintaining their ability to use fully their home language, we will see the merits for the following program features.

- The emphasis is first on oral language development in the target language so that children become fluent in speaking and understanding English.
- There is continued use and skill development in the children's first language. Knowing two languages is a desirable goal.
- The focus of the teacher and students is on meaning, not on form or correctness.
- The learning environment provides many direct experiences, as well as books and media, and stresses talking about them.
- Experiences, instructional materials, and activities represent the children's native language culture, as well as aspects of the target language culture.

- Reading and writing skills are developed in the first language, and are used as a natural part of language learning in the target language.
- Formal grammar is not taught until after literacy is achieved in the second language.
- Teachers are knowledgeable about the children's native language and culture and have access to information about possible language problems from contrastive studies of the two languages.

A good program for children who come to school speaking another language at home is not only a challenge but also a resource. Both the law and our conscience insist that these children be given the respect and support they need as well as excellent instruction.

Language Acquisition of Handicapped Children

Certain children have special problems in acquiring language. Since so much of the source for language development lies in oral conversation—in those special interactions of the young child with adults—deaf children have some difficulty acquiring language. Mentally retarded children, who must process the language they hear, find organizing patterns, and fit new aspects of language into their existing structures, also have special problems in the acquisition of language. Although speech handicaps such as voice problems, articulation problems, and stuttering have a different relationship to the acquisition of language, they concern elementary and middle school teachers. Some speech handicaps are often confused with normal stages in acquisition or have their roots in early language development.

Deafness

Children who are deaf are not exposed to oral language, and although they begin to babble at about the same age as hearing children, they "stop babbling early and later experience great difficulty in learning to talk intelligibly unless hearing aids correct the hearing loss."[40] Even with a great deal of training, deaf children often cannot master natural intonations and rhythm in speech. They tend to have a higher-than-average pitch, speak more slowly, and pause for breath more often. They also have difficulty articulating consonants and vowels, particularly with voiced and unvoiced consonants (like /p/ and /b/) and with nasals and diphthongs. Early intervention, like that in the Nuffield Hearing and Speech Center in England where the very small amounts of hearing the children have is used to help them develop oral speech, shows great promise for deaf children.

Mental Retardation

Mentally retarded children go through the same stages in the acquisition of language as all children, and "their language is almost exactly like that of a normal child of the same *mental age*, which is assessed by comparing their motor skills, memory, and so forth. The same limited set of meanings is expressed in their first sentences, though the rate of development is much slower."[41] A severely retarded child may take a year to make the progress a normal child would make in one month. There is also some evidence that retarded children use many more set patterns, prefabricated routines, apparently relying more on rote memory than on creating their own sentences.

Speech Handicaps

Almost half of speech handicaps involve some sort of articulation problem, and about 10 percent involve stuttering. Many of the problems in articulation are outgrown by age seven or eight. The sound substitution errors that children make are highly systematic and are most often initial consonant sounds. Consonant sounds that cause the most difficulty are /l/ or /r/ (child substitutes /w/); /ð/, the voiced *th-* (child substitutes /d/); /θ/, the unvoiced *th-* (child substitutes /f/ or /t/); /dʒ/ as in *judge* (child substitutes /d/); /ʃ/ as in *sh-* (child substitutes /s/); /t/ (child substitutes /s/ or /ʃ/); and /ɑ/; /j/; /s/; /v/; and /z/. The articulation errors that children make are in the consonants and consonant clusters that require more complex articulation and fine auditory discrimination and are generally mastered later by all children. Parents and teachers should not become unduly concerned about such articulation differences or try too hard to correct them. Many will simply disappear with maturity.

The other speech handicap that seems particularly important to discuss is stuttering. The fluency of speech in the stutterer is disturbed by blocking, repeating, or prolonging sounds, syllables, words, or phrases. There is some evidence of an inherited basis for stuttering, but environmental factors play a significant role. Children who stutter are typically made to pay attention to the way they talk because of their parents' (or teachers') high standards of fluency. All children and adults repeat words or sounds, hesitate, and do everything the stutterer does; it is just less frequent. Over 80 percent of all stutterers recover spontaneously, according to Sheehan. Their recovery is attributed to role acceptance as a stutterer, growing self-esteem, development of adequacy and self-confidence, relaxation, and greater understanding of the problem.[42] It is especially important to provide an atmosphere as free from pressure as possible, avoid overreacting to stuttering or articulatory problems, and to show as little anxiety as possible to the speaker.

While it is important to understand the special problems of handicapped children, the most significant aspect of teaching such children is that what is good for children is good for *all* children. Emphasis on the content of the message, a relaxed atmosphere, and lots of opportunities to interact with adult language in meaningful contexts help special children develop language skills.

Implications for Teaching

There appear to be two distinct implications for classroom practice stemming from the theoretical view presented of how children acquire language. If the basic process of acquisition involves using the language environment as a source for language data, then it is important for the teacher to provide a rich language environment in the classroom. If the rules developed by children about how their language operates are then tested and revised in terms of the feedback they receive as they use language, then there must be many opportunities to use language in various ways.

Need for a Rich Language Source

Providing a classroom environment full of opportunities to hear rich and varied language involves selecting and reading literature with a variety of sentence structures, a wealth of words, and real literary qualities. It also implies that the teacher should not simplify sentence structures or vocabulary unless the children indicate a lack of understanding. Rich language could also be introduced through using various media such as films, audiotapes, recordings, and presentations by guest speakers. This kind of language environment should present language in a meaningful context and offer a variety of experiences from which children can draw language data.

Literature for Children
Literature is a particularly rich source because so many books and poems for children contain imaginative language that children enjoy hearing.

Look at the language used in the following selections from literature and poetry written for children of various ages. Examine the complexity of the sentences and the choice of words used. To get a feeling for complexity in mature language, examine sentence length and the use of clauses. Rich vocabulary is apparent in words that are precise and create vivid pictures in the mind of the reader.

For younger children Skofield's *All Wet! All Wet!* shares a rainy day in the woods.

> *The rainy day begins.*
> *Inside a hollow log, Skunk wakes and yawns,*
> *then steps outside and ambles toward the stream.*
> *Skunk passes spiders, sitting like black stars,*
> *motionless, at the hub of diamond webs.*[43]

In Brittain's *Dr. Dredd's Wagon of Wonders*, a book that will intrigue older readers, Dr. Dredd is described this way.

> *He was well over six feet tall and as gaunt as a dead tree limb. A suit of black wool hung on him like wash on a line, and a string tie of the same color looped down across his shirtfront. On his head was a tall hat of red silk, and in his right hand he clutched a coiled whip of braided leather.*
>
> *His eyes were almost hidden beneath a ridge of brow, and his nose was long and thin, like the beak of a hawk. The cruel slash of mouth put me in mind of a snapping turtle awaiting its prey. His left hand kept moving back and forth across his chest, the fingers ever in motion like the legs of some huge spider.*[44]

Poetry, too, is a rich source of language. Its rhythm and rhyme appeal to children; its words are strange and intriguing. This poem from Adoff's *Eats* about picking strawberries should appeal to children who always like poems about food.

[Untitled]

> *Getting the sweet strawberries*
> *from my fingers down into a basket*
> *without eating all of them up is*
> *the problem*
> *the solution is not*
> *to solve the problem until*
> *you are full*
> *of answers*[45]
> —Arnold Adoff

There is also wonderful language in the next poem below from Paul Fleischman's *I Am Phoenix: Poems for Two Voices*. One reader reads the left-hand part; the other, the right-hand part. When both readers have a line on the same level, they read together.

The Common Egret

First Reader	Second Reader
They call us	
common	common
	egrets.
Common!	
	The injustice!
As if to be so white	
that	
snow	snow
	is filled with envy
clouds	clouds
	consumed with spite
that milk	that milk
	should seem mo-
	lasses
rates as ordinary.	
Gold	Gold
should be so slan-	
dered	
diamonds	diamonds
scorned as worth-	
less	
rubies	rubies
spurned	
	if common
egrets	egrets
	are but
common	common.[46]
	—Paul Fleischman

Through literature for children, the teacher can introduce a variety of language patterns and vocabulary in meaningful ways. There is a rich context for understanding, and concrete imagery to delight and capture the child's imagination.

Research evidence shows that using literature has a positive effect on children's language ability. Studies such as those by Cohen; Fodor; and Cullinan, Jaggar, and Strickland have found literature effective in facilitating some aspect of language acquisition or development.[47] These studies used an activity program or oral discussion as a follow-up to the stories read to the children in the experimental groups. It seems quite clear that what is most helpful is the combination of a rich language input as children listen to the stories and poems and the opportunity to use the language in a meaningful situation. Activities that promote language development after listening to a story or poem are discussing events or ideas in the story, retelling the story (perhaps with puppets or feltboard characters), dramatizing scenes from the story, making up a new element of the story, or doing any other activity that gives students a chance to use language to respond to the story or poem in a way that enhances it for the children. Teachers should be willing to reread favorite stories or poems, which helps to "set" the words and phrasings in the children's minds.

Language of the Teacher

Another source of language input for the classroom is the language of the teacher. Too often teachers working with children in the primary grades attempt to simplify their language so that they will be easily understood. There are, of course, times when this might be necessary for the safety of the children. Other than those few rare times, the teacher can facilitate language development more by speaking in a normal adult way. The context within which language is used helps to clarify much that may not yet be under control of less mature speakers. If the teacher is sensitive to the responses—both verbal and nonverbal—of children, further explanations can make clear any lack of understanding while developing vocabulary at the same time.

Another facet of the teacher's language is the kind of response elicited from children. Teachers must create a need for children to respond to their experiences in a variety of ways. This may occur in individual discussions or as part of a group experience.

Nonprint Media

Another source of a rich language environment that may be provided within the classroom setting is the variety of films, audiotapes, and recordings available. These media also provide a context for language that is meaningful. They should be selected for their inherent interest as well as for their language possibilities.

The content of the nonprint media may involve another subject area, such as mathematics, science, or social studies. Recordings, tapes, films, and filmstrips of both poetry and prose are also available. If the teacher can set up a listening area for independent use, children can select what appeals to them and work individually or in small groups with the materials.

The creation in the classroom of a rich and varied language environment is important for all children. It is crucial for children whose home environment does not provide experiences for children to respond through language. The need to use language to communicate ideas and feelings in an original and creative way is to some extent culturally determined. For teachers working with children who have not experienced this need to use language, the richness of and re-sponse to language in the classroom are vital.

Opportunities to Engage in Language

A major feature of the process of language acquisition and development is the testing and revision of the internalized rules of how language operates. This occurs as children talk and write about their ideas and experiences and share them with others.

Communicating and Explaining

The teacher needs to set up situations that give children opportunities to talk with others. Children need experiences in sharing ideas and explaining things. This may be done with the whole class, with small groups of children, or between individual children. Students should be allowed to talk freely with each other when it will not interrupt class-room activities and as long as that talk is not rowdy or purposeless. In group discussions and in sharing activities, children should be encour-aged to describe and explain and interact with each other. The teacher can accomplish this by asking a variety of questions and by encourag-ing children to ask questions or add their own experiences. Activities that require joint cooperation, effort, and thinking also prompt mean-ingful talk among children.

Imagining and Creating

Through the various avenues provided in oral composition, the teacher can encourage imaginative and creative uses of language. Dramatic activities and storytelling lend themselves to this kind of language use. Inventing new words and using familiar ones in new ways, rhyming and discovering "found" poetry, and telling real and invented stories lead to imaginative and creative uses of language.

Provide opportunities for children to respond to their experiences creatively in various artistic media. This kind of response should be encouraged also in creative language activities. Children even at the early age levels should have an opportunity to tell or write stories and poems. If the task of writing is difficult for them, provision should be made for dictating to others. Children should share orally as well as in written form the stories and poems they have written.

Playing with words and sounds is natural for children. Rhyming words and making up new words are not unusual. It is typical to see this in young children who have not been disciplined so much that their creative responses have been squelched. To foster creative re-sponses by children to their environment, then, teachers must cherish

Children engage in meaningful conversations as they work together on a creative project.

creativity and imagination in children. Students need encouragement and opportunities to work creatively with language in both oral and written forms. They need to hear imaginative language used in both stories and poems.

A Natural Learning Environment

An integral part of early language acquisition is the kind of home environment that fosters learning. This environment is characterized by some qualities that also make a good learning situation at school, although some aspects of the home environment are not possible in a school setting. However, a classroom more like home is beneficial to all learning, and especially to language learning.

Emphasis on Meaning, Not Form

In the language learning that takes place before children reach school age, parents and other adults respond to children to communicate meanings. Little attention is paid to correct form. Children do need to develop skills in using language conventions, but this is a gradual process and comes with real purposes. They want the listener or reader to understand what they are saying or writing. They learn to write good letters when someone they like is away, not when the teacher decides it's time for a unit on writing letters. Handwriting becomes important when they find other people can't make sense of their stories because of the writing or printing. Saying "he doesn't" instead of "he don't" becomes important when they realize that someone they want to impress cares which phrasing is used.

One of the major purposes of language arts instruction is to develop fluency in using both oral and written language. Adults need to be able to speak easily, describing or explaining their ideas fully and transferring these qualities to written expression. Teachers should stress the ability to produce a large quantity and easy flow of language. If teachers insist too soon on correctness—on form, children never really develop fluency of expression. They become too concerned with punctuation or spelling to get their ideas down. They worry about whether to use *lie* or *lay* and about being corrected if they pick the wrong one, and they therefore don't answer the question or tell the story that comes to mind. Too much pressure too soon to use adult forms interferes with language development.

Reduction of Stress

Little stress is placed on the young child learning language at home. Parents are confident that their children will learn to talk, and very few children fail to learn. This is not so with learning to read and write. Cramer points out that "the circumstances accompanying the teaching of reading and writing are often stressful and frequently produce anxiety in the learner. Stress interferes with learning and produces anxiety when it is excessive."[48] While most parents realize that children begin to talk at different ages and continue at different rates, they worry if their child doesn't make at least one year's progress during each school year. Some children may fail to learn to read and write because of the school situation. A bad start, too much stress, not being ready—all may build a barrier to learning both then and later. "Excessive competition, ability grouping, lack of patience, rigid grade levels, parental and teacher ignorance of developmental processes, and inappropriate instructional materials and techniques are among the major factors that lead to failure in reading and writing. Each of these factors is an environmental condition and, hence, can be changed by teachers, schools, and society."[49]

Emphasis on Interrelated Skills

Although, as we have discussed, adults adjust their language when speaking to very young children, in doing so they are not deciding which language skills are needed for speech and then presenting those skills as a sequence of activities. Oral language is acquired naturally, with the child figuring out how language works and then trying it out. Although writing and reading are not completely analogous to oral language, some aspects of learning to talk have parallels in reading and writing. Children need to be read to often and to see their ideas put into printed form as they observe. They need opportunities to look through books and other reading materials to see how important information can be put into print and read by others. A great deal of exposure to written language and encouragement to try it—without any insistence on adultlike form—help children enter the world of print. Writing and reading have parallel oral forms in speaking and listening. Just as listening and speaking interact with each other, so do writing and reading. There is every evidence that they should be taught at the same time to reinforce each other.

Individualization

While adults typically interact on a one-to-one basis with preschoolers, this is not possible in our public schools. At least it is not possible all the time for every student. It certainly is feasible for teachers in a public school setting to have some time each day to listen to a child read, to look at and respond to a story or painting, to listen to something a child has experienced, or to say something special to each child. For many children, five minutes of the teacher's full attention is worth an hour's attention to the group. Oral language typically gets an immediate response, while writing and reading receive a delayed response. A more immediate reaction to children's reading and writing may help them learn.

Summary

Language acquisition occurs as children interact with the people and things in their surroundings. Humans have the capacity for language and can organize information and incorporate new linguistic input. While the rate at which language is acquired varies, there is an amazing similarity in the order in which children acquire particular features of their language. They find patterns in the language to which they are exposed and follow these rules until they get correcting information from other speakers of the language. Their early sentences, therefore, include *hitted*, *reindeers*, and *sheeps*. Later, they learn the exceptions to the patterns and gradually come closer and closer to adult speech.

At first children use single words to express their ideas: "Doggie!" Then they begin to use two- and three-word sentences in telegraphic speech: "Dat doggie. Where doggie go?" Gradually their sentences become longer as they add the "ifs, ands, and buts," and they become adept at using more complex structures.

Learning English as a second language should involve the learner in actively trying to construct meaning while interacting with others who speak English. Meaning rather than correctness should be emphasized as in the acquisition of the first language. Children learning English as a second language should be encouraged to maintain their skills in their native language and culture.

Teachers can enhance children's language development by providing a rich language environment and opportunities to use language and get responses to what they say. Literature is a primary source of such language. Activities that give children a chance to use rich language as they discuss, dramatize, or retell stories and poems will aid them in incorporating new words and new structures into their own language system.

Questions for Discussion

1. What evidence suggests that children figure out their own rules for making language work and then try them out, gradually revising them according to others' responses and new information?
2. Discuss the role of adult correction in the language development of preschool children.
3. Discuss the assertion that bilingualism in the United States is "short-lived and transitional" until the person speaking a foreign language becomes fluent in English. Do Americans want a bilingual society?
4. How do the recommended programs for learning a second language relate to what is known about first language acquisition?
5. What is the role of literature in language development?

Notes

1. Frank Smith, *Understanding Reading—A Psycholinguistic Analysis of Reading and Learning to Read* (New York: Holt, Rinehart & Winston, 1971), 50.
2. E. H. Lenneberg, "A Biological Perspective of Language," in *Lan-*

guage, R. C. Oldfield and J. C. Marshall, eds. (Baltimore, MD: Penguin, 1968), 32–33.

3. David McNeill, *The Acquisition of Language* (New York: Harper & Row, 1970), 2–3.

4. D. McCarthy, "Language Development of the Preschool Child," in *Child Behavior and Development*, Roger C. Barker et al., eds. (New York: McGraw-Hill, 1943), 107–128. E. A.; and Davis, *The Development of Linguistic Skill in Twins, Singletons with Siblings, and Only Children from Age Five to Ten Years* (Minneapolis, MN: The University of Minnesota Press, 1937).

5. Courtney B. Cazden, *Child Language and Education* (New York: Holt, Rinehart & Winston, 1972), 121–125.

6. *Ibid.*, 123.

7. H. Ginsburg and S. Opper, *Piaget's Theory of Intellectual Development* (Englewood Cliffs, NJ: Prentice Hall, 1969), 17.

8. *Ibid.*, 18.

9. A. L. Baldwin, *Theories of Child Development* (New York: Wiley, 1967), 176.

10. Herbert H. Clark and Eve V. Clark, *Psychology and Language* (New York: Harcourt Brace Jovanovich, 1977), 320.

11. *Ibid.*, 327.

12. Dan I. Slobin and Charles A. Welsh, "Elicited Imitation as a Research Tool in Developmental Psycholinguistics," in *Studies of Child Language Development*, Charles A. Ferguson and Dan I. Slobin, eds. (New York: Holt, Rinehart & Winston, 1973), 485–497.

13. *Ibid.*, 490.

14. Susan M. Ervin, "Imitation and Structural Change in Children's Language," in *New Directions in the Study of Language*, E. H. Lenneberg, ed. (Cambridge, MA: MIT Press, 1964), 163–189.

15. Roger Brown and Ursula Bellugi, "Three Processes in the Child's Acquisition of Syntax," in *New Directions in the Study of Language*, E. H. Lenneberg, ed. (Cambridge, MA: MIT Press, 1964), 131–161.

16. Courtney B. Cazden, "Suggestions from Studies of Early Language Acquisition," *Childhood Education* 46 (December 1969): 129.

17. *Ibid.*, 128.

18. David McNeill, "Developmental Psycholinguistics," in *The Genesis of Language*, F. Smith and G. Miller, eds. (Cambridge, MA: MIT Press, 1966), 69.

19. Donald J. Foss and David T. Hakes, *Psycholinguistics* (Englewood Cliffs, NJ: Prentice Hall, 1978), 286.

20. Dan I. Slobin, "Cognitive Prerequisites for the Development of Grammar," in *Studies of Child Language Development*, Charles A. Ferguson and Dan I. Slobin, eds. (New York: Holt, 1973), 191–206.

21. E. H. Lenneberg, *Biological Functions of Language* (New York: Wiley, 1967).

22. Ursula Bellugi and Roger Brown, "The Acquisition of Language," in *Social Research in Child Development* XXIX, no. 1 (1964).

23. Paula Menyuk, "Syntactic Structures in the Language of Children," *Child Development* XXXIV (June 1963): 407–422.

24. Carol S. Chomsky, *The Acquisition of Syntax in Children from 5 to 10* (Cambridge, MA: MIT Press, 1969).

25. Eve V. Clark, "What's in a Word? On the Child's Acquisition of Semantics in His First Language," (unpublished paper) (August, 1971), 12. For further discussion of this theory, see H. H. Clark and E. V. Clark, "Semantic Distinctions and Memory for Complex Sentences," *Quarterly Journal of Experimental Psychology* 20 (1968): 129–138.

26. Lois Bloom, "Why Not Pivot Grammar?" in *Studies of Child Language Development,* Charles A. Ferguson and Dan I. Slobin, eds. (New York: Holt, Rinehart & Winston, 1973), 430–440.

27. Paula Menyuk, *The Acquisition and Development of Language* (Englewood Cliffs, NJ: Prentice Hall, 1971), 182.

28. Walter D. Loban, *The Language of Elementary School Children* (Champaign, IL: National Council of Teachers of English, 1963).

29. Kellog W. Hunt, "Syntactic Maturity in School Children and Adults," *Society for Research in Child Development Monograph* XXV, no. 1 (February 1970).

30. Insup Taylor, *Introduction to Psycholinguistics* (New York: Holt, Rinehart & Winston, 1976), 235.

31. Ursula Bellugi, "The Emergence of Inflections and Negations Systems in the Speech of Two Children," in *The Acquistion of Language,* D. McNeill, ed. (New York: Harper & Row, 1970), 83.

32. F. Grosjean, *Life with Two Languages: An Introduction to Bilingualism* (Cambridge MA: Harvard University Press, 1982), 44.

33. Richard Ruíz, "Bilingualism and Bilingual Education in the United States," in *International Handbook of Bilingualism and Bilingual Education,* Christina B. Paulston, ed. (New York: Greenwood Press, 1988), 539–560.

34. Grosjean, *Life with Two Languages,* 95. The following excerpts are from *Life with Two Languages* by F. Grosjean. Reprinted by permission of Harvard University Press.

35. *Ibid.,* 124.

36. *Ibid.,* 163.

37. D. Alexander and A. Nava, *The How, What, Where, When and Why of Bilingual Education* (San Francisco, CA: R & E Research Associated, 1977), 64.

38. L. W. Fillmore, *The Second Time Around: Cognitive and Social Strategies in Second Language Acquisition* (Ph.D. Dissertation, Stanford University, 1976).

39. F. Grosjean, *Life with Two Languages,* 114.

40. Peter A. de Villiers and J. G. de Villiers, *Early Language* (Cambridge MA: Harvard University Press, 1979), 125.

41. *Ibid.,* 50.

42. J. G. Sheehan, "Speech Therapy and Recovery from Stuttering," *The Voice* 15 (1965), 3–6.

43. J. Skofield, *All Wet! All Wet!,* D. Stanley, illustr. (New York: Harper & Row, 1984), 12. Excerpt from *All Wet! All Wet!* by James Skofield. Text copyright © 1984 by James Skofield. Reprinted by permission of Harper & Row, Publishers, Inc.

44. Bill Brittain, *Dr. Dredd's Wagon of Wonders.* A. Glass, illustr. (New York: Harper & Row, 1987), 12.

45. Arnold Adoff, *Eats* (New York: Lothrop, 1979), 39. From *Eats* by

Arnold Adoff. Copyright © 1979 by Arnold Adoff, reprinted by permission of Lothrop, Lee and Shepard Books, a division of William Morrow & Co., Inc.

46. Paul Fleischman, *I Am Phoenix: Poems for Two Voices,* K. Nutt, illustr. (New York: Harper & Row, 1985), 21–22. "The Common Egret" from *I Am Phoenix: Poems for Two Voices* by Paul Fleischman. Text copyright © 1985 by Paul Fleischman. Reprinted by permission of Harper & Row, Publishers, Inc.

47. Dorothy Cohen, "The Effect of Literature on Vocabulary and Reading," *Elementary English* XLV (February 1968): 207–217; Eugene M. Fodor, "The Effect of the Systematic Reading of Stories on the Language Development of Culturally Deprived Children," *Dissertation Abstracts* XXVII, no. 4 (October, 1966):952; and A. Bernice E. Cullinan, Angela Jaggar, and Dorothy Stickland, "Language Expansion for Black Children in the Primary Grades: A Research Report," *Young Children* 29 (January, 1974):98–112.

48. Ronald L. Cramer, *Children's Writing and Language Growth* (Columbus, OH: Merrill, 1978), 19.

49. *Ibid.,* 20.

Part II

Components of Language

Its Vocabulary, Structure, and Variations

Teachers need to be well informed about the aspects of language they will be teaching. Students need to enlarge their vocabulary, adding new words and new meanings to their repertoires. They need to become increasingly adept at using a variety of language structures, and they need to become familiar with the many kinds of variations that exist in the language.

Because we acquire language naturally, much of our information about language is implicit. We are not really aware of, nor can we explain all that we know about language and how we use it. This section helps teachers identify the major linguistic concepts and suggests practices that will help students become more expert at using language.

Chapter 5 is devoted to teaching vocabulary skills. Experiences and literature in the instructional program form the foundation for acquiring new words and additional word meanings. A variety of activities and games are suggested for giving students the requisite contact with new words or word meanings and the opportunities to use them in appropriate ways.

Chapter 6 presents knowledge about the structure of language—its grammar. Three grammars that may be found in school textbooks are described and discussed. Activities for students are suggested to help them become more flexible in using a variety of structures in their speech and writing. The appendix to this chapter presents traditional grammar for teachers or prospective teachers who may not have dealt with the topic for some time and have forgotten some of it.

Chapter 7 describes the different aspects of linguistic variation that exist in English. A section on the history of English describes historical variation. The chapter identifies the variety of functions that language can serve and its nonverbal aspects. It explores social variations of language in the discussion of the dialects of English. Features of Black English and Spanish-influenced English are included. A section on usage emphasizes learning the appropriate use of formal or correct English patterns. Variations in speaking or writing in response to a topic, audience, or mode are described in a section on registers of language.

Chapter 5
Extending Vocabulary

Extending Vocabulary

Aspects of Developing Vocabulary

Word Meaning

Factors in Ease of Learning

Levels of Word Knowledge

Special Children's Vocabulary

Vocabulary and Concept Development

Vocabulary and Reading

Vocabulary and Writing

Literature as a Source for Vocabulary

Methods of Teaching Vocabulary

Direct and Concrete Experiences

Direct Teaching of Root Words and Affixes

Word Derivations

Making Conscious Associations

Games and Practice Activities

Language uses words to communicate as art uses line and color or as dance uses movement and rhythm. The better a child's vocabulary is, the more effectively he or she can understand others and communicate ideas. Words also help us organize our ideas and experiences; they are a part of thinking.

> Words are the units of speech, of language. Words are experience-namers, and our stock of words influences our view, our perception and conception of the world. . . . Vocabularly development is a matter of seeing conceptual relationships, putting handles on objects and ideas so we can manipulate them effectively. Our ability to *name* things sharply influences the extent of our cognitive skills.[1]

When we tell others about an experience we've had, we need to choose the precise words that will convey that event as accurately as possible. Writing, too, is highly dependent on selecting the words that will communicate vision to others. When there is no voice and only the words are on the paper, those words must be just right or much meaning is lost.

Aspects of Developing Vocabulary

A number of aspects of vocabulary are involved in learning new words and new word meanings. Many English words have several different meanings to be learned. Some word choices are better in some situations than others because of their associations. Children need to become sensitive to these aspects of word choice.

Word Meaning

We must help children develop their word knowledge in two major ways: first, they need to learn many new words; second, they need to learn multiple meanings for the words they already know. In addition to learning the literal meaning of words, children need to develop some sensitivity to the associated or suggested meanings apart from the words' explicit meanings. If you are short, would you rather be called *little, petite,* or *squat?* Were your remarks *brief, curt,* or *succinct?* Which of these is the largest: *massive, huge, enormous, big,* or *mountainous?* Does *massive* suggest anything other than size? Heaviness, perhaps. While it is important to know synonyms, it is equally important to know the shades of meaning by which they differ from each other. These word connotations are a major aspect of vocabulary learning. A thesaurus might give the following synonyms for *hit: batter, touch, smite, strike, knock,* and *smash.* There's a lot of difference between *smashing* people and *touching* them, and *smite* is biblical. We teach children in the primary grades the names of the basic colors such as *green.* When do they learn *emerald, jade, chartreuse, olive, mint, celery,* or *avocado?*

Factors in Ease of Learning

Some words are easier to learn than others; *eat* is easier to learn than *true,* and *circle* is easier to learn than *justice.*

At least five factors play a part in the difficulty or ease of learning a particular word. (1) The degree of abstraction involved is one of these factors. The more abstract words or concepts such as *truth* or *justice* are more difficult than *circle* or *eat.* (2) The complexity of the concept adds increasing difficulty, and so *democracy* or *truth* may be more difficult than *friend.* (3) The frequency with which a word is used is the third factor, and words that are used more frequently are somewhat easier to learn. (4) The amount of context surrounding the word also makes a difference in how easy or difficult a word is to learn. Do you know the word *elute?* No? Now consider it in a high-context sentence: *To elute that stain, use carbon tetrachloride.* The amount of context is not just the number of words; the higher the context, the fewer possible alternative responses exist. Here are three sentences with the same word missing. Notice how the possible responses narrow with increasing amounts of context.

Low context: I need to go to the store to buy a new _____.

Medium context: Perhaps someone will give you a _____ for your birthday.

High context: I keep my money, pictures, and credit cards in my _____.

(5) The fifth factor that affects ease of learning is a person's interest in learning a word. Boys and girls who are fascinated with flight will learn *drag* and *thrust;* they will talk about the *camber* of the wing, the *fuselage,* the *rudder,* and the *ailerons.* These will seem easy to learn, while the concepts of *opposite* and *alternate* may be difficult. Interest as well as experience plays an important role in learning word meanings.

Levels of Word Knowledge

To further complicate the situation, there are different levels of knowing a word. Dale, O'Rourke, and Bamman suggest four categories to describe them:[2]

1. *I never saw it before.*
2. *I've heard of it, but I don't know what it means.*
3. *I recognize it in context—it has something to do with. . . .*
4. *I know it.*

Try classifying the following words into these four categories for yourself: *auger, flounce, gambrel, lyre, bizarre, heinous, dinghy.* The words that you do know will depend on your experiences. If you live near the water, you probably will know that a *dinghy* is a small boat, but you may not know that an *auger* is a tool for boring holes in wood. If you are musical, you may know that a *lyre* is a stringed instrument; those interested in architecture will know that *gambrel* is a style of roof. A *flounce* is a ruffle as well as a way of moving; *bizarre* is odd or eccentric, and *heinous* is hatefully or shockingly evil.

Some of the words that we recognize when we read them might not be understood if we heard them. And even some of those we know when we read or hear them, we never use ourselves in speaking or writing. We may not even know how to say them. Do you know how to say *heinous?* (The first syllable rhymes with *weigh*). Each of us has a speaking, writing, listening, and reading vocabulary. When children enter school, their speaking vocabulary is much larger than their writing vocabulary or their reading vocabulary. By the time they leave school, their reading vocabulary will far surpass the others. How well we know a word, then, depends on both the level of our knowledge and the mode in which the word is being used.

Special Children's Vocabulary

Because vocabulary depends so much on experience, children who have significantly different backgrounds will know very different words. Some of the words they know will not be useful at school; many beginners know *barbecue* and popular brand names of beer, but not *bunny* and *carrot.* Unfortunately for them, typical beginning school materials are full of bunnies eating carrots, but have no barbecues with beer.

Less able children may need more contact with a new word to make it a permanent part of their vocabulary. They will need opportunities to use new words in meaningful ways. The more concrete you can make the meaning, the more easily it will be learned. Also, many children know things they can talk about when they can't write them. Some of your less able readers may be the best storytellers.

Children who come from different language backgrounds have special needs for vocabulary development. Generally speaking, translation from one language to the other is not desirable. Bilingual children need to develop separate language systems; and while occasional translations to make meaning clear are certainly appropriate, translation as a standard practice is not. The bilingual child adds words to his or her vocabulary through lots of talk in the target language about an object, real experiences, role playing, discussion of uses and shades of meaning, and through wide reading in books in the target language. In some ways, speaking another language may be an advantage since English has many borrowed words. Children who speak Spanish, Portuguese, French, or Italian may have the special advantage of being able to relate English words derived from Latin, French, and other languages to parallel ones in their native language. Pointing out these instances will help them think and use what they already know.

As children whose native language is not English begin to write, there are several things that seem to help them become more successful. Ammon suggests that students' motivation to learn is enhanced when the teacher has the attitude that writing is something to take pleasure in but is also something you work at to enhance both the reader's and the writer's appreciation of the product. The more successful bilingual teachers had a good deal of second language input in the form of teacher talk, student talk, and reading. Specifically, they employed metalinguistic activities in which students talked about language itself. The teachers would comment on a particular word or way of saying something or would discuss why sentences were incomplete and how to complete them. These teachers gave their students many opportunities for extended talk in English, and this served as a basis for their writing in the new language.[3]

Clearly, developing a sizable English vocabulary to use in talking and writing, as well as in listening and reading, is an important part of communicating in a second language. The more precise and meaningful words are, the more useful they are to the children. Experiences rich with talk, opportunities to talk about books or dramatize stories, and discussions about words and ways to express ideas help children learning English as a second language to develop their vocabulary in English and become more proficient with the new language.

Vocabulary and Concept Development

We cannot divorce vocabulary development from conceptual development. Words represent the meanings in our language—our concepts. The semantic aspect of language is critical to understanding others and to expressing our ideas. Language reflects our view of reality through word relationships and in the conceptual categories we use.

Each culture simply groups diverse objects, experiences, and events so that its members, in a sense, agree to regard some sets of unidentical things which share certain features, as "the same" or equivalent, and to regard other events, experiences, and objects not possessing certain crucial features, as "different," as belonging to different classes or categories. The words of our language convey our categories.[4]

By understanding the concept associated with a word, we understand the meaning of the word. However, teachers must recognize that saying a word does not guarantee full knowledge of the concept. Children can talk about winter and riding in a "one-horse open sleigh" without ever having seen snow or ridden in a sleigh (and perhaps not even being able to identify one in a picture). Words and concepts become meaningful only with experience; we come to know "ocean" as we run along the shore, wade out to swim, taste the saltiness, and bob up and down with the waves on a summer afternoon. But our concept is incomplete unless we also know it on a windy fall day when the sand whips across our face and the waves are rough and cold. The more experiences we have in an ocean and with different oceans, the more precise and rich our concept of ocean becomes.

Certain concepts are more concrete than others, and the words associated with them are easier to learn. For instance, if you want children to understand the concept of squareness and the word associated with it (*square*), you show them pictures of squares, have them cut out squares, and perhaps even draw squares. The concept is very teachable because it can be demonstrated in very concrete and tangible ways. But how do you teach children the concept of honesty? How do they learn the meaning of the word *honest*? Intangible and emotive concepts such as this are learned through experience—either direct experience, vicarious experience, or a combination of both. When children have had plenty of experiences related to the concept of honesty, they will understand the concept and the word *honest*.

Vocabulary develops through experiences and the association of these experiences with words. Intelligence and environmental factors cannot be overlooked in assessing the depth and breadth of children's vocabularies, but a learning environment that offers a wide variety of experiences can only promote and extend children's vocabulary development.

Vocabulary and Reading

Vocabulary development is a crucial aspect of learning to read. The number of different words a child knows and the number of different meanings for these words both affect reading ability. The more words children know, the more easily they can recognize a word in print.

Knowing just one meaning of a word will help them use word analysis to decode it. If they know *bank* as the place where their parents go to cash a check or the small piggy they put pennies in, then when they see *b—a—n—k* they can sound it out and immediately say *bank*.

But reading comprehension is somewhat different. To comprehend well, children must know the precise meaning of a word as it is being used. If they know *bank* only as a place for money, what meaning can they get from "The boys sat on the bank and dangled their feet in the water." or from "The plane went through the cloud bank at 3,500 feet." How could boys sit on the First National and put their feet in water? Why do clouds have banks? Who would put money in a cloud? For comprehension, children must know *bank* as "the rising ground bordering a lake, river, or sea" and as "a piled up mass of cloud or fog" as well as "a place of business of a money changer."[5] Children who only know *game* as something they play, like tag or monopoly, would have trouble understanding "She soaked the game in vinegar and water before cooking it." Those who know *duck* as the bird that goes quack-quack would surely have trouble with "She bought three yards of white duck." Many children who have well-developed skills in word analysis still have difficulty getting meaning from what they read because they have a limited knowledge of words and their meanings.

The most powerful predictor of excellence in reading comprehension is vocabulary. In factor analyses of reading comprehension, word knowledge explains the variability in comprehension scores better than any other single measure. In fact, the relationship is so strong that Chomsky has said that reading might very well be taught by enriching children's vocabularies so that they can construct for themselves the deeper representation of sounds that correspond so closely to the orthographic forms.[6]

In the relationships between the teaching of vocabulary and improvement in reading, several aspects of vocabulary instruction seem most effective:

- Rich verbal environments that actively involve students in constructing meanings are more successful.
- Long-term programs of vocabulary instruction are more effective, because repeated encounters with words in many different contexts aids learning.
- Motivation to learn words is important in developing a good vocabulary.

These characteristics fit with the view Blackowicz described as the "knowledge position," which holds that conceptual knowledge is the link to reading comprehension because students can use their knowledge to construct meaning from the printed page. In contrast to the "instrumentalist position," which stresses associational links, the knowledge position calls for presenting words and concepts in relational categories that reflect the building of semantic categories.[7]

An important aspect of reading is the development of meaningful context for reading a selection. Context aids readers in two ways: it serves as a check on other decoding cues to determine if a word makes sense, and it serves as a source of information to decode unknown words. Children need to ask themselves, "Does that word make sense here? What word would make sense that starts with those letters?" In combination with knowledge of letter-sound relationships, context is crucial to reading. Context comprehension relies heavily on one's store of words, word meanings, and the relationships among words. This is why the classic prereading activity involves developing the new vocabulary that will be presented in the story.

Newer prereading activities expand this kind of preparation. Strategies such as key-concept mapping help students focus on their knowledge of the concepts involved in the reading selection. After reading, students confirm the accuracy of their initial knowledge and add new information. This focus on words and concepts and their relationships sets the context for reading and helps students with important ideas. In reading, students interact with the text to construct their meaning from it.

Terry and Prater's five steps in key-concept mapping are as follows:[8]

1. *Select the story.* Although key-concept mapping works with many different kinds of reading selections, it is especially useful with those that are more factual.

2. *Select the key concepts.* There are usually two or three essential concepts upon which the story is based.

3. *Map prior knowledge of key concepts.* With a reading group, let the children tell what they know about each key concept and record on chart paper or the board what they say. You should feel free to guide and direct their discussion.

4. *After silent reading, confirm the accuracy of their prior knowledge.* Use the chart made before reading and identify which ideas were confirmed in what they read. If some ideas mapped before reading were not dealt with, leave them alone. Clarify any that were incorrect.

5. *Postmap the key concepts.* Add new knowledge from the reading to the map in a different color or print style. Discuss the entire map integrating both old and new ideas related to key concepts.

By orienting the children to the key ideas and associated vocabulary of the story before they read independently, we provide context for understanding the words and the ideas involved. Postmapping revises that information to leave accurate information. The mapping reflects the relationships among ideas.

The California *Language Arts Framework* section on Learning to Read by Reading states, "Though some students may need more help than others in using contextual or textual clues in reading, all students need background information, vocabulary work, and help in working through a text as they move from words to meaning and from understanding a text to discovery and learning its implications for their lives."[9]

Vocabulary and Writing

Having a rich vocabulary with a real sense of word connotations is an important prerequisite for effective writing. Although sentence structure and rhetorical devices are used to make writing interesting and clear, perhaps the most important device for clarity is word choice. The particular words we select with their connotations and nuances have a great impact on our writing. Others who read what we have written need to make the same connections that we have with the world. The more effective we are in choosing words that convery our thoughts to the reader the better we communicate.

There are certain conventions in written language that make it different from oral language. Students need to develop their sense of which language conventions are appropriate for writing. The changes from oral to written language are often subtle, but with enough exposure to written language, children should recognize when it "sounds right." For example, consider, "I shall be unable to attend." or "I have a previous commitment." Both are appropriate written excuses, but in person we would probably say, "I won't be able to attend. I have already made other plans." It is not a matter of expressing a different idea; it is using appropriate wording for the situation and mode of expression. We do not learn such things in textbooks, but rather through exposure to good writing and the motivation to find out how we can best express ideas. Getting response from others, especially from more experienced readers and writers, is helpful in making the best choices in written language.

The close connection between vocabulary and writing is revealed in the various scales suggested for evaluating writing and in the lists of questions given as examples of what you might ask in conferencing. Nearly all of the evaluation scales have a section on word choice: appropriate and interesting word choice, using strong verbs, using adjectives that describe rather than label, unusual words and expressions, and so forth. The frequency of vocabulary choice as a part of evaluation schemes suggests its importance in writing.

Most of the prewriting or idea generating activities suggested for developing composition skills involve manipulating words in some way. Common idea generators include brainstorming words, "word shaking" (listing words in various categories), mapping ideas in clusters, and outlining. Each activity requires the writer to consider vocabulary—word choice—as an important aspect of writing. The words convey the concepts, which are the backbone of the piece.

Editing, or conferencing between drafts, is another opportunity to examine the words chosen. It isn't that we tell youngsters to pay attention to the words that the writer is using. It is because the words are so important in carrying meaning and because we concentrate so on finding meaning in others' ideas that words are often the focus of students' conference comments. Gere and Stevens contrast teacher conferences with peer conferences and point out that "Students in writing groups tell authors what they think language says, they ask questions about the places which confuse them, and they suggest ways for the writing to do its job better."[10] These authors give some examples of the power of writing group responses by students who were instructed to make only positive comments:

> "Well, I like the way you used the German word, um *Blitzkrieg*."
> " I think the word *sludge* was kind of weird cuz I don't really know what you're talking about."
> "It sounds like you know what you're talking about. But some of the words you used, I didn't really understand."
> "I think your words were kind of strong and might have got just a little bit carried away."
> "I really thought the word *brutally* stood out."

Nearly all of the students' comments dealt specifically with the words the authors had used in their writing. Other comments focused on meaning, such as "Ah, that 'Green Peace'—I didn't really understand what that was." The criticism in these comments, as Gere and Stevens point out, is specifically directed at helping authors convey their meanings more clearly.[11] Making meaning clear is the real purpose of the reader or the responder to writing.

Although there is little direct research on vocabulary and writing, it is clear that a wide word-meaning vocabulary and a sensitivity to connotation and appropriateness in particular contexts enables the writer to make meanings clearer to the reader. Much of the power and impact of writing is due to the words chosen by the writer.

Literature as a Source for Vocabulary

According to research, it is possible to develop and increase a child's vocabulary by reading books aloud frequently.[12] The following story was retold and tape-recorded by a student after a well-known Aesop's fable had been read aloud and discussed. Notice the words and phrases in the child's retelling that have been taken from the original fable—*King of the forest, roars, nibble, paw, trap,* and others.

> *Once there was a mouse. He forgot where he was going and he ran over a poor lion and the lion said, "What do you mean by this?" And he put his paw over the mouse. He was fixing to eat the mouse. And the mouse said, "Oh, King of the forest, please do not do this to me, for one day I may be able to help you." And then he set the mouse free. And a short while later the lion got caught in a trap and he roars and all the animals heard him. And then, the mouse heard him. And the mouse said, "That was the lion that set me free." And then the mouse woke up and came running and never stopped till he came to the lion and the trap was made of rope and the mouse began to nibble the rope. He made a big hole so the lion could get out. And then the lion said, "I'll always remember this: Little friends can be great friends."*

Vocabulary is also increased the more a child reads independently. Therefore, more should be done in a classroom than simply providing a few books for children to read. Make a concerted effort to select a wide variety of books rich in vocabulary that will stretch and extend students' language. Provide time each day to read a book aloud and then place it in the classroom library area. Encourage students to reread it if they are interested, and call attention to other books in the area they may wish to explore and read. Your enthusiasm for and about particular books can have considerable influence on children's reading.

Discussion of particular words after reading a story or poem aloud can extend children's knowledge of words. This poem presents *dozing, sodden, creeping,* and *stillness.*

Wake Up

Dozing in the summer sun,
eyes almost closing,
a bullfrog on a sodden log
appears to be sleeping
. . . a waterbug comes creeping
suddenly frog's leaping
with a jump, clump, thump
to shake the stillness of the lake
urp   blurp   kerchurp![13]
     —Eve Merriam

Because the new words are presented in a meaningful context, children have little difficulty understanding their meaning if they are unfamiliar. Calling attention to certain words and briefly discussing them can ensure that they are noticed. After reading the story or poem, talking about the words or dramatizing them and using them in other contexts help children incorporate them into their own vocabularies. "Show me how the frog looked when he was dozing. What words in the first stanza tell you about how he looked?" ("Eyes almost closing," "appears to be sleeping.") "What do you think *sodden* might mean? Do you know *soggy*? Show me how the water bug moved."

Another poem by this author speaks in a powerful way to the problems of older children:

Conversation with Myself

This face in the mirror
stares at me
demanding, "Who are you? What will you become?"
and taunting, "You don't even know."
Chastened, I cringe and agree
and then
because I'm still young
I stick out my tongue.[14]
   —Eve Merriam

The context of the poem and the situation it describes helps to define *tauntingly, cringe,* and *chastened.* Some further discussion about these words and when they are used, times when a person would feel like cringing or feel chastened, what taunts are and how they make one feel will help to set the words and their meanings for students.

It is just as important to read books and poems aloud to older children as it is to younger ones. After reading aloud a chapter of an intermediate book, spend some time talking about a few of the special words in the story and how the author used them. What are some synonyms, and how do those synonyms differ in the shade of meaning conveyed? Look at the following passage from Babbitt's *The Eyes of the Amaryllis,* a book with many interesting possibilities because of its rich language.

Jenny stood hypnotized at the window, watching as the wall of black came onward. Gradually, the room grew dimmer, the dazzling patch of sky was curtained out. And then the clouds engulfed them. Instantly, the wind began again, shrieking louder than ever, and the world outside was lost in new sheets of rain that swept in the opposite direction now, northward toward the town at the other end of the bay.

Children's vocabularies increase the
more they read independently.

> *This shift seemed to catch the house off-guard. There was a*
> *crash high over their heads, and a sluice of water spread into the*
> *parlor from the fireplace, like blood streaming from a wound.*
> *"Why, the chimney's gone!" Gran exclaimed. She sounded*
> *shocked, surprised. The sudden breaching of her fortress seemed*
> *to jar her own determination; she bent a little in her chair, grip-*
> *ping the wooden head, and her voice had lost a fraction of its*
> *metal.*[15]

For most middle school or junior high school students, some of the words in the description of the hurricane will be new, perhaps *sluice, engulfed,* and *breaching.* Some might be new meanings for familiar words, like *jar* and *metal.* Here context will be a great help in deciding the meaning of the words.

Books for younger children also are rich sources of new words and new word meanings. Wood's *The Napping House* is a cumulative tale about a cozy bed with a snoring granny, a dreaming child, a dozing dog, a snoozing cat, a slumbering mouse, and a wakeful flea who bites the mouse and causes havoc.[16] What wonderful words for *sleeping* the book presents!

In addition to books of fiction, there are many kinds of informational books, alphabet books (for older students as well as for the very young ones), folktales, and concept books that present and explore an idea. Well-written books of any kind for children of any age will present new words and new word meanings in context. Children who have developed an interest in words with teachers who encourage them to pursue this interest will quickly develop their vocabulary and their pleasure in reading. The books listed below are only a sampling of the many fine nonfiction books for students at different ages.

Books Presenting Ideas and Concepts

Anno's Medieval World by Mitsumasa Anno. New York: Philomel Books, 1979. This book with its intricate illustrations describes life in the Middle Ages in a way that appeals to children who still love picture books but are ready for some real content in their reading. "They knew the story about a long-ago king who had asked for the gods to let everything he touched be turned to gold. . . . That was only a fable, but many people still craved gold. Some, who were called alchemists, tried to make it for themselves."

Your Own Best Secret Place by Byrd Baylor, illust. Peter Parnall. New York: Scribner's, 1979. This books tells about a secret place in the desert, and, like Byrd Baylor's other books, lyrically describes in free verse what she found.

Ed Emberley's ABC by Ed Emberly. Boston: Little, Brown, 1978. Students are required to look for animals and objects in the pictures that represent the letters of the alphabet. On the *J* page, we find a jaguar, a jug, a juggler, a jewel, and a jacknife.

Lights! Camera! Action! How a Movie is Made by Gail Gibbons. New York: Crowell, 1985. An on-the-spot look at the making of a movie for younger children who will enjoy its bright colors and learn much from the text. "At the end of the day, all the takes are rushed to the film processing lab to be printed. Each day's film is called a daily. Every morning the producers and director view the dailies from the day before."

Sugaring Time by Kathryn Lasky, photo. Christopher G. Knight. New York: Macmillan, 1983. While presenting accurate information about making maple sugar, this book uses imagery to create a sense of the scene. "Fog swirls through the valley and up into the meadow, covering the hills and mountain tops beyond. Everything is milky white. Snow-covered earth and sky melt together. Pines appear rootless, like ghost trees, their pointy tops wrapped in mist."

Mill by David Macaulay. Boston: Houghton Mifflin, 1983. Like Macaulay's other books, such as *Cathedral: The Story of its Construction* (1973), *Mill* shows architectural details and engineering principles through intricate pen-and-ink drawings. It is clear and complete, a wonderful book for older students who are interested in such factual things. "A strip of wood called a spline fitted tightly into the grooves between every pair of planks. This not only eliminated any air movement between the floorboards that might fan a fire, it also prevented oil dripping from one floor to another and made the floor that much stronger."

They Dance in the Sky: Native American Star Myths by Jean Monroe and Ray A. Williamson, illust. Edgar Stewart. Boston: Houghton Mifflin, 1987. This is a collection of myths about the stars for older students. Along with each is an explanation of what the tale reveals about the culture of the peoples who told it. "The Cherokee believed that the solid sky swung up and down continually. When the sky went up, there was an open place between it and the ground that acted as a door. This belief is illustrated by a story the Cherokee told about a visit to the sun, whom they thought of as a woman."

Town and Country by Alice and Martin Provensen. New York: Crown, 1984. The text of this book, as well as the illustrations, describe what it is like to live in a town and also in the country. The vocabulary is rich and vivid, and younger children will enjoy and learn much from the text and pictures. "But most people who live in the Western world live in a town or in a house in the country. They might live in a hamlet, which is smaller than a village, or a village which is smaller than a town, or a town which is smaller than a city, or a city, which is BIG."

Applebet: An ABC by Clyde Watson, illust. Wendy Watson. New York: Farrar, Straus & Giroux, 1982. This alphabet book is for younger children, but it has complex words in its rhymes so it should appeal to first and second graders as well.

Between Cattails by Terry Tempest Williams, illust. Peter Parnall. New York: Scribner, 1985. This wonderfully descriptive book about nature shows what it is like to enter a marsh through the tall cattails. The language is matched by Parnall's fluid style in the illustrations.

Methods of Teaching Vocabulary

Dale, O'Rourke, and Bamman state that "Vocabulary development in school must be a planned program. . . . Incidental teaching alone, tends to become accidental teaching."[17] There is no doubt that a teacher needs to provide learning experiences that will incorporate the development and expansion of children's vocabularies. Opportune moments for developing concepts and associated vocabulary are often overlooked in the classroom. As an example, a small group of children came to the word *jostled* in their reading. None of the children knew the meaning of the word, but one child attempted to give a definition using the context of the story. The teacher interrupted the child, gave the definition of the word *jostled*, and then announced it was time for the next reading group. What might this teacher have done instead? The students could have been encouraged to predict the meaning of the word by using contextual clues. They might have demonstrated the meaning of the word by participating in a role playing situation, such as being jostled on a crowded bus. Other situations in which one might be jostled could have been discussed, and the word itself could have been found in the dictionary to determine if there were other meanings.

All types of learning and communication experiences offer opportunities to develop a child's vocabulary. "All education is vocabulary development, hence conceptual development; we are studying words and symbols all the time."[18] We do know that planned experiences can be used effectively to extend and broaden children's vocabularies, and they can be incorporated easily into the ongoing learning environment.

Direct and Concrete Experiences

Involvement in direct and concrete experiences helps to develop all types of vocabularies. Children need a variety of sensory experiences—touching, listening, tasting, and smelling. Along with direct experiences are conversations and discussions. By talking with children, a teacher can help them understand concepts and word meanings. For example, a child walked into class one morning carrying a lizard. Instead of placing the lizard aside in a nearby box, the teacher gathered the children around to look and talk about the lizard. They discussed the shape and size of the lizard, its color, and the texture of its skin. One of the children went to the library to get a book about lizards because they wanted more information. They composed stories about the lizard either individually or in a small group with their teacher. That afternoon they built a vivarium for the lizard on the basis of information they had gathered from their reading. Several children pursued their interest in lizards further and recorded new words on a special chart hung above the vivarium. The words on the chart were *habitat, tropical, aquatic* and *terrestrial, camouflage, nocturnal,* and *diurnal,* and the names of the three kinds of lizards—*gecko, iguana,* and *chameleon.* Several days later when the group had finished their extra research, they shared information with the whole class. During the discussion their teacher helped them relate the new words to other words they knew. They talked about *aquariums* and *terrariums* and brainstormed words related to terrariums, such as *terrace, terrain,* and *territory.* One child suggested *terrible;* but when they looked it up, they found it came from *terrēre* (to frighten) instead of from *terra* (earth).

In another class, Ms. Maroni's sixth-graders learned many new words as they worked with a new illustrative medium, *collage*. Working with the art teacher, Mr. Traylor, the class recorded any new words they encountered while experimenting with different types of collage. Their word list included *pattern, texture, dimensional, medium, embossed, contrast, relief, coil, proportion, perspective, unity, vibrant, fabric, material, textile*. Some were completely new words; others, like *medium*, were new meanings for familiar words. Both Ms. Maroni and Mr. Traylor made a conscious effort to use the new words appropriately as they discussed the students' projects. As the words were used by teachers and students, they became a part of the sixth-graders stock of words.

These two examples suggest the potential for learning words during the course of regular classroom events. Almost every activity has such potential, but as a teacher you must recognize it, use the appropriate words and encourage your children to use them too. If you talk about the lizard as a *land animal* instead of *terrestrial* and build a *place* for it instead of a *vivarium*, your students will not learn those new words.

Vocabulary learning can also be structured as a part of other content or study areas. Fourth- or fifth-graders publishing their own newspaper might learn new words such as *cropped, features, graphic, deadline, columnist, editor* or *wire service*. They might add new meanings for *beat* (subject area), a *take* (page), and *copy* (stories). A seventh-grade social studies class studying Greece might learn *rhetoric, pagan*, and *prophecies*. In making a replica of an ancient Greek city they might encounter architectural terms, such as *colonnades, column, cornice, capital* (of a column), *acanthus, Doric, Ionic*, and *Corinthian*. A science class studying oceanography might need to learn *trough, crest, tsunami, impede*, or *salinity*, while younger children studying oceans and currents might learn *tropical, tidal, swells, ripples*, and *current*. Primary-grade children studying symbols might learn *signal, emblem, universal, pictograph*, and *diagram*. Older students studying the same topic would find *amber, semiotic, arbitrary, logo, cuneiform*, and *semaphore* as new words used in learning about symbols.

At least three important ingredients of learning should be present: the students are interested in the activity and are involved in it, the words are encountered in a meaningful context, and there is ample opportunity and need to use the new vocabulary. Teachers can make a special effort to highlight new words and to find out information about the topic and about the words themselves. Teachers can then help the students to relate the new words to each other and to other known words.

Direct Teaching of Root Words and Affixes

Learning various affixes—that is, prefixes and suffixes—and the meanings of common roots has been a traditional way to study vocabulary. Some problems are inherent in such a method, but also some real potential exists. One of the difficulties is that many prefixes do not have a single meaning. For example, the prefix *de-* may mean *from*, or it may mean *down*, or it may indicate *reversal* or *undoing*. Sometimes the prefix no longer has any force or meaning, as in *desolate* or *dedicate*. Then, too, many English words begin with the letters *de* when they do not form a prefix, as in *decorate* and *decoy*. The same problems exist with root words and suffixes.[19]

There are some useful combining forms that have clear, invariant meanings. (Combining forms differ technically from affixes; a combining form plus an affix may form a word, but two affixes cannot.) In this category Deighton lists 26 that appear in some 200 current English words and are often employed in newly developed scientific words:[20]

Useful Combining Forms

anthropo- (human being)
auto- (self, same one)
biblio- (book)
bio- (life)
centro- (center) [*centri-*]
cosmo- (world, universe)
heter- (other, different) [*hetero-*]
homo- (same, similar)
hydro- (water, liquid)
iso- (equal, uniform)
lith- (of stone)
micro- (small, short)
mono- (one, single, alone)

neuro- (nerve, sinew)
omni- (all)
pan- (all, completely)
penta- (five)
phil- (loving) [*philo-*]
phone- (sound, voice, speech)
photo- (light, photograph)
pneumo- (air, lung, respiration)
poly- (many, much)
proto- (first)
psuedo- (false, spurious)
tele- (distant)
uni- (one, single)

He suggests that there are also ten prefixes that have regular, invariant meanings and few words beginning with the same letters where they are not a prefix. These should prove helpful and worth learning. Two others (marked with *) are added to the list although they have more than one meaning because they are so frequently used.[21]

Useful Prefixes

apo- (away from)
circum- (around)
equi- (equal)

mal- (bad, abnormal, inadequate)
mis- (bad or wrong)
non- (not, reverse of)

extra- (outside, beyond)   syn- (with, along with)
intra- (within, during)   *in- (not or into, or to intensify a
                     word) [ir-, il-, im-, en-]
intro- (into, inward)   *un- (not, reverse, remove, completely)

Deighton also recommends two sets of suffixes and combining forms that are worth classroom time. One group is for noun endings,[22] and the other is adjective endings;[23] both lists have invariant meanings.

Noun Endings

-ana (collected items)
-archy (rule, government)
-art (characterized by)
-aster (inferior, worthless)
-bility (capacity)
-chrome (colored)
-cide (killer, killing)
-ee (associated with, small kind of)
-fer (one that bears)
-fication (making)
-gram (drawing, writing, record)
-graph (written or for recording)
-graphy (writing)

-ics (study, characteristic quality)
-itis (disease, inflammation of)
-latry (worship)
-meter (instrument for measuring)
-metry (measuring)
-ology (expression or theory of)
-phore (carrier)
-phobia (fear of)
-ric (having character or nature of)
-scope (means for viewing)
-scopy (viewing, observing)

Adjective Endings

-est (form the superlative of)
-ferous (bearing, producing)
-fic (making, causing)
-fold (multiplied by)
-form (in the shape of)
-genous (producing, yielding)
-scopic (resembling)
-wards (moves or is directed toward)
-wise (in manner of)

-less (without power, unable to)
-able (capable of, liable to) [-ible, -ble]
-most (most)
-like (the same as, resembling)
-ous
-ose
-acious   } full of
-ful

These prefixes, suffixes, and combining forms will give students considerable help in dealing with unfamiliar words. Most of them are probably appropriate for study in the upper elementary, middle school, or junior high school years. A few might be discussed with younger children in an appropriate context.

The most effective way to teach such material is through an inductive approach. You might ask your students to tell you all the words they know that begin with *un-* and write them on chart paper or on the board. Suppose they suggest *unlucky, unable, undone, unhappy, uncovered, unknown, unpaid, unpopular, unwrap, unloved,* and *unpack.* Discuss the collection of words, what each means, or pantomime the actions they represent. Then discuss what the *un-* at the beginning of each means and how it alters the meaning of the base word. Another way to accomplish this inductive kind of approach is for you to present a series of words with the same combining form or affix: *automatic, autograph, autobiography, autocratic, automobile, autonomy, autohypnosis, automat,* and *automation.* Let the students tell you the meanings of as many as they can. Someone can volunteer to look the others up as you discuss them. What then does *auto-* mean?

Once word parts are introduced in such a way, you can provide additional reinforcement and practice through various games. These will be discussed later in the chapter and can provide a good review. Presenting affixes or combining forms in a list on Monday to be looked up, learned, and tested on Friday is ineffective. Children need to be able to interrelate words and have opportunities to use them for real learning to take place. We all need multiple contacts with new words to make them our own.

Word Derivations

Many children can have an enjoyable and profitable time studying the history of words. The study of word origins is intriguing and can entice some students into a lifetime fascination with words. If this study is to be successful, two key points identified by Dale, O'Rourke, and Bamman, are necessary.

> (1) The children must be personally involved, suggesting, contributing, experimenting in terms of history of etymology (at their level), and thereby seeing the relationship of word history to their everyday lives. This goal can be reached by encouraging the children to use key words studied in discussion and conversation (for example, making adjectives such as *jovial* from *Jove, solar* from *Sol, lunar* from *Luna,* etc.). (2) The teacher must become as expert as he can in words and word origins as they relate to general language development. He must, in effect, become "word-conscious," bringing to the classroom a knowledge of the "new" words to be discussed.[24]

Young children might be interested in such word study through tidbits of information you can include in various activities you do. Making pretzels would involve a whole variety of skills such as following directions, recalling sequence, developing new words (*dissolve, knead, sprinkle, coarse*), reading for a purpose, developing fine-muscle dexterity, classifying, and describing. While you are making the pretzels or waiting for them to bake, you might want to tell the class about the origin of the pretzel:

> *A food that got its name from Germany is the PRETZEL. The German word* Prezel *or* Brezel *came from the Latin* brachium *meaning arm. (A* braccialetto, *in Italian, is a bracelet.) Also,* pretium *is Latin for "reward," and in the sixteenth century, monks used to give glazed cakes to children when they learned their prayers. It may be that the twisted shape of the PRETZEL represented the folded arms of the monks. Since these cakes were a reward, they were given the name* pretiola, *or "little rewards." The shape of the PRETZEL stayed the same, but the name changed from* pretiola *to PRETZEL.*[25]

Besides pretzels, Steckler's book tells about other food words, such as *potato, cantaloupe, tangerine, hamburger, ketchup, spaghetti, cereal, waffle, coleslaw, delicatessen, coffee, vinegar, lollipop, chocolate, sandwich,* and *deserts.* Other sections deal with words about people, the animal world, things that grow, things we wear, things we enjoy, and so on. If you don't have access to equipment for baking, why not make some coleslaw?

There are many ways to interest older students in word study. Middle graders should enjoy figuring out how things got their names. They could map words like *hamburgers, wieners, gouda cheese, champagne, frankfurters, Persian cats, Great Danes, Dalmatian dogs,* and *Siamese cats,* or they could compare a map of their region of the country with Europe, looking for similar names. Are some names descriptive of geographical features (*Clearwater, Boulder*)? Are some places named after famous people (*Lincoln, Houston, Columbus*)? Are there Indian names (*Sioux City, Tallahassee*)? Where do their own names come from? There are many books intended for choosing a name for a new baby that tell the meaning of names. Another good reference is *The Tree of Language* by Helene and Charlton Laird (World Publishing, 1975). Hennings suggests many activities to interest older students in word study in *Words, Sounds, and Thoughts* (Scholastic, 1977).

Making Conscious Associations

Since we store information by organizing it in some way, helping children make different kinds of associations may help them store and retrieve information more easily. Some of the associations between words that may be helpful in learning words are described below.

Similarity
Relating new words to known ones because of their similarity of meaning is productive and may lead to discussions of their connotations. There are simple synonyms: *wet/damp, prodigious/enormous.*

Contrast
Apparently one of the ways we commonly store information is through contrasts. Often the first answer given when you do word associations is an opposite or antonym: *steep/flat, docile/violent.* Older students should also be aware that there are different contrasts for many words and be able to choose the appropriate one: *right/left* but *right* answer/ *wrong* answer, *strong/weak* but *strong* smell/*faint* smell, *high/low* but *high* voice/*deep* voice, *rough/smooth* but *rough* sea/*calm* sea.

Hierarchy
Relationships that are hierarchical help us to associate new information and set up new structures. The three that are particularly useful are superordination, coordination, and subordination. Superordination is the higher category. *Animal* is superordinate to *dog. Vegetable* is superordinate to *squash. Vehicle* is superordinate to *automobile.* Coordination categories are equals—on the same level. *Trucks* and *automobiles* are coordinates in a hierarchy where *vehicle* is the superordinate. In the category *fruits, peach* and *apple* are coordinates. Subordination categories are subsumed under a larger category. In the category of *automobiles, subcompacts, compacts, standard size,* and *luxury cars* are all subcategories. Subcategories of apples would include *Granny Smith, Red Delicious,* and *Mackintosh.*

Part-Whole
New words can be understood in the context of a part-whole relationships, as in *yolk/egg, petal/flower.* Understanding which parts make up the entire item are often a productive kind of association.

Derivatives
Making associations of words because they are derived from the same source helps children use the knowledge they have in new ways: *scene/ scenery/scenic, deep/depth.*

   Although there are some other kinds of associations that can be made, these seem to be the most productive for students to use. Examining the associations that help vocabulary learning increases the tie between thinking and concepts, and words. The associations may also form the basis for games or other learning activities.

Games and Practice Activities

Although encounters with new words in a personal situation or within a meaningful context are very important in developing vocabulary because they are so effective, other activities or games structured for practicing new words or learning affixes and combining forms are helpful and do not depend as much on incidental, chance factors.

Charts and Lists

Classrooms at all levels should have lists of words—color words, words that can substitute for *said*, other ways of saying *good* or *bad*, words that tell how things move, size words, etc. In addition, students may want to keep a list of their own new words for the month or for the year. Perhaps a homemade book (directions in Chapter 13) would be good for this. As an alternative, teachers may provide word lists to start a new unit in science or social studies, or words from these new units can be highlighted as the study goes along.

Working with Context

Several games can be developed that involve using context to determine the answer. A form of "Concentration" has pairs of cards: one with a sentence containing a blank for a missing word and the other with that missing word. These are put under slightly larger squares that are numbered from 1 to 20 (or in library pockets on a posterboard) and the children guess the two numbers that they think will match. If they are not right, the sentence or word cards are put back and the next player tries. The cards with the words and sentences could be numbered on the back, but this limits the adaptability of the game for adding new pairs and some children just memorize the number pairs that match instead of learning the words.

"What's that word?" is played with numbered index cards that have a sentence with part or all of one word missing; Figure 5.1 gives two examples. The difficulty level can be varied to suit the class, and different groups can have different sets of cards. A master list num-

---

| 1. Mary Ann makes her own Christmas pr _____. | 2. She watched him go and felt str _____ and lonely. |

FIGURE 5.1   *Sample cards for "What's that Word?" Answers: 1) presents; 2) stranded or strange*

bered with the correct words would enable children to play the game independently.

"Buy a clue" starts with the players or teams having the same number of tokens (poker chips, beans, bottle caps, etc.). In turn they draw a card that has a sentence with a word blank. The object is to guess the word. They can get help by buying a letter or letters—one token per letter. A wrong guess carries a 5-token penalty. The winner is the person or team with the most tokens left.

Working with Categories

Categorizing words in different ways is important in developing vocabulary. Two different games will illustrate this type of practice. In the example shown in Figure 5.2, cards (4 by 6 inches) have five words printed on them, and the student has to tell which word doesn't belong and why. (The same words could have several different correct answers.) Possible answers might be *spatula*, because it's not used to eat with, or *chopsticks*, because there are two of them, or *knife*, because that's not intended to pick up food.

Another category game, shown in Figure 5.3, can be played with the whole class at one time or independently. The teacher or a student sets up a grid with categories of words on one axis and a letter for each column or row on the other axis. Then the children try to fill in each square of the grid with words they think the others won't think of. They get one point for each correct response and an additional point if no one else has their word. Having to think of words others won't put down encourages the children to extend their vocabulary.

Matching Meanings

Working with word meanings can be done in a number of different ways at all levels of maturity. There are several basic game formats that involve matching, and some types of matches can be used with any one of the formats.

A.	chopsticks	spoon
knife	fork	spatula

FIGURE 5.2   Category card:
Which word does not belong?

	Feelings	Colors	Vegetables
B	*bold*		
L			*lentil*
R		*ruby*	*rutabaga*

FIGURE 5.3 *Another category game: Think of a word in each category beginning with the letter indicated.*

For example, you could make up a set of cards (laminating new faces to an old deck of playing cards) with thirteen sets of four synonyms. These would be dealt like rummy, with children "playing" three or four of a kind (the synonyms), or like "Go Fish," where they ask for the synonym they need. A board game might include a set of pictures and a board with a twenty-step path to the end of the rainbow. The players each draw a picture from the set, and if they can correctly name the picture, they move their markers the number of steps indicated. In darts, the players might throw their darts to determine the number of points they will score for correctly giving the meaning required. A variation would be to throw one dart, with the number hit indicating the particular set of questions to be answered or words to be defined.

Game Formats	*Vocabulary Matches*
Card games (like "Go Fish")	Picture to word
Board games	Word to definition
Concentration	
Tic-tac-toe	Word to synonym
Crosswords	
Quiz questions	Word to antonym
Races	
Darts	Definition to word

An interesting synonym (or antonym) game is done like a miniature crossword puzzle with a synonym or antonym as the missing word. This is a good way to introduce students to the concept of a crossword in which the letters must make words both ways. An example of a synonym-antonym game is shown in Figure 5.4. Once the game

```
            Synonym:                        Antonym:

               —                               M
 C   O   M   B   I   N   E         F   A   I   L
               I   —                           S   — — — — — —
               N                               S
               G
               L
               E
```

FIGURE 5.4   *Synonym or antonym game*

gets started the students should be able to take over and set up their own crosswords.

Working with Affixes and Combining Forms

Some of the game formats and matching games can be used equally well with affixes and combining forms. One could match an affix to its meaning, and affix to a root word, or words having the same root. These could be done in any of the formats listed above. There are some other special activities that work especially well for word parts. Give younger children posterboard squares with a number of different words on them, and a set of small cards with affixes on them. The children, one at a time, draw a small card and find a word on their square to combine it with. (Make your own rules about doubling letters or dropping *-e.*). An example is shown in Figure 5.5. Each child's square would have somewhat different words on it. Each would draw a card and play it by putting it on one of the words. Thus, *re-* would cover *call* or *pay; -ly* could go on *quick* or *slow;* and *-ing* would cover *call* or *spell.* The object is to cover all the words on your square.

A variation for older children has roots, combining forms, and affixes on one large card. Two players or pairs use the same card and try to make and write down as many different words as possible from the same set. Figure 5.6 is an example.

Making Word Extensions

Instead of just matching a word with its meaning or an affix with a word, there is the possibility of seeing *how many.* How many words begin with the same prefix? How many words have the same base? How many synonyms are there for this word? Thinking up such extensions can be done in a game format, or it can simply be an ongoing class activity. Instead of boring board work, a prefix or root word could start children scurrying to find answers. A category written on the

Individual square: **On cards:**

see	slow	care
quick	pay	sing
spell	tell	call

-ing
-ly
re-
-er
-ed
-est
-less

FIGURE 5.5.   *Affix game*

pass	im	port
ed	trans	form
de	act	able

How many words can you make from these?

FIGURE 5.6   *Another affix game*

board in the morning or at the beginning of class to be checked just before lunch might be an interesting and profitable activity.

Word study can be a challenging and enjoyable experience for both teachers and children. The prerequisite for an effective program is a teacher who is interested and enthusiastic about learning new words. If the teacher looks for ways to motivate an interest in word study and provides experiences that lead to concept and vocabulary development, the program should be very successful.

Summary

The development of vocabulary—knowing the meanings of many different words and also many meanings for each word—is a critical aspect of language development, and thus comprehension and composing skills. It is important for children whose native language is English and also for children learning English as a second language. Vocabulary is a part of concept development—an essential part of reading and writing.

Vocabulary can be developed through contacts with literature, from direct experiences, and through the study of root words, affixes, and word derivations. Students must practice making conscious associations between new words and what they already know. A variety of games and activities are available to help students develop their vocabularies.

Questions for Discussion

1. Discuss the factors that make a word difficult or easy to learn in terms of its meaning. How do these factors affect teaching strategies for helping students learn more words and word meanings?
2. How is vocabulary related to reading? To writing?
3. Why is literature important in developing larger vocabularies?
4. What kinds of conscious associations will help in organizing and retrieving information? Give a specific example of each.
5. What role does the study of affixes and combining forms play in vocabulary development? How might a teacher help children learn these word parts?

Notes

1. Joseph P. O'Rourke, *Toward a Science of Vocabulary Development* (The Hague: Mouton, 1974), 18.

2. Edgar Dale, Joseph P. O'Rourke, and Henry A. Bamman, *Techniques of Teaching Vocabulary* (Palo Alto, CA: Field, 1971), 3.

3. P. Ammon, "Helping Children Learn to Write in English as a Second Language: Some Observations and Some Hypotheses," in *The Acquisition of Written Language*, S. W. Freedman, ed. (Norwood, NJ: Ablex, 1985), 80–81.

4. J. Lindfors, *Children's Language and Learning* (New York: Prentice Hall, 1980), 44–45.

5. *Webster's Seventh New Collegiate Dictionary* (Springfield, MA: G. & C. Merriam, 1970), 68.

6. N. Chomsky, "Phonology and Reading," in *Basic Studies on Reading*, H. Levin and J. Williams, eds. (New York:Basic Books, 1970), 33–48.

7. C. Blackowicz, "Vocabulary Development and Reading: From Research to Instruction," *The Reading Teacher* 38, No. 9 (May, 1985):876–881.

8. C. A. Terry and D. L. Prater, "Improving Reading Comprehension through Key-Concept Mapping," in *Houghton Mifflin Reading Report* (Boston, MA: Houghton Mifflin, undated). Reprinted by permission of Houghton Mifflin Company.

9. English-Language Arts Curriculum Framework and Criteria Committee, *English-Language Arts Framework* (Sacramento, CA: California State Department of Education, 1987), 9.

10. A. R. Gere and R. S. Stevens, "The Language of Writing Groups: How Oral Response Shapes Revision," in *The Acquisition of Written Language*, S. W. Freedman, ed. (Norwood, NJ: Ablex, 1985), 97.

11. *Ibid.,* 98.

12. D. H. Cohen, "The Effect of Literature on Vocabulary and Reading Achievement," *Elementary English* XLV (February, 1968):209–213, 217.

13. Eve Merriam, "Wake Up," in *The Birthday Cow*, Guy Michel, illustr. (New York: Knopf, 1978), 19.

14. Eve Merriam, "Conversation with Myself" in *A Sky Full of Poems*, W. Gaffney-Kessell, ed. (New York: Dell, 1986), 63.

15. Natalie Babbitt, *The Eyes of the Amaryllis* (New York: Farrar, Straus & Giroux, 1977), 111.

16. A. Wood. *The Napping House*, D. Wood, illustr. (New York: Harcourt Brace Jovanovich, 1984).

17. Dale, O'Rourke and Bamman, *Techniques of Teaching Vocabulary*, 5.

18. *Ibid.,* 215.

19. Lee C. Deighton, *Vocabulary Development in the Classroom* (New York: Teacher's College Press, 1959), 17–23. Used with permission of author.

20. *Ibid.,* 26.

21. *Ibid.,* 26–28.

22. *Ibid.,* 26–28.

23. *Ibid.,* 31.

24. Dale, O'Rourke, and Bamman, *Techniques of Teaching Vocabulary*, 24.

25. Arthur Steckler, *101 Words and How They Began*, J. Flora, illustr. (Garden City, NY: Doubleday, 1979), unpaged.

Chapter 6
Considering Grammar

Considering Grammar

Kinds of Grammars
Traditional Grammar
Structural Grammar
Transformational-Generative Grammar

Grammatical Knowledge

Grammar in the Classroom
Expanding Basic Patterns
Combining Sentences
Finding Movables and Selecting Words
Writing Imitations

Teaching Grammar/Parts of Speech

Appendix: Basic Grammatical Knowledge

The very word *grammar* produces a variety of responses. Historically grammar became associated and almost synonymous with the teaching of English in our public and private schools. Even today some teachers and some parents feel that the schools should teach more grammar, while others are vehemently opposed to any grammar instruction. Part of this wide range of opinion is due to the fact that the term *grammar* is used in several different ways to mean different things.

Traditional grammars or "school grammars" are *prescriptive* in nature. They prescribe or decree what is correct to say or write, basing their prescription on written material by well-known classic authors; and this material, of course, follows the traditional rules of Latin. They include such typical practices as underlining the subjects and predicates of sentences or even diagramming them. Even though it is contrary to research findings, many feel that studying grammar makes one a better writer and a more "correct" speaker. Thus, in one sense of the word, grammar is a set of rules that tells how language should be used.

Newer grammars that have appeared in school textbooks are built upon a completely different basis. Grammar is used to mean a theory of language or a description of how English operates. Instead of prescribing what should or should not be, these more recent grammars have attempted to describe how native speakers of the language actually use that language. The two major kinds of *descriptive* grammars are structural and transformational generative. Both have attempted to look at language in a scientific, analytical way and describe how language is actually used, rather than decreeing how it should be used.

There are still choices of language forms that the speaker or writer must make since English has a number of options. The choice that an individual makes in a particular situation is called *usage*. We recognize, for instance, that "The cat gray here isn't" is not a sentence a native English speaker would say. It is not grammatical, even though we can probably understand what the speaker is trying to communicate. It is a matter of usage, however, when deciding to say, "The gray cat isn't here" or "The gray cat ain't here." In discussing grammar in this chapter and usage in Chapter 7, we use the term *grammar* to describe how language works and the term *usage* to describe the choices or options within the language that one makes. Pooley compares this distinction between grammar and usage to the difference between behavior and etiquette.[1] Grammar, like behavior, is what happens without any judgments being made; usage is like etiquette, and varies because of social and situational forces.

The abstract and rather theoretical study of grammar is not appropriate subject matter for children of elementary school age. The focus on language in the elementary school years should be on helping children become more able to use language to express their ideas and to communicate with others. Teachers should be able to help children put their ideas into words and sentences in a variety of ways. Therefore, grammar-based activities, such as sentence combining, are advocated and discussed later in this chapter.

Kinds of Grammars

Although the abstract and theoretical study of grammar is inappropriate for elementary school children, it is necessary for teachers to become familiar with and understand different grammars. At least three major kinds of grammar are found in school textbooks today: traditional grammar, structural grammar, and transformational-generative grammar. The most recent work in linguistics has centered on the relationship between meaning and structure. Newer grammars such as case grammar[2] and generative semantics[3] have delved into semantics rather than syntax as a prime component of our system of language. This chapter, however, will examine the grammars used with children.

Traditional Grammar

Traditional grammar, mainly based on Latin, classifies words into various parts of speech such as nouns, verbs, adjectives, prepositions, and conjunctions. These parts of speech are defined primarily in terms of meaning or content, as in "A noun is the name of a person, place, or thing." This can present problems to students when using such words as *blue* and *walk*. What parts of speech are they? Blue describes so it must be an adjective, as in "My blue shirt is dirty." But what part of speech is *blue* in "Blue is the best color?" The word *blue* is now a noun. Let's use one other example. *Walk* is quite obviously a verb in "I walk to school," but it becomes a noun in the sentence "The walk is icy."

Traditionally, sentences are classified as simple, compound, complex, or in some cases compound-complex. Sentences can also be described as declarative, interrogative, exclamatory, or imperative. One of the practices most closely associated with traditional grammar is the diagramming of sentences developed by Reed and Kellogg.[4] The most important sentence elements are put on a horizontal line and separated by shorter vertical or diagonal lines. Minor elements of the sentence are placed below the main line in a way that shows their relationship to the other elements of the sentence:

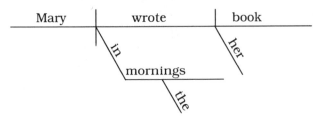

This diagram indicates that *Mary* is the subject, *wrote* is the verb, *book* is a direct object modified by *her*, and *in the mornings* is a prepositional phrase modifying *wrote*.

The most important elements of traditional grammar are the word and the sentence. Little attention is paid to paragraphs or other larger units of writing. Also, there is little emphasis on word order although English, an analytic language, is based on this. The sentence diagrammed above might have read "In the mornings, Mary wrote her book" or "Mary wrote her book in the mornings." There is no way to determine from the diagram how to reconstruct the original sentence.

Recognizing that usage varies, authors of traditional grammars accept the practices of only the best speakers and writers of English as a standard. This implies a prescriptive "best," and therefore traditional grammar in the classroom is usually taught in a highly structured fashion. "Do this!" and "Don't do that!" or "This is right!" and "This is wrong!" become the daily instructional routine for the English teacher in the classroom.

Structural Grammar

Structural grammar is descriptive; it attempts to describe how people use language rather than prescribing how language should be used. An early and exhaustive explication of structural linguistics was made by Charles Carpenter Fries with the publication in 1952 of *The Structure of English.*[5] One of the most important principles of structural grammar is that grammatical function is independent of word meaning. In order to make this point, many structuralists used sentences made up of nonsense words. In *Sligy bobbles wugged ziches, bobbles* is a noun modified by *sligy, wugged* is a verb, and *ziches* is another noun. The fact that we don't know what action *wugging* represents or what a *zich* looks like does not interfere with identifying them as parts of speech.

Fries stated that the grammatical function or structural meaning is signaled by particular devices (such as word endings, articles, and so on). He rejected the traditional parts of speech and defined or categorized words into four major form classes and fifteen groups of function words. Since these do not all correspond to the traditional parts of speech, he gave them names such as *Class 1, Class 2,* and *Group A.* He also used the terms *determiner* for words such as *the, a,* and *an* and *intensifier* for words such as *very* and *much.* Sometimes structural grammar is called "slot-and-filler" grammar because of the pattern substitution concept used to establish the parts of speech in these new categories without referring to the meaning of the words. Class 1, for example, includes all the words that fit in the blank in "The _____ is/are good." Similar "test frames" help describe the nature of the other classes of words.

Structural grammarians also use the stimulus-response (S-R)

model in psychology to explain not only how language functions as a means of communication but also how children acquire language. This theory emphasizes the view that behavior is learned through reinforcement. Lester states that Fries felt that children learn language by associating certain language forms with the situations that called them forth. In dealing with novel sentences, he contended people use analogy to sentences already known. They are able to do this, Fries thought, by using structural signals and sentence patterns.[6]

The emphasis in Fries's *Structure of English* is on sentence structure, a radical departure from traditional grammar. It became known as the "new" grammar or "linguistics," although it represented only part of the linguistic community at that time and today represents an even smaller part.

Transformational-Generative Grammar

Transformational-generative grammar is also a descriptive approach. It attempts to describe not only how language is used but also how related sentences are changed from one form to another (transformed) and how new sentences can be formulated (generated) from our unconscious or conscious knowledge of how our language operates. The person most closely associated with transformational-generative grammar is Noam Chomsky, who first published this theory in 1957 in *Syntatic Structures* and further refined it in his 1965 *Aspects of the Theory of Syntax.*[7]

One of the characteristics of transformational-generative grammar is the distinction made between the surface structure and the deep structure of language. Linguists have noticed that many sentences that appear to be parallel are actually very different. Malmstrom and Weaver give the following example of three sentences that appear on the surface to be formed identically:[8]

> *Jon wanted the guest to eat.*
> *Jon wanted the baby to eat.*
> *Jon wanted the hamburger to eat.*

In the first two, both the surface structures and deep structures (or underlying structures) are similar; the noun preceding *to eat* is to do the eating. The third, although it resembles the other two in its surface structure, is very different. The noun preceding *to eat*, the *hamburger*, is not to do the eating; Jon is. Therefore, the underlying structure of the latter is different from the other two.

Another type of problem sentence that interested transformationalists was the ambiguous sentence that might have more than one underlying structure. An example of this is: "Visiting relatives can be a nuisance."[9] This might mean that it is a nuisance to visit relatives or that having relatives visit you is a nuisance.

A third problem leading to the concept of deep and surface structures is shown by pairs of sentences that do not look similar on the surface but are closely related at the deep structure level because they are nearly synonymous:[10]

> *A new student painted the picture.*
> *The picture was painted by a new student.*

These parallel sentences occur because of the different transformations that have been made in the deep structure before they appear in the surface structures.

Transformational-generative grammar rejected the stimulus-response model as an inadequate explanation of how children acquire their native language. Transformational-generative linguists do not believe that children understand a sentence simply by recalling a prior experience with the sentence. Instead they propose that children attempt to organize a system of language rules according to their cognitive capabilities and language environment. Transformational generative grammar, therefore, attempts to duplicate the rule system that adult speakers of the language employ.

Transformational-generative grammar described two sets of rules. The first set is called *phrase-structure rules* and represents the grammatical relationships indicating meaning between the words in the deep structure of the sentence. The second set of rules, *transformational rules*, accounts for changing the deep structure form into the surface structure form of the sentence.

These phrase-structure rules and transformational rules are helpful to linguists in analyzing language and in understanding what a speaker or writer of English must know in order to use language as they do. Studying such rules is not appropriate for elementary or middle school students. However, there are some practices such as sentence expansion or sentence combining associated with transformational-generative grammar that may make students more fluent in using a wider variety of grammatical structures in their speaking and writing.

Grammatical Knowledge

Although most adults have some instruction in grammar by the time they finish school, most of the rules that they apply in their everyday language have not been learned. Some of these relate to phonemics or pronunciation. For example, the *-ed* suffix on past tense verbs may be pronounced /d/ or /t/ or /əd/. Teachers do not teach children the rules for this, and yet both children and adults can pronounce -ed properly whether it appears in real or nonsense words. Try the following:

walked	prepared	waited
backed	ignored	adopted
priced	hurried	disconcerted
chopped	behaved	headed
zitched	wugged	regicated

The words in the first column, including the final nonsense word, all end with the /t/; those in the middle column all have the /d/ ending; those in the third column all end with the /əd/ phoneme.

Adults unconsciously adhere to rules of syntax or word order. We were not taught the rules for the proper order of multiple adjectives preceding a noun. Even so, if given some examples of possible combinations of these adjectives, we will all come up with the same order or orders. Try the following and see if you agree with others:

small	*green*	*two*	(Martians)
enormous	*red*	*one*	(geranium)
purple	*big*	*four*	(monsters)

The regular order of these adjectives of size, color, and number is (first) number, (second) size, and (third) color. For emphasis, however, the second and third may be reversed. Other "rules" for other combinations of adjectives exist, and all native speakers use them without any formal instruction. Young children operate with these same rules—usually by the time they are four or five years old. Some of the rules are used in all the dialects of English, and others may vary with particular dialects.

The kinds of rules that have traditionally been the job of the English teacher are those for formal or proper usage: *Don't end a sentence with a preposition*, or *Don't use a double negative*. These maxims actually deal with options or choices a speaker may make, depending on dialect, social situation, and mode of communication (whether oral or written). Teachers need to recognize the extensive amount of knowledge about language that children possess and use by the time they enter school, instead of focusing on the knowledge they may lack.

Grammar in the Classroom

The primary aim of the language arts program is to enable children to use language to express their ideas both orally and in writing. The formal study of grammar does not help them meet this goal. Two of the more recent research studies, one conducted by Roland Harris and the other reported by W. B. Elley, substantiate this. In Harris's study, students adhered to the regular curriculum during the first four days of each week, but on the fifth day, half of the students received grammar instruction while the other half wrote stories. At the end of two years, students who had been instructed in grammar wrote less complex sentences and made more errors in writing than those who had written stories.[11] The second investigation, sometimes referred to as the New Zealand study, involved three groups of students and compared three curricula: (1) the study of transformational grammar, (2) the study of traditional grammar, and (3) free reading and creative writing.[12] In summarizing the results of the three-year study, Elley claims there were no significant differences between the performances of the three groups. In the report he says, "It is difficult to escape the conclusion that English grammar, whether traditional or transformational, has virtually no influence on the language growth of typical secondary school students."[13]

Although findings of these two studies agree about the ineffectiveness of grammar instruction, they indicate differences with regard to writing and its influence on students' performance. We know that the mere act of frequent writing does not improve a person's ability to write better sentences or sentences with fewer errors. Therefore, one should ask if instruction accompanied the writing, and if so, what form of instruction occurred along with it.

Substantial evidence exists to show that certain kinds of grammar-based writing experiences can improve students' writing abilities. Research studies indicate that the manipulation of syntax, or sentence building activities such as sentence combining, can influence writing performance. Frank O'Hare reports in a now classic study that seventh-grade students who were exposed to both oral and written sentence combining practice over an eight-month period "wrote compositions that were judged to be significantly better in overall quality than those written by students who did not have the practice."[14] He also generalized from the results of the research: "Although the findings of the present study relate specifically to seventh graders, there is no obvious reason for assuming that sentence combining practice should not be used in elementary and senior high school, as well as junior high school."[15] Other less formal studies support O'Hare's generalization. Their findings have shown sentence combining to be a valuable activity with students at least as early as fourth grade. Younger children can participate in sentence-combining and sentence-expanding activities using an experience story as a base before they can profit from prestructured combining exercises. Considering what we know about young children's cognitive abilities, these findings appear to make sense. Because of the level of reasoning involved, young primary school students who are in the preoperational stage of intellectual development will experience some difficulty, and perhaps even frustration, when asked to do sentence-combining exercises.

Because the evidence in favor of using sentence-building activities to improve students' writing is more than convincing, the following section is devoted to a variety of exercises that a teacher might incorporate into the composition program. It is best that oral discussion precede any written practice since the emphasis is on total language growth. The primary aim, stated once again, is to help students become better able to use language to express their ideas *both orally and in writing.*

Expanding Basic Patterns

Expanding simple sentence patterns in various ways is one activity that can help children be more effective in their use of language. It should be done within the language and the experiences of the child. A format that is particularly useful with this kind of expansion work is the group experience story. Suppose that the children had visited a nearby doughnut shop and were writing about this trip. The teacher could first ask for ideas about what to write. One child might say, "We saw a man cut out the doughnuts." Another might mention, "I like doughnuts." The teacher would then write these ideas on the chalkboard or a large sheet of chart paper. The children would then find various ways to add ideas to the original sentence.

> For: "We saw a man cut out the doughnuts."
>   What could we add about the man?
>   a man in a white jacket
>   a man in the back room
>   a man with a chef's hat
>   a young man
>   What did he do besides cut them out?
>   roll and cut out
>   cut out and twist
>   cut out and fill
>   How did he cut them out?
>   carefully
>   real fast
>   with a knife
>   with a special cutter
>
> For: "I like doughnuts."
>   Why do you like them?
>   because they're sweet
>   because they're good

> Which doughnuts do you like best?
>> chocolate ones with frosting
>> twisted ones with cinnamon

The children could talk about ways to add to the original sentence before writing it on a chart. They might say, "We saw a man in a white jacket cut out and twist the doughnuts," and "I like twisted doughnuts with cinnamon because they're sweet."

Another method of expanding sentences is designed around an exercise format instead of an experience story. Begin with a kernel, or simple, sentence, such as "Jan ran." Then ask the students to tell the different ways that Jan ran. Their ideas should be written on the chalkboard or recorded on a large chart. For example, students might say that

> *Jan ran.*
> *Jan ran slowly.*
> *Jan ran rapidly.*
> *Jan ran fast.*
> *Jan ran backward.*

After a number of suggestions are written, ask the students to tell *why* Jan ran in this manner. They might suggest the following:

> *Jan ran slowly because of his sore ankle.*
> *Jan ran rapidly because he was late.*
> *Jan ran fast because he was in a hurry.*
> *Jan ran backward because he thought it was funny.*

Next, ask the students to add words that will tell *who* Jan is. For example, looking at the sentence, "Jan ran slowly because of his sore ankle," they might say

> *Jan, my brother, ran slowly because of his sore ankle.*
> *My friend Jan ran slowly because of his sore ankle.*
> *Jan, the boy who came in last, ran slowly because of his sore ankle.*

Following the telling and recording of various ideas, students may be given an opportunity to complete similar exercises independently or in small groups. After these are completed, however, some sharing and discussion of the exercises should occur.

Combining Sentences

As research studies have shown, students become more effective in their use of oral and written language if they have meaningful practice with various ways of combining sentences. Group experience stories or charts can be excellent sources of material for sentence combining. For example, suppose a group of students experiment with water erosion and then dictate the following sentences about the experience.

> *We put water in four pails.*
> *We poured it down a hill in two places.*
> *There was grass on one side.*
> *The other side was just dirt.*

The teacher, Mr. Griffin, read it back to them and agreed that it did describe what they had done. But he told them, it sounded choppy with all the short sentences. Then he suggested they try to combine the first two sentences by adding or subtracting some words but keeping the same ideas. They quickly suggested,

> *We put water in two pails, and we poured it down a hill in two places.*

He agreed that the combination worked, although they did not need the second *we*. After struggling with the last two sentences, the students suggested,

> *One side had grass, but the other side was just dirt.*

Sentence combining may be done this way in the context of some group writing the children are doing. Exercises can also be provided to focus on particular ways of combining ideas or sentences that will help children find solutions easily. Younger children may work on simple combinations, such as using compound sentences or compound subjects or predicates. The teacher would provide uncombined sentences for practice. A simple exercise would use "and" as a conjunction. Children would be asked to combine such sentences as the following:

> *I have a dog.*
> *He is brown and white.*
>
> *Rachel has a green sweater.*
> *It has silver buttons.*
>
> *Tom plays tee-ball.*
> *He plays soccer.*

The sentence combining exercises can be made more complex and deal with more unusual ways of expressing ideas for older students. A teacher could instruct students to combine sentences using "who" and reminding them to omit repetitive words.

The skater did triple jumps.
The skater won the competition.

The man walked five miles every day.
The man retired three years ago.

The teacher displayed her students' writing in the hall each week.
The teacher taught seventh grade.

Structured sentence combining practice focused on a particular grammatical element helps students learn about that element and how it is used. After such practice, students may then begin to use the elements appropriately in their own writing.

After structured sentence combining practice, teachers should provide practice in using different ways of combining ideas. This brings students closer to natural writing and exposes them to the many options available to the writer. For example students could be asked how many different ways these three sentences can be combined:

Linda Jo owns a horse.
The horse is gray.
Linda Jo rides her horse every afternoon.

Alternative combinations of these sentences emphasize different ideas. Possible combinations include the following.

Linda Jo rides her gray horse every afternoon.
Linda Jo's horse is gray, and she rides it every afternoon.
Linda Jo owns a horse that is gray, and she rides it every afternoon.
The horse that Linda Jo rides every afternoon is gray.
Every afternoon, Linda Jo rides her gray horse.

For sentence combining activities to be most effective, exercises such as those shown here should be introduced through samples done as a class with the teacher and discussed, then through practice and more discussion on a particular kind of combining, and finally through opportunities to use their repertoire of sentence combining ideas in prac-

Children discuss sentence combining examples with their teacher. They discover how important it is to pay attention to meaning when they are combining sentences.

tice materials and in their own writing. When conferencing with students about their writing, teachers might ask students if they see any sentences in their writing that need to be combined with *and*, for example, or with a *who* clause.

The purpose of sentence combining exercises is to enable students to progress from writing a series of simple sentences to writing longer or more complex sentences. Since sentence maturity is related to a writer's ability to use subordination, to vary sentence length, and to vary syntactic structure, the process of combining sentences seems to give students the skills necessary for writing mature, well-constructed sentences.

Finding Movables and Selecting Words

Certain words or phrases may be placed in different parts of a sentence. For example, the sentence "I knew he had to be my pet when I saw him" can be changed to read "When I saw him, I knew he had to be my pet." Changes such as this sometimes subtly alter the emphasis or effect of a sentence.

There are several ways to use sentences from a reading text, a weekly children's news magazine, or a collection of sentences reproduced on a transparency or ditto sheet. Children may want to use their own writing—moving words, phrases, or clauses around and then comparing the new version with the original piece of writing. Some of the words or phrases that may be used as movables within a sentence are

> Adverbs (*Eventually he moved*/ *he moved eventually*),
> Adjectives (*gigantic orange balloon*/ *orange gigantic balloon*),
> Prepositional phrases (*he walked in the house*/ *in the house he walked*), and
> Clauses (*Since he came early, we*/ *we. . . . since he came early*).

Selecting specific words to convey a particular meaning—or words that are appropriate for a particular kind of writing—is very helpful for the older child. This is the area of *field of discourse* (discussed in the section on register in Chapter 7) that determines what vocabulary or lexical items one chooses for a particular piece of writing. Scientists, for example, make a distinction between *soil* and *dirt*. In the earlier discussion of combining sentences about erosion, *soil* would be preferable to *dirt*.

Other words are chosen for the shade of meaning they convey. Children in the upper-elementary grades might examine a thesaurus that lists synonyms and antonyms. In *Roget's College Thesaurus* the listing for *walk* as a verb is *ramble, stroll, promenade, saunter, travel (on foot), march, parade, tramp, hike, tread, pace, step.*[16] Although these are synonyms for *walk*, there is a difference between *strolling* and *tramping* or between *sauntering* and *pacing*. If you do not want to use a thesaurus, you can have the children list words that have almost the same meaning and conduct a follow-up discussion on the connotations. What are synonyms for the word *thin? Slender, skinny, underweight, bony.* If you are not talking about a person but about material, what words might describe it? *Sheer, fine, delicate, filmy?*

Developing an awareness of the effect of a particular word or of moving a word, phrase, or clause to a different part of a sentence is important in developing writing skills. The function of language in a meaningful situation is the most appropriate way of working with grammar in the elementary school. Working with language in this way offers more potential for improving the quality of children's writing than teaching a formal grammatical description of English through traditional, structural, or transformational theory.

Writing Imitations

In *Teaching Writing K-8*, Jack Hailey summarizes numerous presentations made over several years by teachers and consultants working with the Bay Area Writing Project in California.[17] A variety of sentence-building activities are recommended in the book, and among them is an exercise—"writing imitations"—that relates to literary structures and sentence combining. "Writing imitations" is a "paradigm designed to assist children in building vocabulary power for specific units of writing, such as verbs, descriptors, or nouns."

Hailey describes one form of "writing imitations" as a fill-in-the-blanks game:

> Take a paragraph or selected sentences from a piece of children's literature. Delete the action verbs or the adjectives or the prepositional phrases, and have children fill in the blanks. This activity need not be done individually; pairs or groups of children can work together. . . . Children's internal grammar will lead them to pick a word that fits, and their ears will judge the result.[18]

The following example demonstrates this first form of "writing imitations." Descriptors have been deleted from a selection from *The Castle of Llyr* by Lloyd Alexander.[19]

> *The hut was as the Prince had told them. A _____ layer of dust covered the _____ tables and benches. A spider had spun an _____ web in one corner, but even the web was _____. On a hearthstone lay the _____ remnants of a _____ fire. Near the hearth, a number of _____ crock-pots, _____ and _____ now, had been overturned. _____ bowls and _____ jars, shattered into fragments, were strewn about the floor*
> *The hut was _____; the noises of the forest did not enter.*

The second form of imitation exercise is similar to sentence combining. Students are given sentences from good literature and then asked to write sentences that have the same structure but different content. For instance, consider the following example from Carol Fenner's *The Skates of Uncle Richard*.[20]

> *She glided away on the skates of Uncle Richard, taller and taller and taller, never once falling down.*

Student imitations:

> *I rode away on my new bicycle, straighter and straighter and straighter, never once falling off.*

> *I dove off the high board at the pool, faster and faster and faster, never once closing my eyes.*

> *I rolled down the hill on my skateboard, faster and faster and faster, never once falling down.*

These imitation exercises are most appropriate for older students, but younger children should be hearing stories that contain repetition, refrain, and complex sentence structure. And whenever possible, they should be asked to participate in stories by repeating refrains, verses, and creative sentences.

Teaching Grammar/Parts of Speech

The research on the relationship between studying traditional grammar (parts of speech) and speaking or writing is clear. Knowing traditional grammar does not make anyone a better writer or speaker. It may enable students to determine parts of speech or identify types of sentences and so be able to pass a test that calls for that. Much of the time when we teach grammar, we are only helping children label the words they already use correctly. If they are not using a word appropriately, then we can focus on that usage problem. For example, if a child says, "My books was left on the bus," it will be much more efficient and successful to say, "Lee, in school talk we say *were* when we are talking about more than one thing, so you should say, 'My books were left.' One book *was* left, but two or three or more books *were* left." There is no need to explain subjects and predicates and rules for subject-verb agreements. As adults, we do not think about subjects and objects when we decide what to say even though we know that information. Using language appropriately for a particular situation involves developing a sense of what sounds right combined with self-knowledge of our own usage problems.

Younger children would profit far more from opportunities to develop their capacity to describe, explain, compare, or summarize than from learning that *could* and *should* are modals. Older students in middle schools may benefit from knowing the terminology of grammar to discuss aspects of style or sentence construction in writing or in speaking. Grammar is very abstract, and not really comprehensible to most young children and even to many middle school students.

Most teachers feel that giving clear directions, writing good sentences or paragraphs, being able to tell or write a story, and knowing how to spell or capitalize are more important than knowing declarative and interrogative sentences or being able to label nouns and verbs. Unfortunately some of the test makers at both the national and the state level have kept items that call for children to describe language in such ways. The contrast here is between knowing how to use language and knowing how to talk about language.

When you must teach grammar/parts of speech, it is important to provide many examples of the concept you are teaching. Students can then use their experiences with language and their knowledge of how they use language to help them understand how to talk about it. Simple memorization of definitions has not worked in many years, and there is no reason to believe it will suddenly start to work now. An example in Chapter 1 describes how one teacher modified the traditional lessons on nouns that were in her English book to teach children how to identify a noun, the difference between common and proper nouns, and how to make nouns possessive or plural. The first step was to generate lists of nouns of various kinds and then to label them. The children learned about nouns within a meaningful, purposeful context. The first instructional lesson made sense to them in terms of their own experiences. This approach is equally important for older students who have already had experiences with grammar but have not learned it.

Most students above fifth grade can quickly define a noun, adjective, or verb in a rote way. They are less successful at identifying these parts of speech in a sentence. Why? Their definitions are like a poem, prayer, or song that they have memorized without understanding it. They are like first-graders reciting the "Pledge of Allegiance." They don't know what *allegiance* is, or a *republic*, or what is standing. Later they may come to appreciate the pledge as they understand it more fully, but in the meantime they can participate with others in saying it. However, it does little good to memorize "A verb describes an action or a state of being" if they can't find the verb in a sentence. In deciding to teach a grammatical concept, we need to make sure that children fully grasp it.

First, develop activities that will generate the part of speech involved and all the needed examples. Work with categories of the part of speech, especially in the case of adverbs and pronouns. Most adverbs modify verbs; they end in -*ly* and present few problems for the instructor. Other adverbs that are sometimes called intensifiers, such as *very*, *too*, *extremely*, and *somewhat* look quite different and typically modify adjectives or other adverbs. Adverbs like *there*, *here*, and *where* (also a conjunction) have yet another use. Teaching these at different times and at different grade levels will help students make sense of them. The definition of an adverb—a word that modifies a verb, adjective, or other

learn to identify the type of word when they see it, if asked. Keeping grammar in perspective and focusing on the things that you believe are most important are keys to good teaching. Most parents and teachers want children to use language appropriately—avoiding "he ain't," "she don't," or "them papers was" —rather than to know a gerund from an infinitive.

Summary

Grammar is an abstract and technical description of language. There are several grammars that differ in the aspects of language they emphasize. Traditional grammar defines parts of speech by their meanings and prescribes the correct use of language. Structural grammar defines parts of speech by their functions, positions, and endings. It is a descriptive grammar, like transformational-generative grammar, that explains what we must know to invent sentences and to change them from one form to another.

Most parents want their children to use "good" grammar, by which they mean more formal or correct usage. They are not particularly concerned about typical grammar practices, such as identifying verbs or adjectives, and labeling sentences as interrogative or declarative. They want their children to speak well, to sound well educated, an objective that most teachers share. Children, especially in the primary grades, should concentrate on using language fluently and effectively, not on abstract terminology that describes language. After they have mastered its use, they can appropriately study grammar.

This chapter described some activities that develop students' abilities to use many different grammatical structures, to experiment with different ways of expressing the same idea, and to become increasingly fluent. Activities include expanding basic sentence patterns, combining sentences with phrases and clauses, finding movables and selecting among options, and writing imitations of literary sentences. An inductive approach for directly teaching parts of speech is included. An appendix to this chapter reviews the rules of traditional grammar.

Questions for Discussion

1. How are the newer grammars—structural and transformational-generative—different from traditional grammar in terms of their purposes? What are the main characteristics of each?

2. What evidence indicates that students know more about grammar and how language operates than they can state explicitly?
3. What are some alternatives to learning parts of speech or diagramming sentences that enhance students' abilities to use increasingly complex structures more flexibly?
4. What do you think is the role of grammar instruction in language arts programs? What is most important in helping students to use language?

Notes

1. Robert C. Pooley, *Teaching English Grammar* (New York: Appleton-Century-Crofts, 1957), 106.

2. Jean Malmstrom and Constance Weaver, *Transgrammar* (Glenview, IL: Scott, Foresman, 1973), 259.

3. *Ibid.*, 273.

4. Alonzo Reed and Brainerd Kellogg, "Work on English Grammar and Composition, 1877" in *Linguistics and English Grammar*, H. A. Gleason, Jr., ed. (New York: Holt, Rinehart & Winston, 1965.

5. Charles C. Fries, *The Structure of English* (New York: Harcourt Brace Jovanovich, 1952.)

6. Mark Lester, *Introductory Transformational Grammar of English* (New York: Holt, Rinehart & Winston), 16–20.

7. Noam Chomsky, *Syntactic Structures* (The Hague: Mouton, 1957) and *Aspects of the Theory of Syntax* (MIT Press, 1965).

8. Malmstrom and Weaver, *Transgrammar*, 61.

9. *Ibid.*, 62.

10. *Ibid.*, 63.

11. Roland J. Harris, "An Experimental Inquiry in the Functions and Value of Formal Grammar in the Teaching of English with Special Reference to the Teaching of Correct Written English to Children Ages Twelve to Fourteen," Unpublished Ph.D. Dissertation, University of London, 1962. Summarized in Richard Braddock, Richard Lloyd-Jones and Lowell Schoer, *Research in Written Composition* (Champaign, IL: National Council of Teachers of English, 1963), 70–83.

12. W. B. Elley et al., "The Role of Grammar in a Secondary English Curriculum," *Research in the Teaching of English*, 10, no. 1 (Spring, 1976):5–21.

13. *Ibid.*

14. Frank O'Hare, *Sentence Combining: Improving Student Writing without Formal Grammar Instruction*, Research Report no. 15 (Urbana, IL: National Council of Teachers of English, 1973).

15. *Ibid.*

16. The National Lexicographic Board, *The New American Roget's College Thesaurus* (New York: New American Library, 1962), 399.

17. Jack Hailey, *Teaching Writing K through 8* (Berkeley, CA: Instructional Laboratory, University of California, 1978).

18. *Ibid.*, 80.

19. Lloyd Alexander, *The Castle of Llyr* (New York: Holt, Rinehart & Winston, 1966.

20. Carol Fenner, *The Skates of Uncle Richard* (New York: Random House, 1978).

Appendix: Basic Grammatical Knowledge

Nouns

boy	schools	scissors	happiness
Juanita	playground	rose	success
uncles	Eiffel Tower	chair	democracies
teachers	golf course	giraffe	health

The words listed above are nouns. A noun is the name of a person, place, thing, or idea. Nouns may name one (singular) or more than one (plural). Special endings are often added to indicate plurals, but some nouns change their form in the plural and some retain the same form for both singular and plural.

Nouns may name particular people, places, or things, and these are called proper nouns. Those that name general categories are called common nouns.

Common	*Proper*
city	Chicago
building	Empire State Building
bridge	Golden Gate Bridge
university	Ohio State University

Nouns function in different ways; they can be a subject, direct object, indirect object, object of a preposition, or predicate nominative.

> The **soldier** *fired his machine gun* (a subject, does the action)
> The *captain met the* **soldier**. (a direct object, receives the action)
> The *officer gave the* **soldier** *a letter.* (an indirect object, to whom or for whom the action is done)
> The *package was for the* **soldier**. (an object of a preposition, noun following a preposition)

The winner was the **soldier.** (a predicate nominative, equivalent of subject)

Verbs

walked	appeared	was
climbs	seems	am
pass	looked	are

will be   have talked

should have been   was going

The words listed above are verbs. The traditional definition states that a verb expresses an action or state of being. There are four kinds of inflectional endings characteristic of verbs:

1. *She* **wants** *to go with us.* John **wishes** *he could go.* (Present tense, third person singular: -s or -es
2. *He* **waited** *for ten minutes.* (past tense: -ed)
3. *Annette was* **singing.** (present participal: -ing)
4. *Jack had* **wanted** *a new glove.* (past participle: -ed)

Verbs may be used alone in a sentence (Joel *went* to the pool.) or may have one or more auxiliaries (Shelly *should have been going* to class.) Auxiliaries can be modals (such as *can, should, might, will, must*) a form of *have* (*has, had* or *having*), or a form of *be* (*am, is, are, was, were, been,* or *being*).

Verbs are called "transitive" if they take an object and "intransitive" if they do not.

Verbals: Participles, Gerunds and Infinitives

running	dancing	to balance
waited	baking	to catch
scratching	writing	to decide

The words above are kinds of verbs that are used as other parts of speech in a sentence. They are formed from verbs and so carry the meaning of describing an action, but they are not used as the verb in a sentence.

Participles   Participles (like running, waited, and scratching) are used like adjectives. You may use a participle alone or as part of a phrase—a participial phrase. Participles are used as verbs in the progressive tenses.

> *A* **sleeping** *cat is not unusual.*
> *A* **scratched** *arm is often sore.*

Examples of participial phrases are

> *A batter* **waiting for the ball** *is tense.*
> *They applauded the dancer* **twirling on her toes.**

Gerunds   Gerunds are forms of verbs that end in *-ing* (like a present participle) but that are used in place of a noun in any of the ways nouns can be used.

> **Walking** *may be better exercise than* **jogging.**
> *I enjoy* **cooking.**

Gerunds can also be part of a phrase:

> **Eating too much sugar and starch** *is bad for one.*

Infinitives   Infinitives are forms of a verb with *to* that can be used as a noun, adverb, or adjective.

> **To dream** *is perfectly normal. (as noun)*
> *He raised his arms* **to stretch.** *(as adverb)*
> *The one* **to see** *is Virginia. (as adjective)*

Infinitive phrases have an infinitive and its complements or modifiers:

> **To do a triple jump on the ice** *was his goal.*

Adjectives

pretty	rusty	small
colorful	active	gracious
round	confident	hopeless

The words listed above are adjectives. Adjectives are traditionally defined as words that modify a noun. They usually occur in two positions in a sentence: in front of a noun or after a linking verb as a predicate adjective. (Linking verbs are forms of *be, appear, become, look, seem* and the senses, such as *feel, smell,* and so forth.)

> *She is an* **adorable** *baby. (in front of noun)*
> *The baby is* **adorable.** *(as predicate adjective after is)*

Adjectives can expresss degrees of their quality in two forms: the comparative and the superlative. Most adjectives add *-er* when comparing two things and *-est* when expressing the superlative by comparing three or more. Sometimes *more* is used for the comparative and *most* for the superlative. A few adjectives have special forms, such as *good* (better, best), *bad* (worse, worst), and *little* (less, least).

Sometimes words that are usually nouns are used as adjectives, such as *book* cover, *chicken* dinner, or *gold* watch.

Adverbs

slowly	very	always	here
cautiously	too	never	there
richly	somewhat	soon	where
evenly	quite	often	everywhere
quickly	extremely	yesterday	anywhere

These words are adverbs. An adverb is traditionally defined as a word that modifies a verb, an adjective, or another adverb. It is perhaps more informative to say that adverbs often describe how, when, where, or to what extent.

While many adverbs end in *-ly*, many do not and there are some adjectives that end in *-ly* (e.g., costly, lovely, and friendly).

Some adverbs, like adjectives, can express comparison by adding *-er* or using more for the comparative and by adding *-est* or using *most* for the superlative.

Most adverbs describe the manner in which something happens or describe when or where an action takes place.

> *Do your work* **quietly.** *She jumped* **quickly.** (manner)
> *I went* **today.** *The election was* **yesterday.** (time)
> *Your package is* **here.** *I see trees* **everywhere** *that I look.* (place)

Intensifiers
Adverbs that tell "to what extent" are sometimes called intensifiers. Some of them are *very, too, quite,* and *somewhat.* They modify adjectives or other adverbs.

> *The pioneers were* **incredibly** *brave.*
> *I drove* **very** *slowly through the snow and slush.*

Conjunctive Adverbs
Adverbs such as *nevertheless* and *hence* are called conjunctive adverbs and are used to join independent clauses. They will be discussed under conjunctions.

Pronouns

I	me	my	anyone	this
she	him	her	everything	that
they	us	mine	few	these
you	them	their	several	those

who	myself	whose
what	yourself	that

The words listed above are pronouns. A pronoun is traditionally defined as a word that is used in place of a noun. Pronouns can be used instead of nouns in all of the ways a noun is used—subject, object, or predicate nominative. They can also be used as noun determiners.

Personal Pronouns

Subject or Predicate Nominative		Object—Direct Object, Indirect Object, or Object of a Preposition	
Singular	*Plural*	*Singular*	*Plural*
I	we	me	us
you	you	you	you
he, she, it	they	him, her, it	them

You *can see the flag. (subject)*
Brent saw **them** *at the parade. (direct object)*

Possessive as Noun		Possessive as Noun Determiner	
Singular	*Plural*	*Singular*	*Plural*
mine	ours	my	our
yours	yours	your	your
his, hers, its	theirs	his, her, its	their

Mine *is on the table;* **yours** *is here. (nouns)*
The dog broke **its** *collar. (noun determiner)*

Reflexive Pronouns

Singular	*Plural*
myself	ourselves
yourself	yourselves
himself, herself, itself	themselves

We considered **ourselves** *lucky to meet a movie star.*

Indefinite Pronouns

Nouns		Noun Determiners or Nouns		
anyone	nobody	all	either	some
anything	nothing	any	neither	many
everyone	someone	each	most	few
everybody	somebody	more	several	another
and so forth		no(determiner)	none (noun)	

Each *person will win some prize. (noun determiner)*
Each *has a chance of winning the grand prize. (noun)*

Demonstrative Pronouns

Noun or Noun Determiner

Singular	Plural
this	these
that	those

This *book is too long to read. (noun determiner)*
Those *are really exciting mysteries. (noun)*

Interrogative Pronouns
Asks a Question

Who	What
Whose	Which
Whom	

Who *wants to make cookies?*

Relative Pronouns
Introduces Adjective or Noun Clauses

whose	which
that	who
whom	

I know **who** *won the race. (with noun clause)*
Marie has the ticket **that** *I left here. (with adjective clause)*

Articles and Noun Determiners

a	one	this	my	all
an	four	that	his	each
the	ten	those	their	many

The words listed above are articles and noun determiners. The articles are *a* and *an* (indefinite) and *the* (definite). The term "article" comes from traditional grammar. "Noun determiner" is a more recent term from structural grammar; it indicates that a noun is to follow immediately or after some intervening adjectives. Articles, cardinal numbers, and several kinds of pronouns are used as noun determiners.

Articles

Articles are sometimes referred to as a kind of adjective because they precede a noun and refer to it. *A* is used with words beginning with consonant sounds and *an* with words beginning with vowel sounds. *The* refers to a particular person or thing.

> **A** *girl won the door prize.*
> **An** *orange is sometimes hard to peel.*
> **The** *man we were waiting for had a moustache.*

Cardinal Numbers

These numbers are used the same way as articles and signal that a noun will follow.

> *Mary Ellen bought* **two** *pairs of jeans.*
> **Forty** *men worked on the bridge.*

Demonstrative Pronouns

These pronouns include *this, that, these,* and *those.* They can function as noun determiners (see section on pronouns).

> **That** *skirt is too long for you.*
> *Look at* **these** *miniature vegetables.*

Possessive Pronouns

Possessive pronouns can indicate that a noun will follow.

> *Chuen Li borrowed* **my** *bicycle.*
> *The car had lost* **its** *rear-view mirror.*

Indefinite Pronouns

As discussed in the section on pronouns, certain indefinite pronouns may be used as noun determiners.

*The glove belongs to **another** boy.*
*I saw **more** birds than I have ever seen before.*
***Several** gymnasts can do a double back somersault.*

Prepositions

over	down	under
up	in	to
around	during	off

The words above are prepositions; they indicate a relationship between a noun or pronoun and some other part of the sentence. Prepositions are always a part of a prepositional phrase, such as *across* the water, *near* the desk, *through* those wide doors, *within* five or six minutes.

*I will leave **within** a few minutes.*
*Pierre will stay **until** five o'clock.*

Conjunctions

and	anyway	when
but	consequently	if
or	moreover	since
nor	however	unless
for	otherwise	while
so	therefore	after

The words above are different kinds of conjunctions: coordinating conjunctions (first column), conjunctive adverbs (second column), and subordinating conjunctions (third column). Coordinating conjunctions and conjunctive adverbs can join independent clauses, while subordinating conjunctions join a dependent clause to an independent one.

Coordinating Conjunctions
The six coordinating conjunctions in the first column can be used to connect two independent clauses. (A clause is a subject and predicate—with or without other modifiers—that can stand alone as a sentence.) Coordinating conjunctions can also join words or phrases.

*Betty walked to school, **but** she ran home.* (two independent clauses)
*Burns **and** Allen were a great comedy team.* (two words)

Jackson ran up the stairs **and** *down the hall.* (two phrases—prepositional phrases)
We will meet you at the airport if you come to Atlanta **or** *if you come to Athens.* (two dependent clauses)

Conjunctive Adverbs

In addition to the words listed in the second column above, the following words are commonly used as conjunctive adverbs: *accordingly, also, anyhow, besides, furthermore, hence, indeed, likewise, namely, nevertheless, still,* and *then.* Conjunctive adverbs only join clauses, and may be used in different places in the sentence.

Betty walked to school; **however,** *she ran home.*
Betty walked to school; she ran home, **however.**

Subordinating Conjunctions

These conjunctions are used to join a dependent clause to an independent one to form a complex sentence. A dependent clause is a subject and predicate—with or without other modifiers—that can not make a sentence by itself.

In addition to those in the third column, the following words often serve as subordinating conjunctions: *although, as, because, before, even though, like, so* (that), *though, till, until, where, wherever,* and *whether* (or not). Dependent clauses introduced by subordinating conjunctions function as noun clauses or as adverbial clauses.

I wonder **whether** *Jenny will come to the potluck.* (as noun)
When *you arrive, we will leave for the airport.* (as adverb)

Interjections

Wow!   Yippee!
Oh!   Good heavens!
He ha!   Ouch!

The words above are interjections, traditionally defined as a word that expresses strong emotion and is not related grammatically to the rest of the sentence. An interjection is usually followed by an exclamation point or by a comma if it is not a strong feeling.

Ouch! *That really hurt. Don't pinch me.*
Oh, *do you really think he will?*

Phrases, Clauses, and Sentences

These consist of two or more words that go together in some way, but there are significant differences among them.

Phrase

A phrase consists of two or more words that form a unit but lacks either a subject or a verb. A phrase may have a noun or a verb or verb form but not both.

> *Mr. Waverly,* **the basketball coach,** *applied for the jog.* (noun phrase)
> *He had a chance* **to go there.** (verb phrase-infinitive)
> *That pattern is* **incredibly ugly.** (adjective phrase)
> *The path* **up here** *is narrow and steep.* (adverb phrase)
> *The book* **under the thesaurus** *belongs to me.* (prepositional phrase)

Clause

There are two major kinds of clauses: independent and dependent. Both must have a subject and a verb stated or implied. Independent clauses can stand alone as sentences, or they can be joined together to form a compound sentence with a coordinating conjunction or with a semicolon.

> **Lettie won the competition,** *and* **she got the prize.**
> *or* **Lettie won the competition; she got the prize.**

Dependent clauses also have a subject and a verb, but they can not stand alone as sentences because they express an incomplete idea. They must be added to an independent clause to form a complete sentence. Dependent clauses can be noun clauses, adjective clauses, or adverb clauses.

> *I know* **who will write the best poem.** (noun clause-direct object)
> *Poems* **that rhyme** *are popular.* (adjective clause)
> *You should write a cinquain* **before you try a limerick.** (adverb clause)

When a subject is understood, it is often the word *you* with an imperative form of the verb—giving an order. Sometimes the verb is omitted instead of being repeated or when it is clearly understood

> *Take this report to the principal.* (understood **you** as the subject—**you** *take this report. . . .*)
> *The job was hard; the money inadequate.* (understood **was** as *the money* **was** *inadequate*)

Sentence

A sentence is traditionally defined as a group of words expressing a complete thought and having a subject and verb. Sentences are classified by their structure as simple, compound, complex, or compound-complex.

> *That book is exciting.* (**simple:** one independent clause)
> *That book is exciting, but this one is dull* (**compound:** two independent clauses)
> *If that book is exciting, I want to read it.* (**complex:** an independent clause *I want to read it* and a dependent clause *If that book is exciting*)
> *The book that I read was a mystery, but I usually prefer historical fiction.* (**compound-complex:** two independent clauses—*The book was a mystery* and *I usually prefer historical fiction.* with one dependent clause—*that I read*)

Sentences may also be classified by purpose: declarative (makes a statement), interrogative (asks question), imperative (gives order or request), or exclamatory (expresses strong feeling).

Chapter 7
Describing Linguistic Variations

Describing Linguistic Variations

A History of English

Concepts of Language

Functions of Language

Nonverbal Language

Relationship of Verbal and Nonverbal Behavior

Areas of Nonverbal Communication

Dialects of English

How Dialects Differ

Features of Black English and
Spanish-Influenced English

Considerations for the Classroom

Language Usage

Teaching More Appropriate Usage Patterns

Using Nonsexist Language

Opportunities for Usage Experiences in Oral Language

Opportunities for Usage Experiences
in Written Language

Registers of Language

English as a Second Language

English, like other languages, varies in many different ways. It has changed over time, so that the English of today is somewhat different from that of Shakespeare and very different from that of Chaucer. There are also geographic variations, particularly in how English is spoken. These variations include distinctions between American and British English; they also include differences among New Englanders, Midwesterners, Southerners, and so forth. There are social variations in our use of language; we do not talk the same way to our close friends or family as we do to our minister or school superintendent. We vary what we say and what we write. The words we use when we talk with others in our own field are somewhat different from those we use with outsiders. We also use language for different purposes—sometimes as a way of acquiring information, other times as a way of maintaining social relationships. Language usually suggests words and sentences, but we communicate a great deal without words. A teacher puts an index finger across the lips to ask for silence; a shrug of the shoulders says "Who knows?" Nonverbal communication, intentional or not, conveys a great deal of meaning. For some students in our schools, English is a foreign language. A good language arts program must consider all these variations.

A History of English

English was not the native language in the British Isles. When Julius Caesar explored the island in 55 and 54 B.C., it was inhabited by Celts. About one hundred years later the Roman legions came and conquered the southern two-thirds of the island and remained there until the early A.D. 400s. There were raids by the northern Germanic tribes, who settled in what is now England. When the legionnaires left, the Celts were unable to stop the invaders; and so the Germanic peoples were able to make permanent settlements. The Angles, Saxons, and Jutes all spoke dialects of Low West German that became fused into what we call Old English. The Celts apparently retreated to what is now Scotland, Wales, Cornwall, and Ireland.

Old English at that time was almost exclusively an oral language. There was a means of writing—the Runic alphabet—but it was used only for magic spells and inscriptions. Extended writing was brought by the Roman missionaries who came to convert England to Christianity beginning about A.D. 600. King Alfred the Great, who ruled during the late 800s, had many books translated into English and commissioned a history, *The Anglo-Saxon Chronicle.* But, it was not until the 1400s when the printing press came into use that people other than nobles, those in religious orders, and clerks learned to read and write. The first dictionary to include basic words as well as unusual words and the first dictionary based on usage with dated references both appeared in the 1700s. Several grammars of English also appeared about this time.

One of the characteristics of English is the large number of words that do not come from Germanic roots. Most of these borrowed words come from Latin, Greek, French, or Scandinavian languages. The Scandinavian words entered English at the time of the Viking raids in the 800s. English received an infusion of Latin words twice: once with the Roman missionaries, who by A.D. 700 had made England a center of scholarship in which most writing was in Latin, and then in the 1500s during the English Renaissance. Many Greek words also entered English during the Renaissance. The borrowings from French came with two rulers from France—William the Conqueror in 1066 and Henry III in 1216.

In addition to the development of a written language and the borrowing of many words from other languages, changes in English syntax have also occurred. Old English had word endings or inflections to indicate gender, tense, case, and so forth. These endings began to disappear as an established word order developed in the 1300s and 1400s, and there are very few left today. There have also been significant sound changes, the most important of which occurred between 1450 and 1650, called the Great Vowel Shift. Prior to this time vowels were pronounced much as they are in modern French or Spanish, and short and long vowels had the same general sound, distinguished simply by the length of time they were held. After the vowel shift, the long vowels had the sounds we associate with them today and the short vowels have quite different sounds. Unfortunately, the vowel shift took place after the development of the printing press, which had set the spelling of many words. Thus, the sound shift accounts for most of the inconsistency in spelling vowel sounds.

The chart that follows indicates the major historical events that affected the English language and the progression of changes in the language. Information for the chart comes primarily from L. M. Myer's *Roots of Modern English*.[1] The samples of Old English from *Beowulf*, of Middle English from Chaucer, and of Early Modern English from Shakespeare illustrate the changes that have taken place in the language throughout the last twelve centuries.

Dates	Historical Events	Influence on Language
55–54 B.C.	Britain inhabited by Celts Julius Caesar invades Britain	No English language Celtic languages and Latin spoken
A.D. 43	Roman conquest of Britain	in geographic area of Britain
409	Roman legions withdrawn Celtic inhabitants must resist Pict raids from the north and Germanic raids along east coast	

Dates	Historical Events	Influence on Language
450–650	Anglo-Saxon invasion Angles from Denmark occupy the northern two-thirds of what is now England; the Saxons from northern Germany occupy most of the southern third; a third group (Jutes?) occupies the south-west corner	OLD ENGLISH PERIOD (400–1100) All three Germanic tribes speak Low West German dialects that are mutually understandable; these fuse into what we call Old English; very little borrowing or use of Celtic Probably no written histories of this period; Runic alphabet used for magic spells and in-scriptions; literature transmit-ted orally
597	Roman missionaries begin con-verting England; St. Augustine of Canterbury sent by Gregory the Great with 40 companions	Although people illiterate, the mis-sionaries introduce extended writing; within one hundred years England becomes one of the centers of learning and scholarship; much of writing in Latin as Bede's (ca. 731) *Eccle-siastical History of the English People*, but from 650 on some poetry in English, especially in Anglian dialect
787–886	Danish Viking raids begin in northern England; from 850 or so Danes begin to make perma-nent settlements. In 886 King Alfred the Great, king of Wessex (West Saxony) stops them and by a treaty gives them the north-eastern part of England, leav-ing the southern part free. The Danes are gradually absorbed into the English population. More Danish raids in 900s and early 1000s	The Vikings destroy books that are useless to them and that they fear might contain magic spells their enemies could use against them King Alfred the Great has many books translated into English; there is an English translation of Bede's *Ecclesiastical History* and *The Anglo-Saxon Chroni-cle* is begun

---

SAMPLE OF OLD ENGLISH

"þu eart endelaf usses cynnes, Wægmund inga; ealle wyrd
thou art last remnant of our kin of-Waegumundings; all fate

forsweop mine magas to metodsceafte, eorlas on elne;
swept away my kinsmen to destiny earls in valor

ic him æfter sceal."
I them after must."

c. A.D. 700 *Beowulf*, lines 2813–2816

Dates	Historical Events	Influence on Language
1066	Norman conquest of England by William the Conqueror, who defeats King Harold at the Battle of Hastings; William gains control of all of England and organizes it into one country instead of numerous semi-independent earldoms; redivides land holdings and puts Normans and other Frenchmen in most of the important positions, both secular and religious	Norman rulers speak French and see no reason to change; some English learn French as a way to get ahead; a great many more learn at least some French words and these become a part of English
1100s	Kings and nobels consider themselves Frenchmen who have lands in England	MIDDLE ENGLISH PERIOD (1100–1500)
1204	Normandy lost to the English crown; nobles must choose between English and French holdings	
1216–1272	Henry III is King of England and imports Frenchmen from areas outside Normandy whose speech is more like Central French and unlike Norman French, especially that spoken at that time in England.	The Norman English begin to feel quite English in contrast to the new French in power; more and different French words enter the language By the late 1200s French begins to disappear as the primary language, even with the nobility
1250s	Oxford and Cambridge well established	
1350	English is used in schools	
1362	English required to be used in all lawsuits	English of this period is not a unified language, but a variety of dialects that must be translated to be understood; there is no book of grammar, no dictionary, no spelling book, and not even agreement on the alphabet Many sound changes take place; perhaps more important is the beginning of the loss of inflectional endings (to indicate gender, tense, case . . .) and the development of a standard word order
1387–1400	Chaucer's *Canterbury Tales*	Tremendous number of French words added to English vocabulary from 1200–1400; some are Norman French and some Central French

Dates	*Historical Events*	*Influence on Language*

SAMPLE OF MIDDLE ENGLISH

At nyght was come into that hostelrye
Wel nyne and twenty in a compaignye
of Sondry folk, by aventure yfalle (*aventure = chance*)
In felaweshipe, and pilgrimes were they alle,
That toward Caunterbury wolden ryde.

c. A.D. 1390 Chaucer, *Prologue to the Canterbury Tales*, lines 23–27

1400–1500	Extension of education and more secular education; by 1500 many middle-class men and women learn to read and write English	Careers as authors encouraged
1476	William Caxton sets up first printing press, and London becomes the center of printing	Establishment of conventions of writing, especially spelling London English established as the standard.
		MODERN ENGLISH PERIOD (1500–Present)
1500–1660	English Renaissance	
1642–1660	First Civil War Restoration	Many changes in pronunciation (the Great Vowel Shift) although spelling set Tremendous increase in vocabulary; borrowings from Latin, borrowings from other modern languages, revivals from middle English. This gives English many synonyms to express exact shades of meaning and words that express an idea that might take four or more "native" words to express (e.g., *conflagration:* a number of fires burning at the same time and adding to each other)

SAMPLE OF MODERN ENGLISH—ENGLISH RENAISSANCE PERIOD

But that the dread of something after death—
The undiscovered country from whose bourn
No traveller returns—puzzles the will,
And makes us rather bear those ills we have
Than fly to others that we know not of?

c. A.D. 1600 Shakespeare, *Hamlet*, Act III

Dates	Historical Events	Influence on Language
1660–1800	The authoritarian period	Throughout this period in America new vocabulary from borrowed Indian words and new things (*squash, bluff*) Development of the great difference between how people actually speak and school theory of how they should speak based on concept of a universal grammar
1670–1713	Unsuccessful attempt by Dryden and Swift to set up something in England comparable to the French Academy	
1706	Kersey edition of *The New World of English Words*	First dictionary to include basic vocabulary as well as "hard" words
1714	George I succeeds Queen Anne; he is German and does not even learn to speak English	Movement to set up an English Academy dies
1747–1755	Samuel Johnson's Dictionary	Derived from language actually used and includes meaning, dated references, and a grammatical introduction
1762	Lowth writes *Short Introduction to English Grammar*	Becomes *the* authority on what is correct; authoritarian attitude and concern for regularity rather than actual usage
1800s	Trade with the world and the establishment of the British Empire	Only about two-thirds of the population of the British Isles speak English; others are the Irish, Scottish, and Welsh Vocabulary is growing from 50,000 words in Johnson's dictionary to 450,000 in *Webster's Third New International Dictionary*
1840	Population of U.S.A. surpasses that of England and its individual characteristics affect the English language	Borrowed words from other settlers (*cookie* and *sleigh* from the Dutch) as well as from Indians
1900s	Industrial Revolution	Modern technology adds new words; compound words; acronyms like NATO; brand names like Kodak or Stetson Great changes in the meaning of older words such as *nice,* which once meant *silly,* and *deer,* which once meant any *wild animal* The main structural changes in English since the 1700s are simplification of inflections stopped, further development of

Dates	Historical Events	Influence on Language
1900s		the past and progressive verbs, and an increase in verb-adverb combinations such as *put down, put off, put out*
1932	*Current English Usage* by Leonard completed by National Council of Teachers of English	Revival of interest and acceptability in basing grammar on usage (a theory advanced by Priestly in 1761 but not accepted then); usage classified as literary, colloquial, or popular/illiterate
1952	Fries's *Structure of English*	Grammars developed that *describe* how English operates instead of *prescribing* what is correct or incorrect Structural grammar
1957–1965	Chomsky's *Syntactic Structures* and *Aspects of the Theory of Syntax*	Transformational-Generative grammar
1965–1985	Women's Rights Movement	Nonsexist language with changes in pronoun references and sexist terms (policeman → police officer) Emphasis on sociolinguistics
1990s		Research emphases on composition processes, literary response, and integrated language approaches

There is a strong relationship between historical events and changes in our language. When William the Conqueror invaded England to claim the throne, he and his entourage brought with them many French words that remain in the language. The attempt to set up an English Academy similar to the French Academy failed when George I became King of England because he never spoke English. Recent inventions have brought new words into the language. Political affairs and current events influence the language significantly. By looking down the language column, one can see the pattern of changes in English, changes that are happening today and will continue to happen.

Students are certainly not interested in memorizing historical or linguistic changes, but they are often fascinated by the history of words and how they came into our language. They enjoy making a dictionary of current slang expressions and finding out (and laughing about) slang words that were popular with their parents or grandparents. Finding out about words that have changed their meanings, where words have come from, and how they can be combined helps students develop an interest in language and vocabulary.

Concepts of Language

Some aspects of the nature of language are apparent when we examine its historical development. Other aspects need to be examined in terms of how language is used. The qualities of language affect both what we understand about variations and changes in language and how we feel about those variations and changes.

Language is *systematic*. The changes that have occurred over time are not haphazard; they occur in recognizable patterns. Although many people complain about irregularities in the phonemo-grapheme correspondences, or sound-letter relationships, actually English is very systematic. In fact, changing the spellings of words to reflect their pronunciations more closely would proliferate problems for speakers of all dialects other than the dialect chosen. Would you want everything spelled the way it would be pronounced in Great Britain?

Language is *evolving*. We are constantly adding new words for new things, making new blends like *beefalo*, and revising our sense of whether a word usage is "generally acceptable" or not. We borrow words from other languages—the *chic* look, a *chaise longue*, the *patio*, a *waffle*, *dope*, and *poppycock*. Others borrow from English too. If you listened to a German sportscast, you might hear *dribbeln*, *kicken*, *skoren*, *knockouter*, or *sprinten*. *Charm*, which used to mean only a magic spell, now signifies a compliment. A *villain* was simply a farm worker; now the term is derogatory. The fact that our language changes enables us to adapt to new things and express ourselves very precisely.

Language is *conventional*. We can communicate with each other because we agree on what words mean and what word order signifies. If we agree that the pet that barks is called a gleep, that would be fine as long as everyone called it a gleep. We all interpret *Mary Ann beat Tom* as meaning that Mary Ann did the beating and Tom was the one beaten. Because there are rules about how language works and what words mean, we can talk or write to each other and to people we have never met.

Language is *arbitrary*. There are a few words whose meaning is reflected in the word itself. These are onomatopoetic words like *swoosh* or *ping*. Most words, however, are purely arbitrary; their meaning has nothing to do with them. There is nothing "cardlike" about the word *card*.

Language is *symbolic*. We use a word or a group of words to stand for an idea. The word is not the thing, person, idea, and so forth, but only represents it.

Language is *redundant.* There are many ways to express a concept in language. English in particular uses multiple indicators of certain relationships that enable us to grasp quite easily the speaker's or writer's idea, even if we do not notice each inflection. For example, in "Jim and Paul go to their jobs right after school," there are four indications of plurality—the *and, their* instead of *his, go* instead of *goes,* and *jobs* instead of *job.* This redundancy enables us to read more quickly and listen more effectively.

These characteristics of language—that it is systematic, evolving, conventional, arbitrary, symbolic, and redundant—should help us see its nature more clearly and view more accurately the variations and changes we encounter in it when we communicate.

Functions of Language

Children's experiences with language, even from the very early stages of acquisition, help determine their view of how language is used and what it is for. A child's view of the uses of language may be quite different from that of the teacher, who sees language primarily as a means of conveying information. The child sees many uses for language: to create a new world through makebelieve, sound, and rhythm play; to express individuality; or to control behavior.

In discussing the functions of language, Halliday suggests that language is defined for the child by its uses and summarizes the models of language in terms of the child's intentions.[2]

- *Instrumental function:* Children use language to get something they want—to satisfy their material needs. We hear this when children say, "Give me that one" or "I want some milk now."
- *Regulatory function:* Used to control behavior, as the child hears, "Do what I tell you," or says, "Don't use that piece; use this one."
- *Interactional function:* Used to intervene and maintain personal relationships, or to define who is one of us and who is not. "You could use this one and I will use the other," or "Me and you could do it together."
- *Personal function:* Language expresses the child's personality. Language is a means of making public the self—the self as speaker. "I can do that best of all."
- *Heuristic function:* Uses language as a way of finding out about things by asking questions. "How does this work?" "Why did you say that?" Children also use language to find out about language, so that by school age they know what a *question* and an *answer* are, and what *knowing* and *understanding* mean.
- *Imaginative function:* Used to create a whole new world, an envi-

ronment created linguistically that is focused on sounds. Songs, chants, and play with words are examples of the imaginative function.

- *Representational function:* Language is used to communicate ideas or information. "A fireplace is a place to have a fire, not where firemen live." "That is an ant."

Let's examine a bit of conversation between two three-year-olds playing with some cars in a preschool.

Tom: That's my gold car, Bob.
Bob: No, I want it. You take the red one.
Tom: OK. Watch me. Brrr-brr. It's going to crash.
Bob: Mine's going fast too. It's fast like a rocket. Jet power.
Tom: Look out—there's a big turn up ahead. Better slow down.
Bob: Ohhhh, I'm going to crash, too. Call the ambulance.
Tom: Breaker, breaker. We need an ambulance.
Bob: Get a fire engine. We got a fire.
Tom: Ten-four. We can start to put it out. You and me, Bobby, we can put water on it. All race cars have a fire extinguisher.
Bob: I can do it. I can do like Superman. I am strong.
Tom: You hold it; I'll squirt water there.

In this brief conversation, a number of things are revealed. Both children exhibit some of their knowledge of the world. Bob knows about rockets and that they may have jet power. Tom knows about CB radios and fire extinguishers. They both use language in a variety of ways to serve different functions. Bob uses it as an instrument to get what he wants, "No, I want it" and later "Get a fire engine. We got a fire." They use it to regulate each other's behavior, "You take the red one." The interactional function is revealed with "We can start to put it out. You and me, Bobby, we can. . . ." Bob uses language in its personal function as he says, "I can do it. I can do like Superman. I am strong."

The children shift into full fantasy part way through their conversation. At first the cars represent real ones. They "rev" the engines and drive fast. Then, with the crash, the boys go into a full role-playing situation and call for the fire engine and ambulance on their CB and put the fire out. Here language serves an imaginative function. Tom also uses language in a representational way as he explains, "All race cars have a fire extinguisher." Within a short conversation, nearly all the functions of language are used.

The form that a sentence takes may or may not have anything to do with its function. It would seem that a question would automatically be either instrumental (getting something) or heuristic (finding out through questioning). A question certainly could serve either of those functions, but it could also be interactional (maintain relationships) if the question was "How are you?" or "What are you up to?" It might be regulatory (control behavior) in the case of "What did I tell you to do!" The reverse is also true; a particular function might be expressed in different ways. Suppose you feel cold and want the window closed:

> *Would you please close the window?*
> *Close the window when you get up.*
> *It seems a bit chilly to me. Does it to you?*
> *The weather certainly has changed suddenly.*
> *Would you mind if I closed the window?*

Some of these appear to be questions, some statements. Some request direct action; others are indirect. Yet all of them are intended to serve the same function. They vary in terms of directness, politeness, and authority. How we express a particular function will depend on the person or persons to whom we are talking or writing, according to relative positions of power or authority. It will depend on the social situation and our own personality or style.

This lack of one-to-one correspondence between the form of the sentence and its function can make acquiring language difficult. As their language develops structurally, children add new ways of expressing the various functions. Even very young children can express different functions while using only one- or two-word sentences. In fact, Halliday's functions are listed in the order of their appearance in children between the ages of nine months and eighteen months. With increasing age and experience, children become more fluent and can use a wider variety of structures and functions more easily. Clark and Clark maintain, "Children have to build up structure and function at the same time. As they learn more about structure, they acquire more devices with which to convey different functions. And as they learn more about function, they extend the uses to which different structures can be put."[3]

Children's image of language is very broad in terms of the possible functions it serves. Teachers need to be aware of the multiple functions of language, for they are all equally real to the child. Teachers who fail to recognize that the imaginative function is as valid for children as the representational function may fail to see the needs and opportunities inherent in a given experience. Some children may not meet the demands that school makes because they are not meeting the demands of school language. The teacher must help children develop their language in all its functions, not just concentrate on the representational function.

Talking is one way of learning and of refining one's knowledge. Tough discusses this relationship as follows:

Characteristic of the young child's learning is the need for the actual experience, the information that comes to him through senses. Talk alongside this experience may draw his attention to the important aspects of this experience, will demonstrate a relationship, perhaps, or will help him to structure the whole into something which is coherent and meaningful. Talking that is relevant to his experience may then provide the child with a meaning for the experience different from that which it would have had if it had happened without the accompanying talk.[4]

Although we refer constantly to the need for rich experience, this does not necessarily mean highly unusual experiences. Taking a walk to a nearby store or shopping area, having a room mother demonstrate candle making, or making popcorn can provide rich experiences for children if the talk is right. Talking is one of the major ways that we learn about all kinds of things, not just language.

Nonverbal Language

Communication involves being understood and understanding others. Verbal language is part of this, but nonverbal language also communicates. In fact, nonverbal cues are most often accepted as the real message when they contradict verbal language.

Nonverbal language consists of virtually everything that communicates meaning except for verbal language. It may involve the tone of voice, facial expressions, body stance or posture, gestures, the expressions of the eyes, physical distance, dress, or even the omission of words or deeds. A brief aversion of the eyes or body shift can indicate disagreement or boredom. A lift of the chin and opening of the eyes may show a spark of interest. Some nonverbal language—a gesture of the finger meaning *come* or a narrowing of the eyes to say *no*—is used intentionally. Other nonverbal cues are given without our awareness. This often happens as we try to mask our real feelings with verbal language. Our unawareness of the cue is no indication at all, however, that the cue is not being noticed and responded to.

Relationship of Verbal and Nonverbal Behavior

Nonverbal behavior can add to verbal communication, supplement it, or substitute for it. Knapp lists six ways in which verbal and nonverbal behavior interrelate:

1. *Repeating.* Nonverbal behavior simply repeats what is communicated orally. Pointing to an area while saying "It's there." is an example of this.
2. *Contradicting.* What one says may be contradicted by one's nonverbal communication. Saying "That's good." in an automatic fashion without the corresponding nonverbal enthusiasm reflects this contradiction.
3 *Substituting.* Often a nonverbal message can be used in place of a verbal one. A pat on the back, a smile, and a wink all tell a child that he or she has done well.
4. *Complementing.* Nonverbal messages can elaborate or modify the verbal message. Children's anger can be reflected in the distance from the teacher they take and in the stiffness of their bodies.
5. *Accenting.* The nonverbal message may accent the verbal in much the same way we may underline a word in a letter we're writing. Often this is done with gestures and head movements.
6. *Regulating.* Nonverbal behaviors help to regulate conversation, indicating who is to speak next and so forth.[5]

While the functions of nonverbal behavior are separated here into six categories, they are often inseparable, and one nonverbal behavior may serve more than one function. Pointing to the door while saying "You are excused." repeats the verbal behavior while accenting it. Maintaining honesty and giving complementary rather than contradictory verbal and nonverbal messages is an important aspect of teaching.

Areas of Nonverbal Communication

There are many different ways that we communicate nonverbally. Wiemann and Wiemann suggest four areas of nonverbal communication: the environment and personal space, body movement and orientation, the face and eyes, and nonlanguage behavior.[6] All these relate to aspects of classroom instruction.

The Environment and Personal Space
In school, the environmental factors that are important are the room arrangement and placement of furniture. By altering the room arrangement, the teacher can alter the likelihood that students will participate. A circle or semicircle may encourage children to talk to one another. Sitting in rows facing the teacher focuses attention on the teacher as director. Personal space has to do with how close you want to get to others. Americans generally converse at about arm's length— 1½ to 4 feet. Children tend to sit closest to each other and adolescents

moderately close; adults are more comfortable at the farthest distances. Any number of factors may alter the distances with which people are comfortable, such as the topic of conversation, physical elements like the amount of noise or light, and the relationship between the speakers.

Body Movement and Orientation

Much nonverbal communication is conveyed through gestures, body movement, and orientation. Gestures may substitute for verbal language as when a crook of the finger motions someone to go to the person gesturing or a shake of the head sharply signals "No!" They may add to our meaning as we motion appropriately while saying, "Left to right." Body movement—the way we lean toward someone, for example, or how we sit—conveys messages about tension and liking.

The Face and Eyes

There are certain cues that we transmit with our face or eyes that are somewhat constant and convey an impression. Hair style and grooming are two examples. Most nonverbal communication related to the face and eyes, however, is related to the emotions we express. Researchers in this area have identified six basic emotions—disgust, fear, sadness, happiness, anger, and surprise—and contend that other emotions are combinations of the display features of these six. [Display features in the face are (1) cheeks and mouth, (2) brows and forehead, and (3) eyes and eyelids.] Some of these basic emotions appear to be cross-cultural; that is, the same facial expression conveys the same emotion to peoples from widely divergent cultures.

Eye signals are very important in communicating interest, showing attention, signaling a desire to talk, avoiding interaction, and making a statement about a relationship. Teachers can signal students that they should talk by a look, and children often avoid being called on by not looking directly at the teacher. Students who look directly at the teacher while he or she is explaining something are assumed to be "paying attention."

Nonlanguage Vocal Behavior

The vocal cues that accompany language but which do not have specific content are often called *paralanguage*. They include such things as pitch and tempo, clearing the throat or whispering, yelling, moaning, the intensity of speech, and fillers such as *ummm*, *uhh*, or *er*. Some nonlanguage vocal behavior—such as using the fillers noted above, changing a sentence in midpoint, repeating words, and stuttering—indicate anxiety. Using fillers such as *ah* may provide time for thinking and serve as a way to keep the floor.

An understanding of nonverbal language is extremely important because children's nonverbal language system may differ from the teacher's, which may cause a serious lack of communication. Teachers who are aware of nonverbal cues may use the cues to change the personal interrelationships in the classroom and encourage communication from children.

Teachers who work with children of various cultural groups need to understand the meanings their own nonverbal cues project and to interpret the nonverbal messages they receive from their students. An obvious illustration of this is eye contact. Suburban children habitually maintain eye contact with the teacher to project attention and respect. In Southwestern Indian cultures, however, children lower their heads and eyes to show deference and respect. Nonverbal behavior of children in inner-city schools may be interpreted as rude or insolent when it is not intended that way at all. The more aware a teacher is of the nonverbal behavior of students, the more effective the communication between teacher and students.

Teachers may use their knowledge of nonverbal communication to enhance communication and interaction in their classrooms. To illustrate, consider space and distance—two areas of obvious importance in the classroom. In the traditional classroom the teacher's desk is at the front of the class with the students' desks in rows facing it. The teacher's territory is the area around the desk, from the desk to the board, and from the desk to the first row of pupils. Galloway comments, "More imaginative, fluid arrangements of desks and furniture influence the potential meaning of a learning context."[7] Distance is often maintained by staying in one's own territory or by setting up a table or some other object as a divider. Intentionally removing these can establish closeness, rapport, and more interaction. Physical arrangement of the room, therefore, reveals how a teacher feels about interaction and communication in the classroom. A number of other nonverbal cues will encourage communication: a smile or nod to show enjoyment or agreement, a warm greeting or praise, vocal intonation and inflection patterns that indicate approval and support, a spontaneous attempt to help a pupil, the maintaining of eye contact when listening, and a stance of alert attention. These suggest interest and enthusiasm on the part of the teacher and tend to motivate, setting up the situation for success.

Nonverbal language is not something to be taken lightly. Because it is so subtle, it is very difficult to fake. Perhaps the most important factor in nonverbal communication is that it must be congruent with verbal behavior and with other aspects of nonverbal communication. Just saying "Good!" or "That's fine" is not communicating success unless the voice and the facial expression are saying the same thing.

Dialects of English

Dialects are variations of a language. Speaking a dialect other than the one most frequently used in a particular place or situation means differences in language—but only differences, not deficiencies. The English language is composed of a group of dialects that overlap, and so the dialect spoken in one area is understandable to speakers of a neighboring dialect. Speakers of dialects several regions apart, however, may experience some difficulty in understanding each other. Ashley and Malmstrom suggest that a language is a composite structure of overlapping idiolects, or speech patterns of an individual at a particular time of life.[8]

Dialects are usually determined by geographic regions or areas, although social factors also affect dialects. This is particularly evident when a group of people from one region come to live in a different geographic area but continue to associate mostly with each other for social or economic reasons.

We tend to think that the way we ourselves speak is the right way, and that others are either "affected" or "ignorant." This is partly because we don't really have a clear understanding of dialect variation and partly because the way we speak is such an intrinsic part of ourselves. Somehow we just wouldn't be the same people if we spoke quite differently. Would you be you if you didn't sound like yourself?

In discussing whether one dialect is better than another, we have to define *better*. Better in what way? For the general purposes of communication, no one dialect is better than another. Each dialect is capable of expressing the thoughts of the speaker as well as another. Each particular dialect is also the best way of communicating with other speakers of that dialect. There are, however, some dialects that have greater social acceptability than others. Right or wrong, this is the situation today; and many who wish to become accepted by a different group must alter their language to be accepted. Eliza Doolittle of *My Fair Lady* must change her language to be accepted as a duchess instead of being marked as a flower girl. Perhaps this will change; perhaps it is already changing. Certainly we had several distinct dialects reflected in the language of three consecutive presidents during the 1950s and 1960s—Presidents Eisenhower, Kennedy, and Johnson. There is also a trend in radio and television to drop the single-style national network English for more individualistic language in announcers and performers.

Before discussing the teacher's role in working with children who speak less socially acceptable dialects, let's examine some of the causes for dialect variation in the United States and the kinds of variation that exist in dialects. There are five major dialect regions in this country: the coastal New England region, the northern region, the north midland region, the south midland region, and the southern region. The dialect regions do not follow state boundaries, since those boundaries do not reflect two of the basic reasons for dialect divergence—patterns of original settlement and patterns of migration. Examine the map in Figure 7-1, which illustrates the major dialect regions.

The dialect regions indicate that a person from northern Georgia or Alabama has a dialect more similar to someone from southern Ohio or Indiana than to someone from Florida. Someone from upper New York State would sound more like someone from Wisconsin than someone from southern New Jersey. In today's highly mobile society, however, many individuals have a unique dialect, which is the result of having lived in several areas or having participated in several social contexts. If you examine a map that shows physical features, the division of regions begins to look quite sensible. If you add to it the original settlement areas and trace the migrations westward, the dialect regions make even more sense. Another great influence on dialect patterns has been the impact of major cities on the surrounding area. Cities such as New York, Philadelphia, Charleston, Chicago, St. Louis, New Orleans, and San Francisco were important cultural centers as well as the focus of later immigrations.

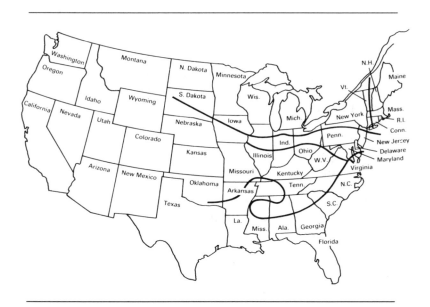

FIGURE 7.1 *The five major dialect regions of the United States*

How Dialects Differ

Just as there are three major areas of contrast in describing a language, the same contrasts describe dialects. There may be *phonological* differences, or differences in pronounciation; *lexical* or *semantic* differences, which involve specific vocabulary; and *syntactic* differences, which involve the addition or omission of words or inflections and changes in the order of words.

The most frequent differences are phonological ones. These differences in pronunciation are very obvious to even a casual listener. They seldom cause real difficulty in understanding, but may cause difficulties in reading—particularly in the area of phonics instruction. Two words that are pronounced differently in one dialect may be homonyms in another. *Pin* and *pen* may be pronounced the same or distinctly differently; *merry, Mary,* and *marry* can be homonyms, or the first two may be pronounced the same, or none of the three may sound alike.

The next most frequent dialect difference occurs in the lexical items used. A carbonated beverage is called many different things: in Rochester, New York—*pop;* in Queens, New York—*soda;* in Boston—*tonic;* in Georgia—*Coke.* A small river may be called any of the following: *creek, stream, brook, run, branch, fork, prong, gulf, binnekill, binacle, rivulet, gutter, kill, bayou,* or *burn.*[9] These differences in words denoting particular things will not usually cause difficulties in understanding.

The least frequent difference is in the syntactic area. When syntactic differences do occur, though, they usually cause real difficulty in comprehension. In Spanish-influenced English, *no* is used before a verb if the verb is followed by a negative word, as in "Sarah no talk to no one." In Afro-American English the inverted word order is used for indirect as well as direct questions, as in "I want to know is he going somewhere." The apparent absence of the possessive *-'s* in this same dialect, as in "My aunt house," may be a syntactic difference, or it may be, as some linguists suggest, simply a difference in pronunciation. The addition of words is exemplified in some dialects: "I might could give you that" in the South, and "The Mr. Smith is here" or "on the Grand Avenue" in Spanish-influenced English.[10]

Features of Black English and Spanish-Influenced English

Teachers in the United States often have students in their classes who speak a black English dialect or whose dialect reflects Spanish. Understanding how these dialects differ is important, especially in helping children to read and spell, and in developing good attitudes toward children who speak differently from their teacher. Since lexical items change so much from place to place and from child to child, these are not listed. They are relatively easy for a teacher to identify. The major phonological and syntactic differences are described below.[11] (Arrows point to the change made.)

Features of Black Dialect

Phonological

Vowels:

1. Omission of glide with long vowels and diphthongs
   ride → rod   oil → all
2. Addition of glide with short vowels
   sit → /siyat/

Consonants:

3. Absence of *r* and *l*
   Paris → pass
4. Absence of final /t/ and /d/
   band → ban   He played ball → He play ball
5. Use of substitutes for *th*
   then → den   nothing → nufin
6. Use of substitutes for nasals, /n/ for /ŋ/
   going → goin

Syntactic

Verb constructions:

1. Nonstandard verb forms
   said → say   were → was   gave → give
2. Perfect construction inflections
   I have walked → I have walk (see also item 4 under "Phonological")
3. Overcorrection of present tense to first and second persons
   -s added: *I walks, you walks,* etc.
4. Expression of future by *gonna* or *goin'* and contracted *will*
   I gonna, he goin', and *I'll go → I go*
5. Use of invariant *be* for habitual actions
   He is busy → He be busy

Other constructions:

6. Inverted word order for indirect questions
   I wonder if he is going → I wonder is he going

7. Negation: use of double negatives and *ain't* as a negative
   He ain't going nowhere → *He didn't do no work*

Features of Spanish-Influenced English

Phonological

Vowels:

1. Use of long vowel sounds for both long and short English vowels
   sit →*seat*   *bet* → *bait*   *bat* → *bait*   *nut* → *not*
   caught → *coat*   *full* → *fool*

Consonants:

2. Use of substitutes for nine English consonants that do not occur
   in Spanish
   v (*very*)   j (*judge*)   z (*zoo*)   sh (*ship*)   ng (*song*)
   zh (*measure*)   th (*with*)   th (*then*)   r (*real*)
3. Omission of certain consonant sounds at ends of words
   All consonants except *d, s, l, r, n,* and *y*
4. Pronunciation of *s* in consonant clusters as a separate syllable
   spot → *es-pot*, and so forth
   sp-   *st-*   *sk-*   *sl-*   *sm-*   *sn-*   *sw-*   *spl-*
   spr-   *str-*   *skr-*   *skw*

Lexical

Although many words are similar in both Spanish and English
(cognates like *segundo-second* and *especial-special*), there are
many Spanish words that look like English words but mean something quite different (false cognates like *pan: bread,* or *fabrica:
factory*)

Syntactic

1. Omission of verb endings, third person singular and past tense,
   and omission of auxiliaries and related inflections
   He plays ball
   He played ball   } → *He play ball*
   He does play ball
2. Omission of some subject pronouns since Spanish verbs have
   pronounlike endings
   Is it red? → *Is red?*   *He is the one* → *Is the one.*
3. Use of double negatives (Spanish places *no* before the verb when a
   negative follows)
   They went nowhere → *They no went nowhere*

4. Omission or inappropriate use of contractions
   I'm going → I going   *Yes, I am → Yes, I'm*
5. Omission of possessive and plural -s
   dogs → dog   *girl's coat → girl coat*
6. Incorrect use of gender references (Spanish gender agrees with the noun modified)
   the table . . . she
7. Use of the definite article with person and place names
   the Miss Watson   *It is on the Prince Avenue*
8. Use of the wrong preposition (In Spanish *en* could be *on, in, at, into, to, for,* and *about*)
   The book is at the table

Considerations for the Classroom

There is no problem in dealing with children who speak a dialect divergent from the teacher's if the dialect they speak is equally socially acceptable. Thus, a teacher from the Midwest who teaches in suburban Boston or Providence does not feel any need to alter the dialect patterns of children in the class even though they are quite different. The problem arises when the teacher is faced with children who speak a different dialect that is not as socially acceptable.

Three factors must be considered in deciding what to do about dialect differences in such a situation. First, teachers need to remember that for purposes of communication no dialect is better than any other, and that each is best for communicating with its own speakers. Second, the way one speaks and the dialect one uses are an integral part of each person. This is particularly true of young children who do not have much knowledge and understanding of the world outside their own family and neighborhood. Teachers who try to change the language used by elementary school children are in essence saying that the way the teacher talks is right and the way the children and their parents talk is wrong. Finally, although some dialects are less acceptable universally in business or social contexts, a person can add a second dialect or change a present dialect as a result of a rational and conscious effort to do so. When children or young adults indicate that they want to change their dialect or learn another dialect, then the teacher can help.

This does not mean that a teacher doesn't need to know about dialects or doesn't have to deal with dialect differences. The teacher must be able to determine exactly what differences exist and how those differences affect the child's understanding of reading and writing instruction. Just as most of us learn to write the *k* in *knot* that we don't pronounce, some children will have to learn to write the *'s* on *aunt* in *my aunt's house.* Phonic programs for reading instruction based on one dialect may not fit the pronunciation patterns of another dialect. Most important at both the intellectual and the action level, teachers need to accept the idea that differences in dialect are only differences and not ignorant, immature, or defective speech.

Language Usage

Language usage has to do with the choices we make among the options available. It involves variations that are primarily social in nature, the etiquette of language. Do you say "can hardly see" or "can't hardly see?" Would you write "I only wanted one, but I received three" or "I wanted only one, but I received three." Would you correct (or want to correct) someone who said, "The four reporters settled the questions between them." What if a child said, "He did it good" or "I'll play if he don't want to." What you choose to say will depend to some extent on your audience, and on whether you are speaking or writing. (Can you imagine saying, "I shall await your reply.") It will also depend on how formal, how "proper," you want your language to be. What do you say when you answer the telephone and the caller asks for you? (1) "This is she (he) speaking." (2) "This is (name)." (3) "This is her (him)." (4) "Yes?" Somehow saying "This is he (she)" seems artificial, strange, but "This is him (her)" doesn't sound right either. Probably your mother and some of your teachers made you say "May I" when asking for permission, rather than "Can I." Do you still do that? Always? Most people adapt their language to the situation, changing some usage forms as language changes.

Traditional school grammar attempted to dictate "correct" usage by tying usage choices to grammatical constructions. Thus, usage becomes very prescriptive. Originally, good usage was the language used by people who were well educated and politically, socially, or economically powerful. Starting in the seventeenth century, grammarians set the rules that are often taught today even though they do not reflect actual practice. For example, traditional grammar teaches that *like* is a preposition, not a conjunction ("That is just like me.") although it is often used as a conjunction in advertising and common speech ("tastes good like a cigarette should," "tell it like it is," or ("Nobody will miss her like I shall"—Dickens). Today, we appear to be returning to the earlier concept of usage and accepting the language of well educated and politically, socially, or economically powerful individuals as a guide to appropriate usage. In recent writing the terms applied to usage more often relate to appropriateness than to correct and incorrect usage. In fact, there is seldom a simple two-part division, a right and wrong. Usage is "better in this situation" or "less appropriate here."

Usage might be categorized as (1) *informal*—relaxed talk or writing with close friends, (2) *conventional*—some attention paid to formal conventions in either speech or writing, and (3) *formal*—carefully planned speech or formal writing situations. In informal usage situations we do not monitor our talk or writing; we don't worry about correctness at all. This is typically talk with close friends or quick notes or letters to someone we know well. Conventional usage is what we use in most situations with people who are not close friends, people we want to think well of us. This is the talk of a group in a discussion, an informal meeting, a class. It is the writing of letters to people we do not know well, business letters, simple reports, and invitations. Formal language is used in a term paper or thesis, a speech given to a large group on a formal occasion, or the wording on an engraved invitation. It is carefully planned ahead of time, rewritten and revised to make use of formal oratorical devices.

Look at the following sentences and see how you would judge them in terms of usage. Are they unacceptable, informal, conventional, or formal?

1. He worked hard to carefully document their work.
2. If everybody would join, they could win the award.
3. That was a long assignment to read, and there's ten questions to answer.
4. John went with Miss Jackson and myself to get the materials.
5. I don't see how this data can help us decide.

The potential problems in these sentences are: (1) the split infinitive (*to carefully document*); (2) *everybody* is singular and so the pronoun *they* should also be singular (*he or she*); (3) *there's* is a contraction of *there is*, but with ten questions following, it shoud be *there are*; (4) *myself* is used as an object of a preposition instead of *me*, perhaps a way of avoiding a decision between *I* and *me*; and (5) the word *data* is plural (singular form is *datum*) and so would be modified by *these*. You can judge for yourself what you would accept in less than formal situations. You will also need to decide which usage forms you will teach depending on your sense of how they are regarded in your community.

Most children's usage choices are a reflection of the language used in their home and immediate environment. There are also regional differences in preferred usage, as well as socioeconomic differences. The amount of formal education of the adults in a child's surroundings determines to some extent the choices that an individual child makes. If a family is bilingual, the other language will influence the child's patterns of English usage. The purpose of instruction should be to help children make usage choices that are appropriate for a particular situation.

Teaching More Appropriate Usage Patterns

When working with students on more standard or more formal usage, several principles are important. Pooley suggests that the teacher must size up each class, noting which usage patterns might need to be worked on. Children must be stimulated to become observers of language—their own and others—and motivated to add to their repertoire more formal usage patterns. Instruction must be part of the natural uses of language, not exercises that divorce language usage from communication for a purpose. Finally, since students learn usage from hearing language, oral practice is preferable. This may be accomplished through storytelling, language games, creative dramatics and role playing, oral reports, and so forth.[12]

Teachers in elementary grades often hear hundreds of "nonstandard" usages, but to be successful can correct only a few. Which ones should teachers concentrate on? Pooley suggests the following:

Speech Forms Subject to Intensive Teaching in Elementary Grades

Verb Forms

ain't or *hain't*
I don't have *no*
learn me a song
leave me go
have ate, *have* did, etc.
he *begun*, he *seen*, he *run*, he *drunk*, he *come*, etc.
I *says*
he *brung*, he *clumb*
we, you, they *was*
was *broke* (broken), was *froze*
knowed, growed, etc.

Pronoun Forms

my brother, *he* (and other double subjects)
him and *me* went, Mary and *me* saw, etc.
hisself, theirselves, etc.
them books, *this here* book, *that there* book
it's *yourn, hern, hisn, ourn*[13]

Similar suggestions are made for the junior high school. Teachers should choose items for instruction that are widely used in the class and that they believe will cause students the severest penalties. An abbreviated list of Pooley's suggestions follows.

Speech Forms for the Junior High School

Pronouns

Will you wait for John and *I*? Let him and *I* do the work.
Us boys want to go.
This is the man *which* did it.

Double Negatives

He *don't have none* . . .
Haven't you never been . . .
Jane don't have no pen.
I haven't nothing to do.

Verb Forms

Irregular past tense forms like *begun, brung, done, drunk, give, run, says, seen, have ate, has began, have broke, have drank,* etc.

Agreement with subject

One of the books *are* lost.
Each of them *are* interesting.
He *don't* play chess.

Other:

You *had ought* to do that.
He *set* in the chair.

Adjectives and Adverbs

a apple
them boys
these kind, *those* kind

Miscellaneous

If he'd *of* come, would *of* come, should *of* come (a spelling error for *have* or *'ve*)[14]

Junior high school or middle school teachers should also use any items from the elementary school list that students persist in using in more formal situations (in school talk).

Using Nonsexist Language

One of the more dramatic changes in American English has taken place in the last twenty to twenty-five years. Nonsexist language is now required by most publishers and requested by many organizations. It is an attempt to treat men and women primarily as people and to focus on shared humanity rather than on gender differences. Neither men or women should be stereotyped.

In language this has affected particularly two aspects of usage: pronoun references to a word that is meant to represent either a male or a female, and words that use *man* alone or as an affix. Traditionally, we used "he" to refer to an unspecified male or female. ("The teacher should do his best to . . .," or "Each student has his own . . .".) Many people now believe that it is fairer to avoid using the male pronoun in such situations. This may be done in several different ways: (1) use plurals ("Teachers should do their best . . ."), (2) use *you* ("You should do your best . . ."), (3) use *he or she* or *his or her* ("The teacher should do his or her best . . ."), or (4) reword to avoid ("The teacher's responsibility is . . ."). It takes little effort to use nonsexist language and thus formally include girls and women in speech and writing.

The use of words containing *man* or *men* as a part of the word is perhaps more difficult to change. Suggestions follow for alternatives for some gender-biased words.

Term	*Alternate Term*
mankind	people, human beings
manmade	artificial, manufactured
the best man for . . .	the best person or candidate for
manpower	workers, human energy
mailman	mail carrier
policeman	police officer
salesman	sales clerk or representative
cameraman	camera operator
chairman	chair, chairperson

Beware of making assumptions about the sex of people in particular roles if you want boys and girls to have the widest possible career options. Avoid, for example, "the secretary and her . . .", "the nurse and her . . .", or "the teachers and her . . .". While there may be more women than men in these occupations, many businesses have a male secretary, hospitals have many fine male nurses, and there are a great many male teachers—even in elementary schools. The reverse is equally sexist ("the principal . . . he," or "the breadwinner and his earnings," or "the lawyer and his client"). There are many women principals, and the breadwinners in many families are single mothers or wives as well as husbands. Nearly half of the students in law school today are women.

It may seem trivial or unimportant to you to use nonsexist language, but research has shown that children—especially girls—do see restrictions on what they can do or on which jobs are available to them. Boys too are often channeled away from jobs that they would enjoy and find fulfilling because of stereotypes reinforced by our language. Each person should have the widest possible choice of activities and career opportunities without reference to gender. If changing the language to reflect nonsexist attitudes will help, it is a worthy objective.

Opportunities for Usage Experiences in Oral Language

There are several ways in which children can become familiar with varying choices in usage. Very young children can be given the chance to become involved in dramatic play. As they play the father, mother, or police officer, they assume the language that is appropriate to that person's situation. Teachers may raise the quality of the dramatic play by adding props such as hats and costumes to the play area, or by intervening with questions that will extend children's thinking about the role or situation. At this stage the children are involved in exploring situations, which is not the time for the teacher to give instruction about what they should say or how they should say it.

Older students can work with role playing. As they are active in taking on various roles, the teacher can discuss what kinds of talk a doctor uses, what a teenager would say, or how a musician or judge would express an idea. Role playing can place the individual in a variety of situations that call for changes in language. What would parents say to their best friend about their child's misbehavior? To the school principal? To the child? How would someone tell about a bad test grade to parents, to friends, or to the teacher? How would you report an accident you had seen to the police officer; how would it be reported on the evening television news; how would you tell it to friends? Using role-playing situations and language changes to create believability in a particular character is both an interesting and an effective way to deal with various usage patterns.

There are also opportunities for working with usage patterns within the framework of classroom discussions and presentations. This is particularly true for children who have had little exposure to formal usage. In informal classroom discussions or conversations, usage choices reveal informality. As you move into presentational discussions, such as round-table or panel discussions, there is a call for a somewhat more formal language. By helping children make distinctions about the formality of the situation, the kind of group involved in the discussion, and the appropriateness of particular usage items, you are helping children grow in their ability to select appropriate usage for particular situations.

Teachers should make clear in any usage lesson that while a word or phrase may be okay in home talk or talk with close friends, it may not be acceptable in formal talk or school talk. Be sensitive to the fact that many dialect-related usages are not the usage patterns of conventional or formal English. This is true of double-negatives "I don't have no . . ."), which are difficult for native Spanish speakers whose language often uses two words to indicate a negative. It is also true in Black dialects of noun-pronoun combinations ("My sister she . . .") and of some irregular past-tense verb forms. However you describe conventional usage, it is important not to counter the students' home and family language.

Teachers often plan instruction on a particular usage item if a number of their students use it inappropriately. Some teachers use a daily oral skills lesson to work on such usage. They present the problem on the chalkboard or on an overhead transparency and ask students to identify errors. In the daily oral language lesson the problem is presented in a sentence or a few sentences. The teacher discusses the usage item with the children, and they discuss what is wrong. The teacher corrects the usage item in sentences, and the students copy the corrected sentences, as in the following examples.

Wrong:

We *was going* over to Jake's house.
Did you say *you was* going with us.
They was going out for ice cream.

Okay:

We *were* going over to Jake's house.
Did you say *you were* going with us?
They were going out for ice cream.

In the discussion, the teacher should point out that with the words *we, you,* and *they,* one uses *were* in school talk; with *I, he, she* and *it was* is used. If the students are familiar with the terms *singular* and *plural,* you could use them in the explanation (although you run into the problem that *you* singular uses *were* as well as *you* plural). It certainly is not necessary to use grammatical terms. *We, you,* and *they* go with *were; I, she, he,* and *it* go with *was.* Make a chant of it; dramatize it. Have three children stand on one side of the room, including a boy and a girl. One child says, "I was," the boy points to the girl and says, "She was," and then the girl points back and says, "He was." On the other side of the room arrange the rest of the class in three groups. One group says, "We were," the second group points to the third group and says, "You were," and the third group points to the other two groups and says, "They were." Do it rhythmically, "I was (clap, clap); she was (clap, clap)" and so forth. Soon it is a game and fun to do, and the conventional form begins to sound right.

Usage items can also be taught inductively using the daily oral language lesson format by presenting sentences with the target word *were* used correctly: What is different about these and the other sentences? When do you use *were* and when do you use *was*? Can you make a rule for this? Now let's try some practice sentences.

Be careful not to say flatly that a given word or phrase is wrong. Probably some of the children's parents, friends, and family all use it, and there is no need to make children choose between teacher and family. Besides, technically it is not "wrong," just "inappropriate." Making distinctions between home talk and school talk or between talk with friends and talk with others can help children become more flexible in their choices. Asking, "How would you say that in school talk?" will often elicit the form you prefer.

Opportunities for Usage Experiences in Written Language

Several kinds of work in written language provide children with opportunities to select among options in usage. These activities are more appropriate for older children for several reasons. Younger children are more involved in simply getting their ideas into written language, and making fine distinctions in written usage becomes too much of a task. Working with the teacher on group stories or recordings of events does help younger children make distinctions between the oral and written modes of expression. Written language is not merely talk written down; there are conventions in writing that do not exist in oral expression, and there are ways of expressing ideas orally that have no parallel in writing.

The teacher can help older students take into account whether the audience is known or unknown, and what the purpose of the writing is, and then determine suitable usage selections. A teacher can structure opportunities for writing that call for various registers of language to be used. Instead of isolated practice that has little meaning, there are real writing situations that call for realistic choices.

Students can assume roles in writing much as they might take roles in oral dramatizing. An event from a story or from real life may be described from several viewpoints. Children who have read *Bridge to Terabithia* might describe Leslie's accident as it would have been reported in the newspaper, as a diary entry by one of his friends, or as Mrs. Myers would have written about it to her daughter.[15] The dedication or improvement of a nature trail or of some new playground equipment for the school might be described by children in a thank you letter to the parents' group who had developed it, in an article for the school system's monthly newsletter, or in letters to their pen pals in another part of the country.

Letter writing offers an opportunity for variations in language usage. A few examples are letters to business concerns ordering free or inexpensive materials for their classroom and letters to a favorite author or to pen pals. Some may want to write to former classmates who have moved away. Although teachers would not necessarily proofread or correct *personal* letters, they can give guidance before the writing period about the kinds of language that might be appropriate. In writing business letters the teacher may want to go over the draft of the letter before it is recopied and sent. Guidance in the prewriting period can be extremely helpful to students when doing this type of letter writing.

Students in the upper grades would be doing some written reporting. At times this may involve describing firsthand observations or the results of a survey or experiment. They might also collect recipes or directions for making something as part of a unit of study. All these reporting situations call for variations in usage.

As children participate in the usage area in either oral or written formats, there are several important principles to remember. Children's language reflects their strong emotional and linguistic ties to family and close friends. There is rarely a way to change language patterns without saying or implying that the teacher is right and family and friends are wrong. The initial goal of the teacher is to develop security in expressing ideas. It is the content of the talk or writing that is important. If children want to change their language at a later time, for whatever reason, they may. In the elementary and middle school, though, the objective is more *fluent* and *flexible* uses of language to express ideas. Viewing usage as a range of choices dependent upon the situation leads children to accept their familiar language and that of other children and adults as variations instead of levels of correctness. Teachers build in choices based on knowledge of how people use language in various situations.

Registers of Language

Three dimensions of variations occur in language: (1) geographical variations—dialect; (2) social variations—usage; and (3) individual variations—registers. Registers overlap to some extent with the other two kinds of variations since each speaker speaks a dialect and reacts to social considerations and education in the usage patterns preferred. Registers of language are patterns of language the individual speaker chooses to use. Register involves considerations of the mode of discourse—oral or written—and of the style or degree of formality. It takes into account the field of discourse (politics or shopping or whatever) and the interaction of the individual's dialect with the mode, style, and field of discourse.

Reflected in the concept of register is the fact that speaking a particular dialect will affect the span of choices available within a particular situational context. This is especially important for teachers to recognize because it explains many of the language differences among children who speak different dialects in the classroom. It accounts for some of the observations that researchers unfamiliar with register variations have made about particular dialect groups. For example, many of the comparative studies of the language of white and black children did not take into account the situation in which the black children were speaking and the kind of language that would be appropriate for them to use in this register in their dialect. The same physical situation is no guarantee of sameness in language because what is appropriate language behavior for one dialect-speaking group in a given situation is not necessarily appropriate behavior for speakers of another dialect.

Children are aware of the need to vary their language depending on particular situations. Even very young children take on different vocabulary, intonations, and sentence structures when playing adult roles. Listen to preschoolers playing house or primary school children playing school. Their language reflects their knowledge about how adults act in those roles. Older children are more adept at making changes in their language. In talking with each other they may say "bugs and stuff" and then change that wording to "insects and other things" when reporting their group's discussion to the teacher and the rest of the class. Adults, too, make similar changes in their language depending on the situation. A teacher may report to the principal or parent that a child "has very little self-control." This same teacher may say to peers or friends that the child "is driving me crazy with all the pushing and hitting."

Many teachers are startled at some of the language used by children in their class who speak a dialect significantly different from their own. This is especially true of younger children who are less aware of appropriate changes to make from an intimate family and friends situation to the more formal classroom situation. Their intent is not to shock or to be unruly; they simply have selected language inappropriate for use in the classroom because of their immaturity and lack of experience. If the teacher can remain calm and suggest that the language they have used is fine in certain situations, but is not appropriate in this situation, the incident becomes useful instruction instead of rejection.

English as a Second Language

In many parts of the United States there are children in our schools whose native language is not English and whose cultural traditions are not American. They must be helped to live in an English-speaking society, but not at the price of alienation from their family and native culture. These children need many of the experiences with language that all children need—opportunities to do or see or hear something and to talk about it. They need an environment rich in English language structures and vocabulary and opportunities to use language in various ways.

Education for children who are bilingual—those who have some language abilities in two languages—usually necessitates recognizing biculturalism. A bicultural component would involve a teacher knowledgeable in the history and culture of the pupil's home language, recognition of the contributions of the child's home culture in all subject areas, and material dealing with that culture and history included in the curriculum.[16]

Bilingual education and the acquisition of English as a second language is discussed at length in Chapter 4, "Acquiring Language." In terms of linguistic variation, people who do not speak English as their first language often retain traces of their first language when they speak or write English. In working with children who are acquiring English as a second language, we need to focus attention on developing fluency and expressing meaning. The conventional patterns of usage are much less important than understanding and communicating with another person.

It is helpful to know something of the patterns of the child's native language to be aware of possible confounding aspects of the two languages. As mentioned in the section on usage earlier in this chapter, native Spanish speakers often use double negatives. This would be expected of French speakers also because both languages use a *no* or *ne* in front of the verb and another negative following it. For example, "I don't know, I know nothing" is "Je **ne** sais **pas**" in French and "Yo **no** se **nada**" in Spanish. It would certainly be understandable for speakers of these languages to say "I don't know nothing."

Another area of differences is in pronunciation. There are many more pronunciation differences than syntactic ones between two languages. Sometimes these variations in how to pronounce words cause the French or Spanish speaker, for example, to make homonyms out of words that are not pronounced similarly in English. In both French and Spanish the letter *i* is pronounced as in *eat* (long *e*.) This makes the word *ship* sound like *sheep* or *pick* like *peak*. Other languages present other pronunciation difficulties. If you know a little about the native language of the children in your class, you will be aware of these usage patterns and can be more helpful to your students. You will also understand the confusion children are experiencing in their attempts to make sense of the two languages.

In elementary schools, children who are not yet proficient in English language skills should be taught within their native language to attain literacy while instruction in English oral skills is begun. The final goal of the program is literacy in English. Such an approach values the child's home language and culture while developing the skills to progress in the English language community also.

Summary

This chapter highlighted some of the kinds of variations that occur in English—historical, linguistic, geographical, and social. Examining the development of English from the time of the withdrawal of the Roman legions and the invasions from the European mainland by the Angles, Saxons, and Jutes to the present day, we find a pattern of continuing changes. Certain historical events have made significant changes in our language, and will probably continue to do so.

English, like all other languages, is used for different purposes or functions. We use it to get what we want, to find out information, and to relate to others. We also create songs, chants, and rhymes to satisfy our creative spirit.

We even communicate without words, nonverbally signalling others. Some nonverbal communication is intentional, like the "thumbs-up" to say "Okay." Other nonverbal communication is done without an awareness of our responses, such as where we choose to sit in a conference room or the distance we maintain depending on how well we know and like another person.

The dialect variations in our language are primarily geographically distributed, although we may attach social prestige to certain dialects and not to others. Depending on what part of the country we live in or grew up in, we pronounce words differently or use different words for the same object. There are also some changes in sentence construction from one dialect to another.

In different social situations we adjust the way we talk, making different word choices in different situations. For some children, speaking with formal language choices is quite different from using the informal language used at home. For others there are fine distinctions to be learned, such as using plural verbs with the word *data.*

Since the 1970s there has been a concerted effort to use nonsexist language that clearly includes girls and women as well as boys and men. *He* is no longer the proper referent for singular nouns that include females as well as males. The label *man-made* is changing to *manufactured,* the *salesman* is a *sales clerk,* and the person running the committee is the *head* or *chair.*

There are many Americans whose native language is not English but who are learning English as a second language. Variations in their learning of English reflect their native language and cause problems in reading and writing that elementary and middle school teachers must be aware of.

Questions for Discussion

1. In what ways have historical events affected the English language?
2. Why is it said that no dialect is any better than any other? Why are some dialects more prestigious than others?
3. What experiences have you had with speakers of another dialect? How much did dialect differences interfere with mutual understanding?
4. How can children be taught to use more "proper" language without hurting their feelings or alienating their families?
5. What is nonsexist language and why might some people resist using it?
6. What kinds of experiences will help students develop their repertoires of registers of language to use appropriately in different situations?

Notes

1. L. M. Myers, *The Roots of Modern English* (Boston: Little, Brown, 1966).

2. Adapted from M. A. K. Halliday, *Explorations in the Functions of Language* (London: Edward Arnold, 1973).

3. H. Clark, and E. V. Clark, *Psychology and Language* (New York: Harcourt Brace Jovanovich, 1977), 373.

4. Joan Tough, *Talking, Thinking, Growing* (New York: Schocken Books, 1974), 112.

5. M. L. Knapp, *Nonverbal Communication in Human Interaction* (New York: Holt, Rinehart & Winston, 1972).

6. M. O. Wiemann, and J. M. Wiemann, *Nonverbal Communication in the Elementary Classroom* (Falls Church, VA: Speech Communication Association, 1975).

7. Charles M. Galloway, "Nonverbal Language in the Classroom " (Columbus, OH: Ohio State University, 1967), 14.

8. Annabel Ashely and Jean Malmstrom, *Dialects USA* (Champaign, IL: National Council of Teachers of English, 1967).

9. Roger W. Shuy, *Discovering American Dialects* (Champaign, IL: National Council of Teachers of English, 1967), 17–24.

10. Jean Malmstrom, and Constance Weaver, *Transgrammar* (Glenview, IL: Scott, Foresman, 1973), 355–378.

11. *Ibid.* This list was adapted and is used with permission of the authors.

12. Robert C. Pooley, *The Teaching of English Usage* (Urbana, IL: National Council of Teachers of English, 1974), 17.

13. *Ibid.*, 18. Reprinted with permission from the author.

14. *Ibid.*, 186–190. Reprinted with permission from the author.

15. Katherine Paterson, *Bridge to Terabithia*, illustr. Donna Diamond (New York: Crowell, 1977).

16. P. E. Woodford, "Bilingual/Bicultural Education: A Need for Understanding," in *The Challenge of Communication*, E. A. Jarvis, ed. (Skokie, IL: National Textbook, 1974), 401.

Part III

Substance and Strategies

Teaching the Language Arts

This portion of the text presents strategies for teaching students the essential oral and written language skills they will use. It is based on the psycholinguistic views of language and on developmental, cognitive learning theory. These theories support a rich environment of experiences, both those first-hand experiences and those presented meaningfully in literature for children.

Chapter 8 focuses on the various oral language arts from sharing or show-and-tell to using simple parliamentary procedures. It presents information on discussion formats and questioning techniques; it suggests a variety of discussion groups for different kinds of reports and discusses storytelling with both teachers and children as storytellers. The chapter also explains how to prepare for reading aloud to students, how to conduct choral reading and choral speaking, and how to teach specialized skills, such as making announcements, giving directions, using the telephone, and conducting meetings.

Chapter 9 presents drama for classroom use. Although drama is a form of oral composition, it is discussed in a separate chapter because it is quite different in nature and purpose from the other oral language activities. The kinds of dramatic activities used in classrooms throughout the primary, upper elementary, and middle school grades include the dramatic play of younger children, movement, pantomime, role playing, and improvisational drama.

Chapter 10 is on listening. It identifies the various factors that affect listening and describes the environment that is conducive to good listening. The major thrust of the chapter, however, is on listening comprehension—how it relates to reading comprehension and how teachers can develop skilled listeners. Television, its impact on listening, and the need for critical listening skills are also discussed.

Chapter 11 describes the writing process that best helps children learn to write well and to love writing. This process follows the steps that professional writers use: choosing and developing the topic, writing drafts and revising them, getting feedback from other students as well as from the teacher, proofreading the final draft, and finally publishing it. Evaluating student writing is discussed, as well as ideas for conferencing with students about their writing.

Chapter 12 considers the various forms that students may use in writing. It begins by discussing the functions writing serves, which then suggest appropriate forms. Journal writing, letter writing, and writing stories and poems are included with suggestions for teaching and using each. The chapter explains the components of an effective writing program and the ways of organizing an effective program. Directions for bookmaking are appended.

Chapter 13 deals with the related writing skills: mechanics of writing, spelling, and handwriting. These skills are developed mainly through students' experiences with writing and through a parallel instruction program for developing these skills.

Chapter 14 details the use of the language arts skills in the other content areas of the curriculum. It illustrates suggested activities in science, social studies, mathematics, art, physical education, and music. The chapter also shows how to plan integrated units of study and presents two webs—one focused on science and the other on social science—that include language arts activities.

Chapter 8

Oral Discourse

Oral Discourse

The Environment that Promotes Oral Language Skills
The Importance of Oral Discourse

Sharing
Teacher-Led Sharing
Student-Led Sharing

Discussing
Planning Discussions
Presentational Discussions
Discussion Procedures

Reporting
Informational Reports
Discussing Literature
Sharing Books

Questioning
Kinds of Questions
Strategies to Improve Discussion
Promoting Child-to-Child Interactions

Storytelling
Telling Stories to Students
Students as Storytellers

Reading Aloud
Reasons for Reading Aloud
Selecting Material to Read
Preparing the Reading

Choral Reading and Choral Speaking
Ways to Read in a Chorus
Planning the Reading
Poems to Begin with

Other Oral Language Skills
Announcements, Introductions, and Messages
Giving Directions or Explanations
Using the Telephone
Conducting Meetings

Mr. Walker's sixth graders had prepared for Richard Chase's visit to their school by reading some of his collection *The Jack Tales*, [1] listening to a record of him telling tales, and listening to other storytellers. They had asked their families at Thanksgiving about stories their parents, aunts, uncles, or grandparents had heard as children. The students shared these stories in class—retelling the tales and playing tape recordings they had made. A small group of students who weren't spending the holiday with relatives had visited a retirement home nearby and had "swapped" some songs for stories. One student said his tale was hard to tell because it had too many characters, so he got friends to help do a dramatic reading of the story with different students taking different parts. Using different voices helped make it clear who was talking.

The day came when Mr. Chase arrived. He was everything they had expected. Looking like some ageless gnome, he told his stories and asked them to tell theirs. They talked about what to say in games, and then exchanged irreverent school rhymes, chants, and songs. He answered all their questions about collecting stories. The glow he sparked got them interested in finding out more about their stories and in finding more stories.

The librarian helped them search out different versions of familiar tales, and they had great fun sharing and discussing these. Mr. Walker had them do some detective work to explain differences in these versions and to infer why certain changes in the stories were appropriate for the country of origin. One group read some Greek and Roman myths and compared these with each other and with Norse mythology.

Two of the girls who had visited the retirement home found that one of the stories they heard there was much like a story told by a boy's grandmother, who had grown up in eastern Canada. They decided to go back to their informant and find out more about where he had heard the story and about his background.

These students were developing important language skills—discussing, interviewing, analyzing, summarizing, storytelling, and dramatic oral reading—and were learning a lot about a special genre of literature. They read stories and information about the countries in which their tales originated to try to explain how the details of a story fit its origins. They delved into history and geography as they tried to explain why the versions differed in detail. The students developed critical listening and reading skills in evaluating the stories they heard and read.

Such integrated learning with an emphasis on oral language development occurs also in primary classrooms. The topic may be different, but many aspects of learning are identical. Ms. Clark's primary-graders took a walk around their school looking for signs of various kinds. When they returned from their walk, Ms. Clark presented replicas of some of the signs they had seen. After a brief discussion, the children decided to make copies of some other signs. When all the signs were completed, Ms. Clark brought out a pocket chart—a large poster board with narrow strips of paper stapled across it to make slots in which the sign replicas would fit. One row was for traffic signs, one for advertisements, and the third for information.. The children selected a sign from the ones they had seen and went up to the chart to put it in the right place. The Burger King sign went into the "Advertisements" pocket, the stop sign into "Traffic," and the street sign into "Information." One of the children put *Buses Only* into "Information." Some of the children protested that it should be in "Traffic." A somewhat heated discussion followed. In the process of that discussion, they came to narrow their meanings of all three labels—"Advertisements," "Traffic," and "Information."

As a follow-up Ms. Clark had the group select one sign, *Railroad Crossing*, and write an experience story about it. They read and reread their story as they were in the process of composing it. When the story was just as they wanted it, she copied it on a large sheet of lined chart paper and they decorated it with cutouts done in poster paint of trains and tracks, of children and cars waiting at a crossing, and of the railroad crossing sign.

The next day one group used an assortment of small boxes, clay, toothpicks, colored paper, and paint to make a table display map of their walk. Three of the children who had wanted to do the experience story on the Burger King sign dictated their own story to a fifth-grader who came to their room three days a week for thirty minutes. Two others decided that there should be a sign for children from their school telling them where to wait for the crossing guard at a busy street nearby. They talked to their teacher about their idea for a few minutes and then went off to get poster paper and paint to make a sign. The rest of the group wrote up their own advertisements for various products, getting help in spelling the words they needed from another fifth-grader.

What are the key characteristics of these two classroom situations that are important in language learning? First, *the students were actively involved in their learning.* The older children collected the stories from their families, told the stories they heard, and introduced and interviewed their speaker. The younger children found the signs they worked on during their walk, built the map, and made up new signs or advertisements.

Second, *the students went into this study in enough depth to develop real understanding.* The sixth-graders did more than read a few stories from one of Richard Chase's books before meeting him and then applaud and go on with their study of prepositions or Twain or whatever. His visit became a renewal of interest in a study of folklore

The Importance of Oral Discourse

Schools tend to focus on written skills, perhaps because children come to school with considerable competence in oral communication skills. While we do need to recognize and incorporate these skills, we also need to develop the various kinds of speaking skills.

For children who are in the preoperational stage of development—approximately two to seven years old—oral discussion experiences are especially important. The egocentrism of children at this stage of development leads them to assume that others know and think the way they do. And when others show that they do not, young children are often exasperated by this lack of understanding. An important way for children to realize that words do not carry all the information they suppose is to allow them many chances to talk with others, to explain their ideas, and to describe their experiences.

At the next stage of development—the concrete-operational period from about seven to about eleven—egocentrism becomes much less apparent and the child develops a social awareness and the understanding of another's point of view. Discussion and conversation are still very important because at this stage of development children still need to communicate their thoughts and refine their concepts. Students at this stage of development cannot work from abstract ideas; their thought processes are still grounded in concrete, firsthand experiences. Their thinking is facilitated by using real objects and events. Through communicating with others, their concepts and views are accommodated into the internalized organizational patterns.

Talk of various kinds is not merely a nice thing to do in elementary- and middle-grade classrooms; rather it is a critical part of the school experiences of children. Oral language activities cannot be dismissed as a nuisance or as unimportant. They need to be considered a major part of the school curriculum for every child—and they are especially important for children whose background of experience does not include conversations or discussions of various kinds with linguistically mature adults.

Sharing

This section is entitled "Sharing" instead of "Show-and-Tell" for several reasons. First, show-and-tell is confined almost exclusively to the primary grades, and older children would feel that having show-and-tell is childish, although they might like to share hobbies or collections if it seemed like a grown-up thing to do. Another reason for using the term *sharing* is that it is more descriptive of the activity at any age or grade level. Show-and-tell implies one person at a time showing something and telling about it without any interaction with listeners. That is exactly what it usually turns out to be—except that those who are supposed to be listening usually are not. Young children are too egocentric to be totally interested in what others say and are really more interested in what they themselves have to say. Too often it is the same few children who get up to do show-and-tell, and they may not be the ones who need the experience the most.

Sharing, on the other hand, is a very adultlike activity. Its name directly implies give-and-take, response from the listeners, mutual participation in the topic. Sharing, however, cannot take place successfully with an entire classroom. Twenty to thirty people of any age cannot participate in a discussion. When show-and-tell shifts from a speaker-audience situation to a sharing activity, it becomes an interactive situation where the listeners' responses, questions, and experiences also have value. This means that the teacher needs to provide a small-group situation for sharing.

Teacher-Led Sharing

Teachers play an important role in sharing. It is their responsibility to encourage personal involvement in the sharing discussion. Through the questions they ask and the strategies of questioning they use, teachers can explore the topics dealt with in greater depth and can extend their students" contributions. The interaction between participants is also part of the teacher's role in sharing discussions.

Teachers often conduct the sharing time, calling on the person whose turn it is to share, directing the discussion, asking the questions, and generally shaping what the children say and suggesting what is appropriate to share. Usually the children tell about some event in their lives or describe objects they have brought from home. The teacher typically responds to each child and decides which questions or comments made by other children are appropriate and therefore "allowed." This sharing activity gives children the opportunity to speak in front of a group and tell about experiences or objects that mean something to them. It gives the teacher an opportunity to listen to each child, one at a time, and evaluate each child's oral speaking ability.

Student-Led Sharing

Less common but perhaps very beneficial are sharing groups run by the children themselves. Michaels and Foster describe such a sharing group of first- and second-graders in which they observed different sharing time styles.[2] In student-led sharing in this classroom, children take turns being the group leader; the leader chooses from among those who wish to share, and they go to a group meeting in an area partially screened on two sides by bookcases. The rules are related to managing the group: only one person can talk at a time, the leader chooses the person to share, and there is one warning about misbehavior before the child must return to his or her seat. There are no rules, however, about the topics for sharing, the style to be used, or the amount of time allowed. "Thus, left to their own devices, sharer and audience together control what gets talked about and how a given topic is developed."[3]

Throughout the year the children developed two styles of sharing. One was a narrative style that often incorporated dramatic modes, such as dialog, sound effects, repetitions, asides, and gestures. Sometimes fantasy events were added to the account or facts were embellished to make a better story. The other style was the lecture-demonstration, usually accompanied by some object or objects related to the topic. This style expects and even depends upon the children's questions and is viewed as informative—"You can learn from it." The mark of a good sharer is not the focus on a single topic or the literate story model valued by teachers, but the sharer's attention to his or her audience. Successful sharers pay attention to the reactions of their audience and shift or modify their topic and style to meet the audience's expectations. "With no teacher to hold the floor open for them, these children try various strategies, including style shifts and the development of novel genres, to hold the audience's attention. Through peer/peer imitation, topping, and evaluation, over time, these children are becoming more skillful in their use of language."[4]

Whether the sharing is led by the teacher or by the children themselves, it is often better placed toward the end of the day than at the beginning. During the day children may do things such as paint or write a story or make something they would like to share, or they might be reminded of experiences they would like to tell about. One successful primary-grade teacher uses a "sharing basket" to encourage participation. Children put notes in the basket during the day about what they would like to share. This has a dual purpose: it reminds them of their ideas and it points out a valid purpose for writing.

Discussing

In addition to conversation and sharing, there are two other kinds of classroom discussion: planning discussions and presentational discussions. These should be used in your classroom when there is a real need to plan or to present something meaningful to the students.

Planning Discussions

Two kinds of discussions are appropriate for planning or generating ideas. These are the brainstorming group and the buzz group. *Brainstorming* has been successfully used by adults as well as by children and is effective in generating ideas, especially innovative or creative approaches to a problem. In brainstorming there is no need to come to a decision or agreement. Every idea is accepted as stated, although others may combine ideas or add to an idea that has been suggested. It is a freewheeling approach that may include a wide range of suggestions from the very practical to the improbable. Most teachers will use it with caution, clearly stating ahead of time that the object is to get a lot of ideas without coming to a decision. *Buzz groups* are also used to get ideas or to plan. In contrast to brainstorming, buzz groups focus on a particular conclusion or decision. A small group or several small groups of students are given a specific problem and a certain amount of time to reach their objective. The discussion may require them to consider a number of pros and cons, but the group eventually reaches closure on an idea or suggestion.

Planning discussions can be used for a wide range of topics in the classroom. Their content may be related specifically to the language arts as children plan, for example, the cover for an invitation to their parents to visit their room. These discussions may also be related to another content area, such as how to care for and record their observations of the gerbils as a part of a science experiment or how to set up a softball tournament between the sixth and seventh grades.

If you allow students to participate in planning activities, you should be willing to agree to any reasonable plan they decide upon. If you feel there should be constraints on what they might decide, then note these ahead of time. You may wish to say what theme should be followed in the invitation, what supplies are available, what the cost or time limits are, and so on. If you have already made some planning decision, then announce it or state the alternatives from which the group may choose.

Presentational Discussions

These discussions are intended as a way for individuals or a group to present to others something they have learned or information they have gathered. The two main kinds of presentational discussions are round-table discussions and panel discussions. The more informal and less audience oriented of the two is the round-table discussion. *Round-table discussions* involve a small group of students and a moderator. They are relatively informal, with the group members sharing ideas or findings with each other or an audience. The moderator's main responsibility is to keep the group moving along and on the topic. You may want to have the moderator summarize the discussion in some way, but keep in mind that summarizing an oral discussion is a rather high-level thinking skill and is fairly difficult even for adults. *Panel discussions* are clearly intended for presenting ideas to an audience. Each member of the panel takes responsibility for some aspect of the topic. The members tend to take turns in presenting their parts, although panel members may add to one another's information as the presentation continues. After the panel has made its presentation, members of the audience may ask questions of the panel as a whole or of one panel member. The panel discussion, in contrast to the round-table discussion, is more formalized and requires more preplanning.

The topics for presentational discussions tend to be primarily in content areas such as science or social studies, although some topics in literature are appropriate. One classroom had been doing a combination study of the stars and constellations: astronomy, astrology, and mythology. Each of the subgroups presented their information in panel discussions. This was the fact-finding part of their work reported orally; later, they extended the activity in many directions. Some went into writing fictitious horoscopes and various kinds of poetry. One group improvised a play about the Pleiades (according to Greek mythology the seven daughters of Atlas who were transformed into a cluster of stars). Another group improvised brief scenes in the lives of famous astronomers as they made their discoveries. One trio actually built a telescope and recorded changes in the positions of the stars. In spite of all the different activities that followed, all the children gained a basic knowledge of astronomy, astrology, and mythology from the original panel discussions.

Discussion Procedures

The purpose of the discussion, whatever kind it is, should be clear to you and to your students. If students have not had much experience with discussion groups, they should be moved into these oral discussions slowly and with a considerable amount of structure. Give clear directions, have some sort of signal to use to stop the discussion if it becomes necessary, and put someone in charge of each group. If the students have to get up and move around to get materials, perhaps one person from each group could be assigned to be the messenger. Keep the early experiences with discussion fairly simple with a clear-cut purpose and some guidelines that are discussed ahead of time. As children become more used to working in groups, less structuring is necessary, and they can work on more complex or involved projects.

Age is not as important a factor as being familiar with working in groups this way.

You may want to start with only one small group working on something jointly while the other students are involved in independent projects. This will leave you free to work with the discussion group and get things started. Then you can add a second group, and finally a third, fourth, or fifth—whatever seems appropriate for their interests and needs. It is important, though, that students' early experiences with discussion work well and that they feel good about the group work.

Students may want to set up their own evaluation of their group work, or you may want to set guidelines ahead of time and then comment on those that were followed and those that they need to work on more the next time. These might include such things as keeping on the topic, listening to others, giving everyone a chance to talk, and doing one's share to reach the group's goal. You might also decide not to evaluate a particular discussion session with your students. Usually, though, it is a good idea for the teacher to keep some record of the discussion session and how children participated in it. This might be done on a checklist basis with each child's name and labeled columns for their performance, as in Figure 8.1. As you move about the room working with the discussion groups, you can make mental notes of individual contributions or responses. These can then be recorded on

Evaluation: Participation in Oral Discussion

Children's names	Actively participates	Adheres to topic	Gives others a chance	Other comments

+ = Positive evidence observed (does this)
− = Negative evidence (does the opposite)

FIGURE 8.1   *Evaluation of discussion*

the checklist. You will not get a chance to check on each student each time, but over a period of time you can record several sessions for everyone.

Reporting

Two typical forms of oral reporting are discussed here: informational reports and book reports. These very words seem to summon visions of children coming, one at a time, to the front of the room and reading a written report (some of which are probably copied directly from other sources). Surely, there must be a better way! The description itself suggests three things to be avoided: standing up in front of the room, reading a written report, and putting down on paper another writer's words. Avoiding the possibility that children will present reports orally in this way can make the reporting situation more appropriate and pleasant for children in elementary and middle school.

Informational Reports

Reporting may be done through a group presentation if students have worked on related informational reports. A panel discussion is less formidable to children than individual reports. If the report topics are not closely related and a group presentation seems unsuitable, there are other ways of helping them present interesting oral reports without reading a prewritten text.

One way to improve oral reporting is to show students how to take notes from the encyclopedia or from other reference materials using their own words. This is not a skill that develops independently without instruction. Note-taking skills can be taught by showing children short paragraphs of material on chart paper or an opaque projector. After they have had a chance to read the paragraph, remove it from their view and have them tell or write down one or two important ideas from the paragraph in their own words. These can be telegraphic in nature rather than written in full sentence form. Your students will need quite a few experiences like this with note taking before they are ready to work with their own research materials. When they make that step, they will still need some help and supervision before they can work completely on their own. Students need to develop confidence in their ability to take notes in their own words instead of relying on copying sentences or even whole paragraphs from other sources.

By changing the format of oral reports, the teacher can do a lot to improve the reporting situation. An effective way is *not* to have the focus of attention entirely on the student giving the oral report. One possibility is to have students prepare chart paper strips with each idea they are going to talk about written on a single strip. These can then be pinned up one at a time as they give the report. This same idea can be accomplished by writing the main ideas on a transparency and using an overhead projector. It is reassuring for many children to think the audience is looking at the main ideas instead of them. The information for the report can also be given in an interview-show technique. You can have your own class version of *The Today Show.* Have children who are reporting prepare three to six questions about the topic for someone else to ask them. They can rehearse their answers with the master of ceremonies who will interview the guests for the day's show. The element of role playing involved makes most children more comfortable. A third possibility for some topics is to have the students prepare slides, gather printed pictures to use with an opaque projector or make their own illustrations to accompany their reports. Students can talk about the pictures as they present information about their topics. Thus, the attention of the class is focused on the pictures—particularly when a projector is being used—instead of on the person giving the report. These are a few of the way you can make children more at ease with oral reporting.

In evaluating students' oral reports, it is extremely important to emphasize *what* the person says, not *how* it is said. The whole purpose of oral reporting is the giving or sharing of information—not oral language usage, projection of voice, and so on. Many teachers like to list (on the board or on a chart) reporting guidelines for children to consider while preparing their reports. If you choose to do this, keep the guidelines very simple and few in number. Too long a list will make anyone feel that there is no way to live up to such expectations. After the report you will no doubt want to make some evaluative comments. Keep in mind that everyone needs to feel successful and good about the experience, and that your comments may serve as instruction for others. You can comment on one or two things that the student did well, and save any further suggestions for an individual conference. Think of evaluation as searching for value in what students do; after all, the word *value* is an inherent part of the word *evaluation.*

Discussing Literature

Teachers of all grade levels discuss stories and books with children. Often, as in the teachers' manuals, most of the questions asked are memory-level questions: "What was the little girl's name? What did her stepmother tell her to do? What did she have to do for her two stepsisters? What was her fairy godmother's warning? What did she use for a coach? What were the horses made from? Where did the coachman come from?" And on, and on, and on. When this happens, it is unfortunate because it offsets the impact of the book or story and suggests that literature is "only the facts." It denies affective response and does not increase children's understanding of the literary elements employed. It reduces literature to the narrative line.

An interesting study done with tenth-graders by Lucking suggests that asking questions in hierarchical order increases students' responses.[5] Experimental group teachers were trained to discuss literature starting with simple recall questions and then progressing to evaluative questions. Whether it was the sequence of questions or simply that the teachers got beyond the memory level and asked a significant number of analytical, interpretive, and evaluative questions is not completely clear from this study. However, it does seem to indicate that significant numbers of higher-level questions are important.

Teachers who want to elicit affective response for discussion may find some of the following questions that Anderson and Groff suggest helpful.

> What could you guess about the characters that is not told about them?
> What did any character in the book do that you would or would not like to do?
> Do you know any people who are like those in the book? Can you describe them?
> What things happened in the book that you would like to happen to you?
> How would you change the story if you could?
> What parts of the book are about things you know are important?[6]

If you want to develop students' understanding about various literary elements in the text, the following questions may be useful:

> *Plot structure:* Can you describe the parts of the book—the beginning, middle, and end? What is the event that the main part of the book builds up to?
> *Characterization:* How did you learn what each of the main characters was like? (Through what the author said? Through what they said or did? Through what others said or how they responded?) Do any of the characters change during the book, and if so, what causes the change?
> *Setting:* Would this story be better or different if it had happened somewhere else?
> *Theme:* What was the author trying to say in the book? Do you think he or she was right? If this book had a moral, what would it be?[7]

Mood: How did the author make you feel the way you did in this book?

Summary: What would you tell a friend this story was about? How well does the title fit the story? What title do you think would be a better one?

Critical summary: What would you say to people who asked you if they would like this book?

These suggestions may help you ask questions about literature that ask students to go beyond the "what happened?" stage. Do not use them all in discussing an individual story or book. Select the ones that will highlight the literary aspects that are most significant. If you want to make sure that the children have understood the story, ask them to retell it. It is much better to ask: *What happened at the beginning of Cinderella? At the middle? At the end?* than to let loose a barrage of comprehension questions like those at the beginning of this section.

Sharing Books

This section is intentionally entitled "Sharing Books" instead of "Book Reports," because the term *book report* usually carries negative connotations. Did you ever have to write and turn in weekly book reports? What was the purpose of all those book reports? To check to see if you had really read the book? The intention here is to present ways that students can share their experiences with books and, at the same time, be motivated to continue their reading. Not every book the child reads has to be shared in some way. Just as adults sometimes read a book they don't find particularly meaningful or a book that is too close to them to want to share, so children should be able to choose what books they want to share.

There are a number of alternatives to formal oral book reports. Books may be shared orally in interesting ways; they may be dramatized; or they may be shared through art. Books may also be shared through enjoyable writing experiences. Consider the following suggestions as examples of alternatives that you might use.

Sharing through Talking

1. Students who have read the same book or who have read books by the same author might discuss the books with each other and with you. This encourages both description and comparing or contrasting, which are important cognitive skills.

2. Once in a while students might enjoy giving sales talks for their books. A sales talk should be finalized with some kind of decision,

which can be a simple vote, or it can be done by listing others in the class who want to read the book after the sales talk.

3. Students might like to tell the story or a part of it to some musical accompaniment of their choosing. This can involve using cutout illustrations, drawings, or a flannelboard.

4. A student can read orally a short scene from a book. The reader should practice this first so that the oral reading is prepared and smooth.

5. Older students might like to hold an interview with one of the characters in the book. The reader prepares the questions for someone else to ask and then impersonates the character in the book, answering the questions as the character would.

6. Students might enjoy preparing a "talking bulletin board" that will motivate others to read their book. Suppose four children have read and enjoyed *Bridge To Terabithia* by Paterson. They might work together in making a display to show the main characters, a favorite scene or episode from the book, and so on. A brief dramatization following the content of the bulletin board would then be recorded on cassette tape.

Sharing through Drama

Dramatic activities based on a book are an interesting and enjoyable way for children to share a book they have liked with others. Some possibilities for dramatizing are as follows:

1. Make stick puppets to dramatize one scene from a favorite book. Students who have read the same book may share this, or one person can ask a friend to help with the presentation.

2. Students may pantomime characters from familiar stories they have read. This might include simple costumes.

3. They might enjoy doing a television commercial for their book. This suggests that less content of the book will be shared, but also that greater selection of ideas is required.

4. If the class has been reading books that are suitable for improvisation, a group who has read the same book might like to do some improvised scenes from the story. They would not memorize any lines, but instead use their own words in the dramatization.

5. Students who have each read a different book can work in pairs and do puppet dramas showing the two main characters meeting and talking. This is particularly effective if the two characters have something in common, such as having lived in the same area at different times, having been president, or having fought in different wars.

Sharing through Art

Art, as a creative medium, is appropriate for sharing responses to another creative medium, such as music or literature. In working with art and literature, try to vary the media used. Crayons and manila paper get pretty tiring after a while and limit potential creativity. Think of painting, crayon engraving, color washes over crayon, chalk, modeling in clay and paper-mâché, collages, sculpture in soap or paraffin, dioramas, and printing using vegetables or corrugated cardboard. Art work done on 9- by 12-inch paper is fine, but other times children need to work with very large sheets of paper. Let the students choose the materials they would like to use, or work with them to suggest various possibilities.

1. Students could make original illustrations for their story. This might be one illustration or a series of them.
2. They might make an original book jacket for their book.
3. They can create a cartoon strip of one special incident in their story.
4. Making a map or time line of events in historical fiction or biography can be an approriate activity.
5. Students can make models or sculptures of characters or objects in the book. This idea can also be extended, and children can create mobiles.

Sharing through Writing

There are many possibilities of writing something that relates to the book read, without doing the standard book report.

1. Write diary or journal entries for one of the characters in the book.
2. Write an outline for a sequel to this story.
3. Write a description of a person or place in the story. This may be done as a simple description or as specifications for sets for a film or play version of the book.
4. Write a letter to the author or to one of the characters.
5. Write end flaps for a new book jacket for the book.

Whatever means you select to have children share their reading, keep in mind two important points: the focus of the reporting activity should be on sharing and stimulating reading, and children should have a choice of how they want to share their book.

Questioning

One of the strategies most frequently used by classroom teachers at all grade levels is that of asking questions. The questions we ask and the means we employ to get children to participate in answering them are especially important because often they determine the level of students'

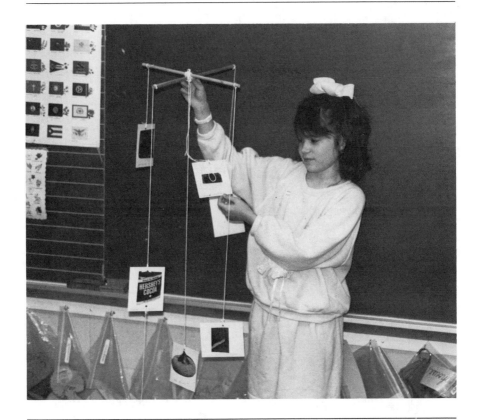

This student created a mobile to share what she discovered about the uses of chocolate.

thinking. If we most often ask questions that require students only to remember and repeat back information, then they are not pushed to think at higher levels or to perform higher mental operations. The more we push students to analyze information, to put together disparate ideas through synthesizing, to cite examples and apply information to new areas, to evaluate according to predetermined criteria, the more they will learn as they make the information their own.

Kinds of Questions

Cunningham developed a model of question categories shown in Figure 8.2 that is helpful in analyzing the various kinds of questions that may be asked.[8] Questions are categorized first as either narrow or

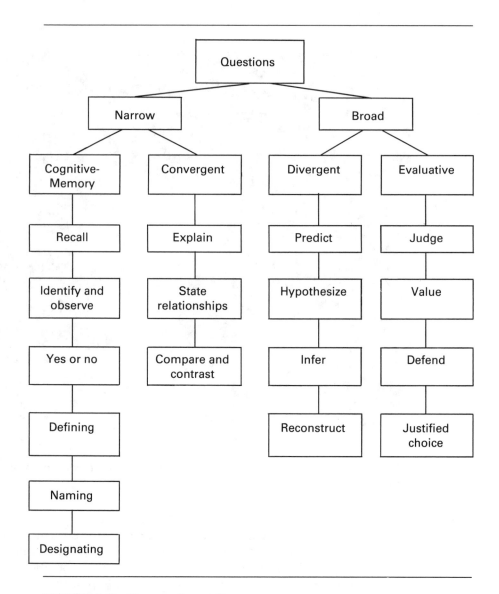

FIGURE 8.2 *Types of questions*   Roget T. Cunningham "Developing Questions-Asking Skills" in *Developing Teacher Competencies*, James Weigand, ed. ©1971, 103. Adapted by permission of Prentice Hall, Inc., Englewood Cliffs, NJ.

broad. Narrow questions focus on a particular correct response; broad questions call for a wide range of responses. Each of these categories is then divided into two subcategories: narrow questions are either cognitive-memory questions or convergent questions, and broad questions are either divergent or evaluative.

Cognitive-Memory Questions

Cognitive-memory questions require the person responding to recall or to recognize information that has previously been made available. Because they involve only remembering answers, these questions are sometimes called "recall questions." The following questions about the familiar tale, *The Emperor's New Clothes*,[9] illustrate the kinds of cognitive-memory questions.

Recall	How many tricksters were there who tried to deceive the Emperor?
Identify/Observe	Who was the first person the Emperor sent to check on the "weavers"?
Yes/No	Did the old minister really see the cloth?
Define	What is a *canopy*?
Name	What do you call the piece of equipment that cloth is woven on?
Designate	Which person in the kingdom finally spoke the truth?

Convergent Questions

The other kind of narrow question is the convergent question. This involves more than simply remembering, but it still leads to a specific correct answer. The aim of the question is to reach a predetermined right answer. The following are examples of convergent questions about the same folktale.

Explain	How did the trickster weavers keep people from telling the truth?
State Relationships	How were the ordinary people taken in by the tricksters just as the palace ministers were?
Compare/Contrast	How was the boy who said that the Emperor wore no clothes different from the adults?

Divergent Questions

Divergent questions are one of the two kinds of broad questions in this scheme. Divergent questions are open-ended and call for a variety of responses rather than a single answer. They are speculative and engage students in projecting information.

Predict	What do you think the Emperor will do to the "weavers" who misled him?
Hypothesize	If you were Emperor, what would you do to your ministers for not telling the truth?

Infer	What effect do you think this parade in underwear will have on the Emperor's love of clothing?
Reconstruct	What do you think led the Emperor to hire these "weavers"?

Evaluative Questions

Other broad questions are evaluative. These questions ask the student to make or support some kind of judgment. Sample questions about the same story follow.

Judge	Who is most responsible for the deception?
Value	What makes this story enjoyable for children?
Defend	Why did you say that the "weavers" are not really the guilty ones?
Justify Choice	Why do you think the Emperor was the most foolish of them all?

These questions illustrate the kinds of each subcategories in the questioning models. It is not important for a teacher to be able to classify questions into such fine types. What is important is that teachers be aware of the level of thinking that is involved in the questions they ask and be able to predict the amount of response a particular question will generate. In attempting to check reading or listening comprehension, teachers too often ask primarily cognitive-memory questions. Even the questions in teachers' guides tend to ask primarily cognitive-memory level questions.

Banton's research indicates that in the teacher manuals used in elementary schools (15 questions from 70 manuals representing 12 publishing companies in use in grades 1 to 6 in Virginia in the 1967–1977 period), 59 percent of the questions given were cognitive-memory level questions, 16 percent convergent, 11 percent divergent, and 13 percent evaluative.[10] Informal checks of newer reading series books unfortunately replicate Banton's findings. If teachers ask the questions given, about three of every five questions will be low-level recall questions. The number of questions given is also appalling, especially in the lower grades. A page with five lines of print may well have eight to twelve questions.

Generally speaking, the broad questions, both divergent and evaluative, provoke the greatest response from several different students. Use cognitive-memory or convergent questions to clarify facts and gain information; then use divergent and evaluative questions to extend thinking beyond that level.

Questions that begin in the following ways tend to increase the number of possible responses from students: What could you tell someone about . . . ? How can you tell that . . . ? What are the differences between . . . ? What things does this picture tell you about . . . ? Under what circumstances . . . ? What reasons can you give for . . . ? What are the possible values of . . . ? What might happen if . . . ? How could you summarize . . . ? What evidence can you find that . . . ? What could have caused . . . ? What are the effects of . . . ?

The teacher's role in questioning, then, is to ask questions that are penetrating and provocative. These are the questions that make one think at a more complex level and that elicit several answers or reasons. Of course you cannot predict ahead of time which way a discussion may lead, but as a teacher you should prepare ahead of time a *few* key questions to ask. During the discussion itself, you can supplement the key questions you planned with others that seem necessary because of the direction the discussion takes.

Strategies to Improve Discussion

In addition to the particular questions that are used during a discussion, there are four strategies for improving discussion.

1. *Ask fewer questions and balance the ones you do ask between broad and narrow questions.* Use narrow questions to establish a common area of information; ask broad questions to extend the thinking of your group.
2. *Balance participation in the discussion by calling on students who do not volunteer as well as those who do.* Do not let a few students who always raise their hands to answer close out others who could also contribute to the discussion. Many students who are less able because of problems with reading and writing are perfectly capable of responding orally in the discussion. They may be shy about answering a question, but they will gladly do so if called upon. You can even refocus a child who is not really involved in the discussion by saying his or her name and then asking a question. However, do not do this to trap someone. Ask a question you think the child can answer.
3. *Use questions that not only allow but encourage several children to answer.* Students are the world's greatest experts at determining what teachers actually want. If you can convince them that there is no preset, predetermined answer for every question and that it is their job to find out what that answer is, your students will reward you with some highly original ideas or solutions.
4. *Improve students' responses to questions by giving them time to think, and ask additional questions to make them correct, clarify, or extend their first answers.* Silence is an uncomfortable

element in a discussion. Too often the teacher who feels responsible for the discussion will give an answer or just go on to another question. If, however, the teacher will make an effort to be quiet, one of the children will break the silence. They often need some time to think, to figure things out, to make connections between the question and their experiences. Give them time. There will be moments when a teacher may want to extend an answer. A puzzled look and perhaps saying "Ohhh?" or "Explain a little more" will elicit additional information.

Questioning plays a very large part in teacher-led discussions. The questions themselves and the strategies of questioning that the teacher uses are significant. Through the questions posed, teachers raise the level of students' thinking and further their language development.

Promoting Child-to-Child Interactions

The questioning strategies above will help develop a pattern of discussion in which the students do more talking than the teacher. Asking questions that do not focus on a single short answer will also promote child talk. After all, the teacher does not really need the experience of explaining, describing, categorizing, and speculating; the necessity to use language in a variety of ways is a part of language development and is therefore what children need. Teachers can deliberately promote interaction among class members by asking them to verify or add to what someone has said, without implying that the first response is incorrect. Another way of facilitating interaction in the classroom is to make students responsible and comfortable in asking questions as well as in giving answers. With young children you can prompt their questions by suggesting what they might ask: "Who would like to ask George what other ways people use to display their collection?" With students of any age, teachers can praise the questions that students ask. If you can make your class feel that asking questions as well as answering them is important to you, they will try to do it.

A critical feature of good discussion as well as of good conversation is a small group in which each participant feels comfortable. With the large group—and perhaps with small groups in the primary grades—children may need to raise their hands and be called on in order to limit constant interruptions. As children have more experience, this should gradually become unnecessary.

Some teachers have found other ways to control interruptions. A "speaker selector" is highly effective if not used excessively. This is an object, something intrinsically interesting such as a marble egg, feather, or large button that is passed around the group. Only the person holding the speaker selector should be speaking. As the object passes around the circle or group, the person having it may talk and then hand it on when finished. If the person who has it does not want to contribute an idea or comment, it is simply passed on. This eliminates the raising of hands and being called on, and it also guarantees that each person will have a turn. Even with young children it is a workable idea—perhaps because of its visibility and the guarantee of a turn. It is difficult to get young children to take turns and not interrupt because of their strong egocentric drive and because of the amount of competition for attention present in the classroom, which is not present at home.

As we move to more interactive situations in the various types of oral discourse—whether in sharing, discussing, or reporting—students will take on a larger share of the responsibility for the interactions. We hope to hear less and less teacher talk and fewer teacher questions, and more and more student talk and student-posed questions. When students are really involved in what they are doing, when they see a reason for sharing information, and when they have a chance to participate, then those sharing sessions, discussion groups, and reports will be richer and more meaningful.

Storytelling

This section describes two kinds of storytelling: telling stories to children and having children tell or retell stories. Both are important classroom practices that benefit both teachers and students.

It is becoming increasingly clear that having a "sense of story"— an idea of what a story is like and what one should expect in a story—is important in reading, and writing stories. Some theorists even suggest that narrative is a mode of thought that is very important for children. Rosen describes narrative as giving coherence to the "virtual chaos of human events," and he believes that narrative is the primary and irreducible form of human comprehension.[11] This sense of what a story is like is developed by hearing many stories, especially those with well-formed plots. These may be stories that are read or told to children or that they read themselves. Narrative is also developed by retelling stories heard and telling events that make up a story. Both listening to stories and telling them are important to further development in reading and writing.

Telling Stories to Students

There is a special quality in storytelling that is not present when you read aloud to children. Storytelling is more direct and more personal.

There is no book to get in the way, nothing between the teller and the listener. Most storytellers respond to their listeners by emphasizing or exaggerating whatever the listener is enjoying. In reading, one is constrained by the words on the page, and few readers feel free to go outside the printed words. Both reading and storytelling are important avenues for stories: each provides special benefits to the listener.

It really is not hard to tell a story to a child or small group of children. We tell stories every day to our friends and family. We recount our troubles getting ready to leave home this morning, what happened on our last vacation, or what happened on our favorite television program or about the latest movie we've seen. Most of us could tell some familiar literary stories without any real preparation if we had to—stories like *Little Red Riding Hood, Goldilocks and the Three Bears,* or *The Three Billy Goats Gruff.* We have heard and read these stories many times; they are so familiar that we can just rattle them off.

This is essentially how you go about learning a new story to tell. Choose a story you really like, one that is memorable for you. Read it over and over, note the pattern or structure of the story, try telling it aloud or in your mind without looking at the print version. Most people find it helps to have visual images of the scenes and characters in the story, so imagine what each character and setting looks like. Then try telling it aloud as if to an audience, or tell it to a close friend or family member. If there are some parts you are unsure of, go back to the printed story and check them. When you have the basic story set in your mind, you can do any polishing you think necessary. You may want to memorize a particular phrase, a magic spell, or an unusual rhyme that appears in the story. You may want to add details of the scene or of characters' dress, based on the original story, its illustrations, or your own mental pictures. Try telling the whole story one more time—perhaps while you are driving to school or waiting for a bus. Then try it with children; they are not particularly critical and will enjoy the story as long as you can make it come out right.

Some advice from expert storytellers is to strip away any pretense of being good or exciting and simply be yourself. Although you may have first encountered the story in written form, you should feel perfectly comfortable in changing some of the details of the story to make it more meaningful to the group you are telling it to. This does not necessarily mean simplifying the story or changing the words to only those known well by your group. In the folktale *Salt*[12] the youngest brother plays the mandolin and sings to the moon; later he is given only beams and boards for a cargo to sell. Even though a harmonica may be more familiar to children, don't take out the mandolin, and don't change the beams and boards to plywood sheets. One of the values in stories—heard, read, or told—is the new words and ideas encountered.

Selecting material for storytelling depends mainly on two factors: first, a story should have a relatively simply plot and sequence of events and clear characterization; second, the overall style or effect of the story should suit the personality of the teller. Because of the need for exciting but simple plot development and characterization, folktales are particularly suited for storytelling. Folktales were originally part of the oral tradition and served a number of functions, some of which are still appropriate. Some of the functions met by various kinds of folklore are education, social protest, escape from reality, and converting work into play. American folklore—as well as the folklore of other lands—offers a tremendous variety of materials to the teacher. There are myths, legends, fairy tales or *Märchen*, and tall tales. A teacher with a soft voice and a quiet way of moving about might be more comfortable with one of the fairy tales or wonder tales rather than the swaggering tall tales or Jack tales. What you choose to tell should seem comfortable for you.

Because folklore was originally part of the oral tradition and was passed from storyteller to storyteller, there are numerous versions of many folktales. How a particular tale with the same basic features can occur in places apparently removed from each other is one of the unsolved mysteries of folklorists. For example, versions of "Puss in Boots" can be found in Sweden, Spain, Poland, the Dominican Republic, Greece, Turkey, India, the West Indies, Africa, and Indonesia. While the basic features of a folktale are similar, the details will vary quite widely. In a 1502 Italian version,[13] the "Puss in Boots" tale begins with the death of a very poor lady named Soriana who leaves her three sons only a kneading-trough, a rolling-board, and a cat.[14] In a Greek version, it is a king who dies after losing all his wealth. He offers his three sons a choice of a golden strap and his curse or the cat and his blessing.[15] The two elder sons, of course, take the strap and the curse, but the youngest son takes the cat and the blessing. In the French version, which is more familiar to most Americans, it is a miller who dies and leaves only the mill, his ass, and his cat. The eldest takes the mill, the second chooses the ass, and the youngest son is left with the cat.

Such variations in tales are opportunities to compare and contrast the different versions. Each country's folklore reflects its values and culture and gives insights into other nationalities. Learning about our country through American folktales is an important part of being an American, and there is such diversity among the peoples who have made America that we have an incredible richness of stories to share.

Storytelling builds a closeness between the teller and the listeners; they experience the story together. As a way of helping children develop their sense of narrative—their sense of story—storytelling becomes more than a nice, "fun" activity. It becomes an important part of learning—learning to read, learning to write, learning about ourselves and our culture.

Students as Storytellers

Children of all ages tell stories; that is one of the ways—perhaps the most important way—that they make sense of all the things happening to them. At home children tell what happened on the playground or on the way home from school. They can tell what happened on a favorite television show or in a book they're reading. Such experiences with narrative are very close to storytelling.

Often young children like to retell a story that they have heard or read. In the retelling the children become more familiar with the story, learning more from it and more about it. Teachers can prompt such retellings by providing feltboard characters or simple puppets for the children to use. For picture storybooks an alternative is to go back through the book showing the pictures and ask children to tell the story with the pictures as prompts. These retellings are most often done in a small group with the children actively taking part. Story retelling may also be done by individual children as a substitute for the standard "book report." This may be informal with the child telling the story to you and to one other person in the room who the child thinks will enjoy it, or it could be done in a small group as part of reading group time, with children sharing their outside reading by telling the stories.

Older students, too, like to tell stories to each other or to younger children. Fifth- and sixth-graders might go to primary-grade classrooms to tell a story. The librarian can assist in selecting a story suitable for the age group, or children can look through folktales and picture storybooks for a favorite to tell. They can practice on each other with the teacher as a final check.

Stories of other countries or cultural groups enrich students' understanding of other places and peoples. Storytelling can occupy a unique place on special days when a celebration is in order. Imagine a middle-school classroom on Halloween, shades pulled and only a candle or shaded lantern flashlight. Instead of silly costumes or a "party," try tales of ghosts or witches or scary events. Storytelling could be a regular weekly event with children taking turns as the storyteller.

Some of the values in storytelling are so important that teachers should make the effort to learn a few stories to tell and encourage their students to do the same. Storytelling is one of the few kinds of talk in the classroom that offers rich, complex, vivid language, which develops students' language in complexity of structure and in vocabulary. Narratives have importance because of their literary value, their prevalence among literary forms, and their connection with thinking. Storytelling plays a special role in oral discourse in the classroom.

Reading Aloud

Reading aloud to students of all ages serves a wide variety of purposes. Most of the time the teacher reads aloud to students, although occasionally students may prepare a story, poem, or description to read aloud to other students.

Reasons for Reading Aloud

The purposes that reading aloud serves more than justify the time spent. Reasons for reading relate to developing comprehension skills as well as composing skills.

Develop a Sense of Story

As in storytelling, listening to stories helps students to develop a "sense of story"—to internalize a definition of what a narrative is. This helps them comprehend better when they read because they can predict more accurately what will happen as they read. Having a good sense of story also gives students a wider variety of structures to use in their own writing.

Develop Vocabulary and Language Structures

Listening to stories helps develop vocabulary. Students encounter words in stories that they have never heard before or whose meaning is not clear. In a charming picture storybook, Wildsmith has a fox and a genet perform at *Python's Party*,[16] and a pelican opens his capacious mouth for the other animals to climb into. Both *genet* and *capacious* are likely to be completely new words for children and for many adults. But an illustration of fox and genet doing their trick can tell the children what a *genet* is. Looking at all the animals in pelican's mouth, they know that *capacious* means big—a large capacity. Through encountering words in a meaningful context and having a chance to use them and to make them their own, students add new words and word meanings to their vocabulary. Language serves as a source for syntax development, and books typically have much richer language than speech. The language of stories and poems with their carefully thought out phrasings expose children to the grammatical constructions they will one day make their own.

Learn the Forms and Conventions of Writing

Hearing the language of stories and poetry and other well-written material gives children a sense of the sound of written language and the conventions used in writing. Although speech can be written down, it usually does not sound like writing. There are certain phrasings, structures, conventions that are part of the written register of language that can be learned partly through listening to written material read aloud. When a child begins a story, "Once upon a time . . ." or when we read in an older child's story, "He loved to bark. Oh, how he loved to bark and howl at the moon!" you know that these children have been read to and have read a great deal. The conventional beginning and the repetition and variation within the exclamatory framework are evidence of familiarity with written registers of language.

Give Information about Other Times and Places

As mentioned previously, listening to stories gives information about other times and places. Someone who has never been to Hawaii can imagine what it is like from reading stories and informational material. Reading about Henry VIII of England and Elizabeth I imparts a sense of what England was like at that time. In hearing stories, children can visit the past and the future. Their knowledge of the world is expanded. They can read about experiences of others that they will never have and understand more fully what other people's lives are like. Lester's *This Strange New Feeling*, for example, relates the stories of three black couples in the 1800s who find happiness and love in spite of the pain it sometimes brings them.[17] Hearing their stories, older children might understand more about slavery and its effects on people's relationships.

Motivation to Read and Write

Hearing stories read aloud provides motivation for young children to learn to read and for older children to become better, more fluent readers. It also motivates them to write stories that will enchant others. Reading is a difficult task for many elementary school children, and listening to good stories provides an ongoing reason to keep working, to keep trying. As students discover the richness in the world of books, the fascinating things and ideas, they may make a greater effort to read and write on their own.

Selecting Material to Read

First, select stories, poems, or excerpts of informational material that interest you, that you enjoy, and that the children are able to understand. Try to select stories that the children would not be reading independently, and stories that the children might not select for themselves, but would probably enjoy. If you expect to be reading a story for a week or more at different times, select a book that has many exciting episodes. Younger children enjoy hearing a story several times and can profit from such repetition, but it is probably better for older children to hear new or unfamiliar stories. Read a variety of things; some children love fantasy, but others want to hear only about real things. Some would never read poetry on their own but enjoy hearing poems read to them. As you select, think about what you wouldn't want them to miss. If you aren't sure, ask your librarian or media specialist.

Preparing the Reading

Never read a book aloud that you haven't read to yourself. Sometimes a book will bring up ideas or words that you do not want to share aloud with a particular group. Sometimes there are words you aren't sure how to pronounce, and you will want to look them up ahead of time.

Decide how dramatic you want to be while you read. Sometimes using a slightly different voice—higher or lower—will help your listeners understand who is talking. Try out the voices you decide to use so you can be consistent.

Practice holding the book if it is a picture book so that the children can see the pictures while you are reading. Usually this means holding the book to the side in your left hand and standing a bit sideways to read it. (Reverse this if you are left handed.)

Don't worry too much if you skip a line or substitute a word. Go on unless the change will be wrong or confusing. In reading everyone makes little substitutions or omissions that don't substantially change the meaning.

After you have introduced a book, you might make a tape recording of it and put the book and tape in a listening center for the children to use again. Encourage parents to read to their children and to take time for the children to read to them. Lists of books for holiday or birthday presents may encourage parents to think of books as a gift. In addition to the splendid hardcover books, there are good, inexpensive paperbacks. Owning some books is an important part of becoming a reader.

Reading aloud is fun for both child and adult; you get a chance to participate in the story with the child instead of viewing it from an adult level. Hearing stories and poems is important to a child's development.

Choral Reading and Choral Speaking

Choral reading or speaking are very special oral language activities that involves children with literature in a rather special way. Choral reading or speaking involve reading or reciting a poem or excerpt from a story together as a chorus sings a song. In fact, all of the ways a chorus presents a song can be used in choral reading: unison, solo voices and chorus, voice sound effects with solos or chorus, and presentation as a round.

Ways to Read in a Chorus

Reading in unison seems simple, but actually it is rather difficult. One person lagging a second behind or saying a phrase differently breaks the unison. It is still enjoyable for the children—even when it is not perfect—and gives them a new and interesting way to respond to literature. Solo voices with a chorus are effective with readers of any age. Many different arrangements can be done with different solo voices and small groups. Some poems suggest a background rhythm or sound effects. "The Pickety Fence" by David McCord seems to demand a group quietly saying "pickety, pickety, pickety, pick" in the background while the poem is being read.[18] Every group that has worked with Myra Cohn Livingston's "Whispers" must use whispering as a sound effect.[19] Very simple and well-known poems work when read as a round.

Planning the Reading

Most books or articles about choral reading presume that it will be done as a performance for the benefit of an audience. Thus, they suggest that the director or teacher plan the most effective way to do the reading and then conduct the practices until the children perform it well. But choral reading should be done in a different way—as response to literature and for self-satisfaction rather than for any audience. In this case, it is critical for the children rather than the teacher to decide how to read the piece. The real learning in choral reading comes when they decide how to read it to bring out the most important ideas. Children need to examine the structure of the poem: Are there repeated phrases, lines, or stanzas that should be emphasized? Do they hear different voices that could be highlighted? What is the mood and tone? Should they read it quietly and rhythmically or boisterously and loudly? As they experiment with different ways to read each piece, they are forced to look at the piece in a new and somewhat analytical way.

Initially, children often choose to read a piece as a series of solo voices. This is perhaps reminiscent of a reading circle and seems fair to them. This style of reading also reflects general inexperience with choral reading. To prepare the students for choral reading, you should help them explore the various ways of doing it. Take several poems and print them on chart paper, on the chalkboard, or on a transparency, or make copies for each student. Recite each poem in several different ways, trying out the possibilities that children suggest. When they seem to know the ways a piece could be done, let them work in small groups. Let them choose a poem from a list or individual cards and ask them to figure out two different ways to read their selection. You may want to tape record their readings so they can listen to them later.

Poems to Begin with

A poem that is easy to do in several different ways and that works well for younger children in unison reading because of its short lines is the counting poem, "Numerical Nursery Rhyme." Even kindergarteners and first-graders who can't read can say the counting lines.

Numerical Nursery Rhyme

One, two,
Buckle my shoe;

Three, four,
Shut the door;

Five, six,
Pick up sticks;

Seven, eight,
Lay them straight;

Nine, ten,
A good fat hen;

Eleven, twelve,
Let us delve;

Thirteen, fourteen,
Maids a-courting;

Fifteen, sixteen,
Maids in the kitchen;

Seventeen, eighteen,
Maids a-waiting;

Nineteen, twenty,
My stomach's empty.

Please, Mother,
Give me something to eat.[20]

Another poem that is easy to read in different ways and in unison and that appeals to older students is "There Was an Old Woman."

There Was an Old Woman

There was an old woman who swallowed a fly;
I wonder why
She swallowed a fly.
Poor old woman, she's sure to die.

There was an old woman who swallowed a spider;
That wriggled and jiggled and wriggled inside her;
She swallowed the spider to catch the fly,
I wonder why
She swallowed a fly.
Poor old woman, she's sure to die.

There was an old woman who swallowed a bird;
How absurd
To swallow a bird.
She swallowed the bird to catch the spider,
That wriggled and jiggled and wriggled inside her.
She swallowed the spider to catch the fly,
I wonder why
She swallowed a fly.
Poor old woman, she's sure to die.

There was an old woman who swallowed a cat;
Fancy that!
She swallowed a cat;
She swallowed the cat to catch the bird,
She swallowed the bird to catch the spider,
That wriggled and jiggled and wriggled inside her.
She swallowed the spider to catch the fly,
I wonder why
She swallowed a fly.
Poor old woman, she's sure to die.

There was an old woman who swallowed a dog;
She went the whole hog
And swallowed a dog;
She swallowed the dog to catch the cat,
She swallowed the cat to catch the bird,
She swallowed the bird to catch the spider,
That wriggled and jiggled and wriggled inside her.
She swallowed the spider to catch the fly,
I wonder why
She swallowed a fly.
Poor old woman, she's sure to die.

There was an old woman who swallowed a cow;
I wonder how
She swallowed a cow;
She swallowed the cow to catch the dog,
She swallowed the dog to catch the cat,
She swallowed the cat to catch the bird,
She swallowed the bird to catch the spider,
The wriggled and jiggled and wriggled inside her.
She swallowed the spider to catch the fly,
I wonder why
She swallowed a fly.
Poor old woman, she's sure to die.

There was an old woman who swallowed a horse;
She died, of course![21]

John Ciardi has written a poem that simply cries out for large-group participation. It is a perfect example of a poem that can be used for choral reading in front of an audience of other children. It allows the audience to participate in the reading by filling in the missing words.

Summer Song

By the sand between my toes
By the waves behind my ears
By the sunburn on my nose,
By the little salty tears
That make rainbows in the sun
When I squeeze my eyes and run,
By the way the seagulls screech,
Guess where I am? At the. . . .!
By the way the children shout
Guess what happened? School is. . . .!
By the way I sing this song
Guess if summer lasts too long:
You must answer Right or. . . .![22]
    —John Ciardi

A poem for inexperienced students that works well with a chorus and a single voice is "The Witch's Song" by Lilian Moore.

The Witch's Song

Hey! Cackle! Hey!
Let's have fun today.

All shoelaces will have knots.
No knots will untie.
Every glass of milk will spill.
Nothing wet will dry.
Every pencil point will break.
And everywhere in town
Peanut-buttered bread will drop
Upside down!
Hey! Hey! Hey!
Have a pleasant day![23]
—Lilian Moore

Poetry is most commonly used for choral pieces, but other material may serve as a source for reading. Speeches or excerpts from them are especially appropriate for holidays. Well-written informational pieces or selections from biographies or autobiographies may make suitable material for reading. Choral readings of part of Martin Luther King's "I have a dream" speech or of John F. Kennedy's "Ask not what your country can do for you" inaugural speech might be effective ways of celebrating national holidays. Today's students seem particularly fond of some of the newer poetry that uses modern language and content.

Whatever the material used, the real learning and enjoyment of choral activities depend on the students' involvement in interpreting the piece, using low and high voices, soft and loud passages, and unison speaking contrasted with solo voices. The overall effect may not be as polished as a program arranged by the teacher, but the learning involved will be considerably greater.

Other Oral Language Skills

A number of other oral language activities might be included in the language arts program at one time or another, but these are not as basic as sharing, discussing, questioning, reporting, storytelling, and choral reading. Some are such an integral part of other activities or of classroom management that they are not obvious to the teacher as oral language skills. Nevertheless, children must be given adequate help in developing these skills.

Announcements, Introductions, and Messages

Students of all ages can participate in making announcements orally. In the early primary grades or with children who have had little experience, the announcements should be very brief. With more age and experience, children can be expected to be more competent in making more complex and lengthy announcements. These can be worked into other content areas or into the regular classroom procedures. Children might report on the temperature or weather or something special about the day or week in the morning opening exercises. Teachers who use a calendar might incorporate these facts with the month, date, and day of the week. This could be a rotating duty all during the year. Other teachers ask someone at each table or group to announce how many students are buying lunch, how many are bringing lunch or ordering milk, and who is absent from their group. In an informal classroom where students help plan some of the activities, individual children might announce special activities that they are planning and that others could share in. Teachers often make many announcements during the day that students in their classes could make, and students need the experience of making them.

Introductions are also part of classroom procedures. Appointing one child per week or per month to welcome visitors to the classroom and to introduce them to others is excellent practice. It also makes visitors feel welcome. Often children do not get any training at home about how to make an introduction, and so you will need to teach or at least remind them how to do this graciously. Instead of instructing the whole class at once in an artificial situation, why not take the three or four students who are the first to be hosts and hostesses and work with them? Role playing is especially effective here. Perhaps you will want to provide signs on strings. In that way, the person who is playing the role of a parent can quickly slip on a sign saying "parent" and enter the room to be introduced to others. Other signs for principal, room mother, guest speaker, university observer, intern, or student teacher, and so on can be used. Role-playing a situation before it actually happens makes it much easier for students, and using those who will actually need to do the introductions establishes a meaningful learning setting. Sometime during the year every student should have an opportunity to assume introduction responsibilities.

Giving accurate messages orally is an extremely important skill for everyone. It requires careful listening and remembering, as well as the skill of relaying information accurately. Pick up on any opportunities that occur to have students practice this skill. As with announcements, the first experiences with this should be simple informational messages. If the information to be relayed is critical, you may want to send a written message along with a child who has had little practice. Every child needs the experience at some time; be careful, therefore, not to limit the privilege to only the more mature children in the group.

Giving Directions or Explanations

Anyone who has asked for directions at a service station or from someone walking by has at sometime thought the informant was deliberately making things difficult or even giving directions to another place. Giving directions is a highly skilled task that requires that persons giving the directions or explanations put themselves in the place of the person asking for help. This makes the task difficult for young children in the preoperational stage of development since their egocentric view of the world makes taking another point of view virtually impossible. They naturally assume that everyone understands by a word or statement just what they do. "Go this way until you get to Julia's house, and then turn." Experiences for young children at this stage of development should involve having them explain things by giving concrete demonstrations as they talk. Older children who are in the concrete-operational stage of development have less difficulty taking another's point of view, but they still need practice in using a step-by-step explanation.

Some teachers have found it very helpful when involving the whole class in a project that requires following directions carefully to work with five or six children first so that they can execute the steps correctly. Then these children can assist the others in their group or at their table by supplementing the teacher's directions or explanations. It certainly minimizes the teacher's being called on for help from every direction at once. Students should also be encouraged to take a leadership role in explaining things to other children. Older children may also work with directions when developing map-reading skills. This kind of map work often starts with mapping some familiar area. The students might then do some role playing in giving directions from one place to another on their map.

Using the Telephone

The telephone is such a vital part of communication that even very young children should be taught to use it to obtain emergency assistance. Older children should be able to answer courteously, get the person asked for, take a message, or handle a wrong number. Many telephone companies provide a kit with working telephones that may be used in the classroom. If this is not available in your area, you can probably borrow a toy telephone from a student or a friend who has young children. Telephone courtesy can be handled in a learning center with a set of situation cards for older students or a tape-recorded problem for younger ones. Every child of school age should know how to call the fire and police departments and be able to give whatever information is necessary (name, address, telephone number, and the problem). If they cannot memorize the police number, they should know how to dial for the operator and explain what they want. In metropolitan areas, this means being able to ask for the correct city department that handles their area. Children need to learn not to tell strangers information about where their parents are or that they are alone in the house. Courtesy is certainly desirable, but safety is an absolute necessity. Using the telephone does not necessarily require a full instructional unit each year, but teachers should verify that the students in their class can use the telephone for emergencies.

Conducting Meetings

Younger children need experiences serving as chair of a group, perhaps during peer sharing time or peer-conferencing on writing. They need experience as chair of a group working on a project. When children start these activities, give them some simple rules to follow and limited responsibility for the outcome. Rules might include the following.

1. Stay on task.
2. Accept other students' ideas.
3. Present your ideas clearly.
4. Help with the group decision.
5. Use your power fairly.

After experiences with small groups, students can practice serving as chairpersons for class meetings and decision making.

Older students should learn the basics of simple parliamentary procedures. This includes how the chair calls the meeting to order, the normal order of events, (reading and approval of the minutes of the previous meeting, treasurer's report, other committee reports, items of old business, new business, and adjournment). Students should learn how to make a motion ("I move that . . ."), and that each motion must be seconded ("I second the motion") before any discussion can be held.

When a participant says, "I move the previous question," it must be voted on immediately and, if passed, the vote on the original motion must be taken without further discussion. During the course of discussion, small changes in the wording may be made with the approval of the person who made the motion and the person who seconded. If major changes are desired by the group, there are two ways to accomplish this. Someone may move to amend the motion (giving the new wording), which must be seconded. Then the amendment is discussed and voted on. If accepted, it becomes part of the original motion, which also must be voted upon. Otherwise, the original motion may be voted down and a new motion presented. Usually votes are taken by voice vote: "All those in favor, say 'Aye;' All those opposed, say 'No.' " If someone in the group believes that the chair made an error, he or she may ask to have those voting each way stand so that the vote can be verified. One does this by saying, "I call for a division of the house." The chair must immediately ask those in favor of the motion to stand to be counted, and repeat the process for those opposed. The meeting ends with a move for adjournment, which must be voted upon right away and, if passed, ends the meeting. The chair can prompt a motion by asking, "Do I hear a motion to . . ." (accept the report? present a play as our project? adjourn the meeting?). Students in the middle grades need experiences working with parliamentary procedure. Otherwise, they may never learn it and then avoid club offices or simply be unable to go to a meeting being conducted using parliamentary procedures and get done what they think should be. Knowing enough to be confident in making a motion, amending one, and in getting on with the business of the group is important throughout life.

Summary

Although much time and attention is paid to reading and writing in school, people use oral language far more extensively. Although children come to school able to talk and to listen to others and understand them, this does not mean that they are accomplished speakers, able to give good directions, participate effectively in discussion, or use parliamentary procedure at a meeting. So much of our time as adults is spent listening and speaking rather than in reading and writing that developing oral language skills is particularly critical.

Sharing is an important aspect of discussion because it leads directly into interactive adult conversations. Questioning is presented as an important teaching technique that involves examining both the questions and the strategies used to get more student response and to ask questions that call for higher levels of thinking. Discussion groups are used to plan and share information in all areas of the curriculum, and different formats can be used for different purposes. Suggestions for improving oral reporting skills are presented to make children more comfortable and their reports more interesting and varied. Literature is the focus of other oral activities such as the suggestions given for involving students in choral reading or choral speaking and also for reading aloud to students. Examples of affective questions and questions focused on literary elements are suggested. Other aspects of oral language include giving oral messages, answering the telephone, and learning to use simple parliamentary procedure.

Questions for Discussion

1. Why are oral language skills often neglected in favor of written skills? Why are they too important to neglect?
2. How can informational reports be improved over the traditional stand-up-and-read-aloud reports?
3. What are some alternatives to the traditional oral book report, and what is their focus?
4. How can teachers ask better questions? What can teachers do to improve the amount of class participation in discussions?
5. What are the benefits of telling stories to children and having them tell stories?
6. Why should students be involved in deciding how to read a poem as a choral reading?

Notes

1. Richard Chase, *The Jack Tales*, illustr. B. Williams, Jr. (Boston: Houghton Mifflin, 1943, 1971).

2. S. Michaels and M. Foster, "Peer-Peer Learning: Evidence from a Student-Run Sharing Time," in *Observing the Language Learner*, A. Jaggar and M.T. Smith-Burke, eds. (Newark, DL: International Reading Association, 1985), 143–158.

3. *Ibid.*, p. 145.

4. *Ibid.*, p. 157.

5. R. A. Lucking, "A Study of the Effects of a Hierarchically-Ordered Questioning Technique on Adolescents' Responses to Short Stories," *Research in the Teaching of English* 10, no. 3 (Winter, 1976):269–276.

6. William Anderson and Patrick Groff, *A New Look at Children's Literature* (New York: Wadsworth Publishing Co., 1972), 229. The two lists are from *A New Look at Children's Literature* by William Anderson and Patrick Groff. © 1972 by Wadsworth Publishing Company, Inc. Reprinted by permission of the publisher.

7. *Ibid.*, 230.

8. Roger Cunningham, "Developing Question-Asking," in *Developing Teacher Competencies*, James Weigand, ed. (Englewood Cliffs, NJ: Prentice Hall, 1971), 103.

9. Hans Christian Andersen retold by Anthea Bell, *The Emperor's New Clothes*, illustr. Dorothee Duntze (New York: North-South Books, 1986).

10. Lee Banton, "The Question: How to Produce Mentally Dull Students and Look Good Doing It," *Virginia Journal of Education* (October 1977): 13–15.

11. Harold Rosen, "The Importance of Story," *Language Arts* 63, no. 3 (March, 1986):226–237.

12. Harve Zemach, *Salt: A Russian Tale*, Margot Zemach, illustr. (New York: Follett, 1964).

13. Thomas F. Crane, *Italian Popular Tales* (Boston: Houghton Mifflin, 1885), 348.

14. Laurits Bodker, Christina Hale, and G. D'Aronco, (eds.), *European Folk Tales* (Hatboro, PA: Folklore Associates, 1963), 197.

15. Jacques Barchilon and Henry Pettit, *The Authentic Mother Goose Fairy Tales and Nursery Rhymes* (Denver, CO: Alan Swallow, 1960), 59.

16. Brian Wildsmith, *Python's Party* (New York: Oxford Press, 1974).

17. Julius Lester, *This Strange New Feeling* (New York: Dial Press, 1982).

18. David McCord, "The Pickety Fence," in *One at a Time* (Boston, MA: Little, Brown and Co., 1974), 7.

19. Myra Cohn Livingston, "Whispers," in *Whispers and Other Poems* (New York: Harcourt, Brace, Jovanovich, 1973).

20. Josephine Bouton (comp.), "One, Two," *Poems for the Children's Hour* (Garden City, NY: Garden City Publishing Co., 1927), 3.

21. "There Was an Old Woman," in *Junior Voices, The First Book*, Geoffrey Summerfield, ed. (London: Penguin, 1970), 24.

22. John Ciardi, "Summer Song," in *The Man Who Sang the Sillies* (Philadelphia: Lippincott, 1961). Used by permission of Judith H. Ciardi.

23. Lilian Moore, "The Witch's Song," in *Spooky Rhymes and Riddles* (New York: Atheneum, 1975). Copyright © 1972 by Lilian Moore. Reprinted by permission of Scholastic Inc.

Chapter 9

Dramatic Expression

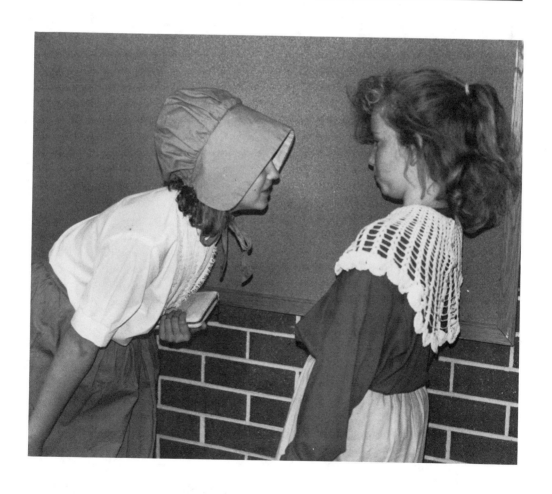

Dramatic Expression

Forces Encouraging Dramatic Expression

Emphasis on Processes

Emphasis on Creativity

Emphasis on Oral Modes

Interdependence of Language-Based Arts

Forms of Dramatic Activities

Dramatic Play

Movement

Pantomime

Improvisation

Readers' Theater

Puppets, Masks, and Flannelboards

Literature for Dramatic Expression

Initiating Dramatic Expression

Role Playing

Warm-up Activities

The Teacher as a Role Taker

Criteria for Dramatic Expression

Concentration

Interchange

Involvement

Skills Developed in Dramatics

Language Skills

Other Skills

Bibliography: Some Books Suitable for Dramatizing

A group of sixth-graders were caught up in their study of World War II—especially the war in Europe. They had seen a television dramatization of the people who hid Anne Frank while other Jews in the Netherlands were rounded up and sent off. Several of the students had just finished reading *Chase Me, Catch Nobody*, by Haugaard.[1] The idea of a fourteen-year-old, Eric, acting as a courier to deliver a package in Hamburg after the man who handed it to him was arrested by the Nazis appealed to the whole class but perhaps especially to the boys. They exchanged their few copies of the book and then acted out various key scenes to share the story with the rest of the class. Their dramatizations were so popular that other groups decided to act out scenes from the books they were reading about the war. One group read *Mischling, Second Degree*, an autobiographical account of a girl who participated in the Hitler Youth movement without being told that her grandmother was Jewish.[2] Another group discovered *Snow Treasure*,[3] which recounts the true story of how some Norwegian children helped get millions of dollars of gold out of Norway in spite of the Nazi occupation troops—in fact, in front of their very eyes—by carrying it on their sleds past the German invaders.

In an elementary school across town a group of second-graders listened to *Bye-Bye, Old Buddy*[4], which details the efforts of Jenny to part with her old baby blanket. This struck home with many of the children who still had favorite comfort toys or blankets, but who, like Jenny, felt quite grown up. In the book Jenny thought of several different ways to dispose of her blanket; the children thought of others and acted them out. Ms. McIlvey had the children work in pairs, each pair figuring out a way to get rid of their "blanket."

Jenny:	Mom, do you need some new coasters for the plants?
Mom:	Well, I guess I do. Are you going to make some?
Jenny:	Yeah. I'm going to cut up my blankie.
Mom:	Great! I've got some cardboard you can glue the pieces onto.

A pair of boys decided to dramatize how they would get rid of their first stuffed toys.

Greg:	I think we should take our animals to the woods 'cause there are lots of tiny animals who could use 'em for a home.
Marvin:	Sure. Lots of little animals like mice and chipmunks and stuff lose their mothers, and our stuffed dogs and rabbits would make 'em feel safer.
Greg:	I'll get Richie to bring his too, and we can go tonight.
Markin:	Okay. Meet ya at seven o'clock back of the barn.

The lines of these improvised scenes were not memorized or even rehearsed. They did not use any costumes or props except for a scarf, a hat, and a package for Eric in the first scene of *Chase Me, Catch Nobody.* For *Bye-Bye, Old Buddy* they used a scrap of old towel and some scissors, which Jenny used to make her plant coasters. The students in both classes did their scenes for the other groups, although of course the wording was a little different each time they went through it.

The authors of the stories that the children chose to dramatize might well flinch at what happened to their carefully chosen words, but they could not help but react favorably to the children's enthusiastic responses to their books. This form of dramatic expression permits students to respond to a book they love in a most meaningful way. "By becoming involved actively in make-believe, children are engaged in direct experience. Certain things happen in drama which do not happen when doing anything else."[5] In the enactment of the story they are gaining experience and developing language skills—listening and speaking—as well as cognitive, affective, and psychomotor skills.

This is dramatic expression, not theater. Drama in the classroom is a way of exploring the world and oneself. It may be based on a story or simply on a situation. Each "performer" will do the same part differently—as he or she sees it, as experience suggests. The *doing* of the play or the scene is the important part. It does not need an audience; in fact, an audience usually inhibits children. It does not require practicing to "get it right," because there is no right way. Sometimes a suggestion of a costume or a prop will help children feel the character, but an old terrycloth towel will do for the wolf's furry back, a paper crown will do for Max as he sails to "where the wild things are," and a yardstick will do for the fishing pole Tom Sawyer uses while rafting downriver. The learning and fun come from participating and not from the applause of an audience. "Theater concerns performances before an audience, whose point of view is included and for whose benefit effects are calculated. Theater is a secondary effect of drama, an outgrowth appropriate only much later, after elementary school."[6]

Forces Encouraging Dramatic Expression

There was a wave of interest in drama in the classroom in the 1970s following the Dartmouth Conference, the Anglo-American Conference on English Teaching, held in 1966. The British participants had already become deeply involved in drama in the process of academic desegregation. In the interim many language educators have remained deeply committed to drama in the classroom. However, in general drama has failed to compete with the pressures for accountability and management by objectives that have prevailed in the 1980s. Recent research and the new emphases on cognitive learning theories suggest that drama should be used more frequently. There are a number of bases for renewed interest in dramatic expression.

Emphasis on Processes

In the past drama meant putting on a play for the PTA or perhaps for another class or two. When students do this, the emphasis is on the product—the play done for the audience. Teachers are coming to the realization that the processes by which students do things are more important for learning than the product, so they choose to spend more time on the process of drama through informal dramatic experiences. Verriour discusses the traditional split between drama "as process" and drama "as product" that has led to the distinction between dramatic play and theater. "This polarization has become so deeply rooted that often these two drama modes are regarded as separate developmental stages in children's education."[7] Whether they are regarded as different stages of drama or simply different emphases, dramatic play with its focus on process seems most appropriate for elementary and middle school students.

In informal dramatic activities, students try out different voices, arguments, and characters. Learning comes from trying out several parts, not from performing one set play for others. Just as we emphasize the process of writing so that students will be able to see *how* to write—not just *what* to write, so we emphasize improvisation rather than theater to focus on the process of learning how to express ourselves effectively.

Emphasis on Creativity

As we increasingly accept diversity in life-style and values, it becomes more important for students to explore a variety of responses to their environment. In society today there is a wide range of attitudes, opinions, and values; some of these contradict one another. Children must learn to cope with these contradictions and even recognize and communicate their own diversity. They must find what is uniquely personal, what their potential is, and where they stand. Language arts teachers are becoming more interested in imaginative writing—in all areas of written composition—where there is an opportunity for original thought and expression. Dramatic activities in the classroom offer a comparable avenue for original and individual oral expression. Dramatizing offers the possibility of trying out attitudes, roles, and emotions and creating new possibilities for students without real risk.

Emphasis on Oral Modes

Schools used to be a place for developing reading and writing skills (along with arithmetic) rather than oral skills. Information from the cognitive psychologists clearly suggests that students need to be active in the learning process, that children of elementary school age who are in the preoperational or concrete-operational stages do not learn by merely reading about things, but from doing them and talking about them. Recent research also indicates that such experiences are important for older students in the formal-operational stage. We also know from the language learning process that students need to use language in a variety of ways. Research on the amount of times most adults spend in oral speaking and listening suggests that writing is not the prime communication channel in terms of functional use. Dramatics offers meaningful practice in both listening and speaking. One must listen to what the other person says in order to respond appropriately. What one says must be clear and meaningful so that someone else can reply. In addition, dramatic expression offers the "intellectual challenge of finding language true to one's subjective experience."[8] The need for developing students' ability to use language orally in an effective way leads directly to increased use of dramatic activities in the classroom.

Interdependence of Language-Based Arts

Language, and especially oral language, is an inseparable part of the entire language arts program. It is the basis for literature, writing, vocabulary skills, and thought development. Literature provides a special way of helping students interact with their surroundings and with others. Through literature they can discover that books offer special satisfaction. "Part of the satisfaction comes from the knowledge, the information, available through literature. This knowledge is not the same as that on the reference shelf; literature is not factual as an encyclopedia article is factual. . . . Literature is concerned with why things happen, on the motivations of man."[9]

One of the ways of helping students respond more deeply to a piece of literature is through dramatizing it. In that process, the individual child moves one step closer to experiencing life in another time, another place, another situation. In the active oral response to the book, students come closer to its view of reality. They are in on the "doing" and are no longer passive receivers. They use the language of the book and make it their own.

Dramatizing stories or situations is an important factor in developing skill in using written language. Dixon asserted that "the neglect of talk and drama has had disastrous effects on writing."[10] Children write best from their own experience just as adults do. Their direct firsthand experience is limited, and they need additional input. Experiences with drama that place them in new situations are a rich source of material for writing. When they write stories of their own, characterization is richer for their having experienced other people's ideas and personalities; setting or environment is more vivid from their insights into other situations; plot is better developed from their observations of the patterns of events.

Language and thought are advanced through dramatizing. Moffett notes that "dramatic interaction [is] . . . the primary vehicle for developing thought and language."[11] Complex cognitive skills are involved in the process of selecting, interpreting, and arranging the material from which the dramatization evolves. Whether the students are working from a piece of literature or from a particular situation, they must choose the relevant and meaningful parts and arrange them so that they are significant. They must select words that carry this significance—words from the book or those directly related to the situation. The more familiar one is with a word and the more importance it assumes, the deeper and richer is its meaning.

These four forces—emphasis on processes, emphasis on creativity, emphasis on oral modes, and interdependence of the language-based arts—point to the necessity for developing dramatic interaction and expression in elementary and middle school classrooms. As we come to know more about how learning occurs, we find more need for active involvement and experience. Participating in dramatizing events, problems, situations, and stories is a uniquely appropriate way of providing this active involvement and experience.

Forms of Dramatic Activities

Although there is no set sequence of dramatic activities that must be followed, there is usually a general progression from simultaneous participation by the whole group to participation by parts of the group while others wait for their turn and serve as an "audience," to performance of scenes for the class or some other small audience. Dramatic expression may take one or more of several forms: dramatic play, movement, pantomime, improvisation, readers' theater, and puppetry.

Dramatic Play

Dramatic play is most often seen in the early childhood years either at home or in the nursery school or kindergarten. Opportunities for this kind of experience should be offered to children in the primary grades—

particularly in areas where children have had little opportunity for this kind of play. Dramatic play involves playing out situations and taking roles. Children may play doctor, house, grocery store, and so on. It is highly informal and not directed by the teacher, although a teacher may intervene briefly to reinvolve a child or to suggest a possibility that may continue the play. All that is needed is some space in the corner of the room and a few simple props or materials for costumes.

Sometimes dramatic play originates after the children have heard a story or when the teacher adds some new element to suggest an idea to the children. A few red firefighters' hats may stimulate a whole series of rescue scenes. An old jacket with some braid may get children involved in ships and sailing. Some empty boxes or cans (opened from the bottom) may initiate a series of grocery store scenes. A telephone, a small toy cash register, and an old typewriter are good props to have available. Hats and scarves, an apron or two, a crown, and some old jewelry help children to become someone else. Through experiences with dramatic play, children learn to work with others to make the play more fun. They also have an opportunity to explore the roles adults take and, in a very special sense, how it feels to be adult.

Movement

This involves developing body-awareness as well as exploring different ways of moving and expressing ideas through movement. Movement might be considered the forerunner of pantomime, although it is not as stylized. Children work on rhythm and moving to rhythms. They also learn about moving in various ways, such as jumping, rolling, twirling, or gliding. An interesting book that may involve children in movement activities is Wildsmith's *Python's Party*.[12] In this story, the python invites all the other animals to his party and suggests a competition to see who can do the cleverest trick. He slithers down a tree, the hyena wobbles along on two round melons, and the elephant comes along with his heavy tread to rescue them.

Poetry, as well as prose, is a good source for experiences with movement. The spaghetti in Eve Merriam's poem almost demands action as it "wriggles."

A Round

Spaghetti,
spaghetti,
heaped in a mound;

spaghetti,
spaghetti,
winds and winds around;

spaghetti,
spaghetti,
twists and turns and bends;

spaghetti,
spaghetti,
hasn't any ends;

spaghetti,
spaghetti,
slips and dips and trips;

spaghetti,
spaghetti,
sloops and droops;

spaghetti,
spaghetti,
comes in groups;

spaghetti,
spaghetti,
no exit can be found. . . .[13]
　　—Eve Merriam

Children can also develop skill in kinesics as they show activities or feelings through body actions and facial expressions.

Pantomime

Pantomime is an outgrowth of movement, although somewhat more formal. It involves postures, facial expressions, and body movements to communicate an idea without using words. Very young children have great difficulty refraining from using language to express themselves, but older children often enjoy the challenge—especially if it can be done in a game situation at first. The class might be divided into small groups with each group selecting an action (riding a bike, climbing a ladder, and so on) and a way of doing something (quickly, cautiously, intensely) to convey to another group. The object of the game is to recognize the action and guess the *-ly* word they are demonstrating.

　　Books too lend themselves to pantomime. *No Bath Tonight*[14] by Jane Yolen seems perfect for younger children to pantomime. It is an account of Jeremy's week and all his reasons for not taking a bath each night. On Monday he built a fortress in the sand and hurt his foot; on Tuesday while picking berries he sat down in a pricker bush; on Wednesday he fell over home plate and hurt his nose. Each day, he does some new activity and finds a new reason for avoiding a bath that night. Children could start with Jeremy's activities of the week and go on to invent their own reasons for not having a bath.

Improvisation

Improvisation is probably the central activity in dramatic expressions for elementary school children. It involves acting out events or situations without using a script and without rehearsing. It is an on-the-spot, impromptu version of what takes place. Improvisations may be based on a familiar story or on a particular predicament. Body actions and language are both used to carry meaning.

Improvisation is an extension of dramatic play as children shift into the dramatic with a more recognizable plot or problem to be solved. One class used improvisation to explore an ecology problem through a mock town meeting. The question before the group was whether the town should allow a new factory to be built. After a unit on ecological issues, each student was assigned a role (mayor, realtor, home owner, group president) and was told to prepare for Friday's town meeting. The hour-long town meeting gave each student a chance to show how a person in a given role would respond to the problem. Another improvisation might simply be to enact what to do if a stranger offers a student a ride. Students can also improvise scenes from a book they have read or from a set of short stories as a unit review.

A series of these dramatizations involving the whole class or a group within the class may explore universal themes. "Daring to Face the Unknown" might involve a dramatization of a Roman centurian off to face the fierce Pictish tribes in Great Britain or of Columbus on his first voyage to America or of a pioneer family crossing the United States to California in a covered wagon. "Decisions" might range from a contemporary of Louis XIV denouncing revolutionary activities to Robert E. Lee resigning his commission in the U.S. Army to fight with the Virginia Militia or someone in the late 1960s deciding whether or not to accept his draft notice during the Vietnam War.

The dramatization of a concept should present some sort of conflict that must be resolved. Although the children may need to search out some information on the topic, their speeches or lines need not be planned. And if the dramatization is repeated with another group of children, a different argument may be presented. A minor character may become a major one. The drama may or may not be repeated depending upon the children's interest and enthusiasm.

Improvisations also may be literature-based. Students could substitute an improvisation from the book they have just read for a formal book report. Sometimes improvisations can extend the story in the book and explore aspects not included. In *Mr. Miacca*[15] Tommy escapes from the Miaccas, who usually eat bad little boys for dinner. Tommy tricks first Mrs. Miacca and later Mr. Miacca. It is interesting to dramatize the scenes that are *not* in the book, such as the couple's conversation when Mr. Miacca gets back from buying spices and herbs and finds that his wife allowed Tommy to return home to bring back some pudding. Is he furious? Does he berate her for being so foolish as to think the boy will come back? When Tommy later escapes from Mr. Miacca, what does Mrs. Miacca say to her husband? Does her response depend on whether he was angry in the first scene or whether he understood how much she loved pudding and consoled her. Such an approach is a good way to explore how other peoples' responses are affected by our actions.

Improvisations are like skits in their fluidity. Even if practiced, they are not formally "set." Doing improvisations allows students a wide range of characters and situations to explore.

Readers' Theater

In readers' theater a story, a section of a book, or a poem is brought to life by the "readers," who prepare the reading so that they can use their voices to create the characters and events. Typically, there are no costumes or props, and the readers sit on tall stools with their scripts in hand during the presentation. Preparations for such a dramatization may include extensive discussion and analysis of the literature. Coger suggests that in readers' theater the readers share their insights into literature with others.[16]

Often, students prepare their own script, which makes readers' theater a perfect blend of literature-based reading, writing, speaking, and listening. Children in the elementary grades can take a favorite storybook and turn it into a script, using a narrator to make explanations, and then can practice reading the parts. Such practiced, rehearsed oral reading is beneficial in developing oral reading skill, and writing the script is good composition practice.

Older students, too, enjoy readers' theater. At a time when they tend to be self-conscious, students seem to find such presentations safe. As in many of the other types of dramatic activities, the learning occurs primarily during the preparation and practice as students work on the way a particular character would say a certain line, why a character behaves the way he or she does, and how a key point can be highlighted in the script.

One class of fifth-graders combined literature and social studies in a look at other cultures through folktales. One activity was readers' theater presentations of four different versions of the Cinderella tale. Each group prepared a script and then performed its variant of the tale, including "Tattercoats," an English version, "Ash Pet," an Appala-

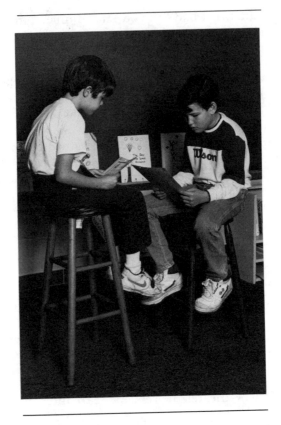

Few, if any, props are needed in reader's theater. Students make the drama come alive through their voices as they read a script.

chian tale in which Cinderella goes to a barn dance; "Little Burnt Face" the Indian version in which Cinderella's sisters become aspen trees who quake in the wind forever; "The Brocaded Slipper" a Vietnamese version of the tale.[17] In this version Tam's father dies, and she is left in the care of her stepmother, who has a daughter of her own named Cam. When the two girls are sent out to catch fish, Tam fills her basket after damming up a channel from the pond to a river. Cam steals all the fish and runs home, leaving Tam in tears as she thinks of the beating she will get for catching none. The students' script was like this:

> *Narrator:*   Just then she felt someone touch her. It was a fairy.
> *Fairy:*   Why are you crying, my child?

Tam: My sister's stolen all my fish, and I don't dare go home empty handed.

Fairy: Look again at your basket. Are you sure it's empty?

Tam: How amazing! There's a fat little fish lying at the bottom.

Fairy: This fish is worth more than all the ones you've lost. Take him home at once and put him in the well. He'll bring you good luck.

Narrator: The fairy vanished and Tam ran home to do as she had been told.

At first the children were upset that Tam had only one stepsister, and the whole business of the fish didn't seem much like Cinderella. But when she got the red brocaded slippers, the beautiful dress, and "the gold and silver and jewels of every description," it seemed more like Cinderella. When Tam went to the celebration where all the young women were invited to try on the brocaded slipper that the crow had dropped at the prince's feet, the children knew it truly was the story of Cinderella. For the prince would only marry the girl whose foot fit the slipper perfectly, and that was Tam, whose slipper had been stolen by the crow when she was drying it.

The children made a chart of all four tales, writing down elements that were similar and different. They speculated about the differences they found and had to find someone who had been in Vietnam to talk about that version.

This was a wonderful experience for the children. Their scripts gave them experience at extended writing, and they were proud of their readers' theater performances. The chart gave each group a chance to be an expert on a tale and to develop skills in comparing and contrasting. Some students were motivated to go to the library to read more about Vietnam because they were curious about the differences they found. They discovered answers to their questions: Why was it a red slipper? Red is considered a lucky color in Vietnam and in China too. Why did Tam have only one sister? Two is a lucky number in Asian folklore rather than three, which is often found in western folklore. There was a real need to do research. The children found this to be fun to do, and they learned interesting facts about Vietnamese culture.

The children had little trouble converting the story into a script. Because they had not learned the fine art of converting description into dialogue, the narrator's part was too long; but the story was clear, the writing was good experience, and the dramatized reading was fun for both readers and listeners. Because all of the children in the class had worked on a Cinderella tale, they were especially sensitive to the variations and were very good listeners.

Puppets, Masks, and Flannelboards

Using puppets, masks, or flannelboards to tell or create a story is fun for students of all ages. Often such activities can introduce a shy or quiet child to drama since it is easy to believe everyone is looking at the puppet or the flannelboard instead of at you. These dramatic media make it easier to depict certain events or characters such as animals, giants, or other magical creatures.

Younger children respond to puppets as if they were real creatures and often enjoy retelling stories or making up new stories as they work the puppets. Puppetry becomes an extension of imaginative play for these youngsters. Older students also enjoy using puppets when they feel too shy to take a particular dramatic part. The puppets do not have to be complex, artistic creations; in fact, the ones the children make from scraps of material, yarn, and paper work wonderfully. The construction of the puppets is an important part of the entire experience. The simplest puppets are cardboard cutouts mounted on tongue depressors or sticks and appropriately colored and decorated. Paper sandwich bags also make simple puppets. The fold at the bottom can become a mouth, and the yarn can be glued on as hair. Facial features can be added with crayon. Styrofoam balls make good puppet heads with cloth bodies added; and a colored sock with the toe split and lined with red for a mouth makes a great animal that can show funny expressions. Felt is useful for puppets because it does not ravel, and scraps of fur or lace and shiny buttons can add to the effect. Such puppets are quickly made and serve just as well as complex papier-mâché creations. For a stage you can tip a table on its side for the children to sit behind and hold up their puppets, or you can make a fine puppet theater from a large, cardboard carton with an area cut out for the stage. One teacher added an inexpensive miniblind for a curtain and covered the carton with contact paper and paint. The students should be involved in planning and making the puppets. Such involvement is more important than having a professional-looking stage or fancy puppets.

Masks help create characters for older and younger students and can be simple paper or posterboard creations. Somehow when you put on a mask, you are no longer yourself, and it is easy to become one of Patrick's dinosaurs or even the queen of France.[18] In addition to facial masks, there are body masks made from large sheets of posterboard or shipping cartons with cutouts for the face and arms. These resemble the old-fashioned scenery boards for funny photographs at the beach. Although they do limit movement somewhat, they are fun for particular characters, such as talking trees and flowers.

Flannelboards are made from stiff cardboard covered with flannel or felt. Then the story characters are cut out from felt, interfacing or lining material, or paper backed with felt or sandpaper. As you tell the story, you place the appropriate characters on the board. This helps the children focus their attention and keep track of a complicated story. Students enjoy retelling the story later using the felt characters, and they can also create characters and make up their own stories at the flannelboard. You may want to make two flannelboards, keeping one in good condition for your own use, and providing another for the children. Appropriately labeled envelopes for the felt characters and important pieces of scenery help to keep things organized.

In all types of dramatic storytelling, the important aspect is that the children are encouraged to participate in telling a story. Much of the real learning involved comes from making the puppets, felt characters, or masks because the children must decide "What makes a giant a giant? How can you show a growing beanstalk?" The puppets, masks, and felt characters get the children involved in retelling a story or in making up a new one.

Literature for Dramatic Expression

Story dramas encourage dramatic expression and provide a good introduction to all kinds of drama. In a story drama the characters are established and the basic plot is provided. The students can act out scenes from the stories they read and gain a greater understanding of them. Doing a drama gets students to look more closely at the story and improves their comprehension.

In planning a story dramatization, you must consider the number of characters, the complexity of the plot, and the complications of various scenes, and try to match them to your students' abilities. Initial experiences should be fairly short and simple and related to stories that the children love and have heard several times. As children have more experiences with dramatizing stories, they can handle more complex stories.

Literature can also serve as background for dramatizations as students turn to books to find information about situations or solutions to problems they encounter. If Paul Revere stopped at your house on his ride to warn the patriots, what might you offer him to eat or drink? How long did his ride take? Did he enlist others to help spread the word? Ongoing dramatic situations provide motivation for such research. Biographies, autobiographies, historical fiction, and informational books help children understand other times and other people in a meaningful context—preparation for dramatic situations in role playing, in puppetry, or any of the dramatic experiences. (See at the end of the chapter for a list of books suitable for dramatizing.)

Initiating Dramatic Expression

There are no hard and fast rules to follow that will guarantee success as you begin working with drama, but there are some general guidelines that should help you work effectively. First, select stimuli for dramatizing—whether stories or situations—that have appeal for both you and your children. You should be genuinely enthusiastic, for your enthusiasm will be conveyed to your students. Heathcote, who has done extensive work in improvisational drama, speaks of the need to arrest students' attention.[19] She insists that drama should not be watered down; it should not be fairies and flowers prancing around in leotards but real situations and real problems to solve.

A second guideline is to start small. Begin with something simple, not an improvisation of an epic by the whole class. In the primary grades, this might be some movement to music or very brief improvisations of scenes from a favorite book you have read to your class, or perhaps pantomimes similar to charades of events in the unit of stories they have just finished. In upper grades, you might start with improvisations of one or two favorite scenes from a book, or pantomimed actions and feelings described earlier in the section on pantomime, or stick-puppet scenes of the most exciting part of the library book the students have read (instead of a book report). Be sensitive to what the students are comfortable doing, and try to make these early experiences a successful, satisfying contact with drama.

A third guideline is that you should do extensive planning of the dramatization even though what the students do will be spontaneous. Unless you have a great deal of experience with the theater and with dramatization, you need to do some careful planning to make the experience work for your students. Consider the best arrangement of furniture in the room. What warm-up or motivational activities might prepare them and make them more comfortable? What extra materials will you need, such as music, fabric pieces for costumes, paper or sticks and paint for puppets. If you plan to have your students dramatize a story, you should analyze the story carefully for possible scenes, characters, movement patterns, and appropriate motivational techniques. If you are working with the whole class in the story dramatization, consider how you can give each student an opportunity to have a part and participate in the dramatization. Selecting a story with a large cast, adding characters or casting new characters for each scene would solve this problem. Although you would not take students through this process, you need to do it yourself. Even though they may take an unexpected direction, your plans can be adjusted and modified as you go along. The thinking-through that you experienced while planning will help you adapt to their ideas; when they need direction, you can be confident that you will be able to provide it.

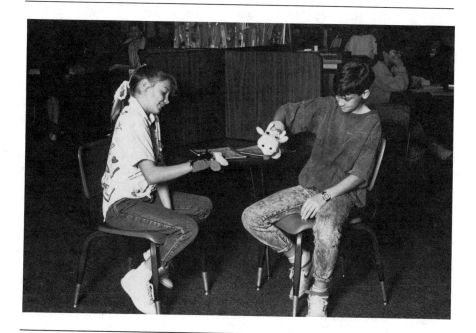

Dramatizations of all kinds require planning. These two students are planning and practicing with their puppets before dramatizing a story.

Role Playing

Role playing familiar experiences is an ideal starting point for young children. It is one way they can verbalize what has happened to them and can find out how some children have shared similar events while others have had different experiences. To the very young, family customs appear to be universal experiences, and at first it will be hard for them to believe that others do things differently. Role playing might begin with something that happens only in the classroom, or that evolves from a discussion of a story or a picture.

Some situations that lend themselves to role playing with young children are celebrating a birthday, going shopping, going out to a restaurant to eat, getting ready for Thanksgiving, buying a new pair of shoes, having a new babysitter, meeting someone new who's moved into the neighborhood, or planting a garden. The children should have experienced the situation themselves, and role playing should result from their familiarity with it. The role play will probably need to be done in small groups since young children all want to participate at once in the dramatizing. The teacher may guide them by asking questions or proposing variations or complications to extend the dramatization.

With older children the situation for role playing should be somewhat familiar, but it need not evolve from firsthand experience. Some situations that might be appropriate for role play in these grades could develop from "unfinished problem" stories or from situations that they might face in the future. These might include returning merchandise to a store, working in an office, selling products door to door, taking a job as a babysitter, taking a driver's license examination, or flying in a plane during an emergency. Role play requires some discussion of the possible situation first, and the teacher may intervene to guide or extend the experience. There should be some problem involved that needs resolution and that could be resolved in several ways. For example, if the group is role playing a babysitting situation, perhaps one of the children gets very ill, or there are warnings of a tornado on the television, or some friends drop in for a visit and break something. This is no time for preaching morals; it is a time for students to discover the alternatives in a situation and the consequences of taking a particular alternative. It is a way of exploring danger and reality in a safe situation.

Warm-up Activities

Before getting students involved in an experience with dramatization, you may want to lead them in some warm-up or motivational experiences. These experiences may include developing the sensory environment, moving to music or to a particular rhythm, pantomime, monologues, or working on dialogues with a partner. The extensiveness of the warm-up depends on the particular group of students and how easily they become involved in the dramatization.

Sensory Exercises
Sensory exercises help children get a sense of the physical environment the drama will explore through a discussion of the various senses. "Here is the bridge the three billy goats will have to cross. Close your eyes; reach down and feel the bridge. What is it like (wood, concrete, cool in the shade, warm in the sun)? What things do you hear (water running over the stones, boughs of trees scraping the bridge railings, a bullfrog down below or some birds calling a warning)? What do you smell (sweet grass in the field across the bridge, clover, apples in a nearby tree)?" If sensory exercises are used, do them first rather than getting the children up and moving about and then asking them to sit down again.

Movement to Music

Movement activities as a warm-up help get the students moving about as the characters in their story or situation might move. "Now you will need to put on your astronaut suit. Be sure you have zipped it all the way up the front. Buckle the straps at you ankles; don't forget those at the wrists too. We will be marching out to the launching pad any moment now, so put your helmet under your left arm and be ready to go when the music begins and I say, 'March!' " [Start some patriotic music.] Now, right foot first and in a line, March!"

Pantomime

Pantomime can be a dramatic activity alone, or it can be used as a warm-up exercise. In pantomime the students work on gestures, postures, and actions that are appropriate for the characters they will portray. "You are Mama Bear fixing the porridge. Measure out the oats. Put some salt in the pan and some water. Now stir it all around and put it on the stove. Perhaps you should set the table now—three spoons and three napkins—that's right, one at each place."

Monologue and Dialogue

The whole class or a group of children usually speak at once during a warm-up. That way they have a chance to assume the voice of the character without being concerned about how well they are doing it. Dialogues are usually done with a partner, with several pairs, or even the whole class, speaking at once. Here are examples of a possible monologue and a dialogue:

Monologue

You are a television reporter at the landing of the space shuttle—the very first one to go to Mars. Can you give us a report of what is happening? Everyone, identify yourself and your station; don't pay any attention to what others are saying or doing; you need to tell your audience what is going on.

Dialogue

Now find a partner. You are now the two astronauts on Mars. Your spaceship has just landed, and mission control has said you can put down the ladder to begin to explore outside. Decide who will go out first, and be sure to tell each other what you find and what you see.

The warm-up activities need to be carefully planned by the teacher so they build the students' self-confidence and prepare them for participation in the dramatization. Not everything you plan will be used, but it is always better to be overprepared.

The Teacher as a Role Taker

Often the teacher assumes a role as a way of getting the students into their roles. Thus, the teacher starts the drama by taking a fictional role. Neelands points out that the role needs "to act as a strong focus for the class's interest, but it needs to be subtle enough to place the group in a position where they will have to make the next move. . . . The teacher should deliberately withhold . . . expertise and knowledge even if that means long embarrassing pauses while the group figures out what to say or do for themselves; it must be the children's work."[20]

Sometimes, especially in the children's early experiences, you may want to intervene in the drama and add some tension. You might ask, for example, if there are any wild animals fleeing from the flood in their area, point out that there has been no report from the other space ship in over 48 hours, or ask if anyone has had any unusual symptoms. Conflict is the essence of drama. It is built in if students are dramatizing literature but may need to be added to situations students choose to dramatize. The teacher, though, is never the star.

Criteria for Dramatic Expression

There are three major criteria for dramatic expression that the teacher can use as general guidelines in working with students: *concentration*, *interchange*, and *involvement*. These are key elements in the success of a dramatic experience.

Concentration

Students must be able to stay within the confines of the drama and not break out of the situation. They should feel as if the situation is real, and they are the actual characters being portrayed. They need to persist in continuing the dramatic experience. Concentration implies an intensification of feeling and a focus on the task at hand. The following questions may help you evaluate their concentration:

Are the students reacting to the drama as if it were real?
Can they continue the dramatization and extend it beyond a superficial level?
Are they beyond the point where minor distractions will interfere with the drama?

You will never be successful with drama if you permit someone to interfere with another student's interpretation of a role or situation. Laughing at someone will not only affect that person but also make the others reluctant to participate if they know they may be ridiculed. When the first happens, the teacher must firmly, but not punitively, stop the laughter.

Interchange

Drama cannot be a solitary experience. Dramatic expression in the classroom involves many students—whether a whole class or a group of children. The participants in the drama must respond to each other in a meaningful way. This means that cooperation is one of the key concerns of the teacher. As the students interact with each other, they participate mutually in the experience. In the interchange process, they come to explore how they react in certain situations and how they respond to others. The verbalizing that goes on in the drama absolutely requires good listening and speaking skills. Since there is no script, there is nothing to fall back on. One must express ideas clearly and listen to what others say. It is at this point that listening and speaking skills develop. To evaluate interchange, these questions may assist you:

> Are students working together in the dramatization, or is it one idea versus another?
> Do the students listen to others and respond to what they have said?
> Does one student pick up on what another has said and repeat or extend the idea?

The teacher may choose to intervene in a dramatization to cue students into an effective idea. This may be done by taking a role within the dramatization for a moment, or simply by making a quick suggestion. It is also possible to wait until the scene is finished and then discuss a variety of ideas. After this, the students may even decide to exchange parts and replay the scene.

Involvement

This is probably the keystone of all experiences with dramatic expression. If students are not really involved and committed to what they are doing, the whole experience becomes unreal. Dramatizing should provide a real learning experience for students. They should not just play at being someone but should actually try to become that person. Participants in classroom dramatizations do not have to worry about conveying feelings to an audience. The drama is done for their sake, not for someone else's sake. The following questions should help you evaluate children's involvement.

> Do you see changes that fit the character each student is playing, or do the students retain their own personality and way of doing things?
> Is the quality of intensity—of becoming someone else—present during the dramatization?

If you continually find the quality of involvement lacking in the students' dramatic expression, it may be that the situation they're dramatizing does not seem right for them. Perhaps you are choosing stories or situations that are too superficial. It may also be that a particular group needs more motivational or warm-up activities before getting into the drama. Go back to basics and start doing some shorter, simpler dramatizations. Perhaps adding some costuming or props will help children become more involved. Try a different time of day or try working in smaller groups. Like so many other worthwhile educational experiences, dramatic expression is not easy, and there is no simple formula for success.

Skills Developed in Dramatics

Although dramatizing stories or concepts is usually an enjoyable activity for children, this is not the primary reason for including dramatics in the language arts program in elementary schools. Drama has a potential for developing language ability that is not paralleled by any other single language arts activity. It offers possibilities for developing more general skills in the cognitive, affective, and psychomotor domains that few other activities possess. It is also an especially fine way to integrate the language arts with each other and with content areas.

Language Skills

One of the two main implications for teaching coming from the psycholinguistic theory of how children develop language is that they need to use language in a variety of ways. Dramatizing stories or situations calls for just this kind of language use. The participants must find language that is true to the character and to the situation they are playing. Through playing a variety of roles, students should experience the language that a variety of people would use. Their language in the dramatization becomes a creative oral composition. Even when the situation being dramatized comes from a story or book that they have heard or read, the language they use in the dramatization is not taken verbatim from the original; they take the idea of what happened and create the language to fit it. Few stories actually require memorization of particular lines; and these lines should be chosen by the students rather than by the teacher. One student teacher whose group was dramatizing the "Three Billy Goats Gruff" tried and tried to get the child playing the troll to say, "I'm going to gobble you up!" He finally was able to repeat the line and the dramatization started. When the moment actually came, he shouted out in a frightened voice, "Hey man, I'm gonna eat you up!" It was so right for him and for the rest of the children, and they were so involved in the dramatization that the student teacher just smiled to herself. When a situation arises that children think requires the exact language of the original story, they either will have it down pat or will ask for it. One specific case where this happens is in dramatizing the "Three Little Pigs." The children want to say, "I'll huff and I'll puff and I'll blow your house down!"

Drama is related to language development and thus to both reading and writing. Research shows that drama appears to improve oral language in several different ways. Researchers have found that children developed greater length and complexity in their language, gained in the number of words spoken and in recognizing problems and projecting solutions, and in facilitating symbolic functioning.[21]

Vocabulary development is another area of language that is increased through drama. In story dramatization children develop both the vocabulary presented in the story or book and the vocabulary used in the dramatization. Students in drama feel the need to express just the right shade of meaning in the words they use. Thus, new words may be presented in the story in a meaningful context, and these words or others may be used in the later dramatization. Finding words in a meaningful context and then having an opportunity to use them immediately is an effective way of building vocabulary.

Research shows that drama is strongly related to reading. Henderson and Shanker, as well as Strickland, found that story drama significantly improved comprehension of literature when compared to workbook skill activities.[22] Galda found that drama promotes a greater understanding of cause and effect and the motivations and responses of characters.[23] Drama is also related to writing. The 1967 Plowden Report on British schools noted, "What is more remarkable now in many infant schools is the variety of writing: writing rising out of dramatic play."[24] Smelstor explains this by pointing out that dramatic performance and good writing have the same thought processes.[25] As drama creates its own special kind of experience, it stimulates students to write; they use experiences with role playing to further define their audience by thinking how others might respond to their writing.

The nonverbal elements of communication are also developed in drama as students use body movement, gestures, and space to develop the characters. Students dramatizing William Steig's *Caleb and Kate* might be asked the following: How can you show that Caleb and Kate are really angry with each other? How close would they stand when arguing? How could Caleb show that he was turned into a dog—without barking? When Caleb comes back home (as a dog), how does he try to let Kate know? How close would he stand to her then? How would the robbers move about their house at night?[26]

All these elements of language are developed through dramatization. They are the expressive part of oral language. The corresponding receptive part—listening—is also well developed through dramatization. Students need to listen to each other in the dramatization in order to respond meaningfully to each other. They need to extend the ideas or refute the arguments presented by others. In story dramatization, they also need to listen carefully to the story to be able to work with it later. Thus, the whole range of oral language skills is represented in dramatic experiences.

Other Skills

Knowledge, or cognition, can be developed through dramatizations as students demonstrate their knowledge at various levels of complexity. Abstract ideas can be shown in a specific context, and students can pull together ideas to form a unique communication. Drama is also a vehicle for exploring affective components and developing appreciation. Drama may influence students in their interests, attitudes, and values as well.

Many students do not have the kind of home life teachers wish they had. Much in the curriculum does not seem real or valuable to such students. As O'Neill points out, "Drama can be a powerful antidote to the kind of alienation many students feel in the school situation, where everything *they* bring to the educational encounter is ignored or rejected. Authentic dialogue and drama can both be effective weapons against alienation."[27]

Within the framework of a dramatization, students can explore how they feel about various ideas and personalities but also how others feel. By playing a scene several different ways, they can explore alternative emotional responses. They can see the consequences of certain behaviors as they take on various roles. Psychomotor skills are also developed through dramatization as children respond to music or rhythm and as they relate their actions to the drama and perform the appropriate physical movement. Finally, creative activities such as role playing and dramatic play are very important in preparing children for the academic work of school. According to Beaven,

> [T]alk alone is not enough to help children organize their concepts and develop their language. They need a structuring activity such as building, creative art and movement, or dramatic play into which they can cast their impressions of the world. A wide variety of studies indicates that one-to-one adult-child play interactions, story-telling, and sociodramatic play using the manipulation of objects, are all good ways to foster growth of language and thought in children.[28]

Summary

Dramatic expression promotes language skills of oral speaking and composing, vocabulary development, language structure development, and listening, as well as other cognitive, affective, and psychomotor skills. An understanding of the skills that are developed through early and continuing experiences with dramatic expression seems to show clearly that dramatizing is more than just fun. It offers opportunities for developing children's abilities in a multitude of ways. Every teacher at every level of elementary and middle school should consider dramatic expression a key area of the language arts. It is a connecting point between language and literature and also serves as a basis for composition.

Questions for Discussion

1. What kinds of emphases in the language arts curriculum should encourage more dramatic activities in the classroom?
2. Why are dramatic activities such as pantomime, role play, and improvisation more highly recommended for elementary and middle school students than putting on plays?
3. Describe readers' theater and its potential for inclusion in the curriculum.
4. How would you evaluate student participation in dramatic activities? What would you look for?
5. If your principal or a parent asked why you spend time on dramatics rather than on basic skills, what would you say? What learning opportunities does drama offer?

Notes

1. Erik C. Haugaard, *Chase Me, Catch Nobody* (Boston, MA: Houghton Mifflin Co., 1980).

2. Ilse Koehn, *Mischling, Second Degree* (New York: Greenwillow, 1977).

3. Marie McSwigan, *Snow Treasure*, Mary Reardon, illustr. (New York: Dutton, 1942).

4. Deborah Robison, *Bye-Bye, Old Buddy* (New York: Clarion Books, 1983).

5. G. Davies, *Practical Primary Drama.* (Portsmouth, NH: Heinemann Educational Books, 1983), 47.

6. James Moffett, *A Child-Centered Language Arts Curriculum K–6: A Handbook for Teachers* (Boston, MA: Houghton Mifflin, 1968), 35.

7. Patrick Verriour, "Drama, Distance, and the Language Process," *Language Arts* 62, no. 4 (April 1985):385–386.

8. Benjamin DeMott cited in *Drama in the English Classroom*, Douglas Barnes, ed. (Champaign, IL: National Council of Teachers of English, 1967), 5.

9. J. N. Hook, Paul H. Jacobs, and Raymond D. Crisp, *What Every English Teacher Should Know* (Champaign, IL: National Council of Teachers of English, 1970), 39–40.

10. John Dixon, *Growth through English* (Reading, England: National Association of Teachers of English, 1967), 89.

11. James Moffett, *Drama: What is Happening?* (Champaign, IL: National Council of Teachers of English, 1967) 63.

12. Brian Wildsmith, *Python's Party* (New York: Franklin Watts, 1975).

13. Eve Merriam, "A Round," in *Finding a Poem* (New York: Atheneum, 1970), unpaged. From *Finding a Poem* by Eve Merriam. Copyright © 1970 by Eve Merriam. All rights reserved. Reprinted by permission of Marian Reiner for the author.

14. Jane Yolen, *No Bath Tonight*, Nancy Winslow Parker, illustr. (New York: Thomas Y. Crowell, 1978).

15. Evaline Ness, *Mr. Miacca* (New York: Holt, Rinehart & Winston, 1967).

16. Leslie I. Coger, "Staging Literature with Minimal Props for Maximal Meaning," *Scholastic Teacher* (October 1971):24–5.

17. F. S. Steel, *Tatttercoats*, D. Goode, illustr. (New York: Bradbury Press, 1976); R. Chase, "Ashpet," in *Grandfather Tales* (Boston, MA: Houghton Mifflin, 1948); "Little Burnt Face" in *The Talking Stones: An Anthology of Native American Tales*, D. Crews, illustr., D. de Wit, ed. (New York: Greenwillow, 1979); and L. D. Vuong, "The Brocaded Slipper" in *The Brocaded Slipper and Other Vietnamese Tales*, Vo-Dinh Mai, illustr. (Reading, MA: Addison Wesley, 1982).

18. Carol Carrick, *Patrick's Dinosaurs*, Donald Carrick, illustr. (New York: Clarion, 1983).

19. Dorothy Heathcote, *Three Looms Waiting* (Time-Life Films, 1972).

20. Jonothan Neelands, *Making Sense of Drama* (Portsmouth NH: Heinemann Educational Books, 1984), 50.

21. The following is some of the research in this area: Sarah Smilansky,

The Effects of Sociodramatic Play on Disadvantaged Preschool Children (New York: John Wiley and Sons, 1968); Kathie Vitz, "The Effects of Creative Drama in English as a Second Language," *Children's Theater Review*, 33 (1984):23–26, 33; Teresa Snyder-Greco, "The Effects of Creative Dramatic Techniques on Selected Language Functions of Language Disordered Children," *Children's Theater Review*, 32 (1983):9–13; and Anthony D. Pellegrini, "Symbolic Functioning and Children's Early Writing: The Relations between Kindergartners' Play and Isolated Word-Writing Fluency," in *New Directions in Composition Research*, Richard Beach and Lillian S. Bridwell, eds. (New York: Guilford, 1984).

22. L. C. Henderson and J. L. Shanker, "The Use of Interpretative Dramatics Versus Basal Reader Workbooks for Developing Comprehension Skill," *Reading World* 17 (1978):239–243; and Dorothy S. Strickland, "A Program for Linguistically Different Black Children," *Research in the Teaching of English* 7 (1973):79–86.

23. Lee Galda, "Narrative Competence: Play, Storytelling, and Story Comprehension," in *The Development of Oral and Written Language in Social Contexts*, Anthony Pellegrini and Thomas Yawkey, eds. (Norwood, NJ: Ablex, 1984), 105–117.

24. B. Plowden, *Children and Their Primary Schools* (Plowden Report) (London, UK: Her Majesty's Stationery Office, 1967.)

25. Marjorie Smelstor (ed.), *A Guide to Using Dramatic Performance and Oral Interpretation in the Writing Class* (Madison WI: University of Wisconsin Press, 1979), 39.

26. William Steig, *Caleb and Kate* (New York: Farrar, Straus & Giroux, 1977).

27. Cecily O'Neill, "Dialogue and Drama: The Transformation of Events, Ideas, and Teachers," *Language Arts* 66, no. 2 (February 1989):153.

28. Mary Beaven, "Learning through Inquiry, Discover, and Play," in *Discovering Language with Children*, Gay Su Pinnell, ed. (Urbana, IL: National Council of Teachers of English, 1980):15–16.

Bibliography: Some Books Suitable for Dramatizing

For Kindergartners, First-, and Second-Graders: Folktales

Asbjornsen P. C. and J. E. Moe. *The Three Billy Goats Gruff.* Illustrated by M. Brown. New York: Harcourt, 1957.

Blegvad, E. *The Three Little Pigs.* New York: Atheneum, 1980.

Cauley, L. B. *Goldilocks and the Three Bears.* New York: Putnam. 1981.

Hyman, T. S. *Little Red Riding Hood.* New York: Holiday House, 1983.

Kellogg, S. *Chicken Little.* New York: Morrow, 1985.

Perrault, C. *Cinderella.* Illustrated by S. Jeffers. New York: Dial, 1985.

Other Stories

Allard, H. *Miss Nelson is Missing.* Illustrated by J.Marshall. Boston: Houghton Mifflin, 1977.

Keats, E. J. *Whistle for Willie.* New York: Viking, 1964.

Lionni, L. *Frederick.* New York: Pantheon, 1966.

Rylant, C. *The Relatives Came.* Illustrated by S. Gammell. New York: Bradbury, 1985.

Sendak, M. *Where the Wild Things Are.* New York: Harper, 1963.

Slobodkina, E. *Caps for Sale.* Reading MA: Addison-Wesley, 1947.

Steig, W. *Doctor DeSoto.* New York: Farrar, Straus, 1982.

Viorst, J. *Alexander and the Terrible, Horrible, No Good, Very Bad Day.* Illustrated by R. Cruz. New York: Atheneum, 1972.

Waber, B. *Ira Sleeps Over.* Boston: Houghton Mifflin, 1972.

For Third-, Fourth-, and Fifth-Graders

Carle, E. *Twelve Tales from Aesop.* New York: Putnam, 1980.

Burch, R. *Ida Early Comes over the Mountain.* New York: Viking, 1980.

Fritz, J. *And Then What Happened, Paul Revere?* Illustrated by E. Thollander. New York: Crowell, 1973.

Grimm, Jacob and Wilhelm Grimm. *Hansel and Gretel.* Illustrated by P. Galdone. New York: McGraw-Hill, 1982.

Mayer, M. (reteller) *Beauty and the Beast.* New York: Harper & Row, Four Winds, 1978.

MacLachlan, P. *Sarah, Plain and Tall.* New York: Harper, 1985.

Ness, E. *Sam, Bangs and Moonshine.* New York: Holt, 1966.

Smith, D. B. *A Taste of Blackberries.* Illustrated by C. Robinson. New York: Crowell, 1973.

Steig, W. *Caleb and Kate.* New York: Farrar, Straus & Giroux 1977.

Van Allsburg, C. *Jumanji.* Boston: Houghton Mifflin, 1981.

Zemach, H. *Duffy and the Devil.* Illustrated by M. Zemach. New York: Farrar, Straus & Giroux 1973.

For Middle School Students

Babbitt, N. *Tuck Everlasting.* New York: Farrar, Straus & Giroux 1975.

Collier J. L. and C. Collier. *My Brother Sam is Dead.* New York: Four Winds, 1974.

Cleaver V. and B. Cleaver. *Where the Lillies Bloom.* Illustrated by J. Spanfeller. New York: Lippincott, 1969.

Engdahl, S. L. *Enchantress from the Stars.* Illustrated by R. Shackell. New York: Atheneum, 1970.

Fritz, J. *Early Thunder.* Illustrated by L. Ward. New York: Coward, McCann & Geoghegan 1967.

Greenfield, E. *Mary McLeod Bethune.* Illustrated by J. Pinkney. New York: Crowell, 1977.

Hunt, I. *Across Five Aprils.* Chicago: Follett, 1964.

Kerr, M. E. *Gentlehands.* New York: Harper & Row, 1978.

Klein, N. *Mom, the Wolf Man and Me.* New York: Pantheon, 1972.

L'Engle, M. *A Wrinkle in Time.* New York: Farrar, Straus & Giroux 1963.
Lewis, C. S. *The Lion, the Witch and the Wardrobe.* Illustrated by P. Baynes.
New York: Macmillan, 1961.
Reiss, J. *The Upstairs Room.* New York: Crowell, 1972.
Sleator, W. *The Green Futures of Tycho.* New York: Dutton, 1981.
Taylor, M. *Roll of Thunder, Hear My Cry.* Illustrated by J. Pinkney. New York:
Dial, 1976.

In addition to the books and stories listed above, there are many, many others
that may be used. Examine the books you and your students love that are in
your classroom or library. Some additional sources are given below.

Folklore of Various Countries

Fitzgerald, B. (ed.). *World Tales for Creative Dramatics and Storytelling.* New
York: Scribner, 1966.
McCaslin, N. (ed.). *Creative Drama in the Intermediate Grades.* White Plains,
NY: Longman, 1987.
Cullum. A. *Aesop in the Afternoon.* New York: Citation, 1972

For Making and Using Puppets

Cummings, R. *101 Hand Puppets: A Guide for Puppeteers of All Ages.* New
York: McKay, 1962
Freericks, M. and J. Segal. *Creative Puppets in the Classroom.* Rowayton,
CT:New Plays, 1979.
Hanford, R. T. *The Complete Book of Puppets and Puppeteering.* New York:
Drake, 1976.

Storytelling

Bauer, C. *Handbook for Storytellers.* Chicago: ALA, 1977.
Ross, R. R. *Storyteller.* Westerville, OH: Merrill, 1975.
Sawyer, R. (ed.). *The Way of the Storyteller.* New York: Penguin Books, 1977.

Stories to Dramatize

Siks, G. B. (ed.). *Children's Literature for Dramatization: An Anthology.* New
York: Harper & Row, 1964.
Ward, W. (ed.). *Stories to Dramatize.* New Orleans LA: Anchorage Press, 1952.
Trelease, J. *The Read-Aloud Handbook.* New York: Penguin, 1982.
Kimmell, M. M., and E. Segel. *For Reading Aloud!* New York: Dell, 1983.

Chapter 10

Listening and Language

Listening and Language

Kinds of Listening

Factors Affecting Listening
Hearing
Listening
Auding

Cultural Differences in Listening

The Listening Environment

Listening and Reading Comprehension
Role of Listener
Aspects of Comprehension

Expanding Comprehension Skills
Setting the Purpose
Developing Background Information
Practicing the Techniques to be Used

Listening to Literature
Listening to Narrative
Listening to Poetry
Listening to Informational Material

Television and Listening
Effects of Children's Viewing
Content of Television

Developing Critical Listening Skills
Teaching Critical Listening
Critical Listening Curricula

Almost everything a child learns before about age six comes from listening. And much of what is learned later in school may come from listening, too, if the studies of the time spent listening are accurate. A study done before the television era showed that three-fourths of a person's communication time is spent in the oral modes—over 40 percent of it in listening.[1] Reports of television viewing of children in 1988 indicate that preschoolers average 28 hours 6 minutes of television per week and that children between six and eleven watch television an average of 23 hours 21 minutes.[2] A great deal of time in school is also spent in listening. A classic study by Wilt[3] found that over half of the classroom time in elementary school is spent in listening, the majority of that to the teacher. Furthermore, the findings of Wilt's investigation indicate that teachers were unaware of how much time they required children to listen, and few of them ranked listening as the most important language skill. The tremendous amounts of time children spend in listening absolutely demand development of skill in this area.

Kinds of Listening

There are different levels of listening. Sometimes we enjoy having music in the background or a television going in another room. At some level we are aware of the sound, but we certainly aren't actively listening.

Other times we listen intently to television or radio because we want to know if our school will be closed that day or if we'll need to carry an umbrella or sweater. We listen to a political debate, mentally refuting the opposition's points; we listen to a friend sympathetically, not making any judgments; we listen to a lecture, taking notes on important points; we listen to a new recipe for a dip; we listen to a record or tape to see if we want to buy it; we listen to the swirl of conversation at a big party, one foot tapping to the music's beat. Different levels of listening are used for different purposes.

The classic categorization of listening comes from a committee of the National Council of Teachers of English[4] and includes four kinds of listening:

- *Marginal:* The listener is somewhat aware of sounds in the environment, but is not actively responding to the stimulus.
- *Appreciative:* Here the listener responds to poetry, music, stories, and so forth primarily for enjoyment and the stimulation of creative or expressive thoughts.
- *Attentive:* The listener focuses on the stimulus to get information, to participate actively. This type of listening is involved in following directions, taking part in a discussion, finding the main idea or sequence of events, and so forth.

- *Analytic:* In this kind of listening, one interprets and evaluates the material heard. Determining bias or point of view, evaluating information, and judging accuracy are all aspects of analytic listening.

More recently listening has been classified by purpose into five categories—appreciative, discriminative, comprehensive, therapeutic, and critical.[5] *Appreciative listening* involves listening to enjoy or to gain a sensory impression from the material. *Discriminative listening* refers to the distinguishing of the auditory or visual stimulus and includes sensitivity to nonverbal communication. *Comprehensive listening* is listening for the purpose of understanding a message. *Therapeutic listening* (or empathic listening) is listening in which the listener serves as a "sounding board" to enable the speaker to talk through a problem. *Critical listening* involves the listener in evaluating or judging the message, taking into account the effects of the language, arguments, appeals, and credibility of the speaker. Other writers on the subject select other ways of categorizing listening, but it seems quite clear that listening is not simply hearing what is said, or even understanding what is heard. Instead it appears to be a cluster of complex skills that relies on thought processes, memory, and language reception skills.

Factors Affecting Listening

Listening is not an unidimensional skill. According to Taylor there are three parts to listening: hearing, listening (comprehension), and auding.[6] Environmental factors and personal factors can affect listening at any one of these stages.

Hearing

Hearing is the necessary first step in listening. Two factors that can affect hearing relate to physical abilities: auditory acuity and binaural considerations. Auditory acuity refers to the ability to hear sounds—the range of tone and loudness we require. Binaural considerations refers to hearing adequately from both ears simultaneously, a necessary prerequisite for locating where sounds come from. Two other factors that affect hearing are situational: masking and auditory fatigue. Low-level but continuous sounds interfere with the things we should hear. These sounds that mask noise are things like the hum of a fan, voices from other groups or other rooms, constant shuffling of feet, a pencil sharpener being used, mowers or airplanes outside, or the hum of traffic on a nearby street. We must work harder to ignore these environmental sounds that mask what we are listening to. Too much listening, trying to concentrate for long periods of time, will lead to auditory fatigue. Our will and concentration diminish if a listening task is too long.

Listening

Listening involves taking in sounds, analyzing, recognizing, and associating them with meaning. Our physical ability to discriminate among sounds is part of listening, but other factors will affect whether or not we associate the proper meanings to the sound we hear. The amount of attention and concentration we give to the task will affect our understanding as will our background experiences. Since listening involves constructing meaning by relating what we hear to our own experiences, lack of experience in an area will greatly affect how much we understand. And making unrelated associations can destroy meaning for us. The speaker's style of delivery and of speech may also affect our listening ability.

Auding

The term *auding* has been used to refer to the higher-level aspects of listening in which we take the meaning from what we have heard and mentally manipulate it by making comparisons, indexing the ideas, noting the sequence, forming sensory impressions, or appreciating it. These mental activities lead to full meaning, which is the desired outcome. At the auding level the factor that affects us more than any other one is our background of experiences. Auding involves the integration of what we hear with everything else we know, and the extent, complexity, and scope of that knowledge greatly determines the meaning we construct.

Some of the factors that affect listening are beyond our control as teachers, but others are not. We certainly can ensure that children do not miss getting orally presented information because they have been asked to listen for too long a time. We should be sensitive to children who seem to have problems hearing—even temporarily because of a cold or ear infection. We may be able to build some additional background of experience for the children or remind them of similar experiences, which will aid them in using new information. Being sensitive to the factors that affect children's ability to listen should give us some clues for making listening experiences more meaningful.

Cultural Differences in Listening

We tend to assume that everyone uses the same cues to indicate they are paying attention and understanding the speaker. This is simply not true. Hall vividly describes the following contradictory aspects of conversation with Navahos: "Unlike middle-class whites, the direct open-faced look in the eyes was avoided by Navahos. . . . I ultimately learned that to look directly at a Navaho was to display anger. . . . Another Navaho taboo was to use the name as a form of direct address. Nor were voices ever raised—except in anger."[7] Imagine the teacher sent to work with Navaho children who had no training in Navaho culture. Typically the teacher raises his or her voice, calls on a student by name, and looks directly at the student, expecting eye contact. The Navaho child looks down to avoid such contact, interpreting the teacher's behavior as *anger*. The teacher, meanwhile, interprets the child's unwillingness to look back directly and respond as evidence of dishonesty or stupidity.

Similar differences in appropriate listening behavior exist in many other cultures. It is true of blacks, Puerto Ricans, Mexican-Americans, Vietnamese, and others. Many teachers are distressed that the black children in their room do not give the expected signs of paying attention: "Basically, the informal rule for black culture goes somewhat as follows: If you are in the room with another person or in a context where he has ready access to you, there are times when there is no need to go through the motions of showing him you are listening because that is automatically implied."[8] Misunderstandings about what children should do when listening can contribute to unnecessary conflicts when children are behaving correctly within their cultural background. Teachers need to become familiar with the nonverbal and verbal aspects of the culture of children they teach.

The Listening Environment

We have talked in earlier chapters about providing a rich language environment for children. In such an environment children are encouraged to converse about topics of interest, share and discuss favorite books, read aloud to book partners, and talk freely with their teacher and peers. This rich language environment is also the rich listening environment. Children are not required to listen to the teacher two-thirds of the time; instead, purposeful listening is continuous throughout the school day. Skills in speaking and listening develop more naturally in this type of learning setting—and rightfully so. *Oracy,* a term originally coined at the Birmingham University School of Education, refers to the skill of listening and speaking, just as *literacy* refers to the skills of reading and writing. The reciprocity between listening and speaking is natural and

*In a rich language environment, children are encouraged to talk
about topics of interest and engage in meaningful conversations
with their teacher and peers.*

can occur within classrooms where teachers value language. In such
classrooms teachers make opportunities for both speaking and listening because it is through them that language develops. But we need to
differentiate between a qualitative and quantitative language environment. If the classroom is organized and managed in a laissez-faire fashion where children merely chat with one another and no direction is
given to their conversations and discussions, little learning of any kind
can take place. Rather, it is the carefully planned and organized environment that facilitates skills in oracy. It is a setting where learning experiences are continuous and not chopped up in little time segments. Andrew Wilkinson, a British educator, describes an effective classroom
learning climate in this way:

> The English teacher has special opportunities for providing a rich
> variety of speech situations, amongst which discussion is prime.
> The traditional English time-table assigned different aspects of
> the subject to different periods. Now we think of the time-table in

terms of a central continuing theme or experience out of which emerge opportunities for various aspects of production (writing and speaking) and reception (listening and reading). We start, not with the skill to be taught, but with the central experience upon which the skills may operate. Within this framework many opportunities for speaking and listening occur naturally.[9]

In such a skillfully organized environment children are actively involved in interesting and meaningful experiences. Skills in both oracy and literacy develop naturally within the framework of the experiences themselves.

Listening and Reading Comprehension

Comprehension is comprehension whether you are trying to understand something you read or something you hear. Of course listening and reading are not identical. Information is gained in listening from the expression and tone of the speaker's voice, from the repetitions of ideas, and even from pauses. In reading, there are graphic cues to help you understand; and you can always re-read a passage you do not understand. Aside from these differences in the mode of presentation of material, the process of comprehending and the skills you use to understand are the same; they are comprehension.

Role of Listener

Our views of comprehension have changed in terms of the relationship between the listener/reader and the text. We used to think the text contained the meaning that the listener or reader was to approximate. Now we realize that different readers get somewhat different meanings from what they read, just as different listeners hear somewhat different messages from the same talk. This is because people's experiential background is different, their vocabulary is different, and the strategies they use to understand are different. Pearson describes the relationship between reader and text in this way:

> Modern theories of comprehension . . . require us as educators to realize that the whole process of comprehension is much more *active, constructive,* and *reader-based* than our older theories suggested. No longer can we think of comprehension as *passive, receptive,* and *text-based.* No longer can we think of meaning as residing "in the text." Instead, we must regard each and every text students read as a blueprint to guide them in building their own

model of what the text means. The text sets some broad bound-aries on the range of permissible meanings, but it does not specify particular meanings.[10]

This is as true of listening as it is of reading.

Aspects of Comprehension

Different theorists have described comprehension using various terms. Perhaps the most widely used description comes from Barrett's "Tax-onomy of Reading Comprehension."[11] This taxonomical listing is pat-terned after Bloom's *Taxonomy of Educational Objectives.*[12] It has four levels: literal recognition or recall, inference, evaluation, and ap-preciation. Literal recognition or recall includes recognizing or recall-ing details, main ideas, sequence, comparisons, cause and effect, and character traits. Inference includes inferring supporting details, main idea, comparisons, cause and effect relationships, character traits, outcomes, and figurative language. Evaluation includes judgments or reality or fantasy, fact or opinion, adequacy or validity, appropriate-ness, and judgments of worth, desirability or acceptability. Apprecia-tion includes emotional response to the content, identification with characters and incidents, reactions to the author's use of language and imagery.

These are the aspects of comprehension that teachers hope stu-dents will be increasingly able to use when working with oral or written materials. To accomplish this goal, students can learn strategies to use in both listening and reading.

Expanding Comprehension Skills

Three sorts of skills are involved in comprehension. These are setting the purpose, developing background information, and practicing the techniques to be used. Each is important in its own way, and none are automatically used by students. These are the skills that teachers should introduce to their students and have them practice.

Setting the Purpose

Part of setting a purpose for listening or reading is the intention to understand. Students must sense a real need to understand and must make a commitment to do so. They need a specific motive for listening (or reading) so that what they should find out or what idea or informa-tion they need is clear.

In fiction, the purpose for listening or reading might be expressed in terms of these questions:

What happened to a particular character?
Why do the characters feel the way they do?
How are these two stories alike?
What did the character do to achieve his or her purpose?

In informational material, the purpose might be presented as follows.

What steps are used to solve a problem?
What facts are there about this topic?
What is the relationship between these two things?
How complete is this explanation or these directions?

Helping students set a clear purpose for listening or reading and an intention to understand are critical to comprehension.

Developing Background Information

Since what readers or listeners know about the topic is the basis for interpreting what they hear or read, you need to help students connect what they know with the new information. You can increase comprehension by developing children's backgrounds of experiences, by helping them relate their experiences to the topic, by helping them understand how knowledge about genre and format can be used, and by developing their knowledge of the vocabulary that will be involved.

Background of Experience
Many children do not have experience with common activities, places, or things. They may never have had a pet or taken care of a small animal or some fish. They may not have peeled or tasted a fresh lemon or orange, nor visited a florist or shoe repair shop, nor seen quarters of beef or pork being cut up. They may never have kneaded yeast dough or used a needle and colored yarn or thread to make designs on burlap or other cloth. They have probably never built an anemometer to tell wind speed or used a prism to split the sunshine into a rainbow. The more experiences you can provide for children, the more you increase their ability to understand as well as their repertoires of things to write about and to draw. It is not necessary to make complicated arrangements to take a bus on a long field trip. Consider a walk-about. Is there a place nearby to visit? Does a neighbor have an interesting collection or skill to demonstrate? If you cannot go somewhere, could someone come to your class? If you cannot have the visitor in person, could you

use the telephone and a speaker so the children can hear and participate in the interview? What about the resources within your school that you may not have considered: Would another teacher who has taken ballet be willing to demonstrate? Will the lunchroom supervisor let you use the kitchen to bake something after serving times? Could you plant a garden outside your door or put out a bird feeder? Does the school secretary know how to tie flies for fishing? Or does the custodian know how to call a square dance? Are there films, videotapes, film strips, records or tapes or other types of second-hand experience that would be interesting? Making things, experimenting with materials, and talking to others about their hobbies and collections can lead to further research, writing, discussion, and to learning. Directly and indirectly such experiences help develop comprehension.

Relating Knowledge to the Topic

Discussing a topic prior to reading about it or listening to information about it can be helpful. Hearing others' experiences may aid or remind us of information we can use. Semantic mapping or webbing of information prior to listening or reading helps students identify the major ideas and relationships in the material they are about to deal with. Before listening to or reading about a topic, the students map out what they know or think they know with the teacher's help. Afterwards, they go back and correct their maps or add to them in light of the new information they have gained. (See the section in Chapter 3, "Learning and Thinking" for illustrations of different kinds of maps or webs.)

Sometimes an analogy may help students understand a concept or idea since it uses familiar information. We might compare our skin with plastic-wrapped food. As long as the plastic is not pierced or torn, no dirt will get on the food wrapped up. If it is torn, then it is no longer protected. So our skin keeps the nerves and muscles, and bone and all protected from the dirt and germs outside as long as it is not pierced or torn.

Knowledge of Genre and Format

Researchers have found that a "sense of story"—knowing what a story is like—is important because the reader can predict more accurately what will happen next. This is true of various kinds of stories, poetry, and informational material. Effective speakers and writers provide structural information for listeners and readers to use. If a speaker says, for example, "There are five common breeds of dairy cows," we know to listen for those five breeds. In a story, we expect a sequence of events. A flashback, in fact, may throw us off if it is not clearly marked. Teachers can make students aware of such cues before starting to listen or read or as the students come across them. The mapping mentioned earlier also helps focus on the structure of the topic or genre.

Vocabulary

Increasing awareness of the usefulness of prior knowledge and background experiences points to the greater importance for developing vocabulary—knowledge of word meanings and associated shades of meaning. Teachers can preview the piece to be read, the tape or film, or consider the topic to determine any unusual words that the students may not know. Also look for meanings that are different from the meaning the students know. For example, although children may know *regular* as meaning "arranged or ordered according to some established rule, principle, or type," as in *at the regular time,* they may not know *regular* as meaning "complete or unmitigated" as in the phrase *a regular scoundrel.* It may be important for students to be aware of special connotations of a word they will encounter, such as *prominent,* which means not only "notable and memorable" (which might apply to a thief or murderer) but also "distinguished and eminent" (which would prohibit our using prominent to refer to them). Students also need to learn to use context effectively to determine word meanings. Practice exercises using cloze procedure, in which a blank replaces certain words, may be done orally to develop this skill. You might also ask students what word could replace an unknown word that would make sense in the context. (See Chapter 5, "Extending Vocabulary," for additional suggestions about teaching vocabulary.)

Practicing the Techniques to be Used

There are some practices that students can use to increase their comprehension, and these techniques can be taught. Often teachers give students no information about how to remember and make sense of what they read or hear; they just ask questions to see if their students can remember the content. Nolte and Singer note, "When teachers ask students questions before or after they read and evaluate only their answers, they are stressing only the *product* of comprehension; they are not teaching students a *process* of comprehending text."[13] The procedures described here focus on the process of comprehending and work well with both listening comprehension and reading comprehension.

Listen and Read Simultaneously

Instead of having students just listen to a tape, film, filmstrip, or story, provide a text to follow while listening. This may not always be possible, but access to copy machines and tape recorders makes it easier. Teacher-made or commercial tapes of favorite storybooks will provide good practice at a listening center. If you can make your own tapes, get a friend or two to speak some of the other characters' voices.

Children read and listen to poems in Jack Prelutsky's book The New Kid on the Block.

Repeat What You Hear or Read

As they listen, have students try to repeat phrases and sentences that they hear. They can reread a piece to themselves or to someone else. Teachers may have students do echo reading where the teacher reads a sentence or phrase and the students then read that same sentence or phrase.

Find the Key Words

As they listen or read, have students try to identify the key words—those that carry the meaning or that identify important structural elements. Students may want to say these aloud or to themselves or to write them down.

Suppose they are reading or listening to this information from Gibbons' *The Milk Makers*, "Next, the milk is 'homogenized,' or forced through tiny openings under great pressure. This breaks up the fatty globules of the cream to give every drop of milk the same amount."[14] The key words are *next, milk, homogenized, or forced through, openings, pressure, breaks up, globules, cream, give, milk,* and *same amount.* The important structure words are *next,* which indicates the sequence, and *or,* which indicates a defining phrase. This use of key words does not give every detail of information, but if students select good key words, they will certainly have the basic idea.

Predict What Information or Event Will Come Next

Active interaction with the speaker or text is critical to real comprehension. So you think, "The milk's been cleaned, pasteurized, and homogenized," the reader might predict that the milk is put in cartons next. Further reading then tests the prediction. On hearing, "It was completely still. Even the leaves hung quietly," the listener might suspect that something loud or terrible is about to happen. A reasonable prediction about a folktale concerning a king with three sons (or three daughters) is that the youngest will outsmart the others and win. Making conscious predictions about what will come next is an important aspect of understanding that is often neglected.

Ask Questions and Answer Them

Active comprehension, according to Nolte and Singer, is a process of generating questions while reading and searching for the answers to them.[15] Students should learn to ask their own questions before, during, and after reading. Questioning helps establish the purpose and causes the listener or reader to interact with the text, confirming or rejecting ideas. Students will need practice in learning to ask questions. Teachers can help by modeling this process as they read with students.

Paraphrase the Content

Students should learn to take time to state in their own words what they are hearing or reading, which helps to ensure that they are following along. Periodic retellings in their own words will help them to understand and also to remember. Students should start by paraphrasing sentences, then paragraphs and even whole pieces.

Summarize Informational Materials

Students should learn to write a summary or to list the important ideas in the text they have heard or read. This may be as informal as jotting a few sentences or as detailed as writing a formal outline. Younger and less experienced students should start out with short texts to work with—a few sentences or a paragraph. As they gain skill in summarizing they can work on longer and more complex materials. At first students will need feedback about their summaries, which might be too complete or too sketchy, or might miss essential ideas or include trivial ones. Discussion of what to include in a summary is often helpful, as well as frequent practice.

Dramatize Episodes in Narrative Material

The act of dramatizing a text forces students to deal with the sequence of events, important aspects of ideas, character traits, and so forth. It is as close to total reconstruction as is possible. Such dramatizations of stories make the literature more memorable and significant.

The eight techniques for improving comprehension all involve active interaction between the listener or reader and the text. They are predicated on a view of comprehension as a process in which the listener or reader tries to construct meaning by interrelating past knowledge about the topic and the structure with new information. Some techniques are more productive for narrative, others for informational materials. Some are easier to do with reading and others with listening. They are all more productive than just asking questions after students have read or heard something that does not help children become better at comprehending materials.

When teaching listening, the most important factor to remember is to integrate. Teachers should help their students practice listening skills—not with special materials for that practice, but with material in the different content areas. Listening should not be an isolated subject in the school curriculum but an integral part of all the language arts and other content areas.

Listening to Literature

"The foundations of good [reading] comprehension are set in early childhood, in listening comprehension."[16] Teale, Hiebart, and Chittenden add that reading aloud to children is the single most important early activity for fostering comprehension. The importance of reading to children throughout the elementary grades and in the middle school cannot be overemphasized. Reading aloud, even after students know how to read for themselves, allows the teacher to share experiences through books that students might not select on their own. It is also a way of sharing poetry that students can enjoy rather than analyze. Listening to literature helps students learn what literature is and what to expect from the various genres.

While simply listening for pleasure to stories and poems is sufficient in and of itself, there may be times when the teacher wants to extend the literary experience. Such interactions with the literature may make it more meaningful for the students. Some extending activities might involve telling and retelling stories—those they just heard and others that are similar in some way, perhaps using the pictures in the text as cues, or using puppets or flannelboard characters. Students could discuss the story, not by answering questions about what happened but by making predictions and inferring information, discussing a character's motivation or development, responding to issues presented by the characters or events, or identifying personally with the characters or events in the story.

After listening to poetry, students might reread selections, participate in choral reading, or mime some of the actions, animals, or people in the poem. Movement activities related to a poem are fun for younger children. Poems, like stories, elicit discussion of their themes, language, and imagery.

Literature is best presented by a well-prepared reader, but there are alternatives to the teacher serving as reader, such as films, tapes, and records of stories and poems. Teachers can make home-made media presentations of stories or poems by audiotaping them and having students do illustrations for them.

Listening to Narrative

An aspect of narratives that children can learn about and use in understanding stories is knowledge of various narrative structures. One such structure is the circular plot. *The Magnificent Moo* by Forrester is an example of such a story structure. The cow is afraid of her own "moo" because it is "so big" and "so loud," but the cat admires it, and so they trade sounds for the morning. Later the cat trades the moo with a duck who trades it with another animal and on it goes until it ends up with a honeybee who gets so busy with honey that she leaves the moo right in the middle of a yellow daisy where of course the cow hears it, eats up the daisy, and decides the sound is delicious.[17]

Before beginning this type of story, you want to tell the students that it is like a circle—it comes back to where it began. Or you may want to diagram the circle (see Figure 10.1) or have five children sit in a circle to represent characters. As they retell the story, the rest of the class can follow the events and see the circle. (Two other picture books with a circular narrative are *The Stonecutter* by Gerald McDermott[18] and *If You Give a Mouse a Cookie* by Laura Numeroff and illustrated by Felicia Bond.[19])

Listening to Poetry

Poetry has its own graphic conventions: longer poems are usually divided into stanzas instead of paragraphs, and each line usually begins with a capital letter even if the word is not the beginning of a sentence. Many poems have short lines that do not fill the width of a page. Poems also make more intensive use of metaphorical language, analogies, sound effects and rhyme, and meter. They are very concentrated so that each word and all that it connotes is important. Poems often make a

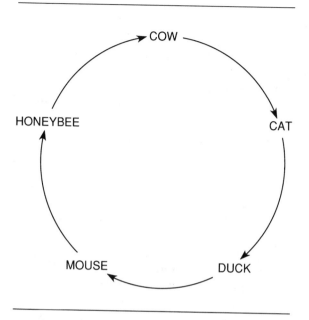

FIGURE 10.1 *Narrative plot structure of*
The Magnificent Moo

comment about life or a statement about values rather indirectly; a reader may lose some meaning if he or she moves on to another one too quickly.

For example, examine "Blow-Up" by X. J. Kennedy.

Blow-Up

Our cherry tree
Unfolds whole loads
Of pink-white bloom—
It just explodes.

For three short days
Its petals last
Oh, what a waste.
But what a blast.[20]
    —X. J. Kennedy

The comparison between a bomb and a cherry tree is so unpredictable that it makes us look at spring's flowering trees in a new way. Several words suggest this comparison: "Blow-Up," *explodes*, and *blast*. Flowering trees are stunning, but they do last only a few days before the grass is covered with fallen petals.

Can children relate the poem to other wonderful things that do not last? What about fireworks or an ice cream cone? There is no need to overanalyze poetry. Sometimes just reading it and enjoying it is enough. Knowing some things about poetry will make children more appreciative if they are not just technical aspects for a test.

Listening to Informational Material

Determining what the children already know about a topic and establishing some specific things to listen (or read) for really develop comprehension and interest. A brief discussion followed by mapping the information the students know before listening, and then correcting and adding to the map after listening is effective. Suppose you were going to read aloud *The Post Office Book* by Gail Gibbons as part of a unit of study on Community Helpers.[21] What do the children already know about the post office and how mail moves? They probably know about where to mail things, about stamps, and about the trucks or cars that deliver mail. They may know their own zip code, but probably not much about what happens after a letter is put in the mailbox. Figure 10.2 shows a map one class made before hearing *The Post Office Book*

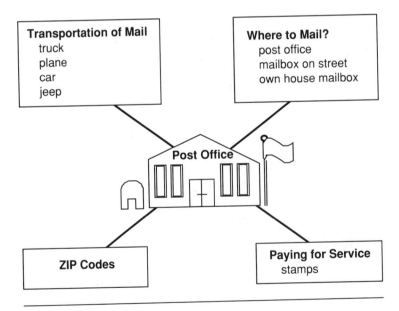

FIGURE 10.2   *Map of knowledge about how mail moves before reading* The Post Office Book

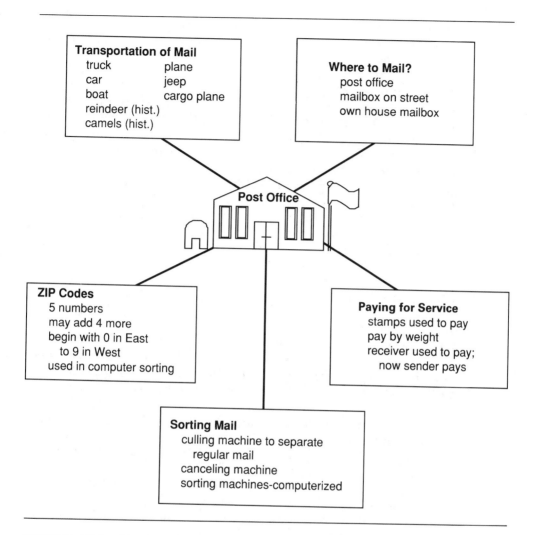

FIGURE 10.3 *Map of knowledge about how mail moves after listening to*
The Post Office Book

read aloud. Figure 10.3 is their map after listening to it and after the
teacher reread some parts. They wanted to visit the post office, but it
was too far away. Instead the teacher invited their local postmaster to
come out to school. He brought a mail truck and a small sorting machine and let the children see how the mail is sorted and stored within
the truck. Later they invented zip codes for their room. Each table had
its own first three digits, and then each person had their own last two
digits. For a while they used the zip code on all their papers, which the

teacher returned to the center of the table for further sorting. They also set up their own mailboxes (wine cases on their side painted blue) with labeled zip code numbers.

Listening to literature is one of the most valuable experiences for children in developing comprehension skills, a sense of story or poem, interest in reading, and language skills. It is important to select good literature to share, and to develop your skill in reading aloud. Students may listen to enjoy a story or poem, or teachers may extend their contact with literature in some way. Extensions should enhance students' responses and make the literature more meaningful and interesting. Literature can serve as the integrating force in the curriculum that allows children to explore their interests and develop literacy skills. "Direct teaching of literature helps students move into, through, and beyond the literary work to a new understanding of themselves and the world around them."[22]

Television and Listening

Television is a source of pleasure for both adults and children, but it is not without problems. In the United States television is certainly a prime consumer of people's time. According to the *1988 World Almanac and Book of Facts* and the *Television and Cable Factbook, 1986*, the following facts describe American viewing habits:

- Children 2 to 5 years old watch television on the average 28 hours 6 minutes per week.
- Children 6 to 11 years old watch television on the average 23 hours 21 minutes per week.
- Teenage girls watch television on the average 20 hours and 33 minutes per week.
- Teenage boys watch television on the average 22 hours and 38 minutes per week.[23]
- There are 196,000,000 television sets in the United States, which is 814 for each 1,000 people.
- In the United States 98 percent of all homes have at least one television set.[24]

What does this mean? It means that the average preschooler watches more than 5,800 hours of television before he or she goes to first grade. This is the equivalent of 145, forty-hour weeks. It means that by the time children enter seventh grade, they have seen more than 13,050 hours of television, or the equivalent of 326, forty-hour weeks or 2,610 whole afternoons (1:00 P.M. to 6:00 P.M.).

Even more alarming is the data showing that 2- to 5-year-olds watch almost five hours per week between 8:00 P.M. and 11:00 P.M., and elementary school children watch more than six hours per week after 8:00 P.M. While school hours vary considerably from place to place, 8:00 to 11:30 in the morning and 12:15 to 2:45 in the afternoon are average. That probably includes one 15-minute recess and a 5-minute bathroom break. Figuring a 180-day school year, that is a total of 1,020 hours of schooling per year compared with 1,214 hours of television.

Effects of Children's Viewing

The effects of so much television viewing by children are not completely clear. "Effects of television on viewers are a result of a dynamic process in which the viewer and the television content interact. Since viewers are different from one another, the same television content can evoke different responses from different viewers."[25]

Television has been called "The Plug-In Drug" by Winn, who lists eight things wrong with watching TV.

1. TV takes time away from other more wholesome activities.
2. TV competes against alternative family activities (like playing a game or listening to a story).
3. TV allows kids to grow up less civilized (because parents do not work at socializing).
4. TV takes the place of play.
5. TV makes children less resourceful (they don't accumulate the skills to fill in time successfully).
6. TV has a negative effect on children's physical fitness.
7. TV has a negative effect on school achievement.
8. Television watching may be a serious addiction.[26]

While one cannot claim that Winn expresses an unbiased view, there is some evidence to support many of her claims. Many professionals suggest similar harms that may be done as a result of excessive television watching.

We should be concerned about even the average television watcher—both about what the child watches and what activities the child gives up to watch. If preschool children listened to someone share one story instead of each hour of television, that would be 5,800 stories by the first grade. While older children are spending 13,050 hours watching television, what games are they giving up playing? What model planes or cars are not being built? What conversation time disappears? What books never get read? What crafts are never tried?

Content of Television

"The content of television is more than a story being told, or information being communicated. It implicitly or explicitly advocates a style of life and a way of dealing with one's conflict with others. It also offers an interpretation of one's surroundings, and some of the national and international events."[27] If we see the same views expressed over and over, we come to believe they must be right. If we always see people living in spacious, carpeted, elegant rooms, then we come to believe that is how everyone else lives. If the characters in our favorite shows drink, then we may view drinking more positively. If people solve their problems through violence, then we may regard this as an acceptable solution. One of the things children learn incidentally from television is how to interact with each other. "In many instances, children imitate the behavior of their favorite stars and heroes in the programs they watch."[28]

There are three main areas of content that present problems for children: separating fantasy from reality, dealing with the violence shown, and TV's messages about sex.

Young children often have difficulty separating fantasy from real life. On television, they see Superman fly, Santa with his sleigh and reindeer coming through the sky, or a man turns into a monster before their very eyes. How are they to know that these are special effects and not at all real? They have very little personal experience to use as a basis for judging. As they move from cartoon characters to real people doing the impossible, they may not recognize these things as unreal.

As for violence, by the time the average American child graduates from high school, he or she will have seen more than 13,000 violent deaths, all of them on television. Some researchers have found that between 80 percent and 90 percent of programs depict violence[29], and that the weekend morning children's programs contain the highest rate of violent action. A recent study of music video programs also showed a high incidence of violence.[30] Moreover, real violence is misrepresented on television because it is more frequent than in real life and it seldom presents the agony of the victim or the turmoil of the perpetrator. Violence is presented as a regular solution to conflict. The killer or the person committing violent acts is often the hero, and violence is depicted as a source of excitement. Is that the view of violence we want children to have?

The messages television gives to adolescents about sexuality should also be of concern. On regular channels sex is implied rather than explicitly shown as it is on pay channels. According to Klein, the messages projected about sex show that a double standard still exists, that men may not be able to control their feelings and may even express them violently, and that amorous techniques are more important than feelings or emotions. The overall view is that sex is secretive and danger-ous.[31] These are certainly not the views that most parents want their children to have.

The content of what we watch on television and what children watch should be of concern to everyone. When you combine the amount of time that children watch television—much of it unsupervised—with the unrealistic views of life, and the amount of violence, and the por-trayal of sex, it is hard to regard 20 to 30 hours per week of television watching as suitable for our children.

Developing Critical Listening Skills

Since both children and adults spend so much time listening—listening to others and to the media—it is particularly important to develop criti-cal listening skills. What is a critical listener like?

> The "critical"-minded are active, not passive, in their reception of the printed and spoken word or the motion picture, television, and radio. They constantly ask: "Is it true? Where's your evidence?" and "What do you mean by 'true'?" They search out hidden assump-tions, unwarranted inferences, false analogies. They are the good-natured skeptics and sometimes, the well-intentioned cynics. They give the ill-informed and inaccurate teacher many a bad moment. And they are our greatest hope for progress.[32]

Children at all grades need to learn to take a critical stance toward what they hear, consciously evaluating it. Critical listening involves applying critical thinking skills to material that we hear. In Chapter 3, "Learning and Thinking," the section on critical thinking listed two essential quali-ties to be considered: adequacy of information and relevancy.

Adequacy can be determined by answering three questions:

> Does this come from a reliable source?
> Is the speaker believable?
> Is this information current?

In judging the adequacy of information, we want to know if it is up to date and if the source of the information is someone or a group that we have reason to believe would be well informed and accurate. We check the believability of the speaker against the facts and against our own background of knowledge.

Relevancy asks us to judge whether what we hear is applicable or not:

Is this fact or opinion?
Is the information pertinent to the problem?
Do the conclusions follow logically?

We should know if a statement is a fact or an opinion. Nothing is wrong with opinions if there are no facts established or if the facts need interpretation. Opinions may well be relevant, although we must consider their source. Another question is whether or not the information is pertinent to the problem. However factual and true something is if it is not related to the issue being considered, it should be excluded. The final aspect of relevancy is whether the conclusions made are logical. The reasoning must be clear and valid.

We need to help students focus on what they hear or read and be skeptical enough to ask such questions. We all should approach information given us with a speculative air—Should I believe that?

Teaching Critical Listening

One of the important things that teachers can do is to model critical listening. As we watch a film or televised program with our class, we can ask, I wonder if she is right about that? Do you think that is true? Where did they get that information. You can give some background biographical information on a speaker that reflects his or her expertise. You can examine the reputation of the filmmaker. When you get some information that seems to be primarily an opinion, you might ask students to try to verify the facts on which it is based. As you model asking critical questions, your example will show students how they might look critically at their world. Advertising is a good topic for activities designed to improve critical listening skills.

Manufacturers would not spend billions of dollars each year on advertising unless they believed that it increased their sales. Students are consumers and will become a major factor in the marketplace. Teachers should examine advertising and the tactics used to get people to buy a particular product. Below are some propaganda techniques that are widely used by advertisers.

Bandwagon: Everybody is doing it. All members of a group are doing it.
Card stacking: Falsehoods that distract. Illogical statements to give the best or worst possible case for an idea.
Glittering generalities: Virtue words like *truth* and *honor.* Empty yet colorful words.
Name calling: Giving an idea or product a bad label.
Plain folks: Attempts to delude an audience into thinking the speaker is just like them.

Testimonial: A respected or hated person who says that a given idea is good or bad.

Transfer: The authority and prestige of something respected are carried over to something else.[33]

You might put together some examples of these techniques that you find in magazine advertising, or tape record some from radio or television broadcasts. See if students can match the ad to the propaganda technique. Have students write ads for an imaginary product using each technique. You may be able to get a film or videotape of Clio Award-winning advertisements—these ads are great fun to analyze.

Start a collection of materials that present different sides of an issue. Different sources of information about a topic under study often present discrepancies in information or different interpretations of the same person or event. When that happens, students are usually startled. How can one source say a mountain is 12,456 feet high and another source gives its height as 12,377 feet? How can one biographer say President Eisenhower treated General MacArthur vindictively while another biographer contends his actions were completely appropriate? If students only read one textbook and do worksheets, they won't find these conflicts and will not learn to judge things critically.

Another possibility for teaching about television and critical listening is to do some classroom activities based on the shows students currently watch to make them more sensitive to what they are viewing.

1. Have students compare their homes or the homes of friends to those shown on television. Are they the same size? What about furnishings? Take a survey and assign different students to research the portrayal of homes on several television shows. Have students survey the job occupations of characters on television as compared to people they know—their parents or neighbors.

2. Have students compare and contrast television news and newspaper coverage of a particular incident or current event.

3. Invite students to discuss how men and women on television are expected to behave. How does this compare with the men and women the students know. Does television reflect reality?

4. When a new program premièrs on television, ask students to watch. The next day discuss and evaluate the program with the students or have them write a review.

5. Ask students to watch a Saturday morning children's show and tally the number of times a character hits or hurts another one. Discuss what they found and talk about why people get angry with others and what alternatives there are. How can such situations be handled without violence?

You can also use children's viewing habits as a basis for other language arts activities. You might get students involved in watching better programs. There are some fine programs that would enrich their lives and provide good material for teaching. Try the following teaching suggestions.

1. Students might like to dramatize scenes from their favorite shows or act out alternative endings.
2. For vocabulary development, have children report new words or phrases they hear. Have them keep a pencil and paper with them during a program to write the phrase or the general context of the word. Remind them not to bring in inappropriate words.
3. Have students practice note-taking skills while watching an informational program. Programs like *60 Minutes, 20/20,* or *Sunday Morning* that have separate story segments work well.
4. Incorporate good informational shows, as appropriate, in what you are studying. Educational networks and local public service television will probably give you an advance guide so you can plan.

In all the talk about television, don't ignore the other electronic media—especially movies and radio. Popular movies are apt to be just as unrealistic, violent, and sex-filled as television. This includes movies students see in the theaters and those at home on VCRs and the radio programs they listen to. Many students have personal radios with earphones that they wear to school or at other times. What is being advertised? What view of life do song lyrics give? What values are expressed?

Critical Listening Curricula

There are two curricula for teaching critical viewing that are appropriate for elementary and middle school grades. The first is *Getting the Most out of Television* produced by the Yale University Family Television Research and Consultation Center for students in grades three through eight.[34] It consists of eight lessons written to go with programs from ABC Wide World of Learning (available in 16mm film or videotape), but the lessons can be used independently of the tapes or films. The second is called *Critical Television Viewing: A Language Skills Work-a-Text* for students in grades five through nine.[35] This material is in book format with a separate teacher's edition. It contains activities, charts, games, illustrations, and photographs to present the skills in ten chapters. There is also a free publication of the federal government that offers suggestions for parents about television from the Children's Bureau of the Department of Health, Education and Welfare called *Children and Television*.[36]

In an age when listening is rapidly becoming a primary means of obtaining information as well as a source of enjoyment through radio, television, and movies, it seems that listening skills deserve more attention that they presently receive in our schools. With an interesting and meaningful learning environment and appropriate instruction, students' listening skills can be improved. Children can become critical thinkers, readers, and listeners.

Summary

Since so much of children's learning and communication in school and at home is spent listening, it is essential for teachers to develop students' listening skills. Children must learn to adjust their levels of concentration to the kind of listening called for by their purpose. Teachers should be familiar with cultural differences in listening and with the factors that may affect students' abilities. Listening comprehension involves setting purposes, developing background information, and practicing techniques useful in comprehension tasks.

Listening to literature is fundamental to good reading comprehension. Different kinds of literature suggest different classroom practices. A major aspect of listening relates to television, which is a prime time-consumer in our nation. The effects of children's viewing are discussed as well as the content of television. This chapter is aimed at making teachers much more conscious of the importance of listening and the significance of developing good listeners with appreciation for oral presentations as well as good critical listening skills.

Questions for Discussion

1. What are some of the factors that affect how well children listen and comprehend what they hear?
2. What techniques can students use to improve their listening comprehension skills? Describe each briefly.
3. What adjustments should be made when listening to stories, to poems, and to informational materials?
4. Why are many educators concerned about the amount of time children spend watching television?
5. Why is critical listening important?

Notes

1. Paul T. Rankin, "The Measurement of the Ability to Understand Spoken Language" (Ph.D. dissertation, University of Michigan, 1926).

2. M. S. Hoffman (ed.), *World Almanac and Book of Facts* (New York: Pharos Books, 1988), 361.

3. Miriam E. Wilt, "A Study of Teacher Awareness of Listening as a Factor in Elementary Education," *Journal of Educational Research* 43 (April 1950):626–636.

4. Commission on the English Curriculum of the National Council of Teachers of English, *The English Language Arts* (New York: Appleton-Century-Crofts, 1952). Copyright © 1952 by the National Council of Teachers of English. Reprinted with permission.

5. Andrew D. Wolvin and Carolyn G. Cookley, *Listening Instruction* (Urbana, IL: ERIC Clearinghouse on Reading and Communication Skills, 1969):7–13.

6. Sam Taylor, *What Research Says to the Teacher: Listening* (Washington, DC: National Education Association, 1964).

7. Edward T. Hall, "Listening Behavior: Some Cultural Differences," *Phi Delta Kappan* 50 (March 1969):379–380.

8. *Ibid.*, 380.

9. Andrew Wilkinson, "Oracy in English Teaching," *Elementary English* 45, no. 6 (October 1968):743.

10. P. David Pearson, "Changing the Face of Reading Comprehension Instruction," *The Reading Teacher* 38, no. 8 (April 1985):734.

11. Thomas C. Barrett, "Taxonomy of Reading Comprehension," *Reading 360 Monograph* (Lexington, MA: Ginn and Company, 1972).

12. Benjamin S. Bloom (ed.), *Taxonomy of Educational Objectives: The Classification of Educational Goals. Handbook I: Cognitive Domain* (New York: McKay, 1956).

13. Ruth Yopp Nolte and Harry Singer, "Active Comprehension: Teaching a Process of Reading Comprehension and its Effects on Reading Achievement," *The Reading Teacher* 38, no. 1 (October 1985):24.

14. Gail Gibbons, *The Milk Makers* (New York: Aladdin Books, Macmillan, 1985).

15. Nolte and Singer, "Active Comprehension," 25.

16. William H. Teale, Elfrieda H. Hiebert, and Edward A. Chittenden, "Assessing Young Children's Literacy Development, *The Reading Teacher* 40, no. 8 (April 1987):775.

17. Victoria Forrester, *The Magnificent Moo* (New York: Atheneum, 1984).

18. Gerald McDermott, *The Stonecutter* (New York: Viking, 1975).

19. Laura Numeroff, *If You Give a Mouse a Cookie*, Felicia Bond, illustr. (New York: Harper & Row, 1985).

20. X. J. Kennedy, "Blow-Up," in *The Forgetful Wishing Well*, M. Incisa, illustr. (New York: Macmillan, 1985). Reprinted with permission of Atheneum Publishers, an imprint of Macmillan Publishing Company, from *The Forgetful Wishing Well* by X. J. Kennedy, Copyright © 1985 by X. J. Kennedy.

21. Gail Gibbons, *The Post Office Book, Mail and How It Moves* (New York: Harper & Row, 1982).

22. English-Language Arts Curriculum Framework and Criteria Committee, *English Language Arts Framework* (Sacramento, CA: California State Department of Education, 1987), 17.

23. Hoffman, *World Almanac*, 361.

24. *Television and Cable Factbook, 1986* (New York: Television Digest, 1986).

25. Ibrahim M. Hefzallah, *Critical Viewing of Television: A Book for Parents and Teachers* (Landham, MD: University Press of America, 1987), 66.

26. Marie Winn, *Unplugging the Plug-In Drug* (New York: Viking Penguin, 1987), 154.

27. Hefzallah, *Critical Viewing of Television*, 66.

28. *Ibid.*

29. Larry Gross, "Television & Violence," in *Television Awareness Training, The Viewers Guide for Family and Community*, Ben Logan, ed. (Nashville, TN: Abington, 1979).

30. Hefzallah, *Critical Viewing of Television*, 88.

31. Marty Klein, "Teens, Sexuality, and Prime Time Entertainment," in *Television and Children* (Summer 1983):20.

32. Edgar Dale, *Audio-Visual Methods of Teaching*, 3rd ed. (New York: The Dryden Press, 1969), 418.

33. Alfred M. Lee and Elizabeth B. Lee (eds.), *The Fine Arts of Propaganda* (New York: Harcourt Brace Jovanovich, 1939), 105.

34. J. Singer, D. Singer, and D. M. Zuckerman, *Getting the Most Out of TV* (Santa Monica, CA: Goodyear Publishing Co, 1981).

35. WNET, *Critical Television Viewing: A Language Skills Work-A-Text*, Student Edition and Teachers' Guide (New York: Globe Book, 1980).

36. Children's Bureau of the Department of Health, Education and Welfare, *Children and Television* (Washington, DC: U. S. Government Printing Office, 1981).

Chapter 11
Written Discourse: The Process of Writing

Written Discourse: The Process of Writing

The Writing Process
Prewriting
Drafting
Conferencing
Revising
Editing
Publishing

Using a Process Approach with Bilingual Students

Assessing Children's Writing Development
Student Folders
Holistic Scoring
Primary Trait Scoring
Analytical Scoring

Most adults learned to write quite differently from the way children learn to write today. There really wasn't any "process" that we followed; we just thought about what we were going to say, and wrote it down as perfectly as possible. Although many people still write that way, professional writers do not. "Real writers" are great revisers; they do a great deal of thinking, and researching, and planning before they write, and they rethink and rewrite many times. They know they are not writing a final copy, so there is no need to worry about spelling or punctuation. They go over their piece many times—rearranging paragraphs or sentences, scratching out portions, and adding others. Today teachers try to emulate the natural process that professional writers use. The instructional emphasis in school is on *how* to write rather than *what* is written; we emphasize the process of writing instead of the product.

How did this change come about? The impetus came from theory and research into writing that has found its way into the classroom. The longitudinal study conducted by Graves and his colleagues is among the most significant studies to impact classroom instruction.[1] The purpose of their research was to observe young children writing. They sat near children as they wrote and kept notes on what they observed. They asked children questions during their composing process, and recorded children's conferences with their peers and teachers when they talked about their writing. Based on their findings, they recommended that writing instruction follow the natural process of writers. Other researchers offer findings to support this recommendation. Hayes and Flower confirm the recursive nature of the writing process, suggesting that composing involves a variety of plans and subprocesses that are implemented throughout the natural composing process as they are needed.[2] Their research evidence strongly contradicts the traditional instructional approach, which adheres to discrete or isolated steps in composing, for example, determine thesis, outline, write, or assign topic, write.

The natural composing process takes place within a meaningful context. Writing has a purpose and occurs for a reason. Moffett and Wagner urge teachers to provide real audiences for children's writing.[3] Frank Smith asks teachers to consider the purpose of composing: "Writing is for stories to be read, books to be published, poems to be recited, plays to be acted out, songs to be sung, newspapers to be shared, letters to be mailed, jokes to be told, notes to be passed, cards to be sent, cartons to be labeled, instructions to be followed, designs to be made, recipes to be cooked, messages to be exchanged, programs to be organized, excursions to be planned, catalogs to be compared, entertainment guides to be consulted, memos to be circulated, announcements to be posted. . . . Writing is for ideas, action, reflection, and experience."[4] This is the way it should be in any classroom where children are engaged in the act of writing.

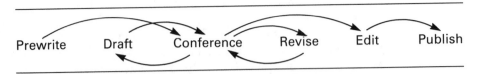

FIGURE 11.1   *Example of one writer's composing process*

The Writing Process

The writing process involves several stages. Some writing authorities divide the process differently, but a six-part process is described here that fits the way children in school usually proceed. The steps include prewriting, drafting, conferencing, revising, editing, and publishing. These stages in the writing process seem to form an orderly way to go about writing, but writers—children or adults—seldom follow them in a sequential order. They go back to earlier steps, skip over a step, go back another time to a step, and so forth. Figure 11.1 is an illustration of how one person might follow the process.

At first glance, the stages in the writing process may suggest a teaching order. This would work only if the process were linear. Actually the process is naturally recursive, as shown in Figure 11.1. As we develop a first draft, we cross out words, insert words, reread to check for clarity. We revise as we go along, and then later revise the piece again before we publish or share it. And if we need some additional information about our topic, we lay our writing aside, do further research, and then begin writing again. Just as experienced writers go through the various stages as they compose, students should experience them as they write, too. For example, here is what Anne did when writing about her dog who had jumped over the fence and had been lost.

Prewriting	Made a list of possible writing topics. Talked with her teacher about the topics. Decided to write about the time her dog ran away.
Prewriting/ Conferencing	Told Leigh Ann what she was going to do. Leigh Ann asked her if she meant the previous Friday when her dog followed the black dog and she answered, "Yes."

continued

Drafting

Wrote her title down. Wrote a few sentences. Drew pictures of dogs jumping fences.

> *(First Draft)*
> Goldie Runs Away
> *Last Friday my dog Goldie ran away. She must have jumped over our fence. We found her with a black dog a couple of blocks away. Dad took us out in the truck driving all over.*

Conferencing/
Revising

Shared it with Leigh Ann. She asked Anne why the dog hadn't run away before and why she jumped the fence that day? Anne explained and decided to put it in the story.

Drafting/
Revising

She read it aloud to herself and decided it needed a better beginning. She also wrote down three new titles.

Goldie Finds a Friend
Goldie Jumps the Fence
Goldie Learns to Jump our Fence

Prewriting/
Revising

She started with the first title and wrote a part of a sentence. Crossed it out. Then went to the last title and wrote the second draft.

> *(Second Draft)*
> Goldie Learns to Jump our Fence
> *One afternoon when I was at school and Mom and Dad were at work, Goldie had a friend come to visit. It was a black dog that moved in on the next street.*

continued

> *That black dog came in the yard and when Goldie saw him jump over the fence, she did the same thing.*
>
> *When I got home, I went out back, but Goldie wasn't there. I called and hunted all over the yard. When Dad came home, he drove us all over the neighborhood looking for Goldie. Finally our next-door neighbor said she had seen them on the next block.*

Conferencing

Shared it with another friend. Don asked how she knew it had followed the other dog over the fence.

Revising

She went back, put in a caret, and added that another neighbor told them how it happened. She had seen them jump the fence on her way back from lunch.

Conferencing/
Editing

Anne shared her story with her regular peer writing group. They loved the title, and wondered why the neighbor who saw it happen didn't do something. They talked about it, but Anne didn't make any more changes in the content. She checked for spelling errors. She read her story aloud to herself one more time. She then added some needed commas.

Publishing

Anne tacked her story and picture on a class bulletin board. Her peers enjoyed reading it.

Prewriting

The first stage in the writing process is usually called *prewriting;* however, Donald Graves prefers to use the term *rehearsal* to identify what we do before we write.[5] Regardless of the terminology, each of us prepares in some way for the writing event. We gather ideas and decide on a focus. We spend time thinking about what we are going to write, and how we are going to write it.

Prewriting experiences that help children get ready to write usually involve talking, writing, or working in groups. Proett and Gill offer the following list of prewriting choices to encourage creative thoughts before drafting.[6]

observing	brainstorming	dramatizing
remembering	clustering	reading
researching	listing	mapping
imagining	detailing	outlining
experiencing	logging	watching films and other media

Let's look closely at how some of these suggested prewriting experiences provide children with ideas or help them plan for writing.

Brainstorming

This technique is excellent for generating ideas, remembering, recalling, and tapping one's brain for stored information. Any exercise in brainstorming stimulates our memory and helps us remember things that often surprise us. Sometimes we brainstorm a list of ideas about our topic as we recall the events or information.

Brainstorming can be done by an individual working alone on a paper; however, it is normally conducted as a group experience. Everyone in the group contributes ideas related to a given topic. These ideas are written down, usually on a chart, a transparency, or the chalkboard. All ideas are accepted during the brainstorming session. After all ideas are exhausted, the group decides which ideas are best and should be kept, and which ones should be omitted. The final collection of ideas may appear in either a group or an individual piece of writing.

Clustering

This strategy, a variation of brainstorming, is extremely useful once it is demonstrated and learned. Rico defines clustering "as a nonlinear brainstorming process that generates ideas, images, and feelings around a stimulus word until a pattern becomes discernible."[7] What instructions should students follow if they plan to use clustering as a prewriting activity? Rico suggests that teachers use the following procedure to teach children how to do clustering:

1. Tell students that they are going to learn to use a tool that will enable them to write more easily and more powerfully, a tool similar to brainstorming.

2. Encircle a word on the board—for example, *energy*—and ask students, "What do you think of when you see that word?" Encourage all responses. Cluster these responses, radiating outward (see Figure 11.2). When they have finished giving their responses, say, "See how many ideas there are floating around in your heads? Now, if you cluster all by yourself, you will have set of connections as unique to your own mind as your thumbprint is to your thumb."

3. Now ask students to cluster a second word for themselves. Before they begin, tell them that the clustering process should take no more than one to two minutes and that the paragraph they will write should take about eight minutes. Ask them to keep clustering until the "Aha!" shift, signaling that their minds are holding something they can shape

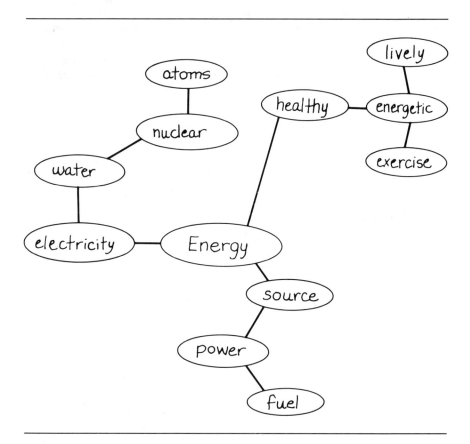

FIGURE 11.2   *Cluster around the topic of energy*

into a whole. In writing, the only constraint is that they come full circle, that is, that they do not leave the writing unfinished.

4. After they finish writing, ask students to give a title to what they have written that is suggestive of the whole.[8]

Young children can engage in clustering as a prewriting activity, although they may do more drawing than writing, as shown in five-year-old Laura's cluster about the word *love* (Figure 11.3). Encourage young children to talk about what they have clustered, and then to write about the topic using their own invented spelling.

Mapping

A map is a structured, visual display of an idea that may be used to organize one's ideas prior to beginning the first draft. In the words of

FIGURE 11.3   *Five-year-old Laura's cluster about love*

Jerome Bruner, "Perhaps the most basic thing that can be said about human memory, after a century of research, is that unless detail is placed in a structured pattern, it is easily forgotten."[9] Mapping is a simple strategy for organizing details. It has major advantages over traditional outlining: (1) mapping illustrates relationships and presents a whole structure; (2) mapping is easily learned and shared.

How does one map? First, brainstorm a written list of ideas about a topic. Second, categorize the list of ideas and label each category. Third, draw a map to show each category and the ideas associated with each category. Look at the map in Figure 11.4. Notice how secondary ideas branch out from main ideas about the topic of pets. Each idea is placed in a category (Dogs, Cats, Fish, Gerbils), yet each one is related to other categories and is interrelated to the whole.

When students finish their maps, encourage them to tell their story to a group or partner. When students have an opportunity to use their maps to tell the story before they write it, they evaluate their organization and planning for the piece of writing. Mapping "helps many students to see *in detail* the composition before or after talking it out. Getting a good fit between visual and verbal images usually results in vivid, strikingly clear writing. If students use their maps to guide them, they can practice visualizing—in meticulous detail—their compositions."[10]

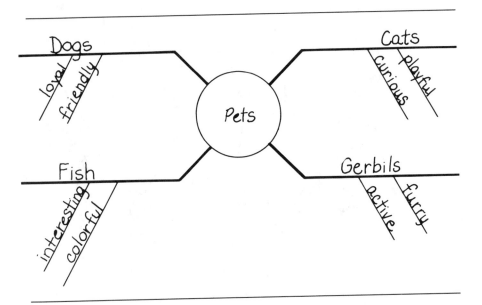

FIGURE 11.4 *Map for the topic of pets*

Logs

Writing logs, which may have a variety of purposes, can be used as a prewriting strategy. Students may keep notes, record observations, or write anecdotes that later become topics for further research and writing. Professional authors often keep writing logs or journals. Donald Murray called his log a daybook, and he said, "I am able to make use of fragments of time because my tools, first and foremost my daybook, are with me at all times."[11] Because the daybook or log is always with him, he is able to jot down an idea the moment it comes. What does a writer include in a daybook? Here are a few items that Murray writes in his:

> Lines that may become poems—or stories or articles or books
> Leads (beginnings), dozens of leads, and often ends
> Titles, hundreds of titles
> Quotations
> Questions that need answers
> Observations of people and places
> Titles of books to read
> Ideas for pieces of writing[12]

Students might be encouraged to keep such a daybook, or writer's log. It can be an invaluable tool for collecting data for future writing topics or for works that are already in progress. They may include the same kinds of things that one finds in Murray's daybook, yet some things will be very different. Children may wish to include drawings, information about their best friends or favorite after-school activities, and so on.

Dramatizing

Drama is perhaps the least used prewriting strategy; yet, through drama students engage in firsthand, concrete experiences out of which rich, meaningful writing grows. A second-grade teacher, Ms. Enoch, describes a successful dramatic event that initiated a piece of writing in her classroom.

> *A little girl crouches down onto the ground until she is very small. Slowly she rises—taller—taller—her arms raise up and wave into the air . . . as she grows and blossoms into a beautiful rose. Silently, the child has created a powerful image through simple body movement and creative play. The other children in the class clap and acknowledge the little girl's interpretation of a blooming flower. Next, the class, with the teacher acting as scribe, creates a poem about the little girl's interpretation of the blooming rose and entitles the poem, "Rose Petal." All the chil-*

dren participate, raise their hands, and share ideas. Finally, after revisions, compromises, and discussions, a poem has been created by the second-grade class. The children eagerly recite their work—over and over—with each other and by themselves. They copy the poem, illustrate it, and anticipate seeing and reading their final masterpiece, "Rose Petal," published in the weekly school newspaper.[13]

Rose Petal

Let the rose smile at you.
Let the rose open your heart to joy and love.
Let the rose feel like red silk on a dress.

The rose makes a diamond dew-drop on color red.
The rose makes a thorn to protect herself from uninvited guests.
The rose brings back faded memories . . .
I love the rose!

Timed Writing/Looping

Timed writing forces students to get ideas on paper. In the beginning, students usually write nonstop for about one or two minutes, quickly jotting down words, phrases, or sentences that relate to a topic. A timer is a useful device to keep track of the minutes, and it also frees the teacher to write along with the students.

As a prewriting strategy for older students, looping is an effective way of generating unconscious thoughts about a topic and focusing those thoughts on a central theme. Elizabeth Cown Neeld developed the technique based upon Peter Elbow's work.[14] The procedures for looping follow.

1. Begin with your topic. Write the topic at the top of the page to focus your thoughts. As you write, you may deviate somewhat from your subject. Continue writing if this happens. You may discover an idea that you didn't think of before starting to write.

2. Write nonstop for [X] minutes. You can write the same words over and over again, but keep your pencil or pen moving. Write as quickly as possible. You want to remove mental barriers where you can write from a stream of consciousness.

3. Read what you have written and find a sentence that tells the central or main idea. This sentence may be perfectly stated or you may have written around it. If you cannot identify such a sentence, make up a sentence that you think presents the theme of the piece. Write this sentence, and then begin another [X] minute loop. When you are finished with the second loop, find and write a main idea sentence for the piece, then begin a third and final loop.

4. Once you have completed the three pieces of timed writing or loops, read over each one. You should discover some useful ideas as well as a topic that has some direction.[15]

The following example illustrates looping as a prewriting strategy. As you read the three pieces of writing about Rosie, notice the main idea sentence in each loop.

Topic: My Dog, Rosie

(Loop One) My dog, Rosie, is white with a brown nose. She is a Bedlington Terrier. This kind of dog is playful, doesn't shed, is smart, learns tricks fast, is good humored—sometimes you can see her smile, and even laugh—sometimes at herself and sometimes at me. She is a friend and companion. She was a wonderful choice for a pet *(main idea).*

(Loop Two) Rosie is a wonderful pet. *Why?* Not all dogs have Rosie's rare personality *(main idea). She has a splendid disposition, and a delightful wit about her. She has lots of friends—yes, she wags her tail, puts on her best smile, and instantly charms any new found admirer. I wonder if all Bedlington Terriers are like Rosie? Certainly not all dogs are like her.*

(Loop Three) My dog, Rosie, has a rare personality. *I am sure she isn't like other dogs. What sets her apart from the average canine? First, she has a splendid disposition. In fact, there are times when I'm in less than a good mood, and who humors me? Rosie, of course. She meets only friends, that is, if they are of the human variety. She wags her tail, puts on her best manners, nudges a leg, tilts her head, smiles in her own way, and pretty soon you are a "gonner." You and Rosie are friends forever.*

Looping is a prewriting strategy obviously intended for older students. It is best that you start with short times—perhaps two-minute loops. As students become more fluent and comfortable with timed writing, you may wish to increase the writing time for the loops.

In many classrooms, little time or attention is given to the prewriting stage, even though many composition authorities consider it the most critical stage in the writing process. Murray states, "The most important writing takes place before there is writing—at least what we usually think of as writing: the production of a running draft. . . . Much of the bad writing we read from inexperienced writers is the direct result from writing before they are ready to write."[16]

Drafting

It is now time for the writer to put words on paper. Encourage young writers to be spontaneous, and let their ideas flow onto the page. The first draft is merely a beginning. Since students need not worry about correctness at this time, they are free to discover and create.

Lead

The creation of a working lead may be an important consideration at this point in the process. Professional writers know the significance of a good lead—a beginning—because it establishes a focus for the piece and first captures the reader's interest. Encourage children to play around with different leads. Older students might even try looping in order to develop a satisfactory lead. Donald Murray suggests that a good working lead becomes "the spine to which everything in the piece is connected."[17]

Time

Time is an important consideration in writing. Students need time to develop a good piece of writing. They may work through several drafts, lay the last one aside, then come back to it with a new reader's eye and fresh ideas. Students and teachers alike must recognize that writing is a process that requires time for ideas to incubate, often through several drafts.

During the drafting stage, students need to make choices of a rhetorical nature. These choices relate to *voice, audience, purpose,* and *form,* and each one influences the outcome of a piece of writing in some way.

Voice

When students consider voice, they need to think of their role in writing a particular piece. Are they writing it as a fan or admirer of a well-known book author? As an interested or scholarly student? As a thoughtful or concerned sibling? As a reviewer or critic? To understand the concept of voice better, students might try writing briefly on a topic using two different voices. Through sharing their writings, students determine which voice is the most effective.

Audience

Students can learn early about the importance of audience when they write. Traditionally, the teacher has served as the primary audience for students' writing, but that tradition is changing. When writing is taught as a process, students engage in writing to different audiences, and as often as possible the audiences are real. Proett and Gill suggest the following questions to get students to consider their audience.

Who is the reader?
How sophisticated on this subject is the reader?
How ready is the reader to receive this "message"?
What help does the reader need?
What pre-formed opinions will this reader have?[18]

Purpose

Purposes for writing include to inform, to persuade, to entertain, to explain, and so on. One's purpose for writing a piece shapes the content and form and influences voice. As students plan and draft a piece, they need to keep in mind their purpose for writing it.

Form

Once students decide about voice, audience, and purpose, the form should be clear. Numerous forms exist, including diaries, letters, poems, plays, notes, and essays. The subject of form and modes of writing are discussed more extensively in the following chapter.

Conferencing

There are many different kinds of conferences that take place in process-oriented classrooms; some are peer conferences, others are teacher-student conferences. While we usually think of a final conference about a piece of writing that is nearly finished, conferences often take place at several different times during the writing process. Many early conferences are quite informal, a student talking for a moment with his or her writing partner about an idea for the next story, or the teacher stopping for a moment to ask a student, "How is it coming along? Do you know what you want to do next?" These conferences are closely tied to pre-writing and may help students get started on a new piece of writing.

During the early drafts students often want to share what they've written. They may do this with a friend or with their teacher. "Does this part make sense? Should I say any more here? Do you like it so far? Don't you think that's funny?" All writers need reassurance that they are on the right track, that their draft is going well. Sometimes, as we wonder whether we should include certain information, we need a response from our audience. These sharing times during the first or second draft encourage children and help reassure them that their writing is going well.

The most typical conferences are those connected with editing and revising. These tend to take a longer time and are somewhat more formal. During these conferences, the students read their writing and discuss possible additions, rearrangements, or deletions of material.

Sharing an early draft with a partner enables a student to get helpful information for revising.

Once these matters are decided, they may proofread for spelling, punctuation, and so on. A closer examination of teacher-student conferences and peer conferences follows because both are critical to the success of the writing program, yet offer the writer quite different perspectives and information.

Teacher-Student Conferences

A roving conference may be held as a teacher walks about the room as children write. This type of conferencing is most effective during drafting; however, as a child approaches the revision stage, a teacher can pull up a chair beside the student and talk about the piece of writing, or teachers may spend a minute or two asking questions or answering children's questions while walking around the room. When a student is ready for a more formal one-on-one conference with the teacher, more time should be set aside. At the beginning of the conference, the student reads the piece of writing aloud. Students learn early that reading one's own writing aloud is an excellent proofreading and revising technique. The chief aim of the teacher during any conference is to foster thinking and to ask questions to draw ideas from the student for revising. To accomplish this task, the teacher should remember the following points:

- Play a low-key role, not dominating or talking too much.
- Show interest in what the child is trying to express.
- Get to know as many of the child's interests as possible.
- Be aware of the child's strengths and weaknesses in writing.
- Leave the pencil in the child's hand.
- Develop the art of questioning; instead of telling what to do, use questions to move the child to find answers.
- Be positive at all times.[19]

As mentioned above, the teacher develops an art of questioning students about their writing. The success of any conference hinges on asking questions that lead students to discover answers for themselves. In *Lessons from a Child*, Lucy Calkins suggests some possible questions for teachers to consider.

Questions that help writers focus

- What is the most important thing you are saying?
- Why did you choose this topic? What's important about it to you?
- Which is the most important part of your story? Why?
- Where do you get to your main idea?
- Is there anything that doesn't seem to fit into your story?
- Do you think you have two stories, or one?

Questions that help writers show—not tell

- Read me the places where you're pleased with your description.
- What makes these sections work better than others?
- Are there places you could described more? I can't always picture it.
- Have you tried to underline the places where you *tell* us something like "he was ugly," and then rewrite those on another sheet of paper, showing instead of telling?
- If I'd been watching you, how would I have known that—as you say in the paper—you felt sad? What exactly would I have seen?

Questions that help writers expand their pieces

- In your own words, tell me all about this. What else do you know about the topic?
- What questions do you think people will have for you? If you answer them now, you can get rid of some of the questions.
- Could you go through your story, reading me a line, then telling me more about it?

- Why don't you try reading your story over and putting a dot on the page wherever there is more to tell.

Questions that help a writer reconsider the sequence

- Let's see; what did you tell first? Second? Third? (They make a list.) Is there any other way you could order this? Why did you decide to put it in this order?
- Have you tried cutting it up and putting it in a different order?
- Could you make this into a flashback?[20]

Peer Conferences

Peer conferences offer an alternative and supplement to the one-on-one teacher-student conferences. In order for children to conference with one another successfully about their writing, a lot of modeling needs to take place. First, they learn conference techniques when they conference with the teacher about their own writing. Second, the teacher can share a transparency of a piece of writing with the class. Students can discuss questions they might pose to the writer in a response group situation. The teacher can guide the class discussion about the piece of writing, and model questioning techniques that are appropriate in peer response groups. Third, students might engage in

During a formal conference, the teacher asks thought provoking questions to get the student to focus on certain aspects of his story. Later the student reads aloud the revised protion to find out if the additional details improve his story.

Partners in a read-around group confer about their pieces of writing. Students then get several peer responses to their writing when the outside circle of the read-around group rotates clockwise.

read-around groups, sometimes referred to as RAGs. How do read-around groups work? Chairs are arranged in two concentric circles and students sit facing one another. Peers sitting across from one another exchange papers for the purpose of conferencing. Students get several readings and responses to their papers when the outside circle of students rotates clockwise. In the beginning, students may be instructed to read only to find what they like best in their partners' pieces. Later, students may be instructed to read for different purposes as they move around the circle. For example, the first pair of readers might focus on content, while the second pair of readers might consider organization. Conferences between students can increase in sophistication as children grow accustomed to the peer conferencing process.

A peer response form, such as the one shown in Figure 11.5, can be extremely useful to students as they conference about their pieces of writing.[21] It should be introduced after students have gained some initial experiences with peer conferencing.

Revising

Prior to any discussion about revising, it is important to mention and underscore that *not all pieces of writing should be revised.* A variety of

```
┌─────────────────────────────────────────────────────────────┐
│                                                               │
│  PEER RESPONSE FORM                                           │
│                                                               │
│        (☺)  - something is well done                          │
│                                                               │
│        (⁇)  - you don't understand something or have a question │
│                                                               │
│        (☺)  - something needs more work                       │
│                                                               │
│                                                               │
│  READ—READ AGAIN AND DRAW FACES—FILL IN BLANKS                │
│  _____  │
│  Author's Name _____      │
│  Title of Piece _____      │
│  I like _____       │
│  Can you tell more about _____       │
│  _____        │
│  Do you need the part about _____       │
│  _____        │
│  You might want to work on _____      │
│  _____        │
│  Editor's full name _____      │
│                                                               │
└─────────────────────────────────────────────────────────────┘
```

FIGURE 11.5 *A helpful form for children who confer with each other about their writings*   Adapted with permission from a peer response form by Cara Keller in Harvey Daniels and Steven Zemelman: *A Writing Project: Training Teachers of Composition from Kindergarten to College* (Portsmouth, NH: Heinemann Educational Books, Inc., 1985).

writing is meant to stimulate fluency—getting ideas down easily on paper—and this kind of writing should not be subjected to revision. Journal entries, timed writing, and impromptu pieces, go through only the drafting stage.

The word *revision* means to "see again." When we apply this meaning to the revising stage in the writing process, we actually look again at our draft to determine how we can improve the quality of what we have written. "Students need to consider such matters as unity, development, order, clarity, emphasis, and word choice" when they are revising. "They also need to examine their work in terms of its organization and the possible need for reasons, examples, or other supporting evidence. They might consider adding further supporting information, qualifying details, concrete examples, sensory details, and transitional words. . . . The degree to which they attend to all these matters will, of course, depend on the skill and maturity of the students."[22]

How can a teacher provide the necessary instruction and help during the revision process? One effective way is to use conferences. A conference involves a one-on-one talk between a teacher and a student, or a student and another student. Small peer groups may also be formed for the purpose of responding to pieces of writing.

Many times both younger and older students need help in revising their writing. Turbill in *Now, We Want To Write*, quotes Sara, a seven year old: "I can't write any more about the calf because I can't fit it on there." (She points to the lines filling the page.) "You just can't move those lines of words up and those words down, you know."[23] Sara did not understand how to insert words or write in the margin using an arrow to indicate the proper placement for additional sentences.

A way of showing children how to revise is to model the process. Compose a class composition on the chalkboard or a large sheet of paper. If you use the chalkboard, do not use the eraser. Revise the composition as a group by crossing out words, inserting words, and drawing arrows. As you revise, talk about such things as word choice, sentence structure, and sequence. Finally, read the revised composition as a class to check for clarity and correctness. If you wish, copy the composition in its final form on a sheet of chart paper and display it somewhere in the classroom.

Modeling good revision techniques is an essential part of any composition program. Too often children are told, rather than shown, how to improve their writing. For instance, children often hear these words or see them on their papers: be more specific; include more details; be more descriptive. How often are they shown how to be specific, how to use pertinent details, and how to write vivid descriptions? Probably not too often in some classes. Rebekah Caplan, Co-Director of the Bay Area Writing Project, realized early in her teaching career that her middle-grade students rarely wrote with any description. They were good at telling, but not good at showing. Caplan explains, "In a description of a student's favorite movie I would read: 'It was fantastic because it was so real!' For a strange person: 'He is so weird.' "[24] In spite of sharing examples with students from well-known authors' works, and writing time-consuming comments on papers, Caplan observes that they still wrote "empty" descriptions—until she made "Show, Not Tell" exercises a part of the daily writing routine. Students wrote descriptive paragraphs just as musicians play their scales regularly, and the results were dramatic. Rich, vivid description emerged in their compositions. What comprises a "Show, Not Tell" exercise or paragraph? Give students a "telling" sentence, such as "The cafeteria is a mess." Students expanded the thought in that sentence into a paragraph that shows rather than tells. They must show, not tell, that the cafeteria is a mess. For example, a student might write:

> *Sticky lines of spaghetti, drenched in red sauce, make creative designs on table tops. Flattened meat balls cling to the green vinyl flooring while chair seats, damp with spilled milk, reek of a distinctive odor. Paper cups and straws dot the room like white punctuation marks that exclaim, "Janitor!"*

The challenge here is to convince one's audience that a cafeteria is a mess without ever using the original statement or telling sentence. The task, suggests Caplan, "is much like charades—a student must get an idea across without giving the whole thing away."[25]

Once students have mastered descriptive paragraphs, they may try writing "Show, Not Tell" sentences. Consider the same telling sentence: "The cafeteria is a mess." Here is a show, not tell sentence for that statement.

> *Red meat sauce coats the once-white tabletops and drips cautiously onto the damp, milk-soaked chairs, while paper cups and straws look up from the cafeteria floor in utter amazement.*

Short writing experiences, such as these exercises or timed journal entries, are important for improving fluency—getting ideas easily and effortlessly on paper. They provide needed practice for honing one's skills as a writer.

Editing

Traditionally, teachers have done the final editing of children's writing, taking their red pens and circling misspelled words, inserting commas, and marking letters that should be capitalized, and so on. Children have been asked to memorize isolated rules that they seldom identify as useful in their own writing. Rules learned out of the meaningful context of students' own writing are rarely remembered. Students are more apt to develop and use good editing skills when they are required to apply them in their own compositions. Lucy Calkins supports this approach to teaching standard writing conventions in her book *Lessons from a Child*. In reporting an informal study of third-graders' acquisition of one editing skill—punctuation, Calkins describes two different teaching situations. One teacher, Ms. West, taught lessons on periods and question marks. She followed the book, gave children worksheets on punctuation, and gave tests before and after each lesson. Her children seldom wrote, and when they did, Ms. West was quick to red-pen any errors. In another classroom, Ms. Howard took a different approach to the teaching of punctuation. Children learned the editing skill through writing, and the concern for correctness was left until the end of the writing process when compositions were polished for sharing or publishing. Lucy Calkins makes the following comments about the results of her study. "In my punctuation mark study, I asked each child from the two classrooms to tell me what each mark meant and how it was used. I found that Pat's third-graders could explain an average of more than eight kinds of punctuation. The children from Ms. West's room who had studied punctuation through classwork, drills and tests, but had rarely written, were able to explain fewer than four kinds."[26]

When children are given the responsibility of editing their own writing, they engage in a meaningful learning experience. They make decisions about comma placements, spelling, sentence structure, and so on. When they check their own drafts for correctness by reading them aloud, or asking partners to read them, they discover their errors and see a need for correcting them. (A more extensive discussion of editing and of teaching supportive writing skills is in Chapter 13.)

Publishing

Children complete a piece of writing with a purpose in mind. The purpose is one of publishing or sharing publicly their writing with an audience. As mentioned earlier, traditionally, the primary audience for students' writing has been the classroom teacher. Students who are involved in an instructional program that centers on writing as a process, however, discover that the teacher is merely one of many audiences for their finished writing. The following list of ideas suggests sources of real audiences for children's writing.

Teacher reads aloud student work to the class.
Students make their own books, writing and illustrating the story, and the books are placed in the classroom library. Submit laminated student collections to the library for check-out.
Display works on bulletin boards.
Make little booklets for selected works.
Create a student newspaper.
Run off copy collections of student pieces.
Develop an end-of-year anthology.
Display student poetry on a "poet tree" made from paper stretched floor to ceiling against a wall.

Students read and share their illustrated books.

Do group sharing, as in a read-around group.
Submit to writing contests.
Create a class book.
Construct a hall bulletin board display.
Make a big book, with everyone using a page.
Feature "special" writing on the bulletin board.
Read to other classes.
Post work in the library.
Hang cord from wall and use clothespins to attach student work
    for display.
Display work as a mobile.
Contribute to the local or neighborhood newspaper or the school's
    literary magazine, if one exists.
Make a newspaper for another class.
Have students choose favorite pieces to publish each semester.
Read student work at daily announcement time over the PA.
Send work to school board to use as addenda to their agenda.
Make an overhead transparency of a good student paper.
Send letters.

Use student writings in presentations to other teachers, with writer's permission.

Share student work with teacher's colleagues or other adults, then write a note to the student concerning adults' responses.

Have mailboxes in the classroom where studens can receive letters and invitations from one another.

Have students record pieces on cassette using a dramatic voice; others can listen to the tape while reading a single piece of a collection.

Write books for young children and exchange with an elementary class; send work to a children's magazine for possible publication.

When students publish a piece of writing, they discover the importance of their own writing. They realize their writing has value and meaning when they share it with an audience. Publishing brings about a sense of accomplishment that inspires young authors to write again and again.

A teacher creates a hall bulletin board display of students' writing.

Using a Process Approach with Bilingual Students

Across the nation there is a growing number of children in schools whose dominant language is one other than English. Should we use a process approach to teach these students to write? The answer is *yes*. Whatever their dominant language, all students are more apt to write well if they engage in writing as a process. Language minority students should participate in prewriting, drafting, conferencing, revising, editing, and publishing stages.

The prewriting stage takes on even greater importance than usual when teachers are instructing language minority students. During this initial stage of the writing process, students discuss orally the content related to their writing topic, receive special help with what they wish to say, and ask pertinent questions. Also, it is during the prewriting stage that these children develop a keen interest in writing in the English language.

A word of advice is in order here, however. Students will more than likely possess varying degrees of proficiency in English and in their dominant language. Consequently, teachers must determine minority language students' readiness for learning to write in English based on their language proficiency in both English and their primary language. Some students may require a rich menu of language activities to improve their facility with basic English as they begin to write in the English language. (A more extensive discussion about teaching the bilingual student is found in Chapter 4.)

Assessing Children's Development in Writing

Effective assessment of students' writing development is an essential component of any instructional program. Informal assessment or evaluation occurs as an ongoing and integral part of the process as students develop a piece of writing. Comments about content and organization occur throughout the prewriting, drafting, conferencing, and revising stages. Students receive feedback about their writing from their teacher and peers. Written documentation develops as students serve as editors, completing peer response or evaluation forms. During one-on-one conferences, the teacher and student discuss ideas and suggestions for improving a piece of writing. When these ideas and suggestions are written on self-sticking notes, they can be placed directly on the page where the revision is needed. Also, individual student folders are kept for the purpose of documenting writing progress and determining where students are in their writing. More formal evaluative measures, such as holistic and primary trait scoring, also have their necessary place in a writing process class. When teachers document children's progress in writing and use evaluative measures to assess students' strengths and weaknesses, they gather essential information for planning an effective classroom instructional program in writing.

Student Folders

Plain manila folders, stapled or taped on each end, are excellent for storing individual student's writing. The entire collection of student folders should be placed in an attractive box and stored in some convenient place in the classroom. Almost everything that a student writes during the year is kept in that student's writing folder. There will be rough drafts along with bits and pieces of writing that may eventually become complete drafts. Final, polished pieces are also placed in the folder, even though some finished works may have appeared in some published form—in class books, on bulletin boards, or mailed to an editor of a children's magazine. Everything that goes into the writing folder should be dated in order to keep a record of writing progress throughout the year. The outside covers of the folder can be used for record keeping, too. On the front cover, a student might keep an ongoing list of possible writing topics, while the back cover might contain titles of completed or published pieces of writing. The inside covers of the folder might document writing skills that need improvement along with skills that have been mastered. Finally, a colored sticker or dot might be placed somewhere on the folder, perhaps next to the name, to identify the peer conference group to which the student belongs.

Sometimes, before students submit a finished piece of writing to their folder, ask them to complete a written evaluation of it. A cover sheet, such as the one shown in Figure 11.6, helps a student focus on certain aspects of the final piece and facilitates the self-evaluation process. Students' involvement in the evaluation process leads to improved writing.

Holistic Scoring

The holistic scoring procedure is used widely to measure the quality of students' writing. It may be used to evaluate students' writing abilities at the beginning of a school year or as a state-wide scoring procedure for mandatory competency tests. The Educational Testing Service (E.T.S.) evaluates thousands of writing samples each year using focused holistic scoring.

What is holistic scoring? Simply stated, it is evaluating a piece of writing as a whole. For example, a teacher or rater reads through a student's finished paper quickly and then responds to it with one

SELF-EVALUATION COVER SHEET

Name _____   Date _____

Title _____

Author's Comments

I proofread my final draft for _____
_____

What I like best about my finished piece is _____
_____

What I like least about my finished piece is _____
_____

I tried to improve the following thing(s) in this piece:
_____
_____

What I think I need work on in my next piece _____
_____
_____
_____

Teacher's Comments: _____
_____
_____

**FIGURE 11.6   *A checklist for children to evaluate their own
writing***

score. It is the only mark that is allowed on the paper. Usually, the
scoring range goes from one to four or from one to nine. A four-point
scale might look something like the following example.

    4 = Demonstrates high competency
    3 = Demonstrates expected competency
    2 = Demonstrates less than expected competency
    1 = Requires extensive help

In focused holistic scoring, specific criteria are developed for evaluating the writing. The criteria are usually based on (1) the type of
writing being done—persuasive, informative, narrative, and so on, (2)
the content presented in the composition, and (3) consideration of an

audience. The evaluative criteria also may include the proper use of mechanics or conventions of writing. A scoring guide, sometimes referred to as a *rubric*, is designed to clearly delineate the established criteria for evaluating each piece of writing. The scoring guide shown below details the criteria for scoring summary writing.[27] To use the guide, a rater reads through a student's summary quickly, determines how well it meets the criteria, and then places the appropriate score on the piece of writing. The rater should be thoroughly familiar with the criteria before scoring any papers.

Scoring Guide—Summary

Score of 4

1. Main events of the story presented in sequence.

2. Introduces main characters

3. Mentions or implies setting if essential to the story.

4. Condenses ideas effectively without sacrificing meaning.

5. Demonstrates comprehension of the story beyond a new retelling.

6. Coherent. Irrelevant details omitted. Ideas flow smoothly.

Score of 3

1. Main events of the story presented in sequence. May include some minor events.

2. Introduces main characters. May include minor characters.

3. Setting is mentioned or implied if essential.

4. May not condense ideas. If they condense ideas, they may lose meaning.

Score of 2

1. Main events are omitted or events not in proper sequence.

2. May not include all main characters.

3. Setting may be omitted when essential.

4. Does not demonstrate adequate comprehension of story.

5. Lacks coherence. Irrelevant details may interfere with flow of ideas.

6. Summary may be either too sketchy or ramble without focus.

Score of 1

1. Main events are omitted or out of sequence.

2. May not include all main characters.

3. Setting may be omitted when essential.

4. Fails to demonstrate comprehension of the story.

Continued

Score of 3 (continued)	Score of 1 (continued)
5. Demonstrates comprehension of the story but may be merely a retelling.	5. Incoherent.
6. Coherent, but may contain some irrelevant details. However, sense of the story remains intact.	6. Lacks focus.

Primary Trait Scoring

This form of evaluative technique is related to focused holistic scoring because it is also based on a set of criteria for scoring a piece of writing. The difference in the two procedures is that with primary trait scoring, a single characteristic or primary trait is evaluated rather than a piece of writing as a whole. For example, the following scoring guide delineates criteria for evaluating a lead—the beginning of the story.

3 = The lead in this story is interesting. It makes me want to read more.

2 = The lead in this story only slightly interests me. Some parts capture my attention and make me want to read more.

1 = The lead does not interest me. It does not capture and hold my attention.

Analytical Scoring

How is analytical scoring different from holistic and primary trait scoring? Analytical scoring involves close reading and the evaluation of the many elements of a piece of writing—content, organization, sentence structure, word choice, spelling, punctuation, and so on. The number of elements will vary depending upon the purpose of the writing and the level of the students. Each element is rated on a scale, usually one to five. Look at the sample analytic evaluation form in Figure 11.7. A teacher has read Ginny's piece of writing to determine how well it meets the criteria of a well-written story. Notice how the appropriate score is circled for each element, and all the scores are added to determine a total score. The teacher also has provided Ginny with some helpful written comments in the space provided at the bottom of the form. In this example, all the elements are given equal weight; however, if one or more elements should receive more emphasis, the scale for those elements may be increased, as shown in Figure 11.8). It is also possible to give two evaluations with two separate total scores, one for content and organization and one for form and correctness.

ANALYTICAL SCORING FORM

Name _Ginny Thompson_   Date _May 6_
Title _The Haunted Classroom_
Kind of Writing _Story_

Elements Scored	Fair	Rating Scale Good	Excellent

Elements Scored	Fair		Good		Excellent
Interesting lead	1	2	3	4	(5)
Sequence of events	1	2	3	(4)	5
Use of dialog	1	2	3	4	(5)
Logical ending	1	2	3	(4)	5
Correctness	1	2	3	(4)	5
(Spelling, punctuation, capitalization)					

Total Score _22/25_

Comments: _Your lead immediately captures my attention. I like the way you have used dialog in your story. The conversations tell me a lot about your characters._

FIGURE 11.7 *In this example, all of the elements are given equal value*

Talk about evaluation and scoring with your students. Share the evaluation procedures and scoring guide with them before they produce a piece of writing that is targeted for evaluation. Try sharing writing samples on an overhead and discussing how well each one meets the evaluative criteria. As a self-evaluation technique, encourage older students to rate their own compositions using a scoring guide, or ask them to help you develop a set of criteria for scoring a particular writing assignment.

Elements Scored	Fair		Good		Excellent
Content	2	4	6	8	⑩
Organization	2	4	6	⑧	10
Correctness	1	2	③	4	5

Total Score ___21/25___

FIGURE 11.8 *In this example, some of the elements receive more value than others.*

Summary

The writing process is recursive in nature but may be viewed as having six stages: (1) prewriting, (2) drafting, (3) conferencing, (4) revising, (5) editing, and (6) publishing. During the prewriting stage, students use strategies such as brainstorming, clustering, mapping, looping, logging, and dramatizing to generate ideas and plan their writing. During the drafting stage, students are allowed time to write. The emphasis during this stage is on content and organization. As students work through several drafts, they revise their compositions based on feedback from partners, and from conferences with peer group members and their teacher. Editing occurs when students prepare to publish or share their compositions. Students are encouraged to share their completed works with a variety of real audiences, not just the teacher.

Teachers who instruct bilingual children follow the same writing process model. Whatever children's dominant languages are, they are more apt to do well if they engage in writing as a process.

Assessing students' development as writers is continuous throughout the process. Assessment occurs when students share and conference about their writing. Formal measures effective in documenting children's progress in writing include: (1) student writing folders, (2) holistic and focused holistic scoring, (3) primary trait scoring, and (4) analytical scoring. Whenever teachers evaluate students' writing, the emphasis is always on *valuing* their written work.

Questions for Discussion

1. How might a map show the stages and concepts associated with the writing process? Share and discuss your map with a partner.

2. Why is prewriting the most significant stage in the writing process?

3. What is the relationship between the art of questioning and improvements in the quality of children's compositions?

4. What are the similarities and differences between focused holistic scoring, primary trait scoring, and analytic scoring?

5. How might you defend the argument that an instructional program for bilingual students should follow the writing process model?

Notes

1. Donald H. Graves (ed.), *A Case Study Observing the Development of Primary Children's Composing, Spelling, and Motor Behaviors during the Writing Process* (Durham, NH: University of New Hampshire, NIE Grant No. G-78-0174, 1981).

2. John R. Hayes and Linda S. Flower, "Identifying the Organization of Writing Processes," in *Cognitive Processes in Writing*, L. W. Gregg and E. R. Steinburg, eds. (Hillsdale, NJ: Erlbaum, 1980), 15–18.

3. James Moffett and Betty Jane Wagner, *Student Centered Language Arts and Reading K–3: A Handbook for Teachers* (Palo Alto, CA: Houghton Mifflin, 1983).

4. Frank Smith, "Reading Like a Writer," in *Composing and Comprehending*, Julie M. Jensen, ed. (Urbana, IL: NCRE/ERIC, 1984), 55.

5. Graves, *A Case Study*, 5–6.

6. Jackie Proett and Kent Gill, *The Writing Process in Action* (Urbana, IL: National Council of Teachers of English, 1986), 3. Copyright 1986 by the National Council of Teachers of English. Reprinted with permission.

7. Gabriele Lusser Rico, "Clustering: A Prewriting Process," in *Practical Ideas for Teaching Writing as a Process*, Carol Booth Olson, ed. (Sacramento, CA: California State Department of Education, 1986), 17–18. Reprinted by permission from "Clustering: A Prewriting Process," by Gabrield Lusser Rico, in *Practical Ideas for Teaching Writing as a Process*, copyright 1986, 1987, California State Department of Education.

8. *Ibid.*

9. Jerome Bruner, *The Process of Education* (New York: Vintage Books, 1960), 24.

10. Marilyn Hanf Buckley, "Mapping and Thinking," in *Teaching Writing, Essays from the Bay Area Writing Project*, Gerald Camp, ed. (Upper Montclair, NH: Boynton/Cook, 1982), 190.

11. Donald M. Murray, *A Writer Teaches Writing* (Boston: Houghton Mifflin, 1985), 68–69.

12. *Ibid.*

13. This prose writing and the following poem are from Julie Enoch's second-grade class, St. Alban's School, Waco, TX, 1988.

14. Elizabeth Cown Neeld, *Writing Brief* (Glenview, IL: Scott, Foresman, 1986). Based on Peter Elbow, *Writing without Teachers* (London, England: Oxford University Press, 1975). Copyright © 1986. Reprinted by permission of Scott, Foresman, and Company.

15. *Ibid.*, 27–28.

16. Murray, *A Writer Teaches Writing*, 17.

17. *Ibid.*, 28.

18. Proett and Gill, *The Writing Process in Action*, 13.

19. Jan Turbill (ed.), *No Better Way to Teach Writing* (Sydney, Australia: Primary English Teaching Association, 1982), 35.

20. Lucy Calkins, *Lesson from a Child* (Portsmouth, NH: Heinemann, 1983), 129–130. Reproduced with permission from Calkins: *Lesson from a Child* (Portsmouth, NH: Heinemann Educational Books, Inc., 1983).

21. Peer Response Form, an adaptation of a handout by Cara Keller, in *A Writing Project; Training Teachers of Composition from Kindergarten to College*, Harvey Daniels and Steven Zemelman, eds. (Portsmouth, NH: Heinemann, 1985), 169.

22. George F. Nemetz, et al., *Handbook for Planning an Effective Writing Program, Kindergarten through Grade Twelve* (Sacramento, CA: California State Department of Education, 1986), 18.

23. Jan Turbill, *Now, We Want to Write* (Sydney, Australia: Primary English Teaching Association, 1983), 35.

24. Rebekah Caplan, "Showing Writing: A Training Program to Help Students Be Specific," in *Teaching Writing, Essays from the Bay Area Writing Project*, Gerald Camp, ed. (Upper Montclair, NH: Boynton/Cook, 1982), 97.

25. *Ibid.*

26. Calkins, *Lessons from a Child*, 35.

27. Doris L. Prater and C. Ann Terry, "Effects of Mapping Strategies on Reading Comprehension and Writing Performance," *Reading Psychology* 9, no.2 (1988):120.

Chapter 12

The Forms of Writing and the Writing Program

The Forms of Writing and the Writing Program

Functions of Writing

Writing to Remember and Organize Ideas

Writing to Learn and Share Information

Writing to Communicate with Others

Writing to Imagine

Learning Various Kinds of Writing

Journal Writing

Writing Letters, Invitations, and Messages

Writing Reports and Informational Material

Writing Stories

Writing Poetry

Basic Components of an Effective Writing Program

Organizing the Classroom for Writing

The Teacher's Role

Physical Room Arrangements

Using Writing Centers

Appendix: Making Books

For many years writing was believed to have only one major purpose—communication. Although we do communicate through writing, it also serves other valuable purposes.

Functions of Writing

Writing helps us remember and organize information; it helps us learn and share ideas and information; we use writing to communicate with others; and we use writing to imagine—to play with language, to create. We use various kinds of writing for different purposes just as we vary how we speak depending upon our purposes.

Writing to Remember and Organize Ideas

We write lists—grocery lists and lists of things to do for a week. We make notes on our calendar and record the amount of our checks in the checkbook. These kinds of writing help us remember things we need to do or get, record information we will need later, and plan our day or week.

Can you imagine doing without lists and calendars?

Writing to Learn and Share Information

Teachers have always had students write, no matter what they were studying. Evidence now suggests that certain kinds of writing actually help us learn material in the various content areas.[1] The kind of writing that is especially effective is that which requires transforming the information in some way. In the process of using the ideas rather than repeating them, we make the ideas our own. Chapter 14, "Learning in Other Content Areas through Literature-Based Language Arts," describes in detail how language, both oral and written, helps us learn and gives specific examples of such classroom activities.

One fourth-grade class, while studying different environments, read Diane Siebert's *Mojave.*

> *And on my mountains, craggy, steep,*
> *I feel the hooves of bighorn sheep;*
> *From shelf to rocky shelf they spring,*
> *Their hoofbeats*
> > *echo . . .*
> > > *echoing.*[2]

The students were enchanted with how beautifully the text and paintings described the desert. One group within the class decided to write a similar book to describe another environment they had been studying—the Arctic. Their book became a popular choice among other students with its pictures of polar bears, bald eagles, pink salmon, and whales, surrounded by immense icebergs and threats of avalanches. By creating a book incorporating their research on climate, landforms, and wildlife of the Arctic, students made the material more meaningful.

Writing to Communicate with Others

February 20
Dear Mom and Dad,
    Thank you for the nice val-
entine card you gave me. I
liked it. It's just like me, espe-
cially when it says giggly. I
love you and thanks for be-
ing my valentine.
                    Love,
                    Janny

People write notes and letters, messages of all kinds to get in touch with each other. Sometimes our writing is formal—when we accept an invitation to a wedding or write to a company for information about its products. Messages may be quite informal, such as a note slipped to a friend in class.

Did you see the way Leigh Ann blushed when HE came
in??!!!   P

In a highly mobile society, we need to keep in touch with our old friends if we move away. It is always a thrill to find a letter from a friend in the mailbox, and we can encourage children from kindergarten on to learn to enjoy and participate in writing to others.

Writing to Imagine

If I Were a Star

If I were a star I would go to the moon or
Venus or Mars and have a good time. But if
I want to go to the sun, I would have to get
a lot of sleep. But I do not want to—not me,
not me. But I am not a star, so that's that!

This second-grader used her imagination to pretend to be something else and go sailing around in space. We almost sense her relief at the end that she is person instead of a star flashing across the universe.

Birds

Birds fly while I try
To learn and read
Birds are show-offs!

The use of rhyme and a wonderful sense of humor in this piece of verse written by an elementary school student illustrates the fun that children can have imagining and playing with language.

Learning Various Kinds of Writing

While the process we use to write something is essentially the same whether we are writing a report, a poem, or a letter, the form that our writing takes varies. We have to consider who will read it (the audience), what information to include, and what format to use. To make those decisions, we rely on what we have learned from other pieces of writing and from instruction.

In general, children start writing and drawing about their own experiences, their family and pets, family celebrations and birthdays. Britton proposes a model of writing development that indicates that children start with *expressive writing* and later move to either *transactional writing* (writing reports, arguments, explanations) or *poetic writing* (stories, plays, poems, songs, and so forth).[3] Moffett recommends that children begin writing about their own experiences primarily for themselves and later write on less familiar topics and less well-known audiences.[4] Journal writing and letter writing, which are the most personal, familiar, and expressive kinds of writing, would therefore precede transactional (reports) and poetic (stories and poems) writing.

Journal Writing

The term *journal writing* actually encompasses a variety of journal types. The most familiar is the diary journal in which children write every day about things they are doing or thinking about. This is a kind of writing that emphasizes fluency and deemphasizes correctness and form, which makes it suitable for younger children to get them started. At first they may draw and write a few words, but as the school year goes on, drawing decreases and writing increases as these beginners become more able to express their ideas in writing. To keep a diary, the children need a special book to write in, one that is used only for this purpose. They need response to their writing and ideas, so the teacher should plan to collect the journals and respond to the children in writing at regular intervals. Usually, responses express reactions to a particular entry or two, and may ask for more information, recount a similar experience, or simply acknowledge the feelings or event. The teacher does not correct the journal, in which only ideas count, not form. Some teachers like to respond on self-sticking notes that the child can remove easily so the diary is still his or her own. The teacher should schedule a time each day for the children to write in their journals. Sometimes a list of ideas to write about may be helpful. The children might paste the list in the front of their journals, occasionally adding ideas as they think of what to write about. Listed topics might include my best birthday, when I was sick, my favorite Saturday activity, my friend, my family, taking a trip, if I were a movie star (singer, teacher . . .), my pet, my sister (brother), the best present I ever received (gave), and so forth.

Children's journals are private, not to be shared with other students without the writer's permission, nor shown to parents or other teachers. You can promise such privacy to the students with the exception that if they write about something that the teacher is legally or morally bound to share with parents or other authorities, the teacher will be free to do so after telling the child of his or her intentions. (For example, in most states teachers are required by law to report suspected child abuse.)

There are also dialogue journals in which the child and teacher take turns writing back and forth to each other. In general, the same guidelines apply, except that the teacher writes directly in the journal. A dialogue journal is like a written conversation between two individuals. This type of journal usually requires more of the teacher's time, although it is both motivating and rewarding.

Older students may keep response journals in which they respond to their reading, class discussions, or other presentations. These journals are less personal in some ways, although they reveal much about the writer's values and preferences. Teachers usually respond to these journals also, focusing on content, not on form. You may ask about something they've missed, point out a part that you like, and agree or disagree with their assessment. Many teachers feel they have a better sense of what students understand from their reading through response journals than through class discussions.

Project journals, or logs, are also effective and are sometimes used in conjunction with other content areas. They are primarily used as prewriting to collect information and ideas, as discussed in Chapter 11. Project journals are kept for a specific time period while students are working on a particular project. Students record what they are observing, take notes on their readings of related information, list their hypotheses, and generally use the journal to keep track of their work on the project.

We should not leave the topic of journal writing without some cautions. Journals take a lot of teacher time as you must respond to them thoughtfully. Therefore, perhaps you should begin with a short-term commitment, and decide later how long you (or the children) want to continue. It is hard to ignore misspellings and the lack of punctuation, but you must! Although mistakes should not be marked in the journal, you may want to keep a separate list of your own and record student's problems with mechanics for future lessons. (If you keep such a list, use it to plan instruction. Do not share it with the students.) Journals provide opportunities to interact with the children and their feelings and ideas. The funny or poignant things they write must be kept confidential; this is private information. The benefits show in the children's increased confidence and fluency in writing. The teacher comes to know the students in more depth than usual. That is what makes all the work worthwhile.

Writing Letters, Invitations, and Messages

We all enjoy getting notes or letters that sound just like the person or that are written with us in mind. Although there are conventional forms for letters, the teacher must not emphasize the form over the contents. Look at these two samples of letters written to an author in terms of form and content:

January 15, 1982
Dear Mr. Burch,
*   Our teacher read Queenie*
Peavie to us. It was a nice
book. Thank you for writing
it. We liked it.
*   Sincerely,*
*   Julianne*

Dear Mr. Burch,
Our teacher read us the story
you wrot about that girl who
was so mean and I wanted
to tell you that lots of girls
are that way cause the boys
are so mean to them and
they half to be that way. You
just made it seam so real
that I could believe it.
*   Your friend,*
*   Julianne*

If you were Mr. Burch, which letter would you prefer to get? The first letter is in perfect form, and probably that student could name the parts of the letter: the heading, greeting, body, and closing. The second letter has a few spelling errors, no date, and some other mechanical errors, but it certainly lets you know that the child was touched by the story she read and sincerely liked it.

Certainly proper form needs to be learned but not at the expense of individuality and ideas. Learning the form may be a slow process that takes place over a number of years. Provide the students with a sample of the correct form, but emphasize what information or ideas will be important and interesting to the receiver. The form becomes an instrument to be referred to when needed; it should not be the focus for writing. It should also not be just "for practice;" writing needs to fulfill a real purpose.

Letter Writing

Both personal letters and what might ordinarily be termed *business letters* may be somewhat informal during the elementary school years. If children are writing for information of some kind or wish to order something, remind them to put their addresses and their full names in the letter, suggesting the proper placement. You may offer to check over the letter if they would like, and to help them with spelling as they are composing. However, the most important thing you can do is to use meaningful situations that call for writing a letter.

You may be able to establish pen pal relationships with a class in another city or in a different part of the country. When one of the children or a group has enjoyed a particular story or book, suggest writing a letter to the author. If you need some free or inexpensive teaching materials, recruit some of the children to order them for you. Keep the addresses of children who move away during the year so that their friends can correspond with them. Write to patients in a nearby veteran's hospital or nursing home. You can encourage the children to write to children's magazines or your local newspaper.

Capitalize on holidays or birthdays to write thank-you notes. The children can make their own note paper, printing or painting designs on it. They can make envelopes or folded notes that do not need envelopes, or you could supply envelopes that fit the paper. Figure 12.1 shows a thank-you note done on a computer, which the girls enjoyed writing and Carol certainly appreciated receiving. The borders and designs that can be done on certain computer programs make writing letters and thank-you notes more fun to do.

Personal Notes

Instead of being upset when children write notes to each other, capitalize on their interest and channel it into good practice in writing. Set up mailboxes for each child somewhere in the room, where they may put notes for one another and where you may also put notices, reminders,

FIGURE 12.1 *A thank-you note*

or notes for them. A special note from the teacher once in a while may be cherished, and writing only two or three a day does not take much time. It's a nice way to compliment someone who does not often get compliments.

Invitations

Children of all ages can help write invitations to others asking them to visit the classroom for something special. If they are too young to write the invitation in letter form, compose some that they can complete: *Please come to_____, Where_____, Time_____, etc.* Even beginning first-graders can copy in the necessary information and make the decorations for the covers. When the children are older, they can write out the full invitation. You will need to remind them of what information is needed, but they can do the actual wording themselves. Perhaps there should be a writer or secretary on the "helpers" chart each week to take care of invitations and thank-you notes. Be sure to give the secretary something to write during the week, even if it is a thank-you note to the cooks for an especially good lunch.

Announcements and Messages

Children need to be able to make announcements and take down messages in written form. The key is providing opportunities for them to have real practice in doing this. However, be sure to have alternative plans for those really crucial pieces of information until your children have had enough practice to be completely reliable.

Literature-Based Letters

The Jolly Postman has served as inspiration for letter writing in many classrooms.[5] The book is a series of envelopes containing letters from familiar fairy tale characters, such as Goldilocks and Jack, the Giant Killer. Students can write their own versions of letters to and from characters in books. Older students often enjoy writing such letters to and from characters in books they are reading currently or in old favorites.

> *Across Weeks and into*
> *Months*
> *Dear Max,*
> *How do you do it? I've been practicing every day so that I can stare in the other wild thing's eyes and tame them like you did. It just doesn't work! How did you do it? Please send me the secret as soon as possible.*
> *Did you finally get some supper? I hope it wasn't all gluey and cold.*
> *Miss ya,*
> *Hairy*

Writing Reports and Informational Material

One of the most difficult tasks for children in elementary school is writing an informational report. Part of their problem is that reporting calls for a more formal style of language than they are accustomed to using, and another part of the problem is that they are told to write a report without being given enough help in how to do this. What also often happens is that they look up information in an encyclopedia or other reference books and then copy whole paragraphs or sections for their report. An earlier kind of informational writing should precede report writing—recording. In written recording children begin to develop skills necessary for more formal reporting.

Recording

Defining Recording Written recording involves some kind of data gathering on a firsthand basis and then converting the information into written sentence or paragraph form. As a beginning step in informational writing, the children use information that they have observed and recorded or have found out personally by surveying, measuring, and so on. Since children of elementary school age do not learn from abstract sources, it is particularly important to involve them in collecting the information they will be writing about.

The observations or survey results should be categorized by the children on some type of chart or graph. This grouping or categorizing helps to consolidate the information they have gathered into a manageable form. Then they are ready to write sentences or paragraphs about their observations.

Learning to record is an important process for children. They learn how to use information and how to organize and write their observations on paper. Not until they have had a lot of opportunities to use the recording process are they ready for written reports which involve library materials and other secondhand sources for their information.

Written recording is an appropriate activity for children in all grades, but is especially valuable for older children who have not had previous experiences with recording. It should be a regular part of the writing program for younger children who need many experiences with written recording before moving into report writing.

Classroom Recording Experiences The kinds of recording experiences that children have should be related to the other activities they are doing; they should not simply be unconnected exercises intended for practice. Recording relates very well to science and social studies where children are observing, comparing, and surveying anyway.

Comparisons: Young children are very perceptually oriented, and the teacher can capitalize on this by challenging them to compare two items. These might be two shells, two rocks of different types, or two plant cuttings. More mature children can compare three or four samples, looking for similarities and differences. An occasional question or suggestion from the teacher may help them make finer distinctions among the items they are comparing.

In comparing plant cuttings, the children will quickly notice the colors of the leaves, their general shape, and perhaps whether they are fuzzy, smooth, or waxy. They may not notice if the leaves grow opposite one another or if they alternate, whether the stem is round or square, and whether the plants have a distinctive odor or not. These are the kinds of cues the teacher may suggest when the children appear to have finished their comparison.

Observations: Children make many observations that can be used for experiences with recording. They may make observations of the living things in their classroom or on the playground, or about the experiments they are conducting in science. As children observe, they should keep some type of log, journal, or chart. If they are recording an event over a period of time, the observations should be made at regular intervals.

One group of second graders made observations about changes that took place during the fall season. They each observed a particular tree on the playground and went out every two weeks to see what changes were taking place. Others kept track of the average daily temperatures and amounts of rain during those same two-week periods. By mid-November they were ready to put together their observations and write about the changes that take place in the fall.

A group from a fourth-grade class made daily observations of the baby gerbils born in their classroom: growth of fur, when the eyes opened, when they began to eat independently, how much they weighed, how well they walked, and so on. After five weeks the gerbils were grown, and the children wrote a description of the growth of baby gerbils based on their recording.

Surveys: Occasionally a disagreement over something or the mention of a favorite program or pet may lead children to take a survey of some kind. Any number of things may be surveyed—favorite sports, foods, colors, television shows, birthday months, types of transportation to school, or state capitols visited. The results of the survey can be easily graphed and written about.

Taking a survey introduces interviewing and is an important way of gathering information for reporting. At first children can survey others in their room, and then children in other rooms, the teachers or other school personnel, or people within the community.

Measuring: Another kind of recording experience involves taking measurements and recording the results. Children may compare standard measures (foot, cup, inch) against nonstandard measures (span of a hand, a glass, a piece of yarn). They may work with various liquid measures (cup, pint, quart, gallon) to find out how many cups make up each of the others, or how many pints in a quart, and so on. Their measuring could involve comparisons between standard measures and metric equivalents.

Recording experiences—A final word: Any number of activities that children regularly do can be used as a basis for recording. Children need many experiences with recording as a basis for the more formal written reports that they will be called on to do later. If they can learn to depend on their own observations and ideas in the early stages of reporting, they will be less prone to copy pages from encyclopedias. Also, the kinds of close observation used in recording form a solid basis for descriptive writing.

Reporting

Moving into Reporting   There are several ways of easing the transition from informal recording activities to more formal reporting. The first written reports might involve topics closely related to the students' interest that could be easily illustrated. The main part of the information could be conveyed with a series of illustrations or a display of some kind. The children could set up a model, diorama, or collection in a table display or a series of illustrations on a bulletin board. The labels or explanations with the illustrations would constitute their report.

One second-grade class wrote about different animals. Figure 12.2 shows a riddle that Chad wrote using information about the giraffe, and Figure 12.3 shows Michael's list of similarities and differences between tigers and cheetahs. Zack wrote about some of the unusual animals in Australia in Figure 12.4. An early form of informational reporting may also be a collection of pictures as shown in Figure 12.5, which shows an interesting variety of birds from chickens to vultures and flamingos.

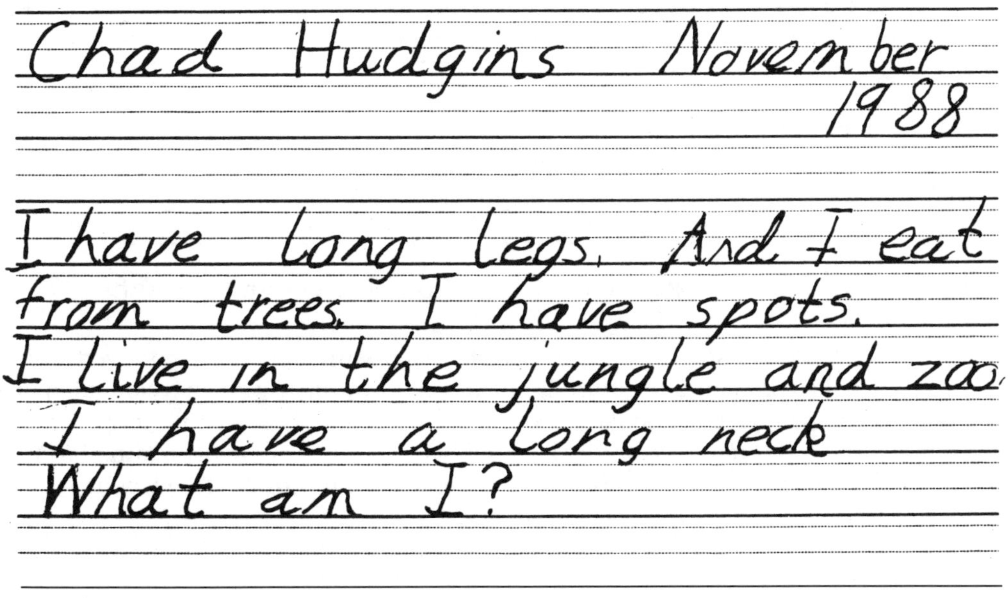

Chad Hudgins   November
                          1988

I have long legs. And I eat
from trees. I have spots.
I live in the jungle and zoo.
I have a long neck
What am I?

FIGURE 12.2   *Chad's riddle: The Giraffe*

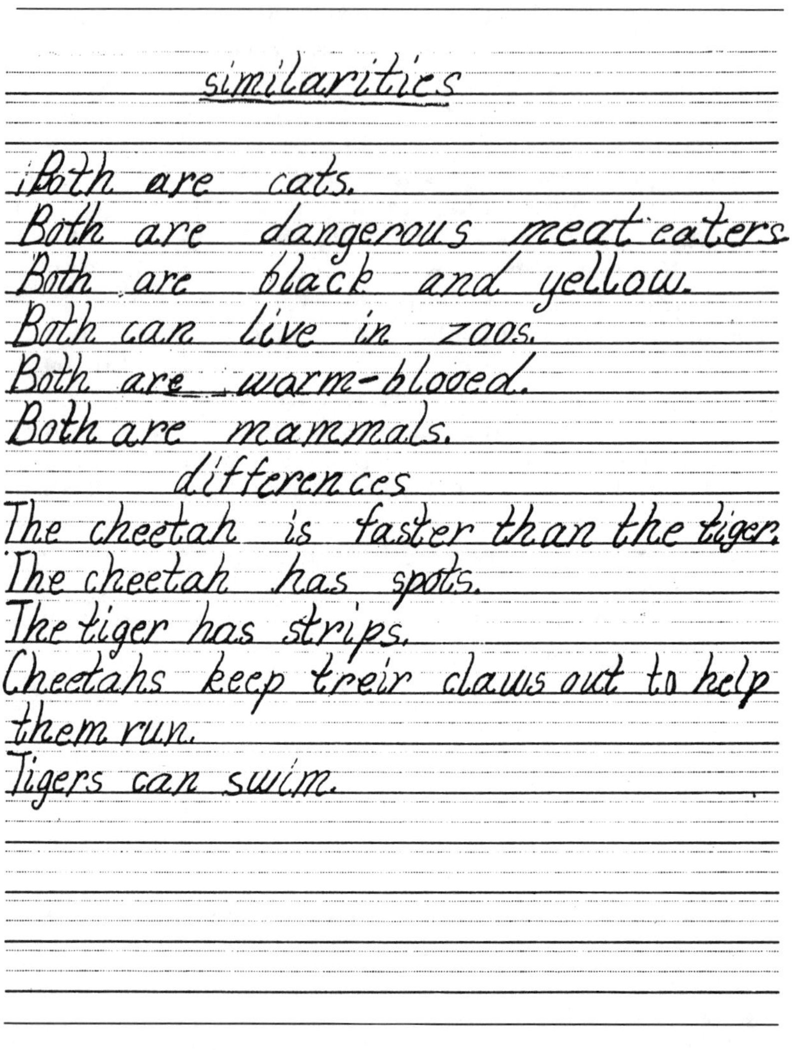

similarities

Both are cats.
Both are dangerous meat eaters.
Both are black and yellow.
Both can live in zoos.
Both are warm-blooded.
Both are mammals.
                differences
The cheetah is faster than the tiger.
The cheetah has spots.
The tiger has strips.
Cheetahs keep their claws out to help
them run.
Tigers can swim.

FIGURE 12.3 *Michael's comparison of tigers and cheetahs*

The first use of reference materials might involve informational books that could be shared. Too often we think only of encyclopedias or similar reference books for reports when there is a wide variety of well-written, illustrated informational books with a range of reading levels. The first kind of report that children write might be a review or summary of one of these informational books.

Developing Reporting Skills   Three major skills are involved in writing reports: taking notes, organizing ideas for writing, and using reference materials. These skills need to be taught. You cannot just send

Zack Geoffrey December 1, 1988
In Australia
Astralia has many, many kinds of
animals like the Koala, the Wombat,
the Bushtailed Possum, the Powerful
owl, the Tawny Frogmouth bird, and
the suger glider. When a baby
koala is born, nobody sees it, not
even it's mother.

FIGURE 12.4 *Animals in Australia*

children to the library with a topic for a report and a set time period
and expect them to be able to write a good report. Each skill needs to be
taught before the children are required to use it.

Taking notes: The problem of copying portions of encyclopedias
and giving them as reports starts with children's inability to take notes
in their own words. Although selecting the main idea from a paragraph
or a larger portion of material is a reading skill that is tested throughout the school years, children select the main ideas from a predetermined set of choices. To prepare children for stating the main idea in
their own words, a great deal of preliminary work needs to be done.

Write out on chart paper or on a transparency a paragraph of
material from a source similar to the ones the children will be using.
Have the children read through the paragraph carefully; then remove it
from their sight and ask them to write down one or two of the main

FIGURE 12.5 *Pictures of birds for a report*

ideas expressed in the paragraph. The instruction may be more effective if done in small groups. When they have finished writing, ask them
to take another look and fill in any details or ideas they missed. Discussion is very helpful. You will want to talk about the main ideas and
details that are important to include. When they have become proficient at selecting the main ideas from materials that you control, they
are ready to work with duplicated materials on their own. This is a
critical time to make sure that they are not reverting to copying whole
sentences from printed sources, but rather formulating the ideas in
their own words. After they have mastered the skill, they are then ready
to take notes independently from library sources.

Organizing ideas: There are a number of ways to organize material collected for writing that are recommended for children. The process of organizing material before writing that is recommended here

has four main steps: listing ideas, grouping ideas, ordering the ideas within groups, and then ordering the groups of ideas. First the child lists all the ideas to be included in the report (in a word or short phrase). Then the child groups together related ideas and sequences for writing the ideas within each group. The final step in organizing is to decide which group of ideas will be expressed first, second, third, and so forth. When that is finished, the child has a rough outline of the report. At any time in the process a particular idea may be discarded or moved to another group.

Teachers may want to go through this process several times before expecting children to be able to do it independently. The first two steps involve categorizing, an appropriate activity for younger children to do simply as a way of organizing information.

Using reference materials: Before starting to use reference materials independently in the library, children need some help in knowing what kind of information is found in what kind of book and how to find out whether a particular book covers the topic of interest. If you can obtain a small collection of reference materials for the classroom, you can help your students learn to use an index and table of contents. Skimming is an important skill in working with reference materials, especially skimming through a segment and reading only the titles and subtitles of sections.

Informational books may provide pertinent material about a subject and at the same time present a format that can be modeled for writing reports. Also, informational books should be available in the classroom as reference sources when students are studying specific topics. Since a wide variety of informational books exists today and these books offer attractive, readable material for different age levels, teachers should consider them as significant resources for students' research and reports. Otherwise, unfortunately, the encyclopedia becomes the single source for information gathering.

Because report writing calls for more formality and often includes secondhand information, students need help learning to write such material. The process of writing is the same as for any other kind of writing—generating ideas and organizing them, writing a first draft, revising it (perhaps after sharing with others and getting their reactions), editing the final draft, and putting it into finished form. Informational reports may be presented in different formats depending on their purpose and the imagination of the writer.

As a fourth grader Paul had to do a report in social studies. He chose the underground railroad as his topic. At the time he lived in Lawrence, Kansas, a city where the underground railroad had been active. In fact, he found out that his church had provided one of the "stations." He interviewed the minister and was able to see the room itself, now a furnace room. He read books about that time period, interviewed someone from the local historical society, and found several different kinds of information in the library. An excerpt from his report follows.

> *Kansas got involved with the railroad in 1854–1863. Some of the people from Kansas were John Doy, John Brown, Richard Cordley, Mary Cox Cordley and Joel Grover. The slaves came from Missouri before they came to Kansas. Some citizens of Kansas knew about the railroad, but the ones who did know about the railroad kept it to themselves. The underground railroad probably started when somebody kept an escaped slave in their house and asked other people to help. Only two or three were kept in an underground railroad at once.*
>
> *The underground railroads often looked like a small basement, but they were all different. They were usually basements and cellars under barns and houses. They were very dark and dirty, and not a very nice place to stay, though it was helping the slaves get north to be free.*

The last section of the report describes famous people from the underground railroad and stories of how they helped rescue former slaves. It is clear that this report was not copied from the encyclopedia. Paul followed the rule that books must be closed when you are writing. It is apparent that Paul not only learned a great deal about his topic, but that this piece of history has human dimensions for him.

Experiences writing different kinds of reports should be done with a real audience in mind, an audience who will enjoy and learn from the information. Like any other kind of writing, doing a paper for the teacher alone is not appropriate.

Writing Stories

Children add story writing to their repertoire of kinds of writing quite early—perhaps because they hear so many stories read to them or watch stories on television, or perhaps because the narrative form reflects how people think.

As children get older and have more experiences with stories, they modify their ideas about the structure or patterns of stories. This "sense of story" influences how well they comprehend and construct oral or written stories. Much of the research in "sense of story" has been done by Applebee who examined the stories of two- to five-year olds to infer what they thought a story should be.[6] Their stories became increasingly complex and contained a thematic center.

Developmental Trends in Story Writing

The stories below were written about one picture and show the general progression of children's story-writing abilities. Although the abilities of children at any one grade level may vary greatly, these stories offer one example of the kind of development that takes place. What kinds of developmental changes can you note?

A First-Grader's Story

I have a Siamese cat. I like my Siamese cat. I like butterflies. They are pretty. Leaves are pretty too. I like them. Sometimes they are brown. I like them. I love animals. I have blue eyes. I have red hair. I like looking at butterflies. I like to catch them. My cat likes to eat them. My cat likes to catch them. Sometimes I catch them. I put them in cages sometimes.

A Second-Grader's Story

It has big green leaves, and the girl is looking at the big butterfly, and the cat's looking at it, and the girl has red hair, and the cat's brown, and it has big blue eyes. It looks like the cat is trying to get a butterfly.

A Third-Grader's Story

Once there was a girl with long red hair and big blue eyes. She was walking through the forest with her Siamese cat. When she saw a big red and black butterfly, she stood there looking at him. She was thinking it was pretty. Her cat was thinking, "Boy would I like to catch him!" All of a sudden he ran after the butterfly. The girl decided to walk back out of the forest because the butterfly was gone.

A Fourth-Grader's Story

I have red hair and blue eyes and a pet cat, and I like to go in the woods and look at butterflies and try to find out what kind they are, and try to find out what kind the leaves are and collect the leaves and look at other animals. One day when I went along with my cat, I saw a butterfly with orange and brown spots; but it flew away, and I never saw anymore like it. One day I saw one almost like it, but it had red spots. But it flew away too. One day I got a butterfly that had all different colors in it, and I kept it for a pet. One day it flew away, but I knew it was happier there with other butterflies so I wasn't too sad.

A Fifth-Grader's Story

There was once a girl who was lost in the woods and couldn't find her way out. She had a pet cat who followed her in the jungle, and the butterfly showed her the way home. After that she made a little place in the woods where the butterfly showed her the way home. When she got older, she lived in this place where the butterfly lived. When winter came, the butterfly had to fly down to Florida; and the girl was sad because he had to fly down south, and she didn't think it would fly back. After winter was gone the butterfly flew back. Then they decided to move to Florida so the butterfly wouldn't have to fly away, and that's where they lived from then on.

Increasing complexity in language: There is increasing sentence length from the three- and four-word sentences that are common in the first-grader's story to the thirteen- or sixteen-word sentences in the fifth-grader's story. This is done at first through coordination (using *and* as in the second-grader's story) to subordination and embedding in the fourth- and fifth-graders' stories ("One day when I went along," "who was lost and couldn't find," "place in the woods where the butterfly").

Greater use of more precise and varied words: The older, more mature writers use pronouns or synonyms to avoid excessive repetition ("fly down to Florida" and "fly down south") and connectives that show order or relationships ("After that," "When she got older," "When winter came," "After winter was gone").

A change from basic description to the development of events: Both the first- and second-grade stories are entirely descriptive. In the third-grade story, the cat chases the butterfly and the girl leaves. The fourth-grade story is similar in that the butterfly leaves, but its author adds other butterflies to the story. In the fifth-grade story we see the development of a crisis when the butterfly goes to Florida for the winter, and the girl fears that she won't see it again. Happily, the butterfly does return, and they move south so that they can be together.

Movement from view of self to the view of others: The first-grader uses the first person, but—more important—many personal notes are added as "I" becomes the central character. "I love animals," "I like them (leaves)," or "I put them in cages sometimes" all appear to be the author speaking. The second-, third-, and even fourth-grade stories may use first or third person, but seem to involve the author as a participant in the stories. The fifth-grader's story is told more from the viewpoint of a disinterested person; certainly there is less involvement of self.

Development from single to multiple events: In the first two stories, the events are not developed. The third-grade and fourth-grade stories suggest a single and similar event—the butterfly goes away. In the fifth-grade story, the butterfly leaves, but when it returns, they all go south to be together.

Increasing use of dialogue: Unfortunately for illustrative purposes, only one of the stories uses dialogue—the third-grader's story. In order to use some dialogue, the story must be viewed as separate from the storyteller, and this is not typical of the early primary grades. It could well have been added to the fourth- or fifth-graders' stories but was not. This may be an individual developmental item, or the result of infrequent opportunities to tell or write stories.

Increasing use of details: In the first-grader's story, the descriptive details include the word *pretty* and the naming of colors. In the second-grader's story, additional details are given—"big, green leaves" and "the cat's brown, and it has big blue eyes." The third-grader's use of details is more frequent and more extensive, with "long red hair and big blue eyes" and "A big red and black butterfly." Both the fourth- and fifth-graders do use descriptive adjectives, but they more frequently supply details in other ways. The fourth-grader adds, "I like . . . to find out what kind they are," " I never saw anymore like it," and "I knew it was happier there . . . so I wasn't too sad." The fifth-grader adds similar details such as "a girl who was lost in the woods and couldn't find her way home," and "made a little place in the woods where the butterfly [had] showed her [the] way home."

The addition of minor events and explanations: This is closely related to the use of details discussed above. We see in the third-grade story an example of the addition of explanations as we find out what the girl and the cat were thinking. In the fourth-grader's piece, there is the idea of the girl as a scientist looking at butterflies and other animals or leaves to identify them. There is also the addition of other butterflies previously seen, "a butterfly with orange and brown spots" that flew away and "one almost like it, but it had red spots" and it flew away too, and finally a butterfly with "all different colors on it, and I kept it for a pet." The fifth-grader adds a series of events as the butterfly shows her the way home; she builds a place in the woods; when she is older, she lives in that place; winter comes and the butterfly goes to Florida; after winter, it flies back; and finally they move to Florida so that it won't have to fly away in the winter.

The trends toward more maturity in the development of story technique and in the language used in writing really need to be examined in multiple samples of children's writing. They indicate the pattern of development, and what will be most evident in older children's writing or with those who have had a fine composition program.

Literature and Story Writing

As children become increasingly familiar with stories, they begin to write their own. Sometimes they may imitate particular story form; other times they appear to use only their own sense of what a story is like. This sense does not come from hearing a story once a week, nor from reading unimaginative or simplified books. It does result from daily exposure to excellence. The need to hear good literature does not end when the child can do some independent reading. It is just as necessary in grades four through eight as it is in kindergarten through grade three.

Literature provides familiar stories to draw upon in imaginative writing and can be important as a specific starting point for writing. Children may draw upon their familiarity with particular kinds of stories and write their own versions. Young children may compose their own ABC or counting books after listening to some and looking at or reading several examples. An ABC book composed by some first-graders and illustrated by them has "Crayons begin with C, dog begins with D, Easter egg begins with E, and fence begins with F." Another group of first-graders used a wide variety of fabrics, paper, buttons, and other materials. They had a real nickel on the N page.

Not all ABC books are intended for young children. Some sixth-graders became intrigued with the words and pictures in *Hosie's Alphabet*.[7] The book inspired them to create their own ABC books illustrated with water color drawings. One student wrote in his book, "D is for devine devilment, L is for the loquacious locust, and Q is for quadrophonic quadruplets." Older students want to write accumulative stories patterned on *The House That Jack Built* or *The Napping House*.[8] They can write their own versions of *Chicken Soup with Rice*[9] using their favorite foods and either months of the year or days of the week.

Older students enjoy writing their own tall tales, parodies of fairy tales, newspaper columns, Mother Goose rhymes, and explanatory tales. Fourth- and fifth-grade groups wrote their own Paul Bunyan stories with Paul solving the problem of a gigantic snowstorm. These are two of their solutions:

> *Paul told the mother snowstorm to tell the father snowstorm to tell the baby snowstorm on the ground to come home or he would spank him!*

> *Paul ate up all of the pepper they had except for one plateful which he put under his nose. Then he sneezed and sneezed. He couldn't stop sneezing and he sneezed the snow away.*

After sharing *Robbers, Bones and Mean Dogs*, a collection of students' essays about what scares them, a teacher discovered that her fifth-graders wanted to compile their own book on the subject.[10]

Preceding any such writing, there should be extensive reading of the story and inductive discussion of its form, format, or characteristics. Books may also inspire writing about a new character, a new adventure, a new event, or an ending to a well-liked story or tale.

These are very direct uses of particular pieces of literature; however, literature also indirectly influences children's writing as they become more familiar with many well-written and enjoyable stories. For example, a group of first-graders were enchanted with the *Winnie-the-Pooh* stories and wrote many of their own based on different characters.[11] Here are three that illustrate what an average group of first-graders can write when they have had many experiences constructing sentences and dictating stories.

Rabbit Invites Pooh Over for a Tea Party

One day Pooh was going for a walk. He met Rabbit and Rabbit invited him over to his house. Rabbit had a tea party. Pooh went out the front door and he got stuck. Rabbit pushed and pulled but Pooh wouldn't move an inch. Pooh said, "Why don't you make your door a little wider?" Rabbit went to find the strongest animal he knew. Pooh was still stuck. Then Rabbit and everyone in the forest pushed and pulled and Pooh shot out like a rocket. And they didn't see Pooh for three years.

Kanga-Roo is Lost!

Kanga was jumping with Roo in her pocket. Then she stopped. Kanga thought that Roo was lost but she was stuck in the pocket. Then Kanga went to Pooh and said, "Pooh would you look in my pocket?" "What for?" said Pooh. "For Roo!" So he did and he found him. He took Roo out. Then they lived happily ever after.

Eeyore Loses His Tail

One day Eeyore was walking along the grass. He heard something fall. He didn't know what it was. He didn't know it was his tail. Eeyore went home and took a nap. When he woke up, he figured out that his tail was missing. He went to Pooh and told him what was wrong. Pooh went to owl. Then Pooh went for a walk. Pooh saw Eeyore's tail lying on the grass. He took the tail to Eeyore, Eeyore said thank you. Pooh put Eeyore's tail back on.

In one sixth-grade room, the students were interested in murder mysteries. It began with Donald Sobol's *Encyclopedia Brown* books. The students wanted more mystery, so their teacher suggested Hildick's *The Case of the Felon's Fiddle* and *Manhattan is Missing*. They read two books by Scott Corbett, *The Case of the Gone Goose* and *The Case of the Silver Skull*. Then she suggested Wright's *Christina's*

Ghost. The students wrote mysteries, they drew mystery pictures, they researched ghosts, mummies, and witches (like *The Witch's Daughter* by Bawden).[12] Here is just one of their many stories.

The Murdering Mummy

As Joe Wilson returned home he felt that somebody or something was watching him. He opened the door to get another pair of shoes.

As he bent down reaching for his shoes, something knocked him back. He saw that it was a whitish figure. The figure pounced on Joe. There was a sound of a dagger ripping through a man's body.

The next day the police were trying to identify the killer. They only found a piece of white cloth. This kept on happening until one day the thing got shot with a gun.

A policeman heard a scream. It was from a house on the other side of the road. He ran as fast as he could go. The lady was dead. The whitish figure kept on running across the yard. The policeman yelled, "Stop or I'll shoot."

The whitish figure fell. He walked over to the whitish figure, "Omigod," the policeman yelled. "A Mummy!"

Story writing gives students of all ages the opportunity to imagine the unknown, to explore in the safety of one's own place what strange, faraway places might be like. It gives the writer a chance to create a story for others to enjoy. Story writing allows you to experiment with language as well as with ideas.

Writing Poetry

Poetry is another kind of writing that should be an important part of every student's school experience. Young children come to school enjoying poems and verse; they enjoy listening to poetry and are certainly willing to write poems. Although poetry uses language somewhat differently than stories or reports, it is not necessarily more difficult. Writing poetry should simply be an alternative way for children to express their personal reactions, feelings, and observations.

Introducing Poetry

Just as children develop a sense of story from listening to or reading many different stories, they can develop a "sense of poem" from listening to and reading many different poems. Their ideas about poetry are influenced by their experiences with poetry. Read them many different poems—rhymed ones and unrhymed ones, poems that are rhythmic and those that are not in meter, poems that involve metaphoric language and those that do not, poems written in various forms and about different topics. Read long poems and short poems, funny poems and serious ones, traditional poems written for children and modern poems. To write poems, students need to know what poetry is.

Students also need to connect pleasure or enjoyment with poetry. It needs to be accessible. Too often their experiences with poetry involve identifying figures of speech, rhyme schemes, and meter or interpreting the author's idea. That is not learning about poetry but about poetic devices.

There are many different ways to enhance students' responses to poems: choral reading, media presentations, dramatizing poetry, writing, discussion, and so forth. One primary-grade class heard the following poem by Aliki Barnstone:

Summer

Deer prance around in our land.
They stretch their necks
to reach the apples in the trees.
Every night we go out
quietly
and try to spot them
I sprinkle salt on the rocks
so they can lick it.

With beautiful antlers
they gracefully run about the fields
till they see us.
They stop and stare
and run.[13]
  —Aliki Barnstone

After listening to the poem a couple of times, the students divided into two groups—people and deer—and moved according to the lines in the poem. The "deer" pranced about stretching their necks to nibble apples, and the "people" quietly walked about looking for deer and sprinkling imaginary salt on rocks, and so on. Then the children changed roles. Later they discussed what words describe deer, how they move, what they eat, where they live, who their enemies are, and how they protect themselves. Most of the children in this class saw deer often in the woods or fields or along the road. Some drew pictures of the deer and wrote about them. For the picture in Figure 12.6, the child-author wrote the following:

FIGURE 12.6   *The deer*

The deer is jumping. He is getting food. He is spoted. He is a boy. He is soft.

For the picture in Figure 12.7, another child wrote:

Their enemies are men, bobcats, and pumas. The deer is large or small. They are shy. The deers have lots of spots. The deer can leap high.

In another class, Lynn wrote a description of deer. Notice how she incorporated much of the language of the poem in her description.

They lick salt. They run swiftly. The baby deer's name is fawn. The legs are skinny. They stare at men, then they run.

FIGURE 12.7   *More deer*

The[y] prance around at night. They have beautiful antlers; their shape is oval. The body is slim. They run gracefully. Some are tall in size, some are short.

Experiences such as these help children relate the poetry to their own experiences in an enjoyable way and foster interest in poetry.

Selecting Poetry to Share

Studies of poetry preferences indicate that children in first through sixth grade like humorous poems about enjoyable familiar experiences, animals, and spooky things.[14] They like poems that rhyme and have rhythm and sound effects. They like limericks and narrative poems. They do not like sentimental or serious poems, or poems that depend on imagery and figurative language, which the younger children don't understand. They do not like to listen to free verse or haiku poetry.

Younger children like traditional poems, while older children tend to like contemporary poetry. However, there were some children at each grade level who liked each poem. So, while we can talk about preferences in terms of the general trends, almost all poems will be liked by some children. In addition, the poems they enjoy listening to may not be the same as those they enjoy writing.

There are many fine poets writing for children today who provide a rich tapestry of forms, topics, and poetic elements. The National Council of Teachers of English presents an Award for Poetry for Children, which is presented to a living American in recognition of his or her work. Works by poets who have won this award are excellent choices to read to children. Recent winners include David McCord, Aileen Fisher, Karla Kuskin, Myra Cohn Livingston, Eve Merriam, John Ciardi, Lilian Moore, and Arnold Adoff. Two other poets who write popular humorous verse for children are Shel Silverstein and Jack Prelutsky. Do not, however, limit yourself to this list of poets; there are other wonderful poems and poets that you and your students will enjoy. Explore, share, discuss, and ask students to bring poems to share. Keep a box or a folder on your desk with copies of the poems you especially like. Then they will be right there when you want to share one. (There may not be time to look one up in the library when you want it—or the book may be checked out.)

You will want a copy of Bodecker's poem below when a child shows off a loose tooth.

Ruth Luce and Bruce Booth

Said little Ruth Luce
To little Bruce Booth;
"Lithen," said Ruth
"I've a little looth tooth!"

Said little Bruce Booth;
"Tho what if you do?
That'th nothing thpethial—
I've a looth tooth too!"[15]
  —N.M. Bodecker

Collect poems that go with books and pair them. "Song of Triumph" by Lois Duncan goes perfectly with Bernard Waber's *Ira Sleeps Over.*[16] The last stanza of Duncan's poem is as follows:

Till finally she sighed
And she told me, "All right—"
So I'm sleeping over
At Ricky's tonight!

After reading the popular *Bridge to Terabithia*, [17] read either Langston Hughes's "Poem" that begins, "I loved my friend," or the poem below by Charlotte Zolotow:

Missing You

Once we laughed together
By the river side
And watched little waves
Watched the waves.

Now I walk
Along the bank
The water's very blue
And I am walking by the waves
  Missing you. [18]
  —Charlotte Zolotow

Collect poems that go with units of study that you teach. Lee Bennett Hopkins has a whole book of poems that younger children will love entitled *Dinosaurs*. [19]

Collect poems that seem to cry out to be discussed. Two that always cause children to want to talk about being independent—more independent than their parents like—are "Where" by Karla Kuskin and "Questions" by Marci Ridlon. [20] Both poems are a litany of parental questions: Where have you been? Where did you go? When did you leave? Who went with you there? and so on. The final stanza in both is the child's answer—a wonderful comparison as well as a guaranteed discussion piece.

Look for poems that are good for choral reading, drama, mime, or movement. One that children love that suggests possibilities for movement is Eve Merriam's poem:

Satellite, Satellite

Satellite, satellite,
The earth goes around the sun.

Satellite, satellite,
The moon goes around the earth.

Satellite, satellite,
I have a little satellite:

My little brother orbits me
And pesters day and night. [21]
  —Eve Merriam

Collect poems that make bright images, those that call for the children's own illustrations. Some students illustrated the "satellite" poem in crayon-resist—crayon designs overpainted with black tempra—with whirling planets, satellites, the Sun, and the Earth. Encourage students to experiment with different media—printing, carving, sculpture, paper folding, or chalk—and not just crayons and manilla paper.

Look for poems that make children want to write their own versions. Perry's "Halloween" served as a model for two students.

Halloween

Hooting
   Howling
      Hissing
         Witches;
Riding
   Rasping
      Ragged
         Switches;
Fluttering
   Frightening
      Fearsome
         Bats;
Arching
   Awesome
      Awful
         Cats;
Long
   Lantern-
      Lighted
         Streets;
Tricks!
   Tasty
      Tempting
         Treats![22]
—P. J. Perry

Holly used this poem as inspiration to write about the ocean but without using rhyme.

Salty
   Sandy
      Sassy
         Water.

Fabulous
  Flawless
    Fascinating
      Shells. . . .

Poetic Forms

Children need many experiences as a base for writing poetry. They need to play with words and with sounds and images. Typical of this is the seven- or eight-year-old who leaned out over the swimming pool watching a bug on the water and made up a word-play poem that he repeated over and over.

Bug off, bug
Go away
Who needs you
On a sunny, summer day?

Children's first attempts at writing poetry are far from being really fine poetry. Before they can write fine poetry, they need frequent opportunities to express themselves poetically. The following suggestions for writing free verse, concrete poetry, invented unrhymed forms, and simple rhymed forms are beginning points in writing. The final objective is the ability to use poetry—rhymed or not—as an alternative to writing prose for those ideas that are especially suited to poetic expression.

Parallel Poems   The editors of *The Whole Word Catalogue*[23] suggest parallel poems and lists as good ways to begin writing poetry. This kind of poetry is based on repetitions; the poems have consecutive or parallel lines that begin or end with the same words. This is a form that many poets have made use of because of its rhythmic, chantlike effect. The structure is there as something to be relied on, and yet its open-endedness invites writers to explore their imaginations. "The beauty of these parallel poem ideas is that they allow students to plug into them at their own level of skill and sophistication."[24]

I Wish
Write a poem in which every line begins with *I wish*. . . .

Colors
Write a poem with a color in every line.

Lies
Write a poem with a lie in every line.
Write a poem with a whopping lie in every line.

I Remember
Write a poem in which every line begins with *I remember.* . . .

Dreams of the Future
Write a poem in which every line begins with *I am going to.* . . .

Comparison Poems
_____*is like*_____. For example: *Thunder is like bowling. Clouds are like a feather.*

Metaphor Poems
Same as comparison poems, except without the word *like.*

Equivalent Poems
In the past they _____*, but now we* _____.

I Used to Be
Has the form *I used to be* (a) _____*, but now I'm* (a) _____. [For example, a first-grader wrote: "I used to be a cookie, but now I am a crumb."]

Free Verse The first writing by children should be very free—something we might call *word pictures.* An example from a first-grader is a poem about time.

THE CLOCK

The clock tells time
  Bedtime
    Suppertime
      Playtime
The best time of all.

Inspired after the teacher had read and talked about free verse, an older student composed the following poem. Notice that he was also interested in experimenting with form—something that may happen when a student has been exposed to reading and writing a variety of poems.

The earth is a large round ball
  Circling the sun, never to be
                    stopped
    By the Human Race . . .

This kind of writing, as it develops, becomes the kind of free verse written by a seventh-grader.

The sky never ends
   up and up forever high
reaching for the top

Darkness spreads like ink
Till the stars shyly peep through
And extend their light

The morning comes thin
   and pinkish paint soaks
the sky
The sun wakes us up

Concrete Poetry   A kind of poetry that may appeal to children throughout the elementary grades is a special kind of picture writing. In concrete poetry the words either outline a visual picture of the topic or
form a more solid picture of the idea of the poem. Laura, a fifth-grader,
contributed the concrete poem shown in Figure 12.8, about fish.

Concrete poetry can be one of the easiest kinds of poetry for young
people to write because there is so much appeal in the visual image,
and there is so little structure that is predetermined. Since the poet

FIGURE 12.8   *Concrete poem by a third-grader*

sets the pattern, the concrete poem can have a very complex form and become a most demanding kind of poetry to write.

List Poems   This form provides an interesting structure for both individual and group poems. One reading group started talking about a book character who was finally happy. They discussed the things that make them happy, and then they wrote the following poem:

> **Happiness is:**
>
> *two kinds of ice cream*
> *learning to whistle*
> *knowing a secret*
> *having a sister*
> *climbing a tree*
> *singing together*
> *learning to tell time*
> *finding your skate key*
> *playing the drum*
> *walking hand in hand*
> > *Anyone and anything at all*
> > *That's loved by you.*

Using "Christmas is . . .," a fourth-grader wrote the poem shown in Figure 12.9. She enjoyed working with the rhymes, and was very successful with them.

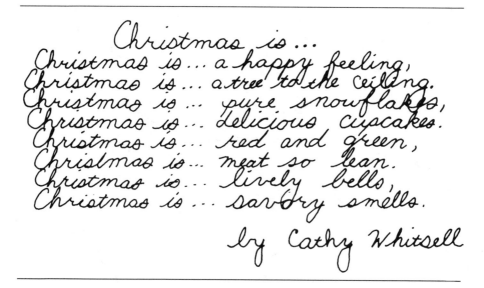

Christmas is . . .
Christmas is . . . a happy feeling,
Christmas is . . . a tree to the ceiling.
Christmas is . . . pure snowflakes,
Christmas is . . . delicious cupcakes.
Christmas is . . . red and green,
Christmas is . . . meat so lean.
Christmas is . . . lively bells,
Christmas is . . . savory smells.
by Cathy Whitsell

FIGURE 12.9   *Definition poem by a fourth grader*

Cinquains The cinquain is one of a number of invented forms that may help children experiment with form and delay dealing with rhyme. Sometimes the invented forms give students structure for composing without being too difficult to use. There are two kinds of cinquains. The first is syllabic with the five lines from which the name comes having a sequence of two, four, six, eight, and two syllables. Another widely circulated kind of cinquain follows a part-of-speech pattern in the five lines—the first line contains one noun, the second contains two adjectives, the third contains three participles, the fourth contains a four-word phrase, and the last line contains one noun.

Syllabic Cinquain

At the Beach

The sea
Patterns of sound
Match the patterns of waves
Match the ridges in burning sand
Echoes

Part-of-Speech Cinquain

Evening

Candle
Bright white
Glowing, shining, sparkling
Such a pretty sight!
Fire

One group of children invented their own cinquain using one, two, three, four, and one word, respectively, in each of the five lines.

Amphibs

Frog
Funky warts
Making foggy sounds
Lovely, madly, slimy, green
Frog

Diamante The diamante is a variation of the part-of-speech cinquain that adds three more lines to make a diamond shape. The poem switches meaning in the fourth line so that the last line is the opposite of the first. It is challenging! Here is sixth-grader Caroline's poem.

Enemy
Strange, untried
Challenging, teasing, ignoring
Opponent, competitor—teammate, pal
Playing, sharing giving
Nice, new
Friend

Students can make up their own invented forms of poems, varying the number of words in various lines, specifying certain kinds of words by part of speech or by category, such as color, size, or name. They can experiment with syllabic forms that are perhaps less restrictive if they are not too short.

Terse Verse   One of the easiest of all the rhymed forms, terse verse consists simply of two rhymed words with a rather long explanatory title.

What the Girl Said to her Mother in the Spring

Green
Scene

Clerihew   Another form of rhymed poetry that children have enjoyed writing is the clerihew, a four-line rhymed poem in which the first line is someone's name. These are more difficult because of the rhyme scheme, and students need to make sure they don't substitute rhyme for meaning.

Casey Jones   *Santa Claus*
Broke all his bones   *Had to pause*
He did it fast   *Bringing toys*
Before he crashed.   *To girls and boys.*

Limerick   Limericks are one of the students' favorite forms of poetry to listen to, but they are very difficult to write. They not only have a rhyme scheme that is quite confining, but they are written in a particular meter. Until students have worked with poetry, especially rhymed poetry, they are unlikely to be successful writing limericks.

There was a young guy in sixth grade
Who thought he had everything made.
  But then he got his report
  Of A's and B's it was short
So he's grounded until seventh grade.

There are, of course, other forms of rhymed poetry with various patterns of rhyming lines. As children become more at ease with poetry, and as they develop a larger vocabulary, they are more able to write rhymed poetry.

Found Poetry   Found poetry is a kind of poetry that children may enjoy discovering. Found poetry comes from prose—a segment of prose that can be rearranged into poetry. You can find poetry in any number of types of prose—advertising, descriptive writing, stories, and so on. The piece of prose, when rearranged in some format, may reveal a shape much in the same way concrete poetry does, or it may be set out like free verse. Here is an example from a magazine article.

> A prickly forest of legs and feelers seethes under a rock ledge 25 feet down in the warm Gulf Stream washing the Great Bahama Bank. Spiny lobsters—hundreds of them—cram a single den no bigger than a pool table. Slowly, several leaders emerge, drawing others into bustling podlike clusters. Gradually the pods string out into lengthening files . . .
>
> Then it begins: a relentless head-to-tail march, a mysterious impulse that drives these crustaceans day and night for miles along the sandy, unprotected shallows.[25]

This might be arranged into a free verse poem by selecting certain phrases and rearranging them into a poetic form, as follows.

> *A prickly forest*
> *of legs and feelers*
>   *h*
>   *ee   e*
>   *s   s*
>   *t*
> *under a rock ledge.*
> *Spiny lobsters*
> *cram*
> *a single den.*
> *S l o w l y*
> *several leaders emerge.*
> *Then it begins*
> *a relentless*
> *head-*
> *to-*
> *tail*
> *march.*

With a shorter passage, the entire piece might be used as a found poem.

Working with found poetry is good experience for many children. It may make them more aware of writing styles and phrasing, and also be a good introduction to poetry about things other than trees, flowers, and fairies. For children who are unsure of their ability to write poetry, found poetry may be an intermediate step to original writing.

A Note on Haiku and Tanka   The oriental forms of haiku and tanka are not included in this section, although they are often recommended as forms of poetry for children. Both haiku and tanka, which are syllabic arrangements, make a comment on life in such a way that the whole poem is a metaphor. Since we have considerable evidence that children have a great deal of difficulty understanding metaphorical language and since writing haiku and tanka calls for making a 17- or 31-syllable metaphorical comment on life, both forms may be too abstract and too difficult for many elementary school children. Also, accepting any 17 syllables arranged in five-seven-five syllable lines without the additional characteristics of the haiku seems to be cheating children by letting them think they have written a haiku when they really have not.

Evaluating Children's Poetry

Evaluation of poetry is a particularly difficult task for anyone, and it is especially important for the teacher not to impose adult standards on children's writing. As in story writing, emphasis on valuing (instead of on grading) is a way to heighten interest and ability. The following guidelines may help in indicating the kinds of things teachers may look for and appreciate in children's poetry.

- *An awareness of an experience:* There is a sense that the child has written about an event that meant something.
- *Sincerity of feeling:* There is an impression of honesty and genuine expression.
- *Appropriate and natural language:* The words are the child's own and fit the topic; there is no obvious straining of sentence structure to make a rhyme; the words are precise without seeming unnatural.
- *Creation of a response in the reader to the poem:* The reader of the poem is somehow touched, amused, or made conscious of something new.

Responding to children's poems by telling them what you particularly liked in the poem and having other children hear and read their poems and tell what they liked stimulates interest in writing poetry and growth in writing. Encouragement does far more good than any grading or evaluation system.

Children as Poets

Children are natural poets. They enter school with characteristic "chatter-patter, mingling and jingling their syllables."[26] Repetitive phrases and word games are part of their everyday play. What poetry does is to make the ordinary extraordinary in some way. Through language and through writing poetry, children learn to channel their thoughts and emotions effectively and to gain a deeper self-understanding as they master written words. Twelve-year-old Hilary Kessler shares what it is like to write a poem in the following example.

> *Poetry starts in the very back of your mind*
> *   and branches out until you are in a different world*
> *Free of worries*
> *Just writing whatever flows from the pencil.*
>
> *Just what you're feeling and how you feel it.*
> *And then when you're all finished*
> *A feeling of satisfaction sweeps over you*
> *And brightens you for the whole day.*

Basic Components of an Effective Writing Program

Successful writing programs may look very different; there certainly is no one right way to develop the writing program in your classroom. However, the following six elements are common to all successful writing programs.

- *Writing is approached as a process:* The focus in the classroom is on the process—how to go about writing something—rather than on the final product. Students use different ways of developing their ideas (using jot lists, explaining orally to someone else, visualizing the topic, clustering, etc.), writing a draft and revising it (perhaps after feedback from others), making another draft and editing it, and publishing it by sharing it with others in some way. It is exciting for both the student and the teacher when a piece of writing really works, but you must remember that the important task is learning how to write, not producing a great piece of writing.
- *Writing is an integral part of learning:* Students will soon find that writing helps them learn the content of many different areas. Some of the writing in science, mathematics, or social studies is

done to help remember important ideas or to organize information, but other writing assignments help students learn about specific topics or concepts. In such writing they transform informational material by taking information and making it their own by using it in a new way. Writing is not restricted to English or Language Arts. Writing permeates the entire school day.

- *Writing builds on student interests and experiences:* Children develop and write about topics that reflect their own experiences and topics. The teacher is not responsible for coming up with a topic or two every day for the students to write about. Students may determine topics by keeping a list of ideas for future writing in the front of their writing folders. The teacher may suggest some possible topics, but choosing the topic is essentially the writer's task.

- *Students write in various modes for different audiences:* They write stories and personal experiences; descriptions of places, people, and events; poems of various kinds; persuasive pieces when they think something should be done; plays or reader's theater scripts to perform; articles for the school newspaper; recordings of experiments or surveys; and so on. Much of their writing is shared with their friends and teacher within their classroom, but writing is also shared with a wider audience, such as the school staff, students in other classes, or students in another school or state. Writing is published by being shared in a peer group or displayed on bulletin boards or in the hall, lunchroom, or library. Several times a year the teacher may put out a booklet of class writings to be sent home. Some local papers publish a children's page with pieces of their writing and drawings. If your school can be adopted by a business, perhaps that will be a new audience. Teachers should seek outside readers if at all possible.

- *Students write on a regular basis:* Although we all enjoy variety, we need some predictability in our lives. This is especially true of children. It helps them when they know they will have time to write every day; this way, they can think about their writing ahead of time and be ready to go when they pick up their pencil. In a world that has so many changes and over which children have so little control, having some pattern to the school day is not boring, it is reassuring.

- *There is a real need to write:* Britton reminds us that children "must practice language in the sense in which a doctor 'practices' medicine . . . and not in the sense in which a juggler 'practices' a new trick."[27] This means that we avoid "writing exercises" and worksheets; instead, we find and develop projects and questions that call for meaningful writing experiences.

In a planned writing program, the emphasis in writing will be different in different grades and with children who have different backgrounds of experience. The focus in the earlier grades is on developing fluent writers—writers who are able to write a considerable amount with a certain ease. This should not imply that correctness does not matter. It does. Students need to learn to spell and punctuate, capitalize, and indent, but such mechanical things should not be the focus in the beginning. In upper grades, the emphasis is generally on sequence, clarity, and experimentations with style in which students develop their own personal voices. But, there is no one "right" way; we each teach using our own strengths and interacting with our students essentially in our own style.

Organizing the Classroom for Writing

The organization of the classroom also is as individual as teacher's teaching styles. The ideas suggested here for you to consider as you plan your own program are derived from the writing process itself and from the known components of good writing programs.

The Teacher's Role

Using a process-centered approach to composition requires that you use a workshop approach. There is just no way to maintain a teacher-directed classroom and still give children control over their writing, letting them make the important decisions about what they write, revise, add, or delete, about what and when they publish, about who they share with along the way, and so forth. As the teacher, you are in charge of the time schedule and the record keeping. You are the most authoritative person to give advice and encouragement, but you are not in charge of the writing. The students are the authors. You are more experienced in writing, especially in its conventions, but the student is more experienced in the topic. You work together, experimenting with new forms and topics, listening to what the author wants to say and how well it is communicated, each contributing to make the piece as good as possible.

With younger children, the teacher can model the writing process by writing in front of children and thinking aloud while doing it. You may want to write on the board, on chart paper, or on a transparency—anything that is comfortable for you and allows the student to see what you are doing as you talk about it. In such a shared writing you can show the steps that writers usually think through. You may model how you come up with an idea to write about, demonstrating brainstorming and the use of lists of ideas from others' writings or from books. Another time you might demonstrate revision—how you check if the piece is in the right sequence, if you wrote enough details for others to understand, if you can make it more interesting, if it sounds complete, and so on. With older students you might model the act of brainstorming ideas and then organizing them prior to writing or you might show how you cluster and associate ideas around a nucleus word to solve writer's block. You could demonstrate revising for stylistic elements such as parallel structure or effective repetition with variation. Such modeling helps students find out *how* to write; it demystifies what goes on in the writer's mind.

It also seems clear that the teacher needs to write. This should be real writing, not a piece done as a child would do it. Use part of the writing time to do your own writing; this forces the students to go it alone for a while. It also means that you share with them what you are writing and willingly take their response and suggestions. You cannot bury your head in your own writing for the entire classtime, however. Students need to confer with you, you need to confer with some of them. Some will need some editing help with their final drafts. Some may be off-task and need encouragement.

Physical Room Arrangements

Just as the writing process calls for a workshop approach and a certain role for the teacher, it also calls for certain room arrangements. Your room needs to take on the aspects of a workshop rather than a lecture hall. If students are going to work together, they need space.

Tables and Folders
Tables are wonderful, but you can group square-topped desks together. Most teachers find that students work well keeping their writing in folders. Regular manilla folders are fine, although the ones with pockets and rivets to hold the writing in place are even better. Organizing the folders by work groups, using different colors or symbols or locations for each set, reduces confusion. Encourage the students to keep all their writing, drafts, and jot lists in the folder. Otherwise, pieces seem to disappear. Teachers can document students' progress in the folders as mentioned in Chapter 11.

References
Students will need an accessible place—or places—to use writers' reference tools such as the dictionary, word books (alphabetic listings without the meanings), thesauruses, rhyming dictionaries, picture diction-

aries, and writing supplies, such as correcting fluid, paper, extra pencils or pens, rulers, scissors, plastic tape (for the reviser who cuts drafts apart), art supplies for illustrating, and so forth.

Room Library

Students need a classroom library with standard commercially published books as well as their own published books. There should be literature of different genres and with different patterns, books of prose and poetry, informational books, and standard reference books. A set of encyclopedias is a wonderful addition. A comfortable place for reading and an appropriate place for taking notes are desirable.

Conference Area

You need to have a place to confer with individual children where you can sit side by side and not at your desk, which represents authority. Present yourself more as a writing colleague with experience who can help. You may also have brief conferences wherever a student is working, but need a special place for the formal conference that you schedule with students or that they schedule with you. Often, such conferences are evaluative and focus on final revisions or final drafts.

Publishing Area

There should be an area for book making, for publishing magazines or duplicated class writings. The chapter appendix gives directions for book binding. Not all stories or other pieces of writing need to be published in a hardcover bound book. Folded and stapled construction paper covers are fine for some pieces. Colored paper covers can be illustrated, laminated, and assembled with brads for a somewhat more elaborate booklet. "Blue books" from college days can be glued inside posterboard covers for a sturdy book with lines that are easy to write on. Some teachers purchase a scrapbook with plastic covered pages to use and reuse all year. Each child has a page for his or her current writing. Ditto masters for children to copy their stories for sharing are also appropriate.

Computers

Access to computers with good word processing programs can facilitate writing. Most students can get their ideas down much faster and easier using computers. Even when they do not know touch typing, their experiences with various video games makes them good at the "hunt and peck" system. Using computers makes revising much easier, and students no longer look upon revisions as a chore. Editing is also easier, and the word processing program may have a spell check program that will help students identify what is wrong if not how to correct it. The final product printed from the computer is much more legible than most

*Computers assist the writing process. Word
processing programs make revising and
editing easier tasks.*

students' handwriting, and copies can be made easily. You need an adequate number of computers; a long line of children waiting for one
terminal impedes progress. You need to be familiar with using the computer yourself and how the word processing program works. Most students need a great deal of help at the beginning. In addition to word
processing programs for students to use in doing their own composing,
there are programs to teach skills such as spelling, punctuation, or
sentence combining, prewriting, and organizing ideas. There are also
programs that students can use to create interactive stories. Be very
selective about software programs, making sure they fit with your view
of writing and your students' needs and abilities. In general, such programs help in motivating students; however, young writers must learn
to generate their own ideas, follow their own prewriting process, and
revise to suit their own sense of what a piece of writing needs.

Using Writing Centers

Writing centers have long been a common approach to involving younger students with writing. They generally display a variety of writing activities based on a theme and provide all of the required materials. In general, centers allow the student to choose a topic and to work at an individual pace. Their drawbacks are two-fold: first, they encourage children to rely on the topics the teacher suggests rather than developing their own ideas; and second, they are too pencil and paper oriented and seldom involve talk, drama, or other prewriting activities.

Sometimes theme centers focused on learning other subjects include writing tasks that are entirely appropriate to language arts. In primary grades, these centers can reflect an area of integrated study that also includes observation, illustration, dramatic activities, and so forth. One third-grade class was studying animals in a fairly standard way until they invited an active bird watcher who lived in their neighborhood to talk to them. But, Ms. H didn't just talk. She took them out around the edges of the school yard to do some active bird watching of their own. Well, that was it! They built feeders of different kinds and put them outside their windows at school and took some home. They read about birds; they listened to recordings of bird whistles; they did a bird census of their own in the neighborhood with Mrs. H's help. The center on bird study that their teacher quickly developed was the hit of the year. There were lots of writing assignments—comparisons of different kinds of bird families: song birds, sea birds, game birds, and birds of prey. They wrote descriptions of the birds they saw and illustrated them. The species in which male and female coloring differed fascinated the children. They drew illustrations of the various nests birds construct and wrote about each. They learned about their state bird, and some students went on to learn about the other state birds. The writing center was successful because the writing served a real purpose and came from the children's experiences.

The writing workshop is a busy place. It is not entirely quiet, but neither is it really noisy. You may find the teacher at one of several places: at the bookcase helping a student find a special book, at the conference table, helping with bookbinding, helping a small group with punctuating dialogue. Papers are not red-penciled; the teachers' responses to pieces of writing, like those of the children, are shared during conferences about the writing.

Summary

We use writing in many different ways for different purposes. Writing is used to remember and organize information, to learn and share ideas and information, to communicate with others through letters, notes, and messages, and to imagine and create. The basic process of writing is an inherent part of nearly all writing.

The form that writing takes depends on the purpose and the audience. Children start writing about themselves and their experiences, and this expressive writing is very much like "talk written down." Later, children move toward transactional and poetic writing. Journal writing does not go through all the stages in the writing process because it is not for publication. Journal writing is "talking on paper," often talking to yourself. Some types of journals such as dialogue or project journals are read and responded to, but essentially journals are for the self. Letter writing, messages, and notes are for communication and have a highly social purpose. We must be careful not to sacrifice content for form when teaching letter writing. Report writing is one of the transactional kinds of writing in which we present our ideas, give information, and make our views known. Learning to write good reports is a complex task that requires direct instruction. Story writing develops as children use their imaginations and their knowledge from stories they have heard. Writing poetry allows them to focus on language and to create images.

The components of an effective writing program reflect the experiences of many teachers who have worked with children's writing at different grades. The final section on organizing the writing program focuses on the role of the teacher, room arrangements, and the use of centers. This chapter, then, illustrates what the writing process described in Chapter 11 might look like in a class setting. The writing workshop model encompasses the various aspects of the process of putting ideas and imaginings on paper for others to share.

Questions for Discussion

1. The purpose for writing has traditionally been for communication; what other purposes does it serve?
2. What are some of the different kinds of journals and what purposes do they serve?
3. Written recording is suggested as an early step in learning to write reports. Describe what it is and how you might plan a recording activity.
4. How does literature—both stories and poetry—help students in their own writing?
5. How would you describe the role of the teacher in a good writing program?

Notes

1. A. Applebee, *Writing in the Secondary Schools*, Research Report 21 (Urbana IL: National Council of Teachers of English, 1982); P. Elbow, "Teaching Thinking by Teaching Writing," *Change* 15 (1983):37–40; T. Fulwiler, "How Well Does Writing across the Curriculum Work?" *College English* 46 (1984):113–125; J. S. Mayer, N. Lester, and G. M. Pradl, *Learning to Write/Writing to Learn* (Upper Montclair, NJ: Boynton Cook, 1982); and M. L. Simpson, "PORPE: A Writing Strategy for Studying and Learning in the Content Areas," *Journal of Reading* 29 (1986):407–414.

2. D. Siebert, *Mojave* (New York: Crowell, 1988). Copyright © 1988 by Diane Siebert. Reprinted by permission of Harper & Row, Publishers, Inc.

3. J. Britton, *Language and Learning* (London, England: Allen Lane, Penguin Press, 1970).

4. J. Moffett, *Teaching the Universe of Discourse* (Boston, MA: Houghton Mifflin, 1982).

5. J. Ahlberg and A. Ahlberg, *The Jolly Postman* (Boston, MA: Little, Brown, 1986).

6. A. N. Applebee, *The Child's Concept of Story: Ages Two to Seventeen* (Chicago, IL: University of Chicago Press, 1978), Chapter 2.

7. H. Baskin, T. Baskin, & L. Baskin, *Hosie's Alphabet* (New York: Viking, 1972).

8. A. Frasconi, *The House that Jack Built* (New York: Harcourt Brace Jovanovich, 1958); and A. Wood, *The Napping House* (New York: Harcourt Brace Jovanovich, 1984).

9. M. Sendak, *Chicken Soup with Rice* (New York: Harper & Row, 1962).

10. B. Berkey and V. Berkey (comps.), *Robbers, Bones and Mean Dogs* (Reading, MA: Addison-Wesley, 1978).

11. A. A. Milne, *Winnie-the-Pooh*, Illustr. E. H. Shepard (New York: Dutton, 1928).

12. D. Sobol, *Encyclopedia Brown* (Nashville, TN: Thomas Nelson, 1973); E. W. Hildick, *The Case of the Felon's Fiddle* (New York: Macmillan, 1982) and *Manhattan is Missing* (New York: Doubleday, 1969); Scott Corbett, *The Case of the Gone Goose* (Boston, MA: Little, Brown, 1961) and *The Case of the Silver Skull* (Boston, MA: Little, Brown, 1974); B. W. Wright, *Christina's Ghost* (New York: Holiday House, 1985); and N. Bawdan, *The Witch's Daughter* (New York: Lippincott, 1966).

13. Aliki Barnstone, "Summer," in *The Real Tin Flower* (New York: Crowell, 1968). Reprinted with permission of Macmillan Publishing Company from *The Real Tin Flower* by Aliki Barnstone. Copyright © 1968 by Aliki Barnstone.

14. Studies of poetry preferences such as C. A. Terry, *Children's Poetry Preferences: A National Survey of Upper Elementary Grades* (Urbana, IL: National Council of Teachers of English, 1974) and C. J. Fisher and M. A. Natarella, "Of Cabbages and Kings: Or What Kinds of Poetry Young Children Like." *Language Arts* 56, no. 4 (April 1979):380–385.

15. N. M. Bodecker, "Ruth Luce and Bruce Booth," in *More Surprises*, L. B. Hopkins, ed. (New York: Harper & Row, 1987). Reprinted with permission of Margaret K. McElderry Books, an imprint of Macmillan Publishing Company from *Snowman Sniffles and Other Verse* by N. M. Bodecker. Copyright © 1983 by N. M. Bodecker.

16. L. Duncan, "Song of Triumph," in *Best Friends*, L. B. Hopkins, ed. (New York: Harper & Row, 1986), and B. Waber, *Ira Sleeps Over* (Boston, MA: Houghton Mifflin, 1972).

17. K. Paterson, *Bridge to Terabithia* (New York: Crowell, 1977); L. Hughes, "Poem," in *A New Treasury of Children's Poetry*, J. Cole, ed. (New York: Doubleday, 1984).

18. C. Zolotow, "Missing You," in *Best Friends*, L. B. Hopkins, ed. (New York: Harper & Row, 1986), 24–25. (Thomas Y. Crowell) Text copyright © 1970 by Charlotte Zolotow. Reprinted by permission of Harper & Row, Publishers, Inc.

19. L. B. Hopkins, *Dinosaurs* (New York: Harcourt Brace Jovanovich, 1987).

20. K. Kuskin, "Where?" in *Near the Window Tree* (New York: Harper & Row, 1975); and M. Ridlon, "Questions," in *That Was Summer* (New York: Follett, 1969.

21. E. Merriam, "Satellite," in *Jamboree: Rhymes for All Times* (New York: Dell, 1984), 50–51. Copyright © 1962, 1964, 1966, 1973, 1984 by Eve Merriam. All rights reserved. Reprinted by permission of Marian Reiner for the author.

22. P. J. Perry, "Halloween," in *Hey-How for Halloween*, L. B. Hopkins, ed. (New York: Harcourt Brace Jovanovich, 1974). Permission to reprint "Halloween" from Phyllis J. Perry, from *Instructor*, copyright © October 1971 by The Instructor Publications, Inc.

23. R. Brown et al. (eds), *The Whole World Catalogue* (New York: Virgil Books, 1972), 49–50.

24. *Ibid.*

25. W. F. Herrnkind, "Strange March of the Spiny Lobster," *National Geographic* (June, 1975):116.

26. E. Merriam, "Some Pearls from Eve Merriam on Sharing Poetry with Children," *Learning* 14, no. 2 (October, 1985): 78.

27. Britton, *Language and Learning*, 130.

Appendix: Making Books

Books are easy to make and children feel that they are very special. They can also provide a purpose for children's writing. The two figures below show the physical and organizational aspects of bookmaking (see Figures A.1 and A.2).

How Books Are Published

Few people know how many people are involved in publishing books. Aliki's well-illustrated *How a Book is Made* gives children a good insight into all the different stages a book goes through before it reaches the reader. (See Figure A.1.)

FIGURE A.1 *Students may enjoy seeing all the aspects of how a book is made by reading this book about making books*   Illustration from *How a Book Is Made* by Aliki (Thomas Y. Crowell) copyright © 1986 by Aliki Brandenberg. Reprinted by permission of Harper & Row Publishers, Inc.

Instructions for Making a Book

Fold the paper in half for the pages (see *A*). Then sew along the fold with a needle and thread or with a sewing machine. If sewing pages is not possible, staple them together along the folded line (see *B*). Next cut cloth or wall paper one inch larger than the book pages on all sides. Lay the pages open and flat to measure as in *C*. Use two pieces of heavy wrapping paper or cardboard about the weight of a shirt cardboard cut, a little larger than the pages as in *D*. Cut two pieces of dry mounting tissue to fit and place between the cardboard and the cloth cover material. If you prefer, glue also works well and may be spread evenly with a damp sponge (see *E*). There should be some space between the

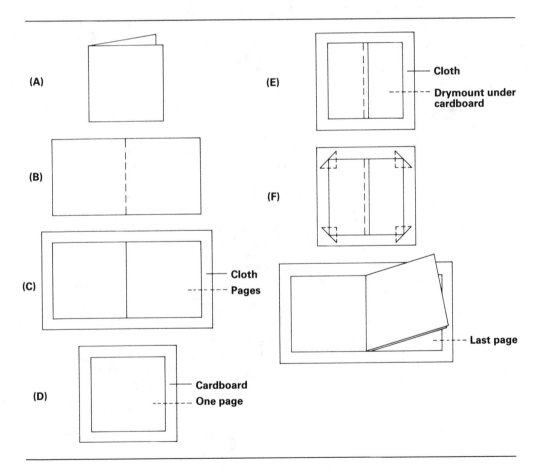

(A)

(B)

(C)   — Cloth
              ---- Pages

(D)   — Cardboard
              ---- One page

(E)   — Cloth
              ---- Drymount under cardboard

(F)

              ---- Last page

FIGURE A.2   *Bookmaking gives children a goal and something tangible for their efforts.*

two pieces of cardboard to allow the book to open and close easily. If you are using dry mounting tissue, press with an iron in a few places to hold the cardboard in place. Then fold the corners of the outer covering in, fold the top down and in, fold the bottom up and the sides in, and iron or glue as in *F*. The final step is to glue or use dry mounting tissue and iron the first and last pages to the cover, as shown in *G*.

Chapter 13

Supportive Writing Skills

Supportive Writing Skills

Skill Development within the Writing Process

Mechanics of Writing: Punctuation and Capitalization

Learning to Punctuate Written Material

Learning to Capitalize Written Material

Student Rule Books

Spelling Instruction

Early Spelling Strategies

Spelling: Part of the Reading-Writing Connection

Regularity in Phoneme-Grapheme Relationships

Sources of Words for Study

Methods of Studying Words

Spelling Games and Activities

Testing in the Individualized Spelling Program

Analyzing Spelling Problems

Handwriting Instruction

Beginning Handwriting Instruction

Materials for the Beginning Writer

Teaching Handwriting within a Meaningful Context

Styles of Handwriting

Teaching Manuscript Writing

Teaching Cursive Writing

Assessing Legibility in Handwriting

Appendix: Handwriting Models

The teacher's goal is to have students who are able to write well—to write fluently and accurately. To reach this goal we must recognize that over-emphasis on supportive writing skills, such as capitalizing, punctuating, spelling, or handwriting, interferes with the flow of ideas and limits fluency. Children must focus attention on their ideas, on choosing the right words, on giving the needed information. If they stop every second or third word to check spelling or to worry whether or not there should be a comma, they lose the sense of meaning they are creating. Calkins points out that word-by-word writing probably destroys fluency just as much as word-by-word reading destroys comprehension.[1]

The only meaningful context for capitalization, punctuation, spelling, and handwriting is within the composing process. If we were not writing down ideas, facts, or imaginings, there would be no need to spell or to know how to capitalize and punctuate, or to learn handwriting. While we can isolate these writing skills and discuss them, they have no meaning outside the writing program. When children write daily about topics of their own choosing and share their writing with each other and with adults, they soon become aware that correct punctuation and capitalization, accurate spelling, and legible handwriting help the reader make sense of written material. As students prepare a piece of writing to share with others, they edit it. This means adding to the ideas, changing wording, or omitting some parts, but it also means checking spelling, fixing up capitalization and punctuation, and rewriting in good handwriting.

In general, there should be a two-part instructional component in developing supportive writing skills. Much of the instruction in writing skills comes about in the process of editing and publishing the student's own writing. In addition, an ongoing program of instruction in the supportive writing skills is needed. In teaching writing mechanics, teach what students need as they need it within a framework of constant use and practice.

Skill Development within the Writing Process

Learning to compose, like other language tasks, does not appear suddenly in fully developed form. Writing is a skill that develops from scribbling through many stages as it approaches mature writing. Very young children use letters and letter-like shapes along with their drawings and believe that others can read them. At an older age, they use what they know of the alphabet and the few words they know by heart to write:

Mi dad plaz wf me.
We pla kowbys and rid whorss

As they have more contacts with print—being read to, writing for themselves or others, and beginning to learn to read—their ability to spell more conventionally increases.

The parallels between the development of writing and oral language development are striking. Children begin talking by using single words to express their ideas, "Doggie!" then they move to two-and three-word utterances, "Doggie bark." As they mature, they use increasingly more complex and varied sentences to express themselves, "That dog barks a lot. Why do dogs bark so early?" and, finally, "You can often follow the mail carrier's route by the barking dogs." A report of one child's development in spelling *like* showed that the child first wrote *L* or *LC*. Later that year, he spelled it *lic* (and *lict* for *liked*), but by the end of the year he spelled it *like*.[2] The same pattern emerged in Bissex's report of changes in her son's spelling of *directions* between ages five and eight-and-a-half—*drakthens* to *drakshins* to *direkshons* to *directioins* and, finally, *directions*.[3] These changes toward conventional spellings were not the direct result of spelling lists or spelling tests. They reflected the children's increasing sense of how words used in their writing and seen in print are spelled.

Calkins suggests that the similarity of the development of writing and the development of oral language may have implications for learning to write. "If we take our cue from how children learn oral language, then we will allow children to learn written language by using it, as best they can, for real purposes, and by having adults see through their errors to what they want to say."[4]

Such an approach allows students to express themselves freely without neglecting correct spelling, legible handwriting, and proper punctuation and capitalization. Neither the quality of the composition nor appropriate skills are slighted when the writing process is followed. Students are encouraged first to put down their thoughts and ideas on paper. The emphasis in the first draft is on the quality of content, not on correct writing mechanics. After the writer is satisfied with the content, the writing is edited; and emphasis is given to correct spelling and proper placement of punctuation and capitalization. After the necessary corrections have been made in this proofreading, the final draft of the composition is prepared. This final copy to be shared with others is done in the student's most legible handwriting.

Figure 13.1 shows Justin's first draft of the beginning of his story, "Marty and the Magic Football," and Figure 13.2 shows his second draft after editing. Notice that he changed the wording between drafts and that the corrections on the second draft are few, including spelling (beautiful, into, attention, seriously) and the capitalization of *Friday*. Changes in other parts of the story included the division of a sentence into two sentences and the addition of some quotation marks to dialogue. When the story suited Justin, the final corrections were

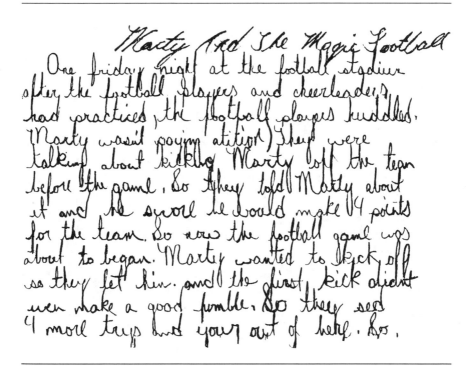

FIGURE 13.1   *Justin's first draft of his story*

made, and the story was ready to be published. Occasionally errors in spelling on a first draft are corrected by the child on his or her own. That happened here with "So they sed 4 more trys," "4 more trys said the coach." The *trys* was corrected in editing and the story was ready to be recopied and displayed. Students should recopy their writing with a purpose in mind. Emphasis on making a paper "letter perfect" calls for providing a means of sharing the piece of writing with others.

Mechanics of Writing: Punctuation and Capitalization

As children write and share what they have written with others, they begin to sense what writing and reading are all about. They notice the marks on printed material that are not letters. They notice that others sometimes have trouble reading what they have written. They notice that when the teacher writes on the board or on charts, he or she uses the same marks found in printed matter. Teachers can build on this

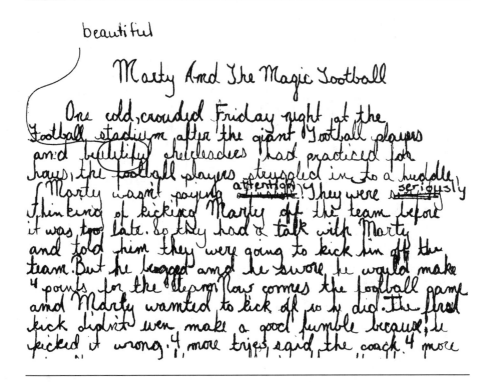

beautiful

Marty And The Magic Football

One cold, crowded Friday night at the
Football stadium after the giant football players
and beautiful cheerleaders had practiced for
hours, the football players struggled in to a huddle.
Marty wasn't paying attention! They were seriously
thinking of kicking Marty off the team before
it was too late. So they had a talk with Marty
and told him they were going to kick him off the
team. But he begged and he swore, he would make
4 points for the team. Now comes the football game
and Marty wanted to kick off so he did. The first
kick didn't even make a good fumble because, he
kicked it wrong. 4 more tries, said the coach. 4 more

FIGURE 13.2 *Justin's second draft of his story after editing*

awareness by commenting as they write on the board, "This is the end of this idea—this sentence—so I'm going to put a period. I'll put a comma between the date and year so it is clear which is which. Notice that when we ask a question, we use a different mark than when we say something." This kind of modeling is helpful in introducing children to basic punctuation. It develops awareness of what punctuation is for and enhances readiness for instruction.

Learning to Punctuate Written Material

As students begin to write conventionally, they may be taught to read their writing aloud to determine if punctuation is needed. Natural pauses in orally read material might suggest commas or other punctuation. If a question mark is missing at the end of a question, oral reading might call attention to the error. Students can learn to listen for possible punctuation when they are reading their own material. Make checking for punctuation a part of the editing process, a natural finishing touch to the process of writing.

When one child needs help with a particular punctuation mark, the teacher can quickly explain and illustrate it within the context of the child's piece of writing. When several children need to learn about a particular punctuation mark, you may form a small group for instruction. The children can help each other proofread for punctuation and thereby gain extra practice.

However we go about teaching punctuation—by modeling it or by giving individual or group instruction as needed—we should be sensitive to children's needs for punctuation at various ages. In considering the punctuation items, or "rules" as they are frequently called, we certainly do not expect the child to learn and apply all of them during the first years in school. We need to focus on those items that the children actually need to use, remembering that not all children need the same things. Perhaps we should look at the kinds of writing that children do at different levels to determine what punctuation items they may need to know.

In the early stages of writing, the primary-grade child uses uncomplicated sentences. They begin writing their names, the date, the name of their school, and so on. They may also compose or copy notes and invitations to take home to their parents. They dictate and write experience stories that usually require only periods, question marks, and commas. We should teach only what they need to use. Asking children to do more than this may be expecting too much at their developmental level.

In the upper elementary grades, children are writing more and more. Sentence structure becomes more complex as the child gets older, requiring more sophisticated mechanics of writing. According to research, dialogue appears in children's compositions at about the age of nine. Older children attend to more detail, and their ability to use a variety of punctuation marks increases. As they begin to use more complex structures and their writing becomes more detailed, children need instruction on the aspects of punctuation they are actually using and need for their writing.

In middle school, students write more formal papers for a wider audience. They begin to develop elements of an individual style in their writing, and consequently need a greater variety of punctuation marks. They begin to use specialized punctuation for specialized purposes. The following lists present items of conventional punctuation that children in elementary school and middle school may need to use in their writing.

Simple Punctuation

Period at the end of a sentence that states something
Period after abbreviations or initials
Question mark at the end of a sentence that asks something

Comma between day and year in writing a date
Comma between city and state
Comma after salutation and closing in a note or personal letter
Comma to separate three or more items in a list
Apostrophe in common contractions like *isn't* or *don't*

More Complex Punctuation

Period after numbers in numbered lists
Period after numerals or letters in an outline
Comma with a conjuntion such as *and* or *but* in a compound sentence
Comma to set off an appositive or noun of direct address
Comma after an introductory phrase or dependent clause
Comma before a quotation within a sentence
Apostrophe to show possession
Apostrophe in less common contractions such as *she'll, he's,* and *weren't*
Exclamation mark at the end of a sentence requiring it
Quotation marks before and after a direct quotation
Quotation marks around titles of poems and stories or chapters within a book
Underlining book titles
Colon in writing time (1:25 P.M.) or after salutation in a business letter
Colon to set off a list that follows
Hyphen when dividing a word at the end of a line
Semicolon between compound sentence clauses when there is no conjunction
Parentheses to set off supplementary matter

Advanced Punctuation

Question mark to indicate uncertainty or lack of information, as in Brutus, Marcus Junius, 85?–42 B.C.
Comma to set off transitional words or expressions, such as *on the contrary and moreover*
Comma to set off brief and closely related clauses instead of a semicolon such as *He came quickly, he was frightened.*
Comma to indicate the place of an omitted word or word group, such as *The 2500 model is used for racing; the 1200, for city use*
Comma to set off inverted names on a list, like *Johnson, Sally*
Comma to prevent misreading, such as *Inside, the cottage was cozy*

Semicolon to separate items in a series that have commas within the items

Colon to introduce a quotation, especially when quotation marks are not used

Colon to separate numbers in ratios (12:6) and in bibliographic references to separate volume and page or chapter and verse

Dash between quotation and author's name and also to indicate omission

Suspension points (three periods or asterisks) to indicate long pauses or an unfinished sentence.

Particular items may be applied in children's writing depending on the method of instruction, the amount of practice or experience a student has in using these items, and when and how the item is introduced. What can a teacher do to help children learn and use punctuation skills? The following list presents a range of possibilities.

1. Have children read their writing aloud to hear intonations and pauses that indicate a need for punctuation.
2. Conduct instruction in small groups for children having similar difficulties in using particular punctuation items.
3. Teach punctuation inductively; let children see how it works and state their own rules.
4. Prepare written materials for children to punctuate or to find punctuation errors after the rule is discovered inductively.
5. Use devices that will illustrate certain punctuation items:
   (a) Show children that a series such as *the wet, cold, icy winter* is the same as saying *the wet and cold and icy winter*.
   (b) When an appositive is taken out of a sentence, the sentence remains complete and meaningful: *Mary Smith, the girl next door, is waiting for you (Mary Smith is waiting for you); He sat in the chair, the one with the broken arm (He sat in the chair)*.
6. Prepare transparency materials to use on an overhead projector. These may be writing samples that require punctuation, or they may contain errors that can be identified and discussed.

Learning to Capitalize Written Material

The need to learn specific capitalization skills also parallels children's writing needs. The young child is concerned with only the most frequently used skills, such as capitalizing the first word of sentences. Older students, whose writing needs are more varied, require a wider knowledge about capitalization. The following lists suggest simple, more complex, and advanced capitalization rules your students may need.

Simple Capitalization

The first word of a sentence
The child's first and last names
The word *I*
The teacher's name and other people's names
The month and day of the week
The name of the school, city, and state

More Complex Capitalization

Proper names such as streets, cities, states, countries, oceans, common holidays, and trade names
The first word of the salutation and closing in notes or personal letters
Mother and *Father* when used in place of their name
Names or abbreviations of titles, such as *Mr., Reverend, Ms.,* and *Dr.*
Names of organizations to which the children may belong, such as *Girl Scouts* and *Little League*
First and important words in titles of books, stories, poems, compositions
First word in a line of verse in poetry
Names of the deity, the Bible, and other sacred writings
The first word of a sentence being quoted
Capitalization as used in outlines

Advanced Capitalization

Derivatives of proper nouns, such as *Americanism* or *Bostonian*
Names of peoples, tribes, and languages
Names of planets, constellations, stars, and asteroids except sun, earth, and moon unless they are listed with other such names
Letters indicating academic degrees: *A.B.* or *Ph.D.*

To help students learn capitalization skills, there are a variety of ways teachers can introduce this instruction.

1. Before children are writing independently, teachers should point out capital letters as they write language-experience charts or labels, or take individual dictation.
2. Have students help each other edit compositions that will be recopied for a final draft.

3. Teach capitalization inductively, letting students discover the rule and state it in their own words.
4. Work with small groups of students who have difficulty with a specific capitalization item.
5. Initiate writing tasks that will cause students to need to use particular capitalization skills.

Student Rule Books

Students can keep their own punctuation and capitalization rule books, either as a section at the front of their personal spelling books or as a separate book. As rules are being used and introduced, the students write them down in their books. Illustrations of the rule should be included, and it would be helpful to have the punctuation categorized by type of punctuation mark. This should make the rules accessible for reference. When the student feels he or she is consistently applying the rule, it can be checked off. Figure 13.3 shows what a student rule book might look like.

Spelling Instruction

The ability to spell correctly is necessary to communicate effectively with others in writing. There is steadily growing concern that too many students are graduating from high school and college who are poor spellers. An instructional program in spelling that is based on current research and applied teaching methods can help all students become better spellers.

First, we must recognize that spelling is a writing skill. No one spells out loud, except perhaps teachers, who *should* not. This means that spelling practice should be written practice, and that any games or

FIGURE 13.3   *Jeff's rule book*

activities intended to teach spelling should involve writing the words or seeing them in written form. Adults tend to use different strategies for spelling words than are taught to children. When students ask how to spell a word, the most frequent answer is "sound it out;" Yet when we aren't sure of how to spell a word, we don't sound it out; we write it down to see if it looks right. That's just what students should do. They should write the word down—using what they know about sound-letter relationships—and look at it to see if it looks right.

When we examine what good spellers do, we find that they are not just smarter. They are persistent and care about spelling correctly. Their characteristic strategy is to write down the word, sometimes three or more ways, and then to look at it to see which is right. When you ask them how they know which one is the correct spelling, they say that they read a lot. They just know the right way when they see it. That is exactly what most adults do who are good spellers. Unfortunately, children who use this approach must figure it out on their own. Few are taught to use this method of spelling. Mostly spelling is memorizing a list of words from the spelling book presented on Monday and taking a test on Friday, and then quickly forgetting the words by the following Monday.

Early Spelling Strategies

Children learn to do many things at home before they come to school, such as dressing themselves, learning to talk, and playing games with rules. Such learning is not organized logically nor segmented into its component parts. It is not done for practice and separated from its real purpose. Writing and spelling should be learned in the same way as these other skills—by doing them. At first new skills are not done proficiently; children frequently fall down, get knots in things, and say *feets* and *holded*. They gain expertise gradually and come to approximate adult behavior. Spelling seems to develop the same way. At first children spell *grl* (*girl*) and *kum* (*come*) and *wateg* (*wedding*), but later, they spell words as adults do.

Children seem to go through five stages in the development of mature, conventional spelling. These are print awareness, dictation, personal invention, beginning conventional, and refined conventional. Sometimes dictation and personal invention coexist, and at school dictation may be used by the teacher as children move from personal invention into beginning conventional.

Print Awareness
Toddlers can usually pick out their favorite cereal, and they know when you have passed McDonald's. They will point to print on the box when

asked, "Where does it say Fluffy Flakes?" Of course, they may be pointing to the words "New, Exciting from Apex Cereals," but pointing to any print indicates they know that print "says" things. They often draw or draw and write letters or letter-like shapes and expect others to read what they have "written."

At this point, we should surround children with print. Reading "Big Books," or very predictable books with enlarged text so that all the children can see the print as it is read duplicates some of the things children learn at home when they are read to. Favorite songs or jump rope rhymes can be put on chart paper or posters and be read aloud. As the teacher points to the words in big books or on the chart, or asks children how many times it says "bowl" or "chair" or what letter *bear* begins with, or what other words also begin with *b*, the children begin to associate the squiggles of print on the page with the words they say.

It is also helpful for kindergarten and first-grade teachers to attach labels to objects in the room, to put the children's names on their chairs and cubbies, and to display charts with song lyrics or finger plays that the children are learning. The knowledge about how print represents words, what words and letters are, where to start reading (front, top, left side), and where to go at the end of a line of print (down and back to the left side) should be developed in as natural a context as possible.

Dictation

Even quite young children will ask how to spell their name, to write *Mommy* or *Daddy*, to write the name of their sister or brother or pet. They want to know how to spell *magic*, or *love*, or *grandpa*. Sometimes they will copy a word from a poster or magazine or a favorite book. This is the earliest form of dictation, and most children ask for such help if they have paper, crayons, and pencils to experiment with and other family members to ask for words.

Dictation is often used at school as children dictate group experience stories or individual stories. Many teachers believe that dictation in the earliest stages of writing helps children record their ideas and have the thrill of authorship at a time when writing and spelling is slow and laborious.

Personal Invention

In the beginning stages of independent writing when children are trying to represent words with letters, their spelling is not at all conventional. Instead, it reflects their knowledge of the sounds they associate with the letters—usually according to their understanding of the alphabet. Consider Cortney's letter in Figure 13.4.

Perhaps your first impression is that the child certainly doesn't

FIGURE 13.4 *Letter from Cortney*

know how to spell. She includes many invented spellings: *Der (Dear)*, *mie (my)*, *sore (sorry)*, *logr (longer)*, and *stire (story)*. But look instead at what she does know: she knows how to spell *I'm* (even using the apostrophe correctly), *was*, *love*—words that she sees and needs to use frequently. She knows to capitalize *D* in *Der (Dear)*, *L* in *Love*, and *C* in *Cortney*. She knows that a note or letter often begins Dear So-and-so and that it ends with Love and your own name. Even though many words are not spelled correctly, they are completely understandable.

How does such writing begin? Many children start with their own names and change initial sounds. Mike put some plastic letters together to spell his name, saying, "That's me. I'm Mike." When asked how he could change it to *like*, he quickly put an *l* at the beginning to repace the *M*. Another child, age five wrote *I no mi abc. wot u ply wf me*—his version of "I know by ABC, won't you play with me?" If children use the alphabet as their basis for writing, the consonants and the long vowels work quite well, but short vowels sounds don't exist (like the *i* in *it* or the *a* in *at*).

Beginning Conventional

This writing is characterized by spelling some words conventionally and still including some invented spellings. Often children will write lists of words on their own that they know or lists of sentences using what they know. One day Amy listed the following sentences:

> *I like Me.*
> *I love Me.*
> *I love Mom*
> *I love Rachel.*
> *I love Dad.*
> *I like Mom*
> *I like Rachel.*
> *I like Dad.*

Sometimes children use very familiar words from their reading books in their writing. One avid reader of Buffy and Mack (the characters in a reading series) wrote the following using a combination of words from those stories arranged in a new way.

> *The sun was up. The lovebug met a groundhog. The love bug met Buffy and Mack and he met the cat and he met the dog. Ther in bg love.*

An even more inventive story in this beginning conventional stage of writing and spelling goes as follows:

> *Small one hid behind the bramble bush with his ears bended back and his eis [eyes] wide opn and vere still. Then hie ran ot of the bramblebosh and saw a snw wit [snow white] fluf of a tale. It was a wit tle dere.*
> > *the Eid*

Although some of the words are not spelled conventionally, most are easily recognizable. Children are apt to be inconsistent in spelling, as in *bramblebush*—spelled once correctly and once incorrectly.

These pieces of writing are typical of first-graders who are getting involved in writing and reading. Being surrounded with words is very helpful: chart lists of colors, ways of moving, describing words, and so forth. Also helpful are personal word books with the words the children know how to spell or have looked up for previous pieces of writing.

Some teachers post frequently used words in alphabetical order as the children begin to learn them. Children often use the word lists or glossaries provided in reading books. Access to words is especially helpful in the editing process. During composing, it seems better to just forget about spelling and get the ideas down.

Refined Conventional

This stage of writing or spelling is reached when children write much as adults do with only an occasional word misspelled. Students need to develop a sense of when a word looks right and how a word could be spelled. They need to learn the most common ways of representing sounds with letters. They need access to a wordbook or dictionary and a thesaurus. Students should work with peer editing groups or partners and focus on independent and guided revision. It is not as important to know how to spell words the first time you write them as it is to recognize when they don't look right and to know how to look them up. Two definitive characteristics of good spellers are that they want their work to be spelled correctly, and they are willing to work to make it right.

Spelling: Part of the Reading-Writing Connection

Language arts specialists used to think that children should become somewhat competent readers before they began to write. Experts now recognize that many children begin writing at home—scribbling and making pictures with letters, letter-like shapes, or words that they believe others can read. Very young children arrange magnetic letters on the refrigerator door to make their name or other words. Montessori also used this method of manipulating letters in her work with children in Rome. She worked in a very directive manner, but the process was essentially the same. The children were given a box with all the consonants and vowels they knew. While the teacher pronounced a word, the children selected the letters to compose it. Montessori comments, "But the reading of the word which he has composed is not so easy. Indeed, he generally succeeds in reading it only after a certain effort. . . . But once he has understood the mechanism of the game, the child goes forward by himself, and becomes intensely interested."[5]

The close connection between writing and reading helps children master both. Writing is an entry into reading as children read back the messages they have written. In an article entitled "Write Now, Read Later," Chomsky suggests that children ought to learn how to read by creating their own spellings of familiar words using sets of plastic letters or alphabet blocks. Instead of words resembling a secret code that only others can break, writing words becomes a way of expressing something that the child knows. She points out,

If we concede that word recognition, or even just the sounding out of words, appears so much more difficult for children than composing words, why do our reading programs as a matter of course expect children to deal with it first? The natural order is writing first, then reading what you have written. To expect the child to read, as a first step, what someone else has written is backwards, an artificial imposition that denies the child an active role in the whole process.[6]

After children have discovered how to read and realize that reading is figuring out what you or someone else has written, they are well on their way to becoming good readers. The more they read, the more they develop a sense of how words should look.

Regularity in Phoneme-Grapheme Relationships

Just as readers need to know what sounds are represented by particular letters or letter combinations, so do writers—spellers. When dealing with sound-letter relationships (phoneme-grapheme relationships), reading and spelling are mirror images of each other. The reader must decide what sound the letters represent, and the speller must decide what letters will represent the sound.

While many delight in pointing out the irregularities in the English language, actually it is quite systematic. One or two letters each will account for a very large percentage of nearly all sounds. Further, the fact that our second-letter relationships are not in perfect correspondence allows for divergent dialect pronunciations. If people wrote words just as they pronounce them, we would have real trouble reading what someone speaking a different dialect had written. Here are some groupings of the consonant sounds and short and long vowel sounds with corresponding spellings; you may find them useful. The information comes from Hanna, Hanna, Hodges, and Rudorf's study[7] of 17, 310 commonly used words in English.

Consonants are the most regularly spelled. Tables 13.1, 13.2, and 13.3 show three groups of consonant sounds with the percentage of time each is spelled as indicated.

Vowels are not spelled as regularly as consonants, but there is enough regularity with both long and short vowel sounds that students can use such information to help them become better spellers. Of these two, short vowel sounds (Table 13.4) are more regularly spelled than long vowel sounds (Table 13.5).

Teachers can use such information in teaching students to spell by encouraging them to learn the letters that might be expected to spell the sounds and to see which spellings look right. Consider the word for

TABLE 13.1   *Consonant Sounds Spelled Primarily with One Letter/Letter Combination*

Sound	As in	Letter(s)	Percentage
/h/	*h*it	*h*	98
/hw/	*wh*en	*wh*	100
/kw/	*qu*ick	*qu*	97
/əl/	rid*dle*	*le*	95
/v/	*v*ery	*v*	99
/w/	*w*et	*w*	92
/th/*	*th*en or *th*ink	*th*	100

*Voiced or unvoiced.

Source: Adapted from Paul R. Hanna, Jean S. Hanna, Richard E. Hodges, and Edwin H. Rudorf, *Phoneme-Graphem, Correspondence as Cues to Spelling Improvement* (Washington, DC: U.S. Dept. of Health, Education, and Welfare, 1966), 35–39.

TABLE 13.2   *Consonant Sounds Spelled with Matching Single or Double Letter*

Sound	As in	Letters Used	Percentage
/b/	*b*at or ru*bb*er	*b* or *bb*	99
/d/	*d*og or fi*dd*le	*d* or *dd*	99
/f/	*f*in or pu*ff*	*f* or *ff*	87
/g/	*g*o or gi*gg*le	*g* or *gg*	93
/l/	*l*ike or fi*ll*	*l* or *ll*	99
/m/	*m*y or hu*mm*ed	*m* or *mm*	98
/n/	*n*o or ru*nn*er	*n* or *nn*	99
/p/	*p*et or cli*pp*ed	*p* or *pp*	100
/r/	*r*ed or pu*rr*	*r* or *rr*	99
/t/	*t*o or pu*tt*	*t* or *tt*	99

Source: Adapted from Paul R. Hanna, Jean S. Hanna, Richard E. Hodges, and Edwin H. Rudorf, *Phoneme-Graphem, Correspondence as Cues to Spelling Improvement* (Washington, DC: U.S. Dept. of Health, Education, and Welfare, 1966), 35–39.

the color of the paper this book is printed on. It could be *whit* or *white*. Does either of those look right? Yes, the second one: *white*. Even if it's not that easy, the process is effective.

Suppose a word includes a vowel sound that is not represented by the most frequent spelling, such as the long *a*. While a long *a* sound is spelled with *a* or *a–e* 79 percent of the time, it can also be spelled numerous other ways. Students will need to learn some of these as they go along; *ai, ay, ai–e, eigh, e, ea, ei,* and *ey* are spellings that are found in ten or more words with this sound. Now, let's take the word that means "to hurt," "to ache," "to be very sore." First, we try *pan* and

TABLE 13.3   Consonant Sounds Spelled with Different Letter Combinations

Sound	As in	Primary Letters	Percentage		Secondary Letters	Percentage
/ch/	check	ch	55	and	tch	31
/j/	gym	g	66	and	j	22
/k/	cat	c	73	and	k	13
/ks/	fix	x	90	and	cs	9
/ng/	ring	ng	59	and	n	40
/s/	so	s	72	and	c	17
/sh/	ration	ti	53	and	sh	26
/y/	yes	i	55	and	y	44
/z/	was	s	64	and	z	23
/zh/	fusion	si	49	and	s	33

Source: Adapted from Paul R. Hanna, Jean S. Hanna, Richard E. Hodges, and Edwin H. Rudorf, *Phoneme-Grapheme Correspondence as Cues to Spelling Improvement* (Washington, DC: U.S. Dept. of Health, Education, and Welfare, 1966), 35–39.

TABLE 13.4   Short Vowel Sounds Spelled with Matching Alphabetic Letter

Sound	As in	Letter	Percentage
/a/	pat	a	96
/e/	pet	e	90
/i/	pit	i	68
		or y	23
/o/	pot	o	93
/u/	putt	u	86

Source: Adapted from Paul R. Hanna, Jean S. Hanna, Richard E. Hodges, and Edwin H. Rudorf, *Phoneme-Grapheme Correspondence as Cues to Spelling Improvement* (Washington, DC: U.S. Dept. of Health, Education, and Welfare, 1966), 35–39.

TABLE 13.5   Long Vowel Sounds Spelled with Matching Alphabetic Letter or Matching Alphabetic Letter and Diacritic e

Sound	As in	Letters Used	Combined Percentage
/a/	acorn or cake	a or a-e	79
/e/	media or scene	e or e-e	72
/i/	idea or hide	i or i-e	74
/o/	roll or pose	o or o-e	86
/u/	unit or tune	u or u-e	89

Source: Adapted from Paul R. Hanna, Jean S. Hanna, Richard E. Hodges, and Edwin H. Rudorf, *Phoneme-Grapheme Correspondence as Cues to Spelling Improvement* (Washington, DC: U.S. Dept. of Health, Education, and Welfare, 1966), 35–39.

pane. Those aren't right; *pan* has the short *a* sound, and *pane* is a piece of glass, a homophone. Well, what next? *Pain, payn, paine?* The only one that looks right is *pain.* An added benefit of this procedure is that students become increasingly able to look up spellings in a word-book or dictionary because if the word isn't spelled as they first think, they have alternative letter combinations to check. The basic strategy, then, is (1) How could it be spelled? (2) Which looks right? (3) If you're not sure, check alternatives.

Sources of Words for Study

Sources for spelling study need to be considered. Each contributes to the spelling program in different ways at different grades. Selection of words from different sources helps to build a complete program.

Students' Writing

Since the purpose of learning to spell words correctly is to communicate with others effectively in writing, the students' own writing is a logical source for spelling words. In fact, a writing component is essential to an effective spelling program. By selecting and writing words, students develop the ability to spell the words they need to use. As needs arise, new words are written, learned, and added to their growing spelling vocabularies.

Younger children may enjoy the way of keeping records suggested by Dunkeld and Hatch.[8] The teacher prepares three envelopes for each child, with the child's name in red on one, in yellow on the second, and in green on the third. As the teacher discovers words that are consistently misspelled in children's writing, he or she writes these words on strips of paper and places them in the red envelope. When the student is in the process of studying the word, it is placed in the yellow envelope; and when it is completely mastered, it is placed in the green envelope. This method gives the teacher a chance to select words for study on the basis of students' actual errors; frequently misspelled words receive special attention; and students can evaluate their progress by seeing how many problem words have been put in the green envelope.

Older students should be encouraged to keep individual spelling dictionaries of their own words. A notebook is alphabetically tabbed for each student, and then when students ask for spellings, look up words, or make mistakes in their writing, the words are placed on the appropriate page. Periodically students should select words from this book for study, checking off the ones mastered, as in Figure 13.5. Teachers use these books, too, as they circulate around the room during writing or editing time and write down the correct spellings of words their students need help with instead of trying to spell aloud.

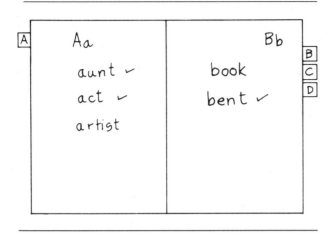

FIGURE 13.5 *Individualized spelling dictionary*

Word Lists

Frequency of use of words is another criterion for choosing words to learn to spell. Researchers have found that about 3,000 words make up 95 percent of all words most commonly used by individuals in their writing. Ten words account for 26 percent of all the words children use: *I, and, the, a, to, was, in, it, of, my.* One hundred words account for 60 percent of all the words used.[9] Unfortunately, frequently used words are sometimes difficult to learn because they have so little appeal and because few of them represent concrete objects.

In Cunningham's "Scratch, Scribble, and Scribe" such frequently used words are written on individual large strips and put up around the room—a few at a time—in alphabetical order.[10] Each day the teacher tells the students to take out a sheet of scratch paper and dictates a test of five words. These may be some of the new words for the day or week or words from earlier sessions. Of course, if students need to look at the word cards, they can, but soon the words are learned, and there is no need. This technique is particularly effective in helping students with frequently used but uninteresting (and often irregular) words.

An appropriate list for younger children might include items from the following lists of frequently used words taken from collected samples of children's writing by Hillerich.[11]

Frequently Used Words in Children's Writing

a	about	after	again
all	almost	also	always

am	an	and	another
any	are	around	as
asked	at	away	back
bad	be	being	because
bed	been	before	best
better	big	black	box
boy	boys	brother	but
buy	by	called	came
can	car	children	Christmas
color	come	coming	could
couldn't	dad	day	decided
did	didn't	do	dog
don't	door	down	eat
even	ever	every	family
father	fell	finally	find
first	five	food	for
found	friend	friend's	from
fun	get	girl	go
going	good	got	had
hair	happened	happiness	hard
has	have	he	heard
help	her	here	him
his	home	house	how
I	I'd	if	I'll
I'm	in	into	is
it	its	it's	just
knew	know	last	later
left	let	like	little
live	long	look	looked
looking	lot	made	make
man	many	me	might
Mom	money	moon	more
morning	most	mother	Mr.
much	my	name	never
new	next	nice	night
no	not	now	of
off	oh	old	on
once	one	only	or
other	our	out	over
people	person	place	play
pretty	put	ran	really
red	right	room	run
said	saw	say	school
see	she	ship	should
sister	snow	so	some

something	sometimes	soon	spring
started	stay	still	take
teacher	tell	that	the
that's	the	their	them
then	there	they	thing
things	think	this	thought
three	through	time	to
told	too	took	tree
two	under	until	up
us	very	want	wanted
was	water	way	we
well	went	were	what
when	where	which	while
white	who	why	will
wish	with	work	world
would	wouldn't	year	years
yes	you	your	

These words were used by about 3,000 first- through sixth-grade children in their weekly creative writing. The children used a total of 8,925 different words in the 379,694 words on their papers. The list above of 255 words includes every word used more than 200 times and accounts for about 70 percent of all the words used by the children.

Spelling Words Taken from Content Areas

Content areas, such as social studies and science, can be sources for spelling words. However, a word of caution is needed here. Words selected for study should be useful to students long after a given topic is completed in a subject area. Too frequently time is spent learning to spell words that will not be needed again for writing. If a child wants to learn some of the more unusual words, this is fine. But a required list of such words to commit to memory is unnecessary. They can simply be listed on chart paper for everyone's use during that unit of study.

Word Families

There are groups of words that can be most profitably studied together. These families are of two types: phonic groupings in which a sound is spelled with the same letter combination and semantic groupings in which the words are related by both meaning and spelling. The phonic groupings are commonly used and help students focus on a particular phoneme-grapheme correspondence such as *hey* and *they* or *few, grew, new, pew,* and *stew.* When using such groupings, it is generally counterproductive to use different spellings of the same sound in one lesson.

Semantic families help children focus on words that come from the same base, carrying similar spellings even when pronunciation changes. The first vowel sound in *courtesy* is difficult, but not when you know that the word comes from *court* and the manners that were appropriate there. Thus, *court, courtesy,* and *courteous* are learned at one time. How is the second vowel in *confidence* spelled? To many it sounds as if it would be an *a* or an *e.* If you associate it with *confide,* however, you know right away that you should use an *i.* Thus *confide* becomes the key to *confidante, confidence, confident,* and *confidential*—all of which carry the *i* in the second syllable.

Both types of groupings can provide children with information to use in selecting the correct spelling. Using several different strategies helps students make the correct, conventional choice.

Spelling Texts

Spelling texts present words in some sort of sequence and may be used to provide continuity from grade to grade. Although commercial textbooks differ, the organization of the basic instructional program usually follows a similar pattern. The test-study-test plan is basic to these spellers and can be a very effective method of learning words if students correct their own tests. The main shortcoming is that such texts encourage all students to study the same words in the same way despite the fact that students differ considerably in the words they can or cannot spell. In addition, texts do not usually provide ways to relate the study of their word lists to students' writing needs in other areas.

Methods of Studying Words

One of the priorities in developing good spellers is to help students see the need for correct spelling. Consequently, it is important to set spelling study within a framework of writing and sharing one's writing with many other people—other students, the teacher, parents, visitors, or students in other classes. No amount of lecturing by the teacher is as effective as seeing someone else unable to read your story because of misspellings.

The steps that a child may take in studying a word are listed below.

1. Observe the word and pronounce it.
2. Close your eyes and mentally picture how the word looks. Write it.
3. Look at the word again and check the spelling with yours.
4. Write the word while thinking about how it looks.
5. Check your written spelling of the word.
6. Try writing the word correctly one more time.

Notice that these study rules involve looking at the word, visualizing it, and checking it in written form. It is not necessary to write the word many times; three times in one study period is about maximum. Concentrated study while writing the word fewer times really works.

For many years we have attempted to teach spelling rules or generalizations to help children learn to spell. Phonic generalizations are not really helpful, except perhaps to check a word after it is written. For example, one rule that is quite regular is that words having double *e* usually have the long *e* sound. For the speller, the problem is not what sound *ee* makes, but what letters to use in writing down the long *e* sound. The study by Hanna et al. indicates that *ee* is used for that sound only 9.8 percent of the time.[12] Because spelling and reading are opposite processes, generalizations that may be helpful in reading are usually not helpful in spelling. Furthermore, many of the generalizations taught do not work well enough to justify teaching them at all. In a study of the applicability of spelling generalizations to words in six major spelling programs, Davis considered the commonly taught rule, "When there are two vowels side by side, the long sound of the first one is heard and the second is usually silent."[13] She found this to be applicable only 32 percent of the time. In 1,893 words with two vowels side by side, 612 conformed to the rule and 1,281 were exceptions. In applying this rule, then, you would be wrong more than two times out of three. But even if the rule worked most of the time, how would it tell you to put two vowels together—much less which two vowels?

The rules that do seem to work are those that can be induced from the charts of sound-letter correspondences given earlier in the chapter.

1. Short vowel sounds are most often spelled with the matching alphabetic letter.
2. Long vowel sounds are most often represented by the matching alphabetic letter or by the matching letter and a diacritic *e*.
3. Consonant sounds are most often represented by the matching alphabetic letter.
4. Consonants are often doubled at the end of words and sometimes in the middle of words.
5. Some consonants double by changing letters: *k* becomes *ck*, *ch* becomes *tch*, and *j* becomes *dge*.

The practices that help students learn to spell involve using a test-study-test program so that students can identify which words they need to study. Research clearly shows that students learn best to spell if they correct their own papers, thus focusing attention on the mistakes they have made as soon as possible. Frequent practice that involves writing the word about three times at a session is more effective than one session in which words are written ten or fifteen times. All practice should involve writing the word, not spelling it out loud. Games may be used for additional practice and for motivation.

Spelling Games and Activities

Occasionally a spelling game or special activity will add motivation and interest to learning to spell. All games should meet two criteria: the spelling should be done in written form and *all* children should participate throughout the activity. This eliminates the spelling bee in its traditional format. An acceptable spelling bee would allow teams to consult on the spelling of a word and the word to be written on the board instead of spelled orally.

Some children enjoy word puzzles of various kinds, and for them crossword puzzles may prove enjoyable. These must be very simple at first as most children do not understand how they work. Early puzzles might have only two or three words but illustrate different spellings of the same sound, as in Figure 13.6.

Another old-fashioned game that still has a great deal of appeal for students is Hangman. In playing this game the players try to find out what word the teacher or another student has selected by guessing what letters might be in it before being "hung." Figure 13.7 shows what would be drawn for a five-letter word after one wrong guess and

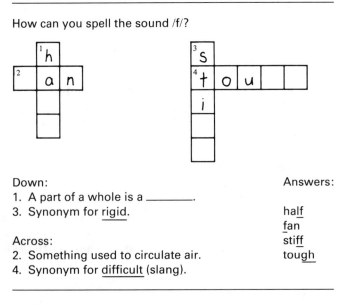

How can you spell the sound /f/?

Down:
1. A part of a whole is a _____.
3. Synonym for rigid.

Across:
2. Something used to circulate air.
4. Synonym for difficult (slang).

Answers:

half
fan
stiff
tough

FIGURE 13.6 *Spelling puzzles*

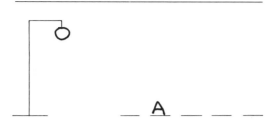

FIGURE 13.7 *Hangman*

one right guess. With each additional wrong guess another part of the person is added to the noose. The students must guess the word before the hanging figure is completely drawn. The teacher may vary the number of guesses allowed by varying the number of parts to the person being hung. That is, only the head, torso, arms, and legs may be used, giving six incorrect guesses; or hands, feet, and so on may be added to the list. Correctly guessed letters are written on the appropriate blanks as clues to the secret word.

Two students take turns as they play the spelling game Hangman.

Classroom versions of television game shows can be adapted to provide interesting spelling games. One such game calls for the contestant to locate words in a line of continuous letters. This is good practice in developing visual awareness of spelling. You can use one line of letters or several rows depending on the students' age and ability. After you give the clue, the students must identify the word by giving its position and saying or writing it. An example of this is shown in Figure 13.8.

Another version of a television game requires a spinner on a wheel with varying number of points marked off around the circle. A preselected title, person's name, or object is shown with a dash for each letter. The players from each team alternate, trying to guess which consonants might be in the mystery word. They may use some of the points they have accumulated to "buy" a vowel (they guess which one), or they may guess the word. If they make an incorrect guess, the next player takes over. The object is to get as many points as possible. If there are two or more repeated consonants in the word, players get the number of points spun multiplied by the number of times the consonant appears.

Team competitions may also be set up by asking students to take turns listing words that have a particular prefix, suffix, or compound part. This could also include writing synonyms or antonyms. For example, use the prefix *un–*:

| *Team A:* | 1. unfriendly | 3. unhappy | 5. unclean |
| *Team B:* | 2. unable | 4. unnecessary | 6. ? |

Team A wins the first round and team B starts the second round. This game is good not only for practice in spelling, but also for vocabulary development.

	1	2	3	4	5	6	7
	n	o	d	d	i	m	e

Clue	Answer:	Position	Word
a. ten cents		4	*dime*
b. strange or peculiar		2	*odd*
c. word that means you		6	*me*
d. opposite of bright		4	*dim*
e. shake your head		1	*nod*

FIGURE 13.8   *Classroom version of a televison game*

The commercial game of Scrabble can also be an enjoyable spelling activity. To score points, players are required to think of a variety of word choices that contain letters or a specified number of letters. Each letter tile has a point value and each word choice must build on letters in previous word choices. Students may also use a dictionary to check word spellings as well as the existence of words.

Games for spelling practice are intended to develop interest in spelling and to make spelling study more enjoyable. They are an excellent alternative to looking up the meaning of each word in the dictionary or writing each word in a sentence week after week—two common practices that have little effect on learning to spell.

Testing in the Individualized Spelling Program

If the spelling words that children are learning are from completely individualized lists, then the testing must also be individualized. If you have an aide or teaching assistant, he or she may give the tests; otherwise the children may test one another. Some teachers prefer to individualize spelling study by using reading groups and alternating which group has individual lists. The test words and sample sentences may also be put on tape by the teacher or by each child, and the tape can then be used to test whenever the child is ready. If it is possible to have a cassette for each student, there are many possibilities for reviewing words.

Perhaps this is an appropriate time to point out that it is not necessary to work with a new group of words each week; there is nothing sacred about Friday spelling tests. Some children may use a four-day study period, others a seven- or nine-day period. Varying when children start a new list to study and when they are tested on the words may help you to individualize their learning.

Analyzing Spelling Problems

An individualized spelling program depends on the teacher's ability to determine the kinds of problems students are having in spelling. Typically, students use particular spelling strategies that cause them to make the same kinds of errors repeatedly. When you can find a pattern in their errors, you can often help your students spell a great many words more quickly.

Some errors indicate less trouble with spelling than others. For example, although *afrade* is not the conventional spelling of *afraid*, we can still recognize the word. Recognizing *thaitch* as *though* is almost impossible and indicates a more serious problem. The types of errors that children make can be classified into seven categories.

1. *Not using the English phoneme-grapheme system:* Children who spell *though* as *thaitch* or who spell *favorite* as falort aren't using letters that could represent the sounds in the word.

2. *Spelling the homophone:* Many words that are pronounced the same have different spellings. These are pairs like *blew* and *blue*, *threw* and *through*, or *see* and *sea*. There are also pairs of words that within some dialects become homonyms: like *on* and *own*, *pin* and *pen*, or *ant* and *aunt*. When children pronounce two words in the same way—whether or not this pronunciation is correct—they are apt to misspell them: like *witch* and *which*, *then* and *than*, or *ask* and *ax*.

3. *Making the wrong choice among options: Cream* could be spelled several different ways: *creme, creem, kreme, criem,* or *creame*. When students choose one of the alternative ways, they are using the English phoneme-grapheme system; they just didn't make the right choice. While this means that the word is not spelled correctly, it is usually still readable and shows that the student knows something about spelling.

4. *Reversing letters in a word:* Often reversing letters occurs when one hurries and the mind is going faster than the pen or pencil. A common reversal is spelling *girl* as *gril* or *also* as *aslo*. This frequently happens when words are studied aloud; children know what letters belong but have not developed a sense of their order or appearance.

5. *Adding or deleting letters when combining words or affixes:* Children often make errors in spelling when they combine two words—*drivway* instead of *driveway*—or when they add an affix to a word and fail to double or drop a letter when they should, or do so when they should not. Thus we get *slideing* instead of *sliding*, *sliping* instead of *slipping*, or *realy* instead of *really*.

6. *Making mispronunciations that lead to errors when children depend on the sounds in the word:* If you pronounce the word *library* as *lieberry*, you are apt to spell it *libary*. *February* is also often mispronounced and therefore spelled *Febuary*. Some dialect pronunciations can also lead children into misspellings: *idear* for *idea* in the Northeast or *den* for *then* among speakers of a black dialect.

7. *Other errors:* There are other errors that do not readily fit into one of the preceding categories. Some seem to occur when children first learn about a diacritic (silent) *e*. They add *e*'s to everything, and so we find *am* spelled *ame* or *stop* spelled *stope*. Then there is *unclet* for *uncle*; perhaps the *t* from *aunt* got transferred here, or perhaps this is creativity appearing. Such unexplainable errors seem to need an "other" category.

Teachers should keep a record of students' errors—or have the students do so—by listing the misspellings along with the correct spelling. Then you can see what patterns emerge in the kinds of errors that individual students are making. Those who are making errors in category 1 need to learn sound-letter representations and to proofread their work to see if they can read it back. Mnemonic devices and special lessons or games may help children who use the wrong homophone, category 2. Working on developing a visual sense of the word and regular proofreading will help children who have category 3 spelling problems in choosing the right option. Reversing letters, as in category 4, and other errors, category 7, may both be helped by careful proofreading and studying words in writing. In Category 5, children, those having problems adding or deleting letters when adding affixes or combining words should be helped by practice with groups of words that drop or add letters. Different word groups should be practiced at different times, so that each is learned thoroughly before encountering another group. Individualized study and concentration on written forms should help children with category 6 errors, which relate to word pronunciation.

Some words seem to be particularly difficult for students, even for those in the middle grades. Unfortunately, many of these difficult words are among the more frequently used words. Many have little intrinsic interest or content, and many use the less common letters to represent their sounds. A list of commonly misspelled words follows, which may help in selecting words for study.[14]

Spelling Demons—197 Words Frequently Misspelled by Elementary Students

about	address	advise	again
all right	along	already	although
always	among	April	arithmetic
aunt	awhile	balloon	because
been	before	birthday	blue
bought	built	busy	buy
children	chocolate	choose	Christmas
close	color	come	coming
cough	could	couldn't	country
cousin	cupboard	dairy	dear
decorate	didn't	doctor	does
early	Easter	easy	enough
every	everybody	favorite	February
fierce	first	football	forty
fourth	Friday	friend	fuel
getting	goes	grade	guard
guess	half	Halloween	handkerchief
haven't	having	hear	heard
height	hello	here	hospital
hour	house	instead	knew
know	laid	latter	lessons

letter	little	loose	loving
making	many	maybe	minute
morning	mother	name	neither
nice	none	o'clock	off
often	once	outside	party
peace	people	piece	played
plays	please	poison	practice
pretty	principal	quarter	quit
quite	raise	read	ready
receive	received	remember	right
rough	route	said	Santa Claus
Saturday	says	school	schoolhouse
several	shoes	since	skiing
skis	some	something	sometime
soon	story	straight	studying
sugar	summer	Sunday	suppose
sure	surely	surprise	surrounded
swimming	teacher	tear	terrible
Thanksgiving	their	there	they
though	thought	through	tired
together	tomorrow	tonight	too
toys	train	traveling	trouble
truly	Tuesday	two	until
used	vacation	very	wear
weather	weigh	were	we're
when	where	which	white
whole	women	would	write
writing	wrote	you	your
you're			

The discussion in this section has centered on a variety of methods and approaches that may be used to facilitate spelling instruction. An effective spelling program does not adhere to a single approach. A method that helps one child to spell better may not help another. And when all is said and done, it is not the method per se that makes good spellers; it is how the method is implemented and how well the children learn.

Handwriting Instruction

The manuscript style of writing, often called printing, first appeared in this country in the early 1920s. After its debut in suburban and private schools, the teaching of manuscript writing spread throughout the public schools. By 1950, this style of writing had become widely accepted in the primary grades, replacing the cursive style of writing which had been learned by young children for years and years.[15]

Teachers, who were concerned with teaching children to read, were delighted to see manuscript writing come into vogue. There was no longer a problem of dealing with two styles of writing—cursive for the purpose of writing and manuscript for the purpose of reading. Now children could focus on one style of writing—print—when first learning to read and write.

Beginning Handwriting Instruction

It is widely accepted that young children should begin to write in manuscript or print. Herrick aptly states the rationale for initial instruction in manuscript.[16] If we consider young children's eye-hand coordination and motor development, the straight lines and circles which are used to make manuscript letters are best. The first-grade child is learning to read, and manuscript symbols correspond to the print children are asked to read. Finally, children's writing is more legible when they use manuscript.

Readiness Experiences

Before formal instruction in manuscript writing, young children can benefit from readiness experiences. The kindergarten child has not yet fully developed coordination of the smaller muscles in the hands and fingers. Experiences that consider children's physical development and help them prepare for writing can be an integral part of the learning environment.

The following activities illustrate the kind of early experiences that might be provided for young children.

- *Painting:* Children need frequent opportunities to paint, either at an easel or on the floor. Children consistently use strokes similar to those needed for manuscript writing when they paint their own pictures. You will readily find simple straight lines and circles, basic strokes in manuscript writing, in their paintings.
- *Making designs:* Children can design their own book jackets, borders for bulletin boards or pictures, fabric for beanbags, and so on. Ideas for using designs that incorporate basic writing strokes are many.
- *Sand or salt trays:* Sand or salt trays are easy to make and loads of fun for children. Using their fingers for drawing, children can make pictures and designs one after the other.
- *Finger painting:* Finger painting offers children the opportunity to explore in a tactile manner lines, curves, ovals, squiggles, and so on.

Children's designs, paintings, or finger paintings can be used in a variety of ways. Those on heavy paper like Figure 13.9A may become book covers or placemats for lunch, snacks or a party. Designs done on long strips like those in Figure B may form a border for a bulletin board or decorate a learning center. Basic writing strokes like those in C may frame a story, a poem, or a picture. Designs on cloth as in D may be sewn into a cushion, a beanbag, or even a pocket on a cover-up shirt. Experiences making these should continue throughout kindergarten, and, for some children, during the first grade in school. Because young children develop physically at different rates, some students will not be ready for formal writing instruction when they enter first grade. They will need many more experiences that will get them ready to write.

Assessing Writing Readiness

The teacher who is concerned with initial writing instruction needs to determine which children are ready to learn manuscript. Berry has developed a list that can be helpful in assessing writing readiness.

Children may be taught to write when

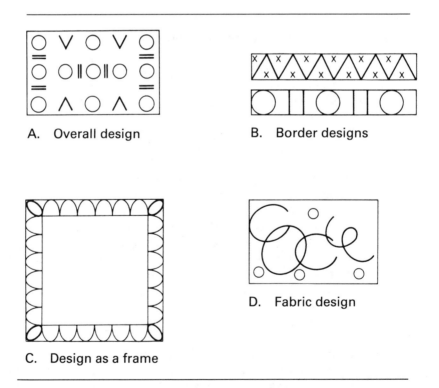

A. Overall design

B. Border designs

C. Design as a frame

D. Fabric design

FIGURE 13.9 *Writing Readiness Designs*

1. they show some interest in writing their own names;
2. they have developed facility in the use of scissors, crayons, paint-brush, and pencil in informal activities;
3. they can copy simple geometric or letter like characters with proper orientation;
4. they have established a dominant hand; and,
5. they sense a personal need to write.[17]

Close observation of each child's physical or motor development is needed to make an accurate evaluation of his or her abilities. It is important for a teacher to understand that certain children, because of their stage of development, cannot be expected to write as well as those children who are already well coordinated.

Materials for the Beginning Writer

- *Paper:* Beginning writers perform best if they are given large sheets of unlined paper. Newsprint or butcher paper works very well because young children need the freedom to use their large muscles for writing. Small sheets of paper require children to use small hand muscles and may lead to fatigue and frustration. Because children's eye-hand coordination is still developing, unlined paper is recommended for use throughout grade one. Also, writing without lines helps beginners focus attention on letter formation.
- *Easels and chalkboards:* Children can write on paper that is attached to an easel or practice manuscript strokes or letters on the chalkboard. Both provide the area that young children need when beginning to write.
- *Writing instruments:* Large crayons or primary pencils are frequently recommended as writing instruments for young children. The primary pencil or readiness crayon is approximately twice the thickness of a conventional no. 2 pencil and is intended to be easier for beginning writers to hold. However, research studies indicate that most young children do very well with a standard-size writing instrument, with which many children are already familiar because they have used them at home.
- *A manuscript alphabet:* Sample alphabet cards are familiar in the elementary school classroom. You frequently find them placed above the chalkboard in the front of the room. To make the manuscript alphabet easier for children to see and use, try taping a sheet containing the alphabet to the top of each student's desk or table. Looking up to the front of the room and back to one's paper is difficult. The alphabet sheets may be laminated or covered with clear contact paper for protection from wear and tear, and this way children can see the letters as often as they wish.

Teaching Handwriting within a Meaningful Context

Instruction in handwriting should occur within a meaningful context. Practicing and mastering isolated strokes and letters before writing words belongs to the past. Young children can first learn to write their names, addresses, telephone numbers, the name of the school, and their teacher's name. They can keep their very own book or diary for recording each day's date along with something special to remember for the day. Meaningful writing experiences may also include writing notes to parents, labeling objects, recording observations of the classroom hamster or fish, writing messages to a pen pal within the class, or attaching captions to their drawings and paintings. Children may copy dictated experience stories or begin writing their own stories using their own spelling system.

Styles of Handwriting

There are many different styles of writing, and teachers should learn to form their letters—both manuscript and cursive—according to the writing system adopted in their school system. There is a surprising amount of difference in the letter shapes. Herrick compared nineteen commercial writing systems and found agreement only on *i* and *o* in lowercase manuscript; only on *P* in uppercase manuscript; and only on *a, i, e, m, n, s,* and *t* in lowercase cursive.[18] There was no agreement on any uppercase cursive letter. In manuscript, there were five forms of the lowercase letters *y, p,* and *g* and seven forms of *q*. In lowercase cursive writing, *c* and *r* had the greatest variations with six forms, and then *g* and *y,* which had five forms. Uppercase letters were even more varied.

Two styles of writing commonly used today are reproduced as an appendix to this chapter for your reference. One is the more traditional "ball-and-stick" style of print from Zaner-Bloser; the other is an "italic" style from Scott Foresman.

Teaching Manuscript Writing

Letter Groupings of Manuscript

It is critical to start children off well so that they will develop correct writing habits. For children to begin writing properly, the teacher needs to show them individually how to form the letters, where to start each letter, and what makes a letter different from another similar one.

In handwriting, "similar" and "different" take on somewhat new meanings. In geometry, a triangle is a three-sided shape, and no matter how you turn it, it is still a triangle. But now children are confronted with the following:

The same: $aaAaa$

Different: $dbpgq$

What differences do make a difference? To help them learn what we know about this, it is important to teach letters in groupings that will contrast what is similar yet different. The emphasis in beginning writing must be on the order and direction of formation of the letters, not on similarities of appearance in the finished letter. Observe students as they write to ensure they are making their letters in the right order and direction.

Manuscript Lowercase Letters   There are five basic groups of letters in lowercase manuscript, according to direction and order of formation.

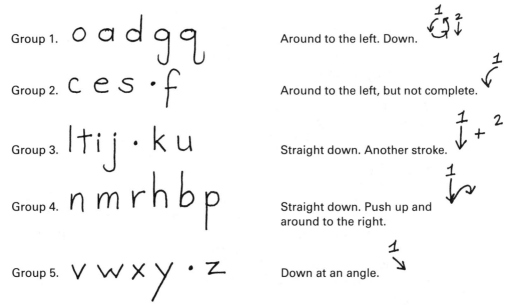

Group 1. o a d g q   Around to the left. Down.

Group 2. c e s · f   Around to the left, but not complete.

Group 3. l t i j · k u   Straight down. Another stroke.

Group 4. n m r h b p   Straight down. Push up and around to the right.

Group 5. v w x y · z   Down at an angle.

Teaching letters in these groupings will help children avoid confusion with reversals because *b* and *d* are widely separated, emphasizing that *d* is like *a* (except with a longer line) and *b* being is more like *h* (except completely closed). *S* is often reversed as ε. Associating *s* with *c*, should help prevent reversals because the first curve is made in the same direction as *c*. Sometimes children are unsure about the second line of *y*, making it Ɣ. Again, associate *y* with *v*, *w*, and *x*, whose first strokes are the same.

Manuscript Capital Letters   Most capital letters are taught after the lowercase letters, although children may know a few—the ones in personal and familiar names. These letters should be taught in three groupings based on similarity to a corresponding lowercase letter, with subgroupings by direction of formation.

Group 1. Similar to lowercase.

COS · TKPU · VWX · Z

Group 2. Partly similar to lowercase

FJ · MN · Y

Group 3. Different from lowercase

AHILE · DBR · GQ

Beginning Instruction in Manuscript

The beginning instruction in forming manuscript letters should be done carefully, with the teacher checking each child individually to make sure each letter is being formed correctly —that is, in the proper direction and order. You cannot look at, an *O* and tell if it was formed clockwise starting at the bottom or counterclockwise from the top. You need to be walking around while children are practicing—checking their letters, the way the pencil is held, and the way the paper is placed. No more copying from the board while the teacher takes lunch count or works with reading groups!

After children have gone through the initial stages of learning to form the letters in manuscript, the teacher needs to individualize hand-writing instruction. Some children may be reversing letters, others may need help with spacing, and a few may be unable to write certain letters. Children who have similar writing problems can be grouped together for instruction. Using the overhead projector, chalkboard, or prepared worksheets, the teacher can easily give these children special help.

Starting the Left-Handed Writer

Because most children in elementary school classrooms are right handed, those who are left handed are frequently slighted. Without special guidance, the left-handed writer will naturally follow the instructions for right-handed writers. Too often, left-handed children develop the habit of hooking the wrist when they write because they have learned to slant the paper in the same direction as that of right-handed children.

It is the primary teacher who gives children their start in both manuscript and cursive writing. What must this teacher consider when teaching the left-handed writer? According to Enstrom, teachers should consider the following techniques.

1. The paper for the left-handed writer should slant about 30 degrees to the right for both manuscript and cursive styles of writing, or slightly more slanted than for a right-handed person and in the opposite direction. Getting the child to position the paper in the proper direction is the first step toward making a successful writer. See Figure 13.10
2. The left-handed child should hold the pencil farther back from the point than the right-handed child.
3. The child's elbows should be kept rather close to the body.
4. The blunt end of the pencil or pen should be directed back over the shoulder.
5. The desk should be high enough for the child to see the pencil or pen as it touches the paper.[19]

Working with Children with Special Needs

Children with learning disabilities of various kinds may need special help with writing. If there is a specialist who works with such children, he or she may be able to suggest specific approaches to be used. If not, try using multisensory practice and reducing as many distractions as possible.

While most children do not need tactile or kinesthetic practice—

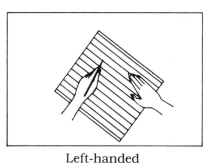

Left-handed   Right-handed

FIGURE 13.10 *Positions for writing paper*

making letters in sand or salt, tracing around sandpaper letters, or making large letters in the air with the whole arm—such practice may be helpful to children with learning disabilities. Lined paper is distracting, especially the kinds recommended for young children by companies producing handwriting materials that are filled with rows of straight lines in two colors with dotted lines interspersed. Such paper is disastrous for learning-disabled children. To reduce distractions, use unlined paper or paper with single lines. Children who are color-blind will also have trouble with lined paper using two colors. Give them unlined paper or paper with only single-color lines, or mark the line they should write on until they can distinguish the special shade of gray that denotes the line.

While most manuscript systems have letters that are made with separate strokes, it may be helpful for some children to do more retracing or to use an italic system that is more similar to cursive letters, as in Figure 13.11. A special focus on legibility rather than on perfect letter form seems appropriate.

Teaching Cursive Writing

Although nearly all schools help children convert from manuscript to cursive writing, there are several arguments for children continuing to write in manuscript style. Using research and theoretical evidence, those who favor continuing manuscript make the following points.

- There is no difference in speed between manuscript and cursive writing when children have had comparable practice in both.
- When children are under pressure to write quickly, manuscript writing remains more legible.
- A signature does not have to be written in cursive writing to be legal.
- Children who develop slowly could benefit from continuing manuscript writing throughout elementary school.

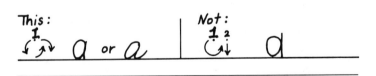

FIGURE 13.11 *Modified letter forms for exceptional children*

- Time spent learning cursive writing could be better spent in creating, composing, and expressing ideas in the writing style that children have already mastered.
- The primary concern of secondary schools is legibility, and manuscript writing is more legible than cursive. Note the frequency of "PLEASE PRINT" on forms.[20]

In spite of numerous logical reasons for continuing manuscript writing, it is difficult to break with tradition. Many parents want their children to learn cursive style, and many children look forward to the time when they will learn to write in "real writing." Certainly all students should be taught to read cursive writing, and many would choose to learn to write it.

Suggestions for Teaching the Reading of Cursive Handwriting

Reading cursive should begin before formal instruction in this style of writing. The second- or third-grader will initially find cursive writing difficult to read and will need some special help. Several weeks before instruction in cursive, take the following steps.

- Write the day's date on the chalkboard each morning in cursive.
- If you are writing brief instructions on the chalkboard for children to read, write them in both manuscript and cursive, as in Figure 13.12.

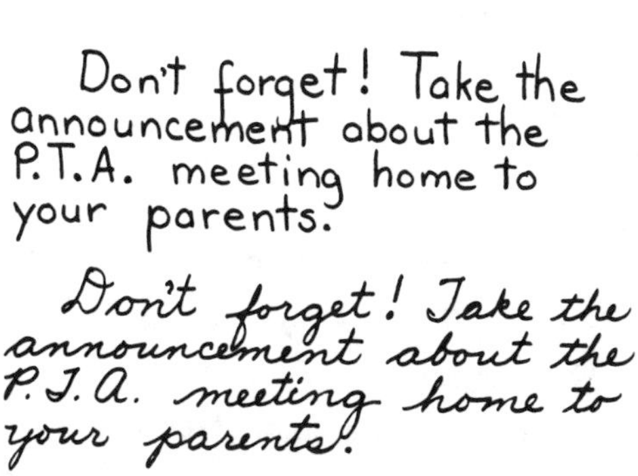

FIGURE 13.12 *Instructions written in (top) manuscript and (bottom) cursive*

- Prepare ditto sheets that have sentences written in both manuscript and cursive writing styles. As a class activity, read and discuss the sentences. Invite comparisons between the formation of corresponding manuscript and cursive letters.
- As the children become more adept at reading cursive writing, start writing more of your instructions or announcements entirely in this writing style.

Letter Groupings of Cursive Writing

Most of the letters in cursive writing are very similar to their corresponding manuscript form except for the connecting strokes or loops that help join the letters within a word.

Cursive Lowercase Letter Groups   All but six lowercase letters can simply be connected, and we have instantaneous cursive writing. Look at Figure 13.13

Show the children this. Let them try it a few times. Then take these twenty letters in groups of four or five and practice. Now make words and write them. Try *all, at, that, chain, cat, dog, chicken, pig, cow, goat, toad, big, two, dot, can, no, not, milk, jump, cold, cool,* and *yowl.* Have your students go on a word hunt for words without *s, r, f, e, z,* and *b.* Practice writing all the words they find, gradually slanting the letters and working in cursive without referring to the print.

Then go on to teach the six letters that look different in cursive writing or are made in a different order-direction. Take time with each letter and practice using them in words as you go along.

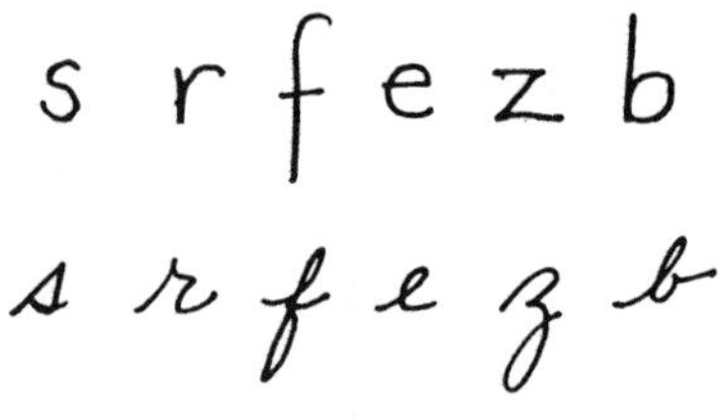

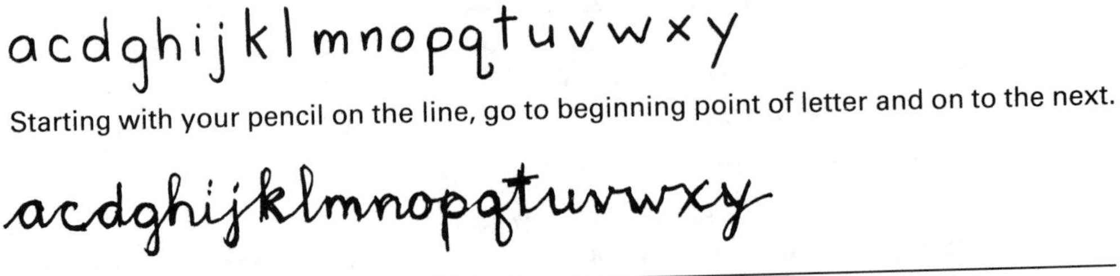

FIGURE 13.13   *Connecting manuscript letters to form cursive letters*

Cursive Capital Letter Groups   For a while the students can use their manuscript capitals as they develop skill in the cursive lowercase letters. When you are ready to teach the capital letters, consider the groups and subgroups shown

    Group 1: Similar to lowercase letters

a c o · m n v u y z w · p

    Group 2: Partly similar to lowercase letters

K X

    Group 3: Different from lowercase letters

B R · F T · G S · I J · L · E · H · 2 · D

Midpoint Connectors   One other group of letters in cursive writing may need special attention. These are the midpoint connectors:

b o v w

All the other letters start and end at the baseline; these four end at midpoint and cause students great difficulty when they are followed by *s, e,* and *r* in particular, but sometimes also *k, l,* and *i.* When the upstroke from the line is not present, the letter changes appearance. These combinations need special practice.

    bring, bite, tubs, bean, black   *br*

    ostrich, toe, ore, coke, old, coin   *os*

    very, vivid, village   *ve*

    flows, west, wring, winter, wise   *wr*

Some children have trouble with *m* and *n* that can be alleviated by starting all letters at the baseline and emphasizing that *m* has three down strokes while *n* has two down strokes—true even after a midpoint connector.

m n am an omit on

Students need to observe how letters are formed. A teacher may use an overhead projector and the chalkboard to demonstrate letter formation, uniformity of size, slant, and how particular letters are connected.

Some Thoughts on Practice

Practicing handwriting is not a very exciting task, and anything the teacher can do to make it more interesting seems worthwhile. Children may use the chalkboard or an overhead projector to work on particular groups of letters. They also enjoy using colored felt-tip pens and brightly colored paper. Even while they are learning to write in cursive style, they need opportunities to maintain some facility with manuscript writing. Making signs, labels for displays, or titles for bulletin boards helps them stay in practice.

Assessing Legibility in Handwriting

Early evaluators of handwriting emphasized its esthetic qualities, and instruction emphasized beautiful writing. Current methods emphasize teaching for legibility, since the entire purpose of writing is its readability. What factors influence legibility? Four factors are the most important in determining legibility: letter formation, spacing, size or proportion, and slant. Two other factors may affect legibility: alignment and line quality. The letters formed should be the correct shape, well rounded, and properly connected. Spacing should be even and appropriate between letters, words, and lines of writing. The size of the letters should be even, not too large or too small, with enough contrast between tall letters and mid-size ones. The slant should be regular, not too far forward or backward. (Some backward slant may be appropriate for left-handed writers.) Alignment means that the letters are on the line, not above or below it. The line quality of the writing should be even and not too light or too dark.

To complete the evaluation of students' writing, the teacher should check the position of each student's body and paper as well as how the writing instrument is held. This should be done often in the early grades and less frequently in later grades. When you are teaching an upper grade and have students holding a pencil incorrectly or writing left-handed with the wrist hooked, it may be difficult to get them to change. This is why it is critical to get students started correctly in the lower grades.

One of the main ways to improve handwriting is to improve the quality of instruction in the initial stages of writing. Developing legibility and speed is then an individual problem. Conferences with the teacher are helpful in getting children to see what particular problems they have and how they can make their handwriting more legible. Before such a conference, the teacher should observe the child writing. This helps in assessing handwriting speed and facility as well as in helping to determine if a child is forming letters correctly. Teacher-student conferences to determine the particular skills the children should work on provide direction and purpose to their practice.

Merely copying from the board will not improve students' writing. They must focus their practice on the major problem they are having. If they need to work on the *c–e–s–f* group in manuscript, they need words with lots of those letters. If they need to work on midpoint connectors in cursive followed by an *e* or an *r*, they need words with *b–o–w–v* plus *e* or *r*. Don't have them copy poetry; it makes for poor handwriting practice and turns them away from poems.

Students should be involved in evaluating their own writing. A quick way is to have a set of samples ranging from excellent to poor. These may be prepared by you or may be available from publishers of handwriting materials, such as Zaner-Bloser.[21] To use such a scale, students compare a sample of their writing with the writing specimens given on the scale. When they find a specimen that closely resembles theirs, they read the corresponding rating score and evaluative comments. Students can determine what factors, such as letter size and slant, they can improve the quality or speed of their writing.

Students should also keep samples of their writing to be used for evaluative purposes. It is best to begin a handwriting folder for each person at the first of the school year. From time to time, new handwriting samples are added to the folder. By dating each sample, students can compare papers written in September with those placed in the folder in October, November, December, and so on. The growing collection of handwriting samples can be used by students to assess their own handwriting progress. When later samples are compared with earlier written samples, students can determine if the quality of their handwriting is steadily improving. They also can diagnose problem areas that need further improvement. Individualization, allowing students to work on their own handwriting problems, is essential to an effective handwriting program.

Summary

The supportive writing skills are referred to as *supportive* because they support composition but are not used independently of writing or composing. They should be learned within the context of writing experiences and imaginings to share with others. Children learn punctuation, capitalization, spelling, and handwriting when they see the need for such skills in their own writing. Thus, the primary instruction in these writing skills should be within the context of writing. There should also be an ongoing program of instruction, especially in spelling and handwriting, to support individual communication and to help with writing skills. The impetus for such study should evolve from students' needs. Using conventional spelling, standard punctuation and capitalization, and legible writing are courtesies to your readers.

Students should practice these writing skills in the way that a doctor practices medicine or a lawyer practices law—not pretending, but using the skill in meaningful ways. Students should be active in examining how words are spelled and how sounds are represented in writing. They should puzzle over how to mark a sentence so the reader will know if it is meant to be funny or sad. Figuring out the rules, figuring out how something works as you need to know helps you remember the rules because they have meaning for you. The supportive writing skills should be viewed as communication aids and should never divert attention from the presentation of ideas.

Questions for Discussion

1. Why should children wait until after a piece of writing is completed before correcting spelling, punctuation, or capitalization? Why not look it up when they first write the word?
2. What are some reasons for not having children practice spelling by spelling aloud?
3. What are some ways that spelling instruction can be individualized?
4. Why should you watch children as they write, particularly when they are first learning to form letters?
5. How can handwriting instruction be individualized after the initial stage of learning to form letters?

Notes

1. Lucy M. Calkins, *Lessons from a Child* (Exeter, NH: Heinemann Educational Books, 1983), 33.
2. Donald H. Graves, *Writing: Teachers and Children at Work* (Exeter, NH: Heinemann, 1983), 185–186.
3. Glenda L. Bissex, *Gnys at Wrk: A Child Learns to Write and Read* (Cambridge, MA: Harvard University Press, 1980).
4. Lucy M. Calkins, *The Art of Teaching Writing* (Portsmouth, NH: Heinemann, 1986), 36.
5. Maria Montessori, *The Montessori Method* (Cambridge, MA: Robert Bently, 1967), 283.
6. Carol Chomsky, "Invented Spelling in First Grade," unpublished paper, Harvard Graduate School of Education (May 1974):11–12.

7. Paul R. Hanna, Jean S. Hanna, Richard E. Hodges, and Edwin H. Rudorf, *Phoneme-Grapheme Correspondences as Cues to Spelling Improvement* (Washington, DC: U.S. Dept. of Health, Education and Welfare, 1966), 35–39.

8. Colin Dunkeld and Lynda Hatch, "Building Spelling Confidence," *Elementary English* 52, no. 2 (February 1975):227.

9. Robert L. Hillerich, *A Writing Vocabulary of Elementary Children* (Springfield, IL: Thomas, 1978), xiii.

10. Pat Cunningham, "Scratch, Scribble, and Scribe: Can't-Fail Writing Recipes," unpublished paper, Alamence County Schools, NC: undated.

11. Hillerich, *A Writing Vocabulary.*

12. Hanna, Hanna, Hodges, and Rudorf, *Phoneme-Grapheme Correspondences,* 35.

13. Lillie S. Davis, "The Applicability of Phonic Generalizations to Selected Spelling Programs," *Elementary English,* 49, no. 5 (May 1972): 706–713.

14. E. B. Fry, J. K. Polk, and D. Fountoukidis, *The Reading Teacher's Book of Lists* (Englewood Cliffs NJ: Prentice Hall, 1984), 55–56. Copyright © 1984. Used by permission of the publisher, Prentice Hall, Inc., Englewood Cliffs, NJ.

15. Gertrude Hildreth, "Manuscript Writing after Sixty Years," *Elementary English* 37, no. 1 (January 1960):3–13.

16. Virgil E. Herrick, "Children's Experiences in Writing," in *Children and the Language Arts,* V. E. Herrick and L. B. Jacobs, eds. (Englewood Cliffs, NJ: Prentice Hall, 1955):271–272.

17. Althea Beery, "Readiness for Handwriting," *Readiness for Reading and Related Language Arts* (Champaign, IL: National Council of Teachers of English, 1950).

18. Virgil E. Herrick, "Manuscript and Cursive Writing," *Childhood Education* 37 (February 1961):264–267.

19. Eric A. Enstrom, "The Extent of the Use of Left Hand in Handwriting and Determination of the Relative Efficiency of the Various Hand-Wrist-Arm-Paper Adjustments," *Dissertation Abstracts* 17, no. 5 (1967):1036–1037.

20. Gertrude Hildreth, "Manuscript Writing after Sixty Years," *Elementary English* 37, no. 1 (January 1960):3–13.

21. *Guiding Growth in Handwriting Scale* (Columbus, OH: Zaner-Bloser Company, 1969).

Appendix: Handwriting Models

Parker Zaner Bloser*

*Reproduced with permission of Zaner-Bloser, Inc. for the series *Creative Growth in Handwriting*, © 1975, 1979.

D'Nealian™ Manuscript Alphabet*

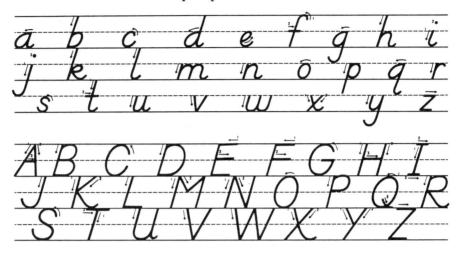

D'Nealian™ Cursive Alphabet

D'Nealian™ Numbers

*From *D'Nealian™ Handwriting* by Donald N. Thurber, copyright © 1978, Scott, Foresman and Company. Reprinted by permission.

Chapter 14

Learning in Other Content Areas through Literature-Based Language Arts

Learning in Other Content Areas through Literature-Based Arts

┌─ **How Language Advances Learning**
│   Remembering Information
│   Finding Information
│   Organizing Information
│   Making Information More Precise
│   Applying Information
│
├─ **Why Integrated Learning Works**
│
├─ **How Literature Fosters Learning**
│   Introduce a Topic
│   Provide Information on a Topic
│   Make a Topic Accessible and Challenging
│   Selecting Books for a Topic
│
├─ **Oral Language across the Curriculum**
│   Group Discussions
│   Individual Oral Presentations
│   Panel and Round-Table Discussions
│   Interviews
│   Debates
│   Storytelling or Retelling
│   Dramatizations
│   Talking Displays
│   Comparisons and Contrasts
│
├─ **Writing across the Curriculum**
│   Stories and Poems
│   Journals, Logs, and Diaries
│   Descriptions
│   Books and Booklets
│   Reports
│   Writing for Radio, TV, or Newspapers
│
├─ **Integrated Units of Study**
│   Unit Planning
│   Webs as Planning Strategies
│
└─ **Bibliography: Children's Books Used in Webs**

This textbook has presented a view of the language arts in which the various aspects of language are not taught in isolation as separate language skills, but rather as interrelated skills that make sense only in the context of real communication for real purposes. Thus, spelling and handwriting are not isolated and taught as subjects separate from composing but rather as an integral part of the writing process. Language usage—proper English—is viewed as an aspect of communicating through oral or written language. Literature study enriches writing as it provides motivation, defines genres, and defines structures for composing.

This chapter extends the uses of oral and written language beyond studies of language, literature, and composition to other curricular areas, such as mathematics, science, music, social science, and art. Language is used to learn—to learn more and at a more meaningful level.[1]

In the past language and writing were considered only as a means of communication. Studies show, however, that language skills help us remember things, find information, organize our ideas, make what we know more precise, and apply what we know to new situations. To maximize effectiveness, language must be used not merely to duplicate or repeat information, but to reorganize, transform, and interpret ideas. As we move from reiterating facts to the concepts that interrelate the facts, we gain knowledge in a powerful way.

How Language Advances Learning

Teachers in the various content areas as well as teachers in self-contained elementary classrooms use language as they explain information or have students explain ideas and as they lead discussions about topics or concepts that they want students to know more about. Students write during math, science, social studies, and so forth. But much of this discussion and writing is focused on remembering information, as teachers check that their students have read and understood the textbook. Although this is one important aspect of learning through language, language can also be used to increase learning by having students move beyond recalling and reproducing information to analyzing, synthesizing, and applying it.

Remembering Information

People write lists of things to do, grocery lists, or lists of presents we need to write thank you notes for; we take notes in class of important ideas to remember; we keep a record of the checks we write or of expenses we can be reimbursed for or that we can deduct from our taxes. Some people keep a journal, writing down their activities for each day, their observations and ideas. Many people make notes on a calendar to help them remember. In school teachers list on the board the work assignments or the schedule for the day. They keep written records of who has homework due, who is line leader, or when an assignment is due. Why? It helps teachers *and* students remember things.

Finding Information

We often ask someone how to find something we need: the date of an assignment, the name of the book, or a fact. We write for a catalog or brochure or to an expert in some area for information. We read books, articles, pamphlets, and newspapers to get information. We listen to the radio for the traffic reports in the morning or for the news at noon, and we watch television to find out what has happened in the world or what the experts say about a topic of interest. We use language constantly to find out things.

At school, we ask students to go to the library to find out about nocturnal animals, the French Revolution, the origin of mosaics, or conditions for growing a fungus. We assign material to read for information. We suggest they call the power company for data on electric power consumption or that they write to the Italian Consulate for booklets on Roman ruins. We all ask for information, nearly all the time.

Organizing Information

Most of us write down some kind of outline or ordered list before we start to compose something. Even when writing something quite short, we plan it in our head before we begin. We think through the items we want to talk about before making a business call. We use language to organize our ideas, especially in writing. We often use lists to organize our day—things to do first, things to do if there is time.

Students who try to organize their information and ideas on a subject invariably find areas where they need to know more or how the parts are related to each other. Mapping information or ideas is a good way to do this. Organizing information involves examining order, similarity and difference, and interrelationships.

Making Information More Precise

As we explain an idea, orally or in writing, we must be absolutely clear. When we begin to share an idea or give directions or explain how to do something, we may find that we only have a somewhat general idea. Sometimes what we thought we knew is quite vague, or the order doesn't seem right. Explaining thoughts to someone else forces us to make them clear and orderly. When we have a problem, it often helps to tell someone else about it—not because they tell us what to do, but because in the telling it becomes clearer. The very act of putting ideas into words forces us to include all the information needed and in the right relationships.

Telling or writing down how to do something—find a square root, change a song to a different key, or describe the structure of a story or poem—serves as a good check on how well that particular concept is understood. Mathematics and science teachers find that having students keep a journal in which they record their understanding of new procedures or interpretations of their observations forces the students to be clear about their ideas and to fill gaps in their knowledge. Then too, in reading the journals the teacher can find out precisely what misinformation exists or what concepts need clarification.

Applying Information

We use language as we make connections between the familiar and the new. The processes of learning and thinking involve taking in new ideas, experiences, and information and relating them to previous experiences. Language helps us manipulate ideas and to use what we know in dealing with the unknown. Having words as labels for ideas or concepts makes the concepts more accessible.

Students need to become independent learners—able to use what they know and the skills they have to learn more. Experiences applying information to new situations, projecting relationships, checking out projections, and trying out ideas to see if they work help students become increasingly able to figure out things on their own. Teachers must be careful to focus on processes and ideas more than on facts. Assignments must challenge students to do more than reiterate information from their teachers and textbooks.

Why Integrated Learning Works

Students learn more and at a deeper level when subjects are integrated. The main reason for this is that using language—written or oral—helps students go beyond the facts to the ideas and feelings that control facts. There is a purpose for finding out information and a way to use what they have learned. Integrated learning lends itself to opportunities to individualize assignments without a great deal more teacher planning. The students can select a focus for their learning that interests them within a broad topic, which makes the course itself more interesting and the presentations more varied.

An example of such integrated study is reported by Zarnowski who worked with seventh graders in an integrated social studies-language arts study of the American Revolution.[2] The students did independent research on some aspect of the Revolution—The Battles of Trenton and Princeton, The Intolerable Acts, the defeat of the British at Saratoga, the Second Continental Congress, and so forth. They wrote a report on their topics. Then they began the second part of the project—writing a piece of historical fiction incorporating some of the real events, places, people found in the report research. Students were to create a character who would play a major role in their story and who would know real historical figures and participate in real events. Writing the story led to further research because students needed to know details, such as how long it would take to ride a horse from Boston to Lexington, or what a mug of cider would cost at the tavern, or who would assume command if the Major were mortally wounded. It was through writing the story that the Revolution came alive. Students could appreciate the sacrifices that the patriots made to achieve independence. They could see history, not as a collection of dry facts to be memorized but as events that touched people and forever changed them. The most important characteristic of integrated study is that significant concepts become clearer and that students develop skills for further learning.

How Literature Fosters Learning

Literature, when it is carefully researched and well written, has the power to bring the past alive, to make faraway places seem accessible, and to explain complex processes or ideas. "If children are to become real readers, they should meet good books not only at reading time, but also as they study history, science, the arts—all subject areas."[3]

Books greatly enhance studies in science, social studies, mathematics, health, music, art, and so forth. Many books are classified as informational books—those written specifically to explain people, places, or things. Biographies and autobiographies can make historical figures seem real, thereby giving life to the study of their time. Well-written historical fiction also has the potential to make other times and places familiar. Often historical events seem to bear little relationship to students' lives, and students fail to sense their common humanity with people of the past. Literature can fulfill special functions in history as in other content area studies. It can initiate study, supplement the regular textbooks, and extend information to students with special needs or interests.

Encourage students to go beyond the content area texts to find information about topics. Biographies, autobiographies, historical fiction, and informational books enrich units of study.

Introduce a Topic

Students should begin a unit of study or a new topic with some curiosity—a sense of wanting to know something—because students who feel like this will learn more. Often a book or an excerpt will arrest the students' attention or give a sense of reality to events in other parts of the world or in the past.

One book that might serve in such a way for a study of Colonial America is *A Lion to Guard Us* by Clyde Bulla, which tells of three children who come to Jamestown from London to find their father.[4] After a shipwreck on Bermuda, they eventually get to Jamestown and find their father, who has just barely survived the 1609–1610 Starving Time. The early settlements seem unreal to most young children; they were so long ago and mostly concern adults. Using this book as an introduction to the time period has the potential of making the whole unit more interesting and more relevant.

Older students may think of geography as dry and irrelevant, but *African Journey* by John Chiasson will quickly dispel that idea.[5] Chiasson depicts six distinctive regions of Africa replete with photos that show how people's lives are shaped by the area in which they live. Nothing dry or distant here; suddenly geography has something to do with life, not just maps.

Provide Information on a Topic

Most textbooks by their very nature give overviews of an area of study, summaries of the most important events, and generalizations about the topic. Informational books tend to focus on specific events or examples and may include much more detailed information about certain ideas, events, or people. Often these additional details are what makes the topic interesting and understandable to students. Sometimes informational books are more up to date than textbooks because of the time involved in completing textbooks and in the adoption processes and finances of schools. An additional bonus of using informational books by many different authors is the opportunity for critical reading. Students can compare authors' presentations and interpretations.

Younger children studying animals will find color photos of baby snakes, lizards, and other scaly creatures in *Scaly Babies: Reptiles Growing Up* by Ginny Johnston and Judy Cutchins.[6] Few textbooks about reptiles have more than two or three photographs—not a whole book full. The younger children may enjoy learning in more detail about the first years of life of reptiles.

The extensiveness of information in good books for older students is exemplified in *The Way Things Work: From Levers to Lasers, Cars to Computers—A Visual Guide to the World of Machines* by David Macaulay, which has nearly 400 pages of elaborately illustrated machines of all sizes, shapes, and descriptions, each with a clear explanation.[7] No middle school textbook physics unit on levers and pulleys will be as complete.

Make a Topic Accessible and Challenging

A persistent complaint of content area teachers in the middle school is that the children cannot read their textbooks. Primary grade teachers deal with children who are reading at the second-grade to the sixth-grade levels, but who have only fourth-grade science books if they are in the fourth grade. One way to cope with varied reading abilities when studying a particular topic is to provide many different books about the subject on different reading levels. Students can find a book they can learn from and that interests or challenges them. The slower reader can work productively, the child with a particular interest in some aspect of the topic can read about it in more depth, and brighter students can find materials to challenge them.

For the "mad scientist" in the lower grades there is *Lots of Rot* by Vicki Cobb, which introduces children to experiments they can do to learn about mold, mildew, and bacterial decay.[8] The book includes a section with a word and picture clues to help students identify what they grow. With little hard reading, this is a high interest book for slower readers.

Middle school students involved in a study of desegregation as part of their history class or as part of Black History Month will find a new sense of history in *The Friendship* by Mildred Taylor.[9] The story is drawn from a boyhood experience of the author's father—the friendship of a black man and a white man in the 1930s in Mississippi. It won the Coretta Scott King Award in 1987, and it helps to make events of that time seem immediate.

Selecting Books for a Topic

Informational books, historical fiction, biography, and autobiography—like realistic fiction, fantasy, or any other genre—should be well written and appropriately illustrated. It is particularly important that the author(s) have some expertise in the subject so that the content is accurate. Textbooks in children's literature typically have one or two chapters devoted to books in other subject areas, with examples and recommendations. Journals that review children's books are good sources of information. The Children's Book Council publishes an annual list of recommended books for science in *Science and Children*, and for social studies in *Social Education*. *The Kobrin Letter* is published ten times a year and reviews informational books by topic—a useful resource for teachers. The National Council of Teachers of English publishes *Adventuring with Books* (preschool to grade six) and *Your Reading* (junior high and middle school), which have recommended books of all kinds organized by topic and type.[10] If there are particular books your students would enjoy using, contact the school librarian or the library your students use and request that the books you would like to have be ordered when funds are available. There are wonderful books waiting to be used.

Oral Language across the Curriculum

There are many kinds of oral language activities that offer opportunities for learning information in various content areas. To maximize the effectiveness of these activities, the students should be involved in interpreting the information in some way, not merely remembering and recalling it. Thaiss points out that children understand and remember only what they have had the opportunity to talk about and perhaps also to write about, sing about, draw, or dramatize.[11] Through such activities, students become active participants in their learning.

Group Discussions

Teachers often discuss material that is important in class, which helps focus students' attention on important ideas or sequences. The most effective discussions are those in which there is a real opportunity to do more than repeat ideas from the book, film, or lecture. Discussions should do more than give the predetermined correct answers; they should give students the opportunity to analyze or speculate and to present their own ideas. Topics for group discussions might include the following:

> Why were American Indians treated badly and moved to reservations in the Southwest?
> Why has there been an increase in the popularity of country music at a time when people are moving away from rural areas?
> Should the United States have used the atomic bomb to bring a quick end to World War II?
> Does historic preservation interfere with progress?
> What is progress?

Individual Oral Presentations

Individual oral presentations are often useful and interesting if they focus on something the presenter knows well and that the children are interested in. "How To" presentations are one such activity:

> How to make a kite
> How to propagate plants
> How to add and subtract in a base-5 system
> How to draw a dinosaur

Individual oral presentations may resemble oral reports in which students share information they have collected. Encourage them to use charts, transparencies, or other visual aids to make their reports more interesting and themselves more comfortable. Topics for oral reports might include the following:

> Windmills as an energy source
> The fate of Japanese-Americans during World War II
> Meteors

Panel and Round-Table Discussions

Instead of giving individual oral reports, students can be assembled in a panel or round-table discussion format, seated as a group at the front of the room. Other students can ask questions of the panel members, who are often less self-conscious than when doing an individual report. Each member can make a brief presentation of his or her subtopic or area of expertise, and then the discussion is open to interchange between panel members and the audience. Topics for panel discussions might include, for example:

> Insects—friend or foe?
> The many uses of computers
> How to plan an exercise program
> The role of the United States in global politics in today's world

Interviews

Obtaining first-hand information is vital to students as they try to understand their world. Teachers can often provide opportunities for personal or telephone interviews.

> Interview other students or teachers on ways to improve your school
> Interview the president of the local historical society about significant historical sites in your area
> Interview the school cafeteria workers about how they plan and cook lunches
> Interview a professor of ecology in a nearby university about how to save water

Students may also do mock interviews in which they become the expert and provide questions for the interviewer to ask them. A partner or the teacher may play the role of interviewer.

> Interview famous inventors or mathematicians.
> Interview a person who lived in the period of history you are studying.
> Learn about primates and interview students as curators of important exhibits of monkeys and apes.

Debates

Older students need experiences with debating—at first informally but later following the rules of formal debate. There should be opportunities for deciding which side to take and time for getting and organizing information. Debates work well as a culminating activity and may reveal the true extent of knowledge on a topic more than a test would.

> Proponents versus opponents: Should we rely on nuclear power plants for our energy needs?
> Fishing industry representative versus ecologist: How should sea mammals that interfere with commercial fishing be managed?
> Patriots versus Tories: Should the colonies seek independence from Great Britain?

Storytelling or Retelling

Because folktales and myths reflect different cultures, they often provide important cultural information about countries and groups of people. Stories of events may also be retold in historical fiction or in informational books, adding much to the study of a topic. Storytelling possibilities include

> Creation myths of various cultures
> American Indian tales (Seminole, Apache, etc.)
> Retelling *The Incredible Journey of Lewis & Clark*,[12] which recounts the explorations of Lewis and Clark that led to westward expansion of the United States

Dramatizations

Informal dramatizations of particular times or places can require students to put information together in new and different ways. Sometimes small groups might want to dramatize a particular event or scene; other times the whole class might participate in dramatization.

> How our community helpers help us
> The D-Day team meetings of June 4 and June 5, 1944
> A town meeting or city council meeting in which a new industry tries to get a zoning variance to build a large plant
> A state educational committee discussing "No Pass-No Play" laws

Talking Displays

An alternative to individual oral reports is the talking display. The student makes up a display—poster or bulletin board—with pictures, charts, labels, and so forth. He or she also makes an audiotape to go with the display, explaining and giving additional information. The tape recorder and tape are placed at the display, and other students, parents, or visitors can listen to the tape and look at the display as they choose. This is especially helpful for shy students as it helps to build their confidence for making such presentations in person. Topics for talking displays might include

> Animals on the farm
> Different geometric figures
> Various types of storms
> Elements of the judicial system

Comparisons and Contrasts

Individual students, pairs, or small groups can present categorizations and charts that involve comparisons and contrasts on a wide variety of topics. Rearranging information to show similarities and differences forces clarity and aids comprehension. Students might compare and contrast

> Bodies in the solar system
> Binary and other number systems
> Forms of currency—today and in the past

All of these kinds of oral language activities help children learn more about other curricular areas. They involve students in using information in ways that make it more memorable. Sheppard gives a new perspective on the question of what is basic: "Natural to learning are processes that enhance learning; therefore, the 'basics' become those processes that focus on communication."[13] Real language use for real purposes is the key to planning oral activities to enhance learning in other content areas.

Writing across the Curriculum

Students are so familiar with taking notes as a part of studying or answering questions from textbooks that they tend to think of these as sufficient writing experiences. They are not. We must do more than record the information, ideas, or concepts; we must restructure the material and make it our own.

Writing gives us opportunities to revise our ideas and add to them; we can re-read what we have written and change it to make it clearer. Oral expression is fleeting and hard to reexamine, but writing can be modified later. We can go back to our written work and review it. For students, however, written language is more time consuming to produce and perfect. A good balance between oral activities and written ones is desirable.

Stories and Poems

Most children are familiar with the narrative and find it an easy writing format. Within the framework of the story, students can include a great deal of information. The stories should grow from what the students are studying and should incorporate real events, problems or people. Fiction is not necessarily fantasy, and even fantasy must be grounded in reality to be effective. Students might

> Write a story of someone's search for oil
> Write a story of someone their age going on the Oregon Trail in the 1840s
> Imagine what school might be like in 2030 because of new technology

Some students love writing poems or song lyrics. These can offer opportunities for adapting information or concepts in different ways. The kind of poem will depend on the age of the child and his or her experience in writing poetry. Younger children might enjoy

> Concrete poems in geometric forms
> Free verse poetry about their favorite animal

Older students might write more complex poems:

> Limericks about people who missed being famous
> Ballads of famous historical events
> Lyrics for a familiar melody about their city or state

Journals, Logs, and Diaries

Informal writing can reveal a greater depth of thinking than students may be willing to share in class. Both information and misinformation can be found in the students' explanations and descriptions of their learning:

> Keep a project journal during your study of fossils
> Keep daily summaries of your reading and class work in algebra

Keep a writing log while planning a piece of historical fiction with plot summaries, research problems, and character sketches

Diaries may also be fictional—the entries of an imaginary person or of a famous person writing about events during a part of his or her life:

The groundhog's entry for February 2
A confederate soldier's diary of his war experiences
A medical researcher working on cancer research
Someone's diary of their train trip across the United States

Descriptions

We may not at first think of descriptions as an appropriate writing format for other content areas. But descriptions may take the form of first hand "how-to" accounts or of lab reports—depending on the content base:

Describe different kinds of storms (tornado, hurricane, typhoon)
Describe how to plan and plant a garden
Describe how to use a computer for work and play

After conducting some experiments, students can

Describe how magnets work
Describe how different kinds of seed germinate
Describe light refraction

Books and Booklets

An interesting format for a report can be a booklet or brochure. Creating a finished product, illustrated and bound with a cover, motivates students to do their best and most careful work. The booklet format requires students to order their information carefully and to present it for readers who may not know about the topic:

A brochure entitled Visit Historic _____"
A book entitled *All about Trees*
A booklet on caring for your teeth

A variation of this format is the ABC or counting book, which can be written by younger children or by older students at a more sophisticated level:

Animals from Alligator to Zebra
The ABC's of Rocks
A counting book in base 2, base 3, and base 5

Reports

Reports are perhaps the most familiar kind of writing in other content areas. Often they are not well written, but there are ways to help students write good reports. Chapter 12 discusses report-writing techniques as well as alternatives to the formal report.

The report may be in a conventional format on topics such as:

Bicycle safety
Shaft and strip mining
Arctic and Antarctic creatures and their adaptations to their environment
Statehood for Alaska

The report content may also be presented on a poster or bulletin board with both visual and written descriptions:

Poisonous plants
Our national park system
How to mix colors

If the report is on a person, it may be done as a biographical sketch or as a collection of mini-biographies:

My favorite person
Musicians and composers
Olympic gold medalists and their records

Information for a report can also be presented in a chart format showing similarities and differences or interrelationships found in the information. Charts might compare these topics:

Different biographies of the same person
Plane and solid geometric figures
The students' state or geographic region with another

Writing for Radio, TV, or Newspapers

Students' familiarity with radio and television may lead to some interesting writing assignments that will capitalize on their familiarity with the broadcast media. Newspapers also provide a different writing format and style that may be attractive to student writers.

Radio or television scripts for presentation in class—with microphone and booth for radio scripts and costumes or props for television shows—can be written by individual children or pairs or small groups:

> "You Are There" script describing the Wright brothers' flight at Kitty Hawk in 1903
> The news report of Martin Luther King's 1963 speech "I Have a Dream"
> Television commercial for an anti-drug campaign

The newspaper style, which allows an editor to delete closing paragraphs if necessary, requires a different organizational pattern for writing. Advertisements also offer interesting opportunities for presenting information in new ways:

> Ads for travel in their city or state
> A report of the 1929 stock market crash
> A entire issue—news, sports, advertising, comics—for the first walk on the moon or for the United States' declaration of war in 1941

Writing across the curriculum as a way of learning more about other subjects requires that the content be at the center of the writing. As in other kinds of communication, students need audiences for their writing. They need to follow the same process of writing that they would follow in English or language arts classes. This means spending time on prewriting activities so that students write from real knowledge. A major part of the preparation for writing involves collecting information from a wide variety of sources and doing a considerable amount of reading. It means helping students while they are writing their drafts and not just evaluating the final product. It means letting students share with each other, helping with revision and editing. If their writing involves interpreting and adapting information rather than merely parroting it, other students will be interested in reading the products and so will you.

Integrated Units of Study

Using oral language or writing to learn information in the content areas requires little additional planning time and pays off in increased learning, students who are busy and involved, and a more interesting class for everyone. It is not a shortcut in terms of teacher time, although the teacher's time is spent somewhat differently. The teacher's role shifts from "source of information" to "assistant in locating information." No longer will all students read the same material at the same time and write out answers to the same questions. They will need a variety of books—informational books about all aspects of the topic, realistic fiction or biographies, and so on. The text, or better yet several textbooks on the topic will be used, but other sources will become equally important. Students will work on different aspects of the topic. They will work alone, in pairs, or in small groups. They will go to the library, bring books or tapes to class, call people for interviews and write for information. The teacher will be the organizer, the helper, the advisor.

Unit Planning

In planning a unit, there are three primary tasks. You must determine what the children should learn as a result of the unit of study. You must plan the activities through which the children can encounter and master the important ideas and information. And, finally, you must figure out how these experiences and activities can be organized or scheduled most effectively.

Determining Content Objectives

To plan a unit, the first step is to determine the content objectives. These purposes or goals will guide your selection of all activities and research topics. They will form the basis of the oral and written activities. Objectives should call for real inquiry, for synthesizing information and applying it. Content objectives for three different areas might include the following:

Unit on Energy Sources

1. Explain the potential of solar energy for heating and for other home or industrial uses.
2. Demonstrate how solar energy can be stored efficiently.
3. Argue the advantages and disadvantages of fossil fuels as energy sources.

Unit on The American Colonies

1. Locate major settlements on a map, identify settlement patterns, and explain the effects of patterns on later settlement.
2. Explain what factors strengthened or weakened a colony.
3. Understand the cultural diversity of groups that immigrated to the American colonies.

Unit on The Solar System

1. Explain the current scientific theory of the origin of the solar system.
2. Analyze the possibilities of space travel in the solar system.
3. Compare Earth with other bodies in the solar system.

Decide on Learning Experiences

Once you have determined what knowledge or concepts are important for students to have grasped by the end of their study, you can examine and list various activities to meet the objective. Look specifically for ideas that have potential for writing or for some oral activity. Many teachers find it helpful to keep the topic in mind—looking at the objectives—and to go through a list of language-based possibilities.

Ask yourself, "In this unit, which learning experiences would work best: group discussions, individual oral presentations, panel and round-table discussions, interviews, debates, storytelling or retelling, dramatizations, talking displays, or comparisons and contrasts?" Are there possible writing activities you could use—stories and poems; journals, logs, or diaries; descriptions; books and booklets; written reports, posters, charts, biographies; or writing for radio, TV, or newspapers?

Students' oral or written language activities are a reflection of experiences they have had, experiments they have tried, or information they have collected. Active participation in learning leads to deeper knowledge. The following learning experiences might enrich students' studies in a unit on energy sources.

1. Take the temperatures of a cup of water in the sun and a cup of water in the shade. Compare the two and write it in your journal.
2. Build a solar still to collect water. Then prepare to tell others how to build one.
3. Telephone someone in the solar construction business. Ask how homes can be built using solar energy, what supplementary energy sources are typically included, and how the building costs of conventional and solar energy compare?
4. Write magazine advertisements for solar energy.
5. Make a chart with at least five energy sources and compare them as to cost, environmental impact, and world supply.

Organize the Unit of Study

The final step in planning an integrated learning unit is to organize the activities and assignments. With younger children, give fewer choices at a time. You might want all students to complete at least one activity related to each objective. Remember that students learn from one another, so set up specific ways for them to share their work. If some students are producing books or brochures, display them and provide time for other students to read them. If there are poster displays or talking bulletin boards, set up a time for other students to see or hear them.

Some teachers set up the unit in a learning center; others examine the planned experiences in terms of long-term or short-term assignments. If students need to send away for materials or conduct experiments over a period of time for their information, these activities should be started at once. As children's experiences are under way, you may want to introduce some short, whole-class activities to revitalize their enthusiasm. Perhaps there's a speaker or a film they should see, something to try out or observe. During the unit study, you will want to confer frequently with the students to see that they know what to do and are doing it. Older students can usually work more independently for longer periods of time, but keep a check on progress.

Webs as Planning Strategies

Webs are one way of setting up an overview of your plans for a unit, showing the activities relating to an objective or a subtopic. A web is a kind of mapping or clustering (discussed in Chapter 3) that may make planning easier as it helps you to visualize many elements at one time.

A web for a unit on "Weather Forecasting and Climate" for older students is shown in Figure 14.1. Notice that within all topic areas (which relate to content objectives), there are observations and experiments, as well as language-related activities. There are projects that will involve the whole class and some that will be done individually. There is a balance of written and oral activities, and while most activities are based on facts and information, there are some opportunities for creativity in presenting them.

Another example is a social studies web for third through fifth grades, presented in Figure 14.2. It has a strong literature base and includes books in the picture storybook format and also chapter books for better readers. Its focus is on understanding and appreciating the variety of Indian cultures in our country, finding common ideas in their folktales and legends, and developing a better understanding of Indians in the 1800s and today. Full bibliographic information for the books in this web, as well as those in the weather and climate web, are in the appendix to this chapter.

When using these webs or those you develop, you may not use every activity. Students' interests may lead you to expand one area and minimize another. Certainly no one student will do every activity. The purpose of a web is to have a visual display organized by topics and content objectives that shows some possibilities for using language more effectively to learn.

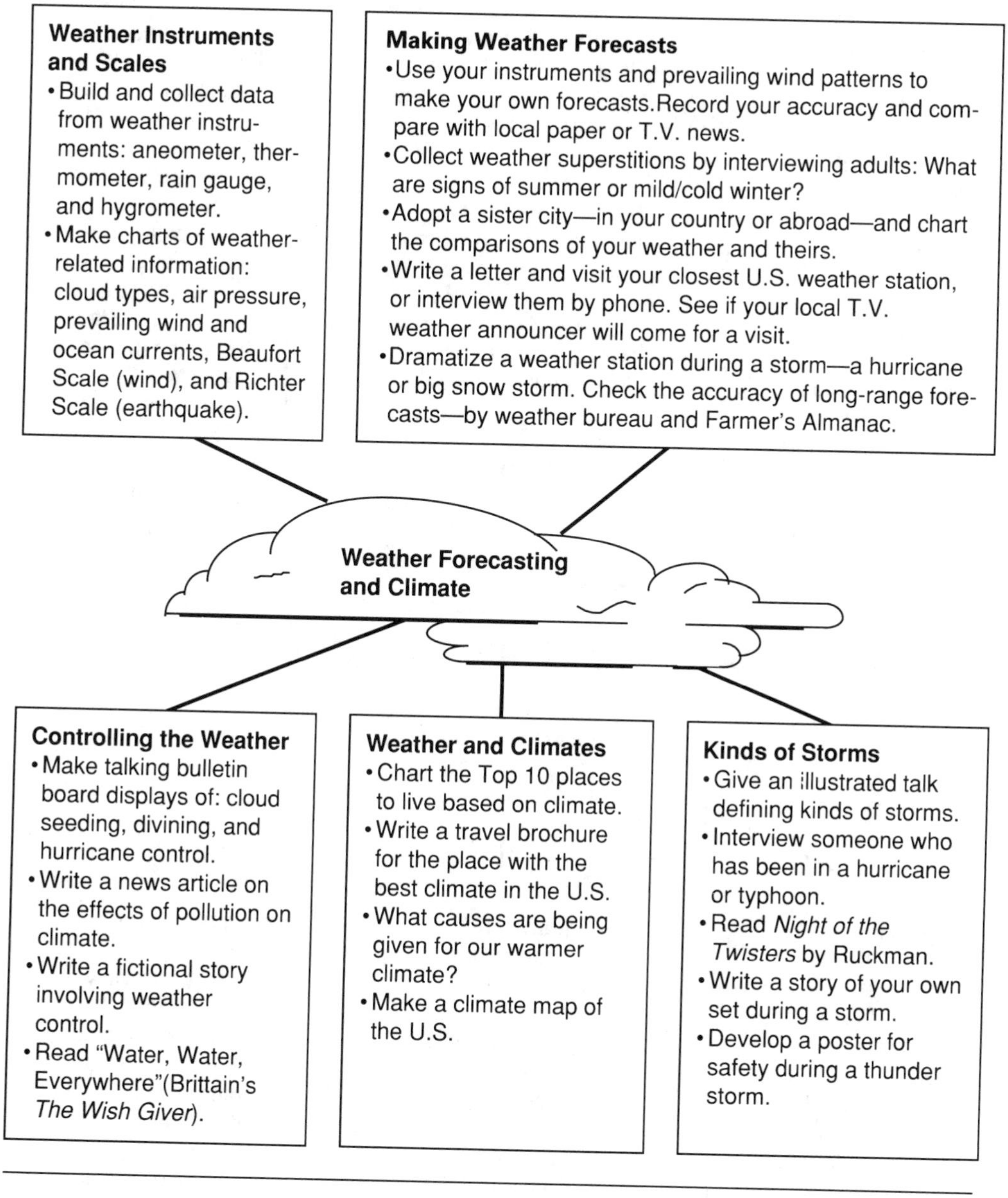

Weather Instruments and Scales
• Build and collect data from weather instruments: aneometer, thermometer, rain gauge, and hygrometer.
• Make charts of weather-related information: cloud types, air pressure, prevailing wind and ocean currents, Beaufort Scale (wind), and Richter Scale (earthquake).

Making Weather Forecasts
• Use your instruments and prevailing wind patterns to make your own forecasts. Record your accuracy and compare with local paper or T.V. news.
• Collect weather superstitions by interviewing adults: What are signs of summer or mild/cold winter?
• Adopt a sister city—in your country or abroad—and chart the comparisons of your weather and theirs.
• Write a letter and visit your closest U.S. weather station, or interview them by phone. See if your local T.V. weather announcer will come for a visit.
• Dramatize a weather station during a storm—a hurricane or big snow storm. Check the accuracy of long-range forecasts—by weather bureau and Farmer's Almanac.

Weather Forecasting and Climate

Controlling the Weather
• Make talking bulletin board displays of: cloud seeding, divining, and hurricane control.
• Write a news article on the effects of pollution on climate.
• Write a fictional story involving weather control.
• Read "Water, Water, Everywhere"(Brittain's The Wish Giver).

Weather and Climates
• Chart the Top 10 places to live based on climate.
• Write a travel brochure for the place with the best climate in the U.S.
• What causes are being given for our warmer climate?
• Make a climate map of the U.S.

Kinds of Storms
• Give an illustrated talk defining kinds of storms.
• Interview someone who has been in a hurricane or typhoon.
• Read Night of the Twisters by Ruckman.
• Write a story of your own set during a storm.
• Develop a poster for safety during a thunder storm.

FIGURE 14.1   A web on Weather Forecasting and Climate

Graphic Designs and Crafts
- Make hand looms and weave using Indian designs.
- Make pottery from coils of clay.
- Borrow a rock polisher and mount polished rocks on wood cubes.
- Experiment with natural dyes and make a display.
- Books: *Art of the Southeastern Indians* and *Art of the North American Indians*

The Indian Territories
- On a U.S. map locate the different Indian tribes' original territories.
- Make a map of the Trail of Tears.
- Make a detailed map of Indians in your geographic area.
- Compare and contrast two tribes from different parts of the country.
- Make a talking bulletin board about one particular tribe.
- Books: *This Land Was Theirs* (Oswalt), *Hollering Sun* (Wood), *Indian Tales* (Raskin), *The Dancing Stars* (Rockwell).

Folklore and Legends
- Retell Indian tales.
- Dramatize a favorite tale.
- Compare two tales of the same type.
- Make a cartoon strip of an interesting tale.
- Books: *The Star Husband* (Mobley), *When the Corn Is Red* (Shor), *The Dancing Horses of Acoma* (Rushmore), *The Great Fish* (Parnall).

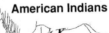

American Indians

Indians in Today's World
- Compare demographic data on Indians and non-Indians in U.S. today.
- Read realistic fiction about Indian life.
- Books: *Higher than the Arrow* (Van Der Veer), *Life on a Cool Plastic Ice Floe* (Cheatham) *The Whipman is Watching* (Dyer), *The Owl's Song* (Hale).

Language and Communication
- Learn how to mark trails.
- Make an exhibit of totem designs.
- Display the Cherokee alphabet and show samples of their newspapers.
- Books: *Talking Leaves, The Story of Sequoyah* (Kohn), and *Arrow to the Sun* (McDermott).

Indian Heroes and Heroines
- Role play interview of heroic Indians.
- Write a brief biography of an Indian hero or heroine from the point of view of Indians and non-Indians.
- Make a book about famous Indians.
- Books: *Custer's Last Battle* (Goble), *Sitting Bull* (Anderson), *Maria Tallchief* (Tobian).

FIGURE 14.2   *A web on American Indians*

Summary

This chapter is intended to help teachers plan classroom study in the content areas, particularly science, social studies, and mathematics. Literature that is well written and researched has power to make information more accessible to students. Activities such as discussion, debate, journal writing, writing stories or radio scripts, and so forth, help students become more actively involved in their own learning. Through talking and writing they are forced to clarify their ideas, which helps them learn. The special uses of literature in content area learning are discussed, and a number of examples of different kinds of oral and written activities are given to illustrate the range of possibilities. A section on integrated units of study applies the concept of webs to the process of teacher planning.

Questions for Discussion

1. What kinds of language use help students go beyond remembering information to actually learning more?
2. What are some ways literature helps students learn material in the content areas?
3. What kinds of oral and written language activities might be used to help students learn information about a topic?
4. Describe a web and explain how it may be used as a planning strategy for integrated learning.

Notes

1. J. Emig, "Writing as a Mode of Learning," *College Composition and Communication* 28, no. 2 (May 1977):122–128; G. M. Pradl and J. S. Mayer, "Reinvigorating Learning through Writing," *Educational Leadership* 42 (1985); and W. F. Weiner, "When the Process of Writing Becomes a Tool for Learning," *English Journal* 75 (1986).

2. Myra Zarnowski, "Helping Students Write Historical Fiction," in *Activities to Promote Critical Thinking*, J. Golub (chair) and the Committee on Classroom Practices, eds. (Urbana IL: National Council of Teachers of English, 1986), 139–143.

3. C. S. Huck, S. Hepler, and J. Hickman, *Children's Literature in the Elementary School* (New York: Holt, Rinehart & Winston, 1987), 614.

4. Clyde Bulla, *A Lion to Guard Us* (New York: Crowell, 1981).

5. John Chiasson, *African Journey* (New York: Bradbury Press, 1987).

6. Ginny Johnston and Judy Cutchins, *Scaly Babies: Reptiles Growing Up* (New York: William Morrow, 1988).

7. David Macaulay, *The Way Things Work: From Levers to Lasers, Cars to Computers—A Visual Guide to the World of Machines* (Boston, MA: Houghton, Mifflin, 1988).

8. Vicki Cobb, *Lots of Rot* (New York: Lippincott, 1981).

9. Mildred Taylor, *The Friendship* (New York: Dial, 1987).

10. Recommended books for science in *Science and Children* (Washington DC: National Science Teachers Association); books for social studies in *Social Education* (Crawfordsville, IN: National Council for the Social Studies); *The Kobrin Letter* (732 N. Greer Road, Palo Alto, CA 94303), and *Adventuring with Books* (1985) and *Your Reading* (1983) (Urbana, IL: National Council of Teachers of English).

11. Christopher Thaiss, *Language across the Curriculum in the Elementary Grades* (Urbana IL: National Council of Teachers of English, 1986), 6.

12. R. Blumberg, *The Incredible Journey of Lewis & Clark.* New York: Lothrop, 1987).

13. Ronnie Sheppard, *Enhancing Learning through Oral and Written Expression: Strategies for Subject Area Teachers* (Columbus, OH: The National Middle School Association, 1985), 1.

Bibliography: Children's Books Used in Webs

Books in Weather Forecasting and Climate

Brittain, Bill. *The Wish Giver.* New York: Harper, 1983.
Ruckman, Ivy. *Night of the Twisters.* New York: Crowell, 1984.

Supplementary Sources:
Ames, Gerald and Rose Wyler. *The First Book of Volcanoes and Earthquakes.* New York: Harper & Row, 1958.
Ayelsworth, Thomas G. and Virginia L. Ayelsworth. *The Mount St. Helens Disaster.* New York: Watts, 1983.
Bendick, Jeanne. *The Wind.* Chicago, IL: Rand McNally, 1964.
Branley, Franklyn. *Flash, Crash, Rumble and Roll.* New York: Crowell, 1985.
Gribbon, John. *Weather Force.* New York: Putnam, 1979.
Pringle, Laurence. *Lives at Stake.* New York: Macmillan, 1980.
Williams, Terry and Ted Major. *The Secret Language of Snow.* New York: Sierra Club/Pantheon, 1984.

Books in American Indian Web

Anderson, L. *Sitting Bull, Great Sioux Chief.* Champaign, IL: Garrard, 1970.
Cheatham, K. F. *Life on a Cool Plastic Ice Floe.* Philadelphia, PA: Westminister Press, 1978.

Dyer, T. A. *The Whipman is Watching.* Boston: Houghton Mifflin, 1979.

Glubok, S. *The Art of the Southeastern Indians.* New York: Macmillan, 1978.

Glubok, S. *The Art of the North American Indians.* New York: Harper & Row, 1964.

Goble, P. and D. Goble. *Custer's Last Battle.* New York: Random, 1969.

Hale, J. C. *The Owl's Song.* New York: Avon Books, 1976.

Kohn, B. *Talking Leaves: The Story of Sequoyah.* New York: Prentice Hall, 1969.

McDermott, G. *Arrow to the Sun.* New York: Viking, 1974.

Mobley, J. *The Star Husband.* New York: Doubleday 1979.

Oswalt, W. *This Land Was Theirs.* New York: Wiley, 1973.

Parnell, P. *The Great Fish.* New York: Doubleday, 1973.

Raskin, J. and E. Raskin. *Indian Tales.* New York: Random House, 1969.

Rockwell, A. *The Dancing Stars: An Iroquois Legend.* New York: Crowell, 1972.

Rushmore, H. with Wolf Robe Hunt. *The Dancing Horses of Acoma.* Cleveland, OH: World, 1963.

Shor, P. *Why the Corn is Red.* Nashville, TN: Abingdon Press, 1973.

Tobias, T. *Maria Tallchief.* New York: Crowell, 1970.

Van Der Veer, J. *Higher than the Arrow.* New York: Camelot Books, 1975.

Wood, N. *Hollering Sun.* New York: Simon & Schuster, 1972.

Index

General

A

Acquisition (*see* Language acquisition)
Adaptation, 65, 96
Affixes, 151–153, 159–160
Analogies, 84–86
Analytical scoring, 368–370
Announcements, 272
Assessing writing, 364–370
Auding, 313
Audio-lingual method, 115
Autobiography, 51

B

Bilingualism, 109–117, 230–231
  characteristics of program, 113–117
  children's strategies, 113–114
  code switching, 114–115
  English as a second language, 230–231
  extent of, 110–111
  goal of, 111–112
  method of teaching, 115–117
  programs, 112–113
  students' writing process, 364
Biography, 51
Black English features, 216–217
Book(s):
  and booklets, 489–490
  comparisons, 81–82
  for dramatizing, 305 (*see also* Drama)
  informational, 51–52
  making bound, 345, 420–421
  reports, 250, 252
Brainstorming, 345
Buzz groups, 345

C

Capitalization 429, 433–435
  lists of rules, 434
  teaching, 435
Categorizing (*see* Classifying)
Cazden, Courtney, 33
Children, characteristics of, 69–71

Children's Books, Poems, and Authors

This constitutes a continuation of the copyright page.